Children's Views and Evidence

Children's Views and Evidence

David Burrows
Solicitor-advocate

Bloomsbury Professional

Bloomsbury Professional
An imprint of Bloomsbury Publishing Plc

Bloomsbury Professional Ltd
41–43 Boltro Road
Haywards Heath
RH16 1BJ
UK

Bloomsbury Publishing Plc
50 Bedford Square
London
WC1B 3DP
UK

www.bloomsbury.com

BLOOMSBURY and the Diana logo are trademarks of Bloomsbury Publishing Plc

British Library Cataloguing-in-Publication Data

A catalogue record for this book is available from the British Library.

ISBN: PB 978 1 52650 317 6
Epub 978 1 52650 318 3
Epdf 978 1 52650 319 0

Typeset by Phoenix Photosetting, Chatham, Kent
Printed and bound by CPI Group (UK) Ltd, Croydon, CRO 4YY

Preface

Representation of children and their rights

This book is about child law: the rights of children and the way they give evidence and express views in courts. But rights are of little meaning if you do not know about them; or you do not have someone who can help to understand and represent those rights. When I was working on **Chapter 6** of this book and trying to reduce the law into a manageable form for those who represent children, I realised what a fractured set of principles is the law of representation of children's rights in family proceedings. It often has no clear logic and is not easy – even for specialist children lawyers – to understand.

Children Act 1989 (*CA 1989*) changed the statutory face of children law; and much of the 1989 Act (subject to often prolix amendment) is the same now as in 1989. Procedural law in relation to child representation – now Family Procedure Rules 2010 (FPR 2010) Pt 16 – has remained largely unchanged. It has not been amended in substance (apart from early amendment in 1992) since introduction of Family Proceedings Rules 1991.

The result is a scheme under the Act and Pt 16 which even a children lawyer of the calibre of Lady Black (Black LJ as she then was) has described as 'of complexity' (in *Re W (A Child) (Care Proceedings: Child's Representation) Practice Note* [2016] EWCA Civ 1051, [2017] 1 WLR 1027). I quote the full passage in her judgment (considered more fully at **6.88**):

> '[18] There was some divergence of view as to which precise part of Rule 16 FPR 2010 should be the focus of the court's attention. This was explored during the hearing but I do not propose to go into the details because there was, in fact, agreement as to the "test" that determined whether or not FW was entitled to be separately represented. I should make clear that when I speak of FW being separately represented, this is a loose term not entirely reflecting the complexity of the scheme under section 41 of the Children Act 1989 and Rule 16 FPR 2010 [ie FPR 2010 Pt 16]. What I seek to convey by it is a situation in which FW separates from the children's guardian appointed to represent her interests, and gives her own instructions to a solicitor, as occurred in the original care proceedings....'

As explained at **6.116**, it is possible that even after that explanation the Court of Appeal did not find the correct way, in law, through the 'complexity'. For example, there was probably no need in the early stages of the case for a children's guardian to be appointed (recovery order proceedings under *CA 1989* are not 'specified proceedings': s 41(6)). Had the court got that right originally the appeal is unlikely to have been necessary; the girl's lawyers need not have done so much work free ('*pro bono*'); and we would not ever have heard of the case.

There are at least four separate schemes for child representation in family proceedings: in care proceedings (*CA 1989, s 41*); in private proceedings where the child applies for an order (*CA 1989, s 10(8)*); child abduction (Hague Convention) proceedings; and where a child applies to join in proceedings which concern him or her (*CA 1989, Pt 2* or Hague Convention). In each of these the law and rules as to a child's representation are different. They can be found in different statutes and proceedings rules. In each an assessment of the 'understanding' of an older child will be necessary; though the law is not always clear on exactly when and by whom this assessment is to be done (see **Chapter 6**, **Part 4**).

Legal aid for child representation

And, as can be seen from **Chapter 6**, **Part 6**, the legal aid scheme which applies to all this is beset by its own semantic contortions. Definitions do not parallel those in the children proceedings scheme. For example, the reader must distinguish between 'specified proceedings' (*CA 1989, s 41(6)*; and see **6.12**) which tell the child whether she or he should have appointed a children's guardian (*CA 1989, s 41(1)*).

By contrast, to establish whether or not legal aid is available the child must work out whether her or his case is:

- A 'special Children Act 1989 case' (**6.108**); or is it
- A 'a public law case' (eg because it is not a 'special Children Act 1989 case') (**6.112**); or, yet again, is it
- Any other form of case where ordinary civil legal services representation may be available (**6.114**)?

All this needs to be kept clear; since in the *Re W* case it seems the courts (including the Court of Appeal) may have got it wrong (see **6.116**).

I have said here that the child must work out whether she is entitled to legal aid. And of course, most children will have help, probably from a lawyer. But for the mature – that is, the *Gillick*-competent child – that is not guaranteed. That child may have to work through the procedural and legal aid rules to understand what his or her rights to representation are. In the *Re W* case the lawyers who were dealing with the child's case (though against her wishes) got the law wrong.

That any children are confronted – whether represented or not – by a law which even a senior children judge finds 'complex' – and may wrongly construe – is a blot on our justice system. (W was busy studying for and sitting exams, so she probably had little time in any event to study the minutiae of *CA 1989, s 41(6)*, FPR 2010, Pt 16 and aspects of the legal aid scheme.)

Gillick and children's rights

In the light of the House of Lords in *Gillick v West Norfolk and Wisbech AHA* [1985] UKHL 7, [1986] 1 AC 112, [1986] 1 FLR 224 and the Cleveland Inquiry report and of other impetus for child law reform in the 1980s, children's rights to be heard were intended to be given greater prominence by *CA 1989*. By 2016, *CA 1989, s 1(3)(a)* – that the views of a child of age and understanding should be taken into account when the court is considering an order in relation to that child's future – had been elevated to a 'fundamental principle' of our law (by Ryder LJ in *Re D (A Child) (International Recognition)* [2016] EWCA Civ 12, [2016] 1 WLR 2469, [2016] 2 FLR 347) (see **Chapter 4**).

Things are changing when it comes to children's views and, for example, of courts' observation of the United Nations Convention on the Rights of the Child 1989, Art 12.1: that a child 'who is capable of forming his or her own views' should be guaranteed 'the right to express those views freely in all matters affecting the child'. The child's views should be 'given due weight in accordance with the age and maturity of the child' (**Chapter 5**).

Yet some things do not change very much. Between *CA 1989* receiving Royal Assent and its coming into operation in October 1991 in *R v B County Council exp P* [1991] 1 FLR 470 the Court of Appeal was confronted by a judicial review application, the only way a local authority's failure to call live evidence (as opposed to rely hearsay) could be done then. The challenge was to a decision that a child (J, aged 17 and 3 months) need not give evidence against her step-father. She alleged that he had abused her sexually. The local authority said that they would rely only on her statement which was covered by the then recently introduced Children (Admissibility of Hearsay Evidence) Order 1991. The Court of Appeal held – on a more or less technical judicial review basis – that the decision not to call J was within the local authority's discretion and could not be set aside by judicial review.

Nicholls LJ at 478 said:

> 'The stepfather's case is that J's statements are a tissue of lies. She is an accomplished liar with ample motive for concocting such dreadful allegations. So there is a head-on conflict of testimony between the two of them. Only they know which of them is telling the truth.
>
> The time-honoured means of resolving this type of dispute is for the two individuals to attend before an impartial judge who hears both of them. Each may himself, or through an adviser, ask the other questions, so as to test the other's veracity. The judge listens and observes. At the end the judge has little difficulty, in most cases, in deciding which of the two is being truthful and which is not....
>
> It is against this elemental background that I have a sense of grave disquiet in the present case....'

Children proceedings: a fair trial

How different were things in 2016? As explained at **3.70**, in *Re S (Care Proceedings: Case Management)* [2016] EWCA Civ 83, [2017] 1 FLR 1476 the Court of Appeal was confronted by a 15-year-old (K) whose statements to a social worker and children's guardian had led to a judge to decide – though in the absence of hearing live evidence from K – that her young niece should be found to be suffering significant harm. This decision was upheld by Black and Vos LJJ.

The third member of the Court of Appeal, Gloster LJ, would have allowed the father's appeal and required K to give evidence, albeit with special measures (see **Chapter 3**, **Part 7**). She said:

> '[58] … This case has left me with a deep sense of unease…
>
> [64] … There was no adequate consideration by the judge of the impact on the appellant's case of the inability of his counsel to cross-examine K as to the allegations and her retraction of, or unwillingness to proceed with, them. The consequences for the appellant, and his infant children, leaving aside his relationship with his partner, were monumentally serious if K's allegations against him were accepted….
>
> [65] …. In my judgment, the judge failed to appreciate that the critical issue was whether or not the appellant could have had a fair trial without the ability of challenging K's evidence in any realistic way.'

In both cases, over 25 years apart, a father was condemned by a family court on the untested, hearsay evidence of a 'child'; but a 'child' who is competent to give evidence in criminal proceedings (*Youth Justice and Criminal Evidence Act 1999, s 53(1)*). In *Gillick* terms the child witness would have been well able to express views and to be heard. In both cases the father had no opportunity to cross examine – even to put questions in writing – to his accuser. In criminal proceedings, anyone charged with a criminal offence has right to 'examine or have examined witnesses against him' or her (European Convention 1950, Art 6.3(d)); albeit with use of special measures (*Re D (a minor)) v Camberwell Green Youth Court* [2005] UKHL 4, [2005] 1 WLR 393; and see **3.22**). In family proceedings that basic right – part of the Art 6 right to a fair trial – is not available.

This book examines these rights and other aspects of the law in relation to children and their evidence. The working out of the recommendations for children in family proceedings (following the work of the Vulnerable Witnesses and Children Working Group (considered in **Chapter 1**)) remains to be seen. The effects of EU withdrawal will be felt in children law as it will in many others.

The law is stated as I understand it to be at 4 September 2017.

Contents

Table of Statutes

[*References are to paragraph number*]

Table of Statutory Instruments

[*References are to paragraph number*]

Table of EU Law

[*References are to paragraph number*]

Table of International Law

[*References are to paragraph number*]

Table of Cases

[*References are to paragraph number*]

Q

R

1

INTRODUCTION

1 CHILDREN PROCEEDINGS AND THE RULE OF LAW

Clarity in family law

1.1 It may be thought that this introduction says more than need be in a book on children proceedings and on such topics as the framework of the law; the common law and statute law; delegated legislation and the variety of guidance and other forms of quasi-legislation which the child confronts – whether or not he or she is represented – in children proceedings. This is necessary because, unfortunately – even where parties are represented – the family courts occasionally misunderstand the law. This is not necessarily to blame the judges. As the mature child who wishes to try to represent him or herself – as they are entitled to do[1] – will find, children law, especially procedural law, is 'complex'[2] (and perhaps needlessly so?).

1.2 Lord Bingham said, as the first rule of his *Rule of law*:[3]

> 'First, the law must be accessible and so far as possible intelligible, clear and predictable. This seems obvious: if everyone is bound by the law they must be able without undue difficulty to find out what it is, even if that means taking advice (as it usually will), and the answer when given should be sufficiently clear that a course of action can be based on it.'

1.3 How many of the few children who may be required to represent themselves in family proceedings will find that children law complies with Bingham's fist rule; or, indeed, that procedural law complies with the statutory

1 As explained in Ch 6.

2 As even Black LJ asserted in *Re W (A Child) (Care Proceedings: Child's Representation) Practice Note* [2016] EWCA Civ 1051, [2017] 1 WLR 1027 where she considered 'the complexity of the scheme under section 41 of the Children Act 1989 and Rule 16 FPR 2010' (ie FPR 2010 Pt 16), and as explained at 6.12 and 6.88. And, it is possible that Black LJ may, with respect, have got some aspects of Children Act 1989 and legal aid provision wrong, as explained at Ch 6, Part 6.

3 On 16 November 2006, the Centre for Public Law held the sixth in the series of lectures in honour of Sir David Williams. The lecture, entitled 'The Rule of Law' which was given by The Rt. Hon Lord Bingham of Cornhill KG, House of Lords, see www.cpl.law.cam.ac.uk/sir-david-williams-lectures/rt-hon-lord-bingham-cornhill-kg-rule-law.

requirement that rules by which children law is regulated must be 'simple and simply expressed'? This is a requirement of *Courts Act 2003, s 75(5)(b)*.[4]

Judges and the rule of law

1.4 A scattering of examples, explained more fully in the succeeding chapters, will serve to illustrate the point of judges at the highest level sometimes misunderstanding the law:

- In *Local Authority X v HI and Others*[5] the court failed to note[6] (perhaps the judge was not told by the variety of lawyers in the case?), that the common law (as now set down in Family Procedure Rules 2010 (FPR 2010)) prescribes a procedure for the application in question;[7] and that, at the highest level of authority,[8] what the judges did in that case has been frowned upon. It was said over ten years ago by the House of Lords that 'no such procedure [of permitting a parties' advocate, to the exclusion of his or her client, to see material in the case] should be followed in future'.[9]
- In *Re W (A Child) (Care Proceedings: Child's Representation) Practice Note* [10] the judges at first instance and in the Court of Appeal did not record the rights of a child in, for example, United Nations Convention on the Rights of the Child 1989, Art 12: namely that a child is entitled to be heard; and, as explained in **Chapter 3**, FW (the 16 year old concerned) was probably not a party to the Children's Act 1989 (CA 1989), s 41(6) 'specified proceedings', so – the feature which started the rot in the case – appointment of a guardian, need not have happened in the first place.
- In *Re E (A Child) (Evidence),*[11] as McFarlane LJ laments, and as is explained below,[12] judges are still not taking proper account of the Supreme Court decision in *Re W (Children) (Abuse: Oral Evidence)*[13] as to when a child can be expected to give evidence in children proceedings.

1.5 It is, accordingly, proposed to spend a little time (in **Part 3**) on the framework of the law, predominantly the common law, which is the evidential and often the procedural basis upon which most children cases proceed. Accordingly, this chapter proceeds as follows:

---

4 See further at 1.37.

5 [2016] EWHC 1123 (Fam), [2017] 1 FLR 1362, Roberts J.

6 As explained at 10.48.

7 FPR 2010, r 21.3, as explained in *West London Pipeline and Storage Ltd v Total UK Ltd* [2008] EWHC (Comm) 1729 Beatson J.

8 *Somerville and others v Scottish Ministers (HM Advocate General for Scotland intervening)* [2007] UKHL 44, [2007] 1 WLR 2734; and *Browning v The Information Commissioner & Anor* [2014] EWCA Civ 1050, [2014] 1 WLR 3848.

9 See 11.29.

10 [2016] EWCA Civ 1051, [2017] 1 WLR 1027.

11 [2016] EWCA Civ 473, [2017] 1 FLR 1675, [2016] 4 WLR 105.

12 See 1.53.

13 [2010] UKSC 12, [2010] 1 FLR 1485.

- **Part 2** offers a few notes on rules of evidence; but leaves the subject mostly to be dealt with in other parts of the book. A short section covers hearsay evidence in children proceedings.
- **Part 3** deals with the structure of the law: statute law; the common law and how it is formed; and discretion and law contrasted.
- **Part 4** summarises the position as to delegated legislation, practice directions and quasi-delegated legislation; and at how each of these at their varying levels of authoritativeness apply in children proceedings.
- **Part 5** moves on to the more general subject of precedence and stare decisis; and how these contrast with the inherent jurisdiction of the High Court in family proceedings.
- **Part 6** looks at 'straws in the wind': possible areas of law reform in the foreseeable future. For the reasons explained the work of the Vulnerable Witnesses and Children Working Group seems to be stalled; and it remains to be seen whether the lost February bill to protect complainants of domestic abuse being cross-examined by their alleged abusers resurfaces in the government's proposed Courts Bill (as looks likely); and if so in what form. And the EU (Withdrawal) Bill is touched upon.

Extra-judicial discussion and debate

1.6 Senior specialist judges in appellate courts have led discussions of where children law might be going, especially in the field of listening to children and hearing their evidence.

1.7 For example, Lady Hale, formerly Brenda Hoggett, has been in the van of family law reform since at least the 1980s, when she was – as a Law Commissioner – one of the leading architects of the then Children Bill. And, as many pages of this book will show, she is prominent amongst judges in the House of Lords and Supreme Court in child law reform as the common law develops children law and practice. Her address to Association of Lawyers for Children on 20 November 2015 *Are we nearly there yet?*[14] considered progress in the field of children's evidence, especially since her watershed judgment in *Re W (Children) (Abuse: Oral Evidence)*.[15] It concluded with her saying she was glad that the subject of children's evidence was 'firmly on the agenda'; but that she was 'less clear exactly where we are heading and whether it is in the right direction'.

1.8 Lady Hale's baton was taken up a year later by Eleanor King LJ in *Giving Children a Voice in Litigation: Are we there yet?*;[16] and in her address to Association of Lawyers for Children in November 2016. She looked at the history of taking children's views into account, especially since the introduction of CA 1989 in

14 http://alc.org.uk/uploads/Keynote_speech_2015.pdf.
15 [2010] UKSC 12, [2010] 1 FLR 1485.
16 http://alc.org.uk/uploads/Keynote_speech_by_LJ_King_18_Nov_16.pdf.

October 1991. But she ends with a note of caution, recalling Lady Hale's words in *Re M (Abduction: Zimbabwe)*:[17]

> '[46] ... These days, and especially in the light of Art 12 of the United Nations Convention on the Rights of the Child 1989, courts increasingly consider it appropriate to take account of a child's views. Taking account does not mean that those views are always determinative or even presumptively so. Once the discretion comes into play, the court may have to consider the nature and strength of the child's objections, the extent to which they are "authentically her own" or the product of the influence of the abducting parent, the extent to which they coincide or are at odds with other considerations which are relevant to her welfare, as well as the general Convention considerations referred to earlier. The older the child, the greater the weight that her objections are likely to carry. But that is far from saying that the child's objections should only prevail in the most exceptional circumstances.'

1.9 Both speakers, it must be said, were hampered by the fact that the Vulnerable Witnesses and Children Working Group[18] had reported when they spoke; but that its recommendations remain still – at the time of going to press and as each of them spoke – on a shelf in the Ministry of Justice.[19]

2 RULES OF EVIDENCE: SOME NOTES

Rules of evidence

1.10 No dedicated chapter has been devoted to law on the rules of evidence in relation to children proceedings; but the subject crops up in a number of guises throughout the book, including:

- Rules in relation to relevance of evidence; that the onus is on him or her to prove an assertion; and standard of proof (**Chapter 3**).
- Disclosure: legal professional privilege; other forms of privilege from disclosure and applications to override confidentiality and privilege (**Chapter 9**, especially in **Part 2**).
- Withholding disclosure (**Chapter 10**) balanced against the rights to full disclosure for a fair trial.
- Control of evidence especially under FPR 2010, r 22.1 (**Chapter 10**, **Part 5**).
- Closed material procedures (**Chapter 11**).
- Public interest immunity (**Chapter 12**).
- Self-incrimination privilege (**Chapter 9**, especially in **Part 5**).

17 [2007] UKHL 55, [2008] 1 FLR 251
18 See 1.65.
19 As explained – resources issues, perhaps? – at 1.65.

1.11 A little will be said later in this Part on the subject of hearsay evidence in children proceedings.

Evidence at a hearing

1.12 Subject to the above aspects of the rules of evidence it can be said, in outline, that judges make their decisions based on the admissible evidence they receive about a case. Evidence is the means whereby a party establishes his or her case; and it is the means whereby another party responds to and opposes that case. In *Re H (Minors) (Sexual Abuse: Standard of Proof)*[20] Lord Nicholls explained the function of evidence:

> 'The starting-point here is that courts act on evidence. They reach their decisions on the basis of the evidence before them. When considering whether an applicant for a care order has shown that the child is suffering harm or is likely to do so, a court will have regard to the undisputed evidence. The judge will attach to that evidence such weight, or importance, as he considers appropriate. Likewise with regard to disputed evidence which the judge accepts as reliable. None of that is controversial....'

1.13 A party's evidence – and it may be that of the child (as explained in **Chapter 3**[21]) – is the means by which facts are proved. That evidence depends on what issue the court is considering and on the relevance of the evidence called. That evidence is then tested by the judge, in civil proceedings, against the balance of probabilities (or probability standard):

> 'Evidence is the means whereby relevant facts are proved in court. What the evidence is required to establish depends upon the issue the court has to decide. At some interlocutory hearings, for instance, the issue will be whether the plaintiff has a good arguable case. The plaintiff may assert he is at risk of the defendant trespassing on his land or committing a breach of contract and that, in consequence, he will suffer serious damage. When deciding, whether to grant an interlocutory injunction the court will not be concerned to resolve disputes raised by the parties' conflicting affidavit evidence.'

Written statements and affidavits: evidence and forms of hearing

1.14 Evidence in chief of witnesses in family proceedings is, as a general rule, by written statements filed and served before the hearing; or in certain cases by affidavit. In the case of children and vulnerable witnesses – and to help the witness

20 [1996] AC 563 sub nom *Re H and R (Child Sexual Abuse: Standard of Proof)* [1996] 1 FLR 80 at 98 and 99.

21 And see, eg, *Wolverhampton City Council v JA & Ors* [2017] EWFC 62 (18 August 2017), Keehan J discussed at 8.102.

prove their best evidence – the evidence may be provided to the court with the assistance of special measures.[22]

1.15 Parties and their witnesses will then be heard by the court at a final hearing, by their oral evidence (subject to what is said below about statements[23]); and in writing at all interim hearings[24] (where there is a need for evidence: eg case management hearings will normally be dealt with on submissions from the parties or their advocates). FPR 2010, r 22.2(1)[25] deals with this as follows:

> **'22.2 Evidence of witnesses – general rule**
>
> (1) The general rule[26] is that any fact which needs to be proved by the evidence of witnesses is to be proved –
>
> (a) at the final hearing, by their oral evidence;[27] and
>
> (b) at any other hearing, by their evidence in writing.'

Content of statements and affidavits

1.16 The statement provided to the court represents the party's own version of events, even though in many cases it will have been prepared by a solicitor. The individual who signed the statement bears responsibility for what is stated. The Bar Professional Standards Committee has prepared guidance – helpful to anyone who may be required to prepare a statement – where one of its members is instructed to prepare a witness statement (other than in criminal proceedings). Amongst other advice the guidance includes (at para 6(d)(iii)) the following: that a statement:

> '(iii) Must contain all the evidence which a witness could reasonably be expected to give in answer to those questions which would be asked of him in examination in chief. The witness statement should not be drafted or edited so that it no longer fairly reflects the answers which the witness would be expected to give in response to oral examination-in-chief in accordance with the witness's oath or affirmation.'

1.17 Evidence is limited to that 'which [the individual who is making the statement] would be allowed to give orally'.[28] It is the statement of the witness, not a pleading or a substitute for legal argument (though a chronology within the statement may be helpful and make it easier to follow in appropriate cases). It should not contain evidence which is not admissible, such as evidence which may

22 As explained in Ch 3, Part 7
23 FPR 2010, r 22.6 (final hearing where a statement has been served)..
24 FPR 2010, r 22.7.
25 Largely derived from Civil Procedure Rules 1998 (CPR 1998), r 32.2(1).
26 (2) The general rule does not apply – (a) to proceedings under Pt 12 for secure accommodation orders, interim care orders or interim supervision orders; or (b) where an enactment, any of these rules, a practice direction or a court order provides to the contrary.
27 CPR 1998, r 32.2(1)(a) adds the words 'in public'. Family proceedings are generally in private: FPR 2010, r 27.11; and see 13.45.
28 FPR 2010, r 22.4(1).

be excluded by privilege or confidentiality,[29] hearsay evidence (rare in children proceedings: see below); or evidence which is irrelevant to the issues before the court.

Hearsay in children proceedings

Survival of the hearsay rule

1.18 For witnesses in children proceedings the complexities of the hearsay evidence rules were intended to be eliminated by Children (Admissibility of Hearsay Evidence) Order 1993 (C(AHE)O 1993). The rule against hearsay in civil proceedings – and thus in children proceedings – was soon afterwards made less complex generally by *Civil Evidence Act 1995* (*CEA 1995*).

1.19 Nominally, hearsay applies to evidence which has been heard or has been written down by a witness (ie set out in a document); and which in both cases are sought to be repeated as evidence in court. Accordingly, *CEA 1995, s 1(2)* defines hearsay as:

(a) 'hearsay' means a statement made otherwise than by a person while giving oral evidence in the proceedings which is tendered as evidence of the matters stated, and

(b) references to hearsay include hearsay of whatever degree.

1.20 A combination of *CEA 1995* and *C(AHE)O 1993* means that any rule against hearsay rule will be no real relevance in children proceedings. *C(AHE)O 1993, Art 2*, under the heading 'Admissibility of hearsay evidence' provides as follows:

> '2 In –
>
> (a) civil proceedings before the High Court or a county court; and
>
> (b) (i) family proceedings, and
>
> (ii) civil proceedings under the Child Support Act 1991 in a magistrates' court, evidence given in connection with the upbringing, maintenance or welfare of a child shall be admissible notwithstanding any rule of law relating to hearsay.'

1.21 Use of the term 'in connection with the upbringing, maintenance or welfare of a child' is intended to be a flexible form of words applicable in most children proceedings. The concept of a question with respect to the upbringing of a child is part of the welfare principle under *CA 1989, s 1*. The effect of the Order is to make relevant evidence admissible regardless of whether – strictly speaking – it is hearsay.

29 As explained at Ch 10.

3 STRUCTURE OF THE LAW

Statute law

Statute law and delegated legislation

1.22 Statute law overrides all other law, and repeals, revokes or otherwise overrides any law which conflicts with it (save, at present, in the case of EU law[30]). Most obviously, it can change existing common law; though if that common law defines existing or fundamental rights, any statute passed by Parliament must state in terms how it is intended that those rights will be altered or otherwise lost. This was stated in clear terms by Lord Hoffman in *R v Secretary of State for the Home Department, exp Simms R v Secretary of State for the Home Department, exp O'Brien*:[31]

> 'Fundamental rights cannot be overridden by general or ambiguous words. This is because there is too great a risk that the full implications of their unqualified meaning may have passed unnoticed in the democratic process. In the absence of express language or necessary implication to the contrary, the courts therefore presume that even the most general words were intended to be subject to the basic rights of the individual. In this way the courts of the United Kingdom, though acknowledging the sovereignty of Parliament, apply principles of constitutionality little different from those which exist in countries where the power of the legislature is expressly limited by a constitutional document.'

1.23 These words were approved recently by the Supreme Court in *R (Miller & anor) v Secretary of State for Exiting the European Union*.[32] It remains to be seen to what extent the *exp Simms* principle will be honoured in the forthcoming EU Withdrawal legislation.

1.24 Much statute law depends for its effectiveness on delegated legislation. This will be explained in **Part 4**.

Common law

1.25 The common law is judge-made law, either where a judge comes across, or has come across in the past, areas of dispute where there is no answer readily provided by statute or in earlier cases; or where a judge may be asked by parties to a dispute to define an aspect of statute law where parties differ as to what it may mean. This was explained by Supreme Court in *R (Miller & anor) v Secretary of State for Exiting the European Union*[33] as follows:

30 See Ch 7, Part 2.
31 [1999] UKHL 33; [2000] 2 AC 115 at 131.
32 [2017] UKSC 5, [2017] 2 WLR 583, and see 7.7.
33 [2017] UKSC 5. [2017] 2 WLR 583.

'[42] … The law is made in or under statutes, but there are areas where the law has long been laid down and developed by judges themselves: that is the common law. However, it is not open to judges to apply or develop the common law in a way which is inconsistent with the law as laid down in or under statutes, ie by Acts of Parliament.'

1.26 In *R (Cart & Ors, on the application of) v The Upper Tribunal & Ors*[34] the Queen's Bench Division Divisional Court (Laws LJ) explained this interpretative role of the High Court. He was dealing with a claim by the government, as a defence to judicial review proceedings brought by Mr Cart and others. The government said that because a statute (in that case Tribunals, Courts and Enforcement Act 2007) asserted that a court (ie the newly set up Upper Tribunal[35]) was a 'superior court of record', then that assertion must be correct. The Upper Tribunal was therefore immune from judicial review. The Administrative Court disagreed (and so too, in due course, did the Supreme Court[36]). Laws LJ explained his view that the High Court must remain responsible for explaining and interpreting statutory provisions as follows:

'[37] The principle I have suggested has its genesis in the self-evident fact that legislation consists in texts. Often – and in every case of dispute or difficulty – the texts cannot speak for themselves. Unless their meaning is mediated to the public, they are only letters on a page. They have to be interpreted. The interpreter's role cannot be filled by the legislature or the executive: for in that case they or either of them would be judge in their own cause, with the ills of arbitrary government which that would entail…. The interpreter must be impartial, independent both of the legislature and of the persons affected by the texts' application, and authoritative – accepted as the last word, subject only to any appeal. Only a court can fulfil the role.'

1.27 Many of the principles laid down in the European Convention for the Protection of Human Rights and Fundamental Freedoms 1950 (the Convention) derive from the common law, since much of the drafting of the Convention was done after the Second World War by English common lawyers. In particular, a number of the principles on which Arts 6 and 10[37] are based derive from English common law doctrines; and they still derive from English common law despite the passing of the *Human Rights Act 1998* (as will be shown shortly in relation to the open court principle).

Common law and family courts

1.28 The common law applies in exactly the same way to family courts as in any other jurisdiction. One of the more controversial areas of procedure is whether

34 [2009] EWHC 3052 (Admin) [2010] 2 WLR 1012; this decision was upheld in the Court of Appeal and in the Supreme Court.

35 *Tribunals, Courts and Enforcement Act 2007*.

36 *Cart v The Upper Tribunal* [2011] UKSC 28, [2012] 1 AC 663, [2012] 1 FLR 997.

37 For text of Art 6 and 10 see Ch 5, Part 3.

a hearing should be in private or in open court.[38] The general rule is a common law rule, now confirmed by the Convention, Art 6.1, that all hearings should be in open court with one or two exceptions (mostly, but by no means entirely, in family law[39]). Indeed, the main case on the subject, which is still routinely referred to, is a divorce (ie family proceedings) case, namely *Scott & Anor v Scott*.[40] Over 100 years ago the House of Lords were astonished – that is not too strong a term – that a judge should have required that nullity proceedings be heard in private, and should have made an order that Mrs Scott and her solicitor be held to be in contempt of court for breach of the privacy requirement. The hearing in *Scott* should have been in open court, said the House of Lords;[41] and the Lords explained the principles of open justice.

1.29 In *R (ota Guardian News and Media Ltd) v City of Westminster Magistrates' Court (Article 19 intervening)*[42] the Court of Appeal was considering whether or not *The Guardian* was allowed to see court documents read by the judge, where the hearing itself had been in open court.[43] The case turned on whether the open court principle applied also to the documents. In effect, the Court of Appeal had to make new law: there was no clear answer in existing case law on the subject. The court allowed *The Guardian*'s appeal and said the newspaper could have the copies they had applied for.

1.30 In giving the lead judgment, Toulson LJ included his clear assertion of the roots of the open court principle in the common law; and he distinguished those roots from the much more recent European Convention 1950:[44]

> '[88] I base my decision on the common law principle of open justice. In reaching it I am fortified by the common theme of the judgments in other common law countries to which I have referred. Collectively they are strong persuasive authority.... The development of the
>
> common law did not come to an end on the passing of the Human Rights Act. It is in vigorous health and flourishing in many parts of the world which share a common legal tradition...'

38 See Ch 13, Part 2.

39 That said the leading case on the open justice principle is *Scott & Anor v Scott* [1913] UKHL 2, [1913] AC 417.

40 [1913] UKHL 2, [1913] AC 417, discussed in Ch 13.

41 Divorce and nullity – if ever contested, or even as to grant of a decree, must be in open court, as must committal proceedings (both an exception to FPR 2010 r 27.10 (see 13.45).

42 [2012] EWCA Civ 420, [2013] QB 618, [2012] 3 WLR 1343, considered further in 13.6 where the full common law background to the open court principle is explained.

43 See 13.50.

44 This passage has since been approved by Supreme Court in *A v British Broadcasting Corporation* [2014] UKSC 25, [2015] 1 AC 558.

Law and discretion

Discretion and decision-making

1.31 Children law demands close attention to whether a decision of the court depends on law, or on the discretion of the individual judge or court. Many areas of children law depend largely on the court's discretion; but always provided that that discretion has been vested by statute in the judge. No court can decide – as it were – to take the law into its own hands and to exercise a discretion for which there is not statutory foundation.

1.32 Thus, for example, the court has wide powers to make a child arrangements order (*CA 1989, s 8*), subject only to the restrictions in *CA 1989, s 9*, where a question arises as to the welfare of a child:

> '(1) In any family proceedings in which a question arises with respect to the welfare of any child, the court may make a section 8 order with respect to the child if –
>
> (a) an application for the order has been made by a person who –
>
> (i) is entitled to apply for a section 8 order with respect to the child; or
>
> (ii) has obtained the leave of the court to make the application; or
>
> (b) the court considers that the order should be made even though no such application has been made.'

1.33 In exercise of this discretion the court – judge or magistrates – is constrained only by the checklist (at *CA 1989, s 1(3)*) and other matters in *CA 1989, s 1*. As relevant here, s 1 is as follows:

> '**1 Welfare of the child**
>
> (1) When a court determines any question with respect to –
>
> (a) the upbringing of a child; or
>
> (b) the administration of a child's property or the application of any income arising from it,
>
> the child's welfare shall be the court's paramount consideration.
>
> (2) In any proceedings in which any question with respect to the upbringing of a child arises, the court shall have regard to the general principle that any delay in determining the question is likely to prejudice the welfare of the child....
>
> (3) In the circumstances mentioned in subsection (4), a court shall have regard in particular to –
>
> (a) the ascertainable wishes and feelings of the child concerned (considered in the light of his age and understanding);
>
> (b) his physical, emotional and educational needs;

(c) the likely effect on him of any change in his circumstances;

(d) his age, sex, background and any characteristics of his which the court considers relevant;

(e) any harm which he has suffered or is at risk of suffering;

(f) how capable each of his parents, and any other person in relation to whom the court considers the question to be relevant, is of meeting his needs;

(g) the range of powers available to the court under this Act in the proceedings in question.

(4) The circumstances are that –

(a) the court is considering whether to make, vary or discharge a section 8 order, and the making, variation or discharge of the order is opposed by any party to the proceedings; or

(b) the court is considering whether to make, vary or discharge a special guardianship order or an order under Part IV.

(5) Where a court is considering whether or not to make one or more orders under this Act with respect to a child, it shall not make the order or any of the orders unless it considers that doing so would be better for the child than making no order at all.'

1.34 By contrast the basis on which a care order may be made by a family court is based at the initial stage entirely on law. *CA 1989, s 31(2)* which vest in the family courts the power to make a care or supervision order states the threshold which the court must find that a local authority applicant has passed if an order is to be contemplated by the court; and this depends on facts being found by the court which are sufficient in law to establish 'significant harm'. *CA 1989, s 31(2)* states:

'(2) A court may only make a care order or supervision order if it is satisfied –

(a) that the child concerned is suffering, or is likely to suffer, significant harm; and

(b) that the harm, or likelihood of harm, is attributable to –

(i) the care given to the child, or likely to be given to him if the order were not made, not being what it would be reasonable to expect a parent to give to him; or

(ii) the child's being beyond parental control.'

1.35 This demands a forensic focus on the evidence presented by the local authority to prove not just harm to a child, but – as the law requires – 'significant harm'. It is a matter of law and evaluation of evidence as to whether the s 31(2) threshold has been crossed; and there is a variety of case law at the highest level [45] to explain the meaning of this and related legal terminology.

4 SUBSIDIARY LEGISLATION AND QUASI-DELEGATED LEGISLATION

Delegated legislation and court rules

Legislation delegated by Parliament

1.36 Law is a combination of statute law, the common law and a variety of delegated legislation (mostly court rules, such as FPR 2010) and of sub-delegated – or quasi-delegated – legislation (such as practice directions, guidance, practice notes and protocols). A substantial proportion of modern legislation is delegated by Parliament to government ministers or others on Parliament's behalf. In modern life, this is inevitable. Children law, save in respect of court rules (ie Family Procedure Rules 2010), is relatively light on properly so-called delegated legislation (rules, regulations etc); but it abounds with a variety of sub-delegated legislation, guidance and the like, as explained below.

1.37 The making of court rules is delegated entirely to Family Procedure Rules Committee. They are confirmed in Parliament by the negative resolution procedure. The *Courts Act 2003, s 75(1)* sets up that Committee. Sections 75 and 76 deal with the content and scope of the rules and include, as relevant here, the following:

> **'75 Family Procedure Rules**
>
> (1) There are to be rules of court (to be called "Family Procedure Rules") governing the practice and procedure to be followed in family proceedings.
>
> (2) Family Procedure Rules are to be made by a committee known as the Family Procedure Rule Committee.
>
> (3) Family proceedings" means—
>
> (a) proceedings in the family court, and
>
> (a) proceedings in the Family Division of the High Court which are business assigned, by or under section 61 of (and Schedule 1to) the Senior Courts Act 198, to that Division of the High Court and no other....
>
> (5) Any power to make Family Procedure Rules is to be exercised with a view to securing that—

45 See, eg: *Re B (Children)* [2008] UKHL 35 [2009] 1 AC 11, sub nom *Re B (Care Proceedings: Standard of Proof)* [2008] 2 FLR 141; and *Re B (a Child)* [2013] UKSC 33 sub nom *Re B (Care Proceedings: Appeal)* [2013] 2 FLR 1075.

(a) the family justice system is accessible, fair and efficient, and

(b) the rules are both simple and simply expressed.

76 Further provision about scope of Family Procedure Rules

(3) Family Procedure Rules may modify the rules of evidence as they apply to family proceedings in any court within the scope of the rules.'

1.38 A definition of 'family proceedings' can be found in the *Matrimonial and Family Proceedings Act 1984, Sch 1, para 3* which defines the 'business' which is assigned to the Family Division as family work.

Rules of procedure

1.39 The function of rules is to say how cases should proceed, not to create law or to extend or re-define the jurisdiction of the courts. In response to counsel's argument that a new rule (in that case CPR 1998, r 52.17[46]) Buxton LJ said in *Jaffray v The Society of Lloyds*:[47]

> '[8] That approach is quite misconceived. The CPR, being rules of court, cannot extend the jurisdiction of the court from that which the law provides, but can only give directions as to how the existing jurisdiction should be exercised. That is very trite law, but if authority is needed for the proposition it can be found in the speech of Lord Herschell LC in *British South Africa Co v Companhia de Mocambique* [1893] AC 602 at p 628.'

1.40 The purposes of procedure and the rules on which it is based is to define how a case comes to trial (or final hearing). In particular it regulates evidence and, for example, how costs and enforcement of orders (where applicable) are to be dealt with. The main subjects set out below fall within FPR 2010.

Practice directions

Practice directions and rules contrasted

1.41 Rules are made formally by the Family Procedure Rule Committee (FPRC) under powers delegated to them under *Courts Act 2003, s 75(2)*, as explained above. Practice directions are incorporated into the rules or issued separately by the President of the Family Division with the approval only of the Lord Chancellor. Rules are approved – nominally at least – by Parliament. There is no such democratic control in the case of practice directions (still less of the remainder of the forms of 'guidance', 'practice notes', 'protocols' and so on considered later).

46 Power of the Court of Appeal to set aside its own decision.

47 [2007] EWCA Civ 586.

1.42 However, practice directions have a formal statutory basis. Some are part of the rules (for example *PD12G* which supports FPR 2010, r 12.73 (communication of information)[48] or *PD16B* which deals with representation of children[49]) and have the approval of the FPRC. Others are freestanding and are issued by the President with Lord Chancellor approval;[50] though these are relatively rare in family proceedings. An example of a practice direction, which applies in family proceedings can be found as issued by the Lord Chief Justice in *Practice Direction of 9 April 2001: Citation of Authorities*.[51]

1.43 The practice direction has no power to change procedural rules, still less to change the law. For example, in *U (A Child) v Liverpool CC*[52] the Court of Appeal, per Brooke LJ, said:

> '[48] The status of a practice direction has been authoritatively delineated by Hale LJ in *Re C (Legal Aid: Preparation of Bill of Costs)* [2001] 1 FLR 602 at §21, May LJ in *Godwin v Swindon Borough Council* [2001] EWCA Civ 1478 at §[11], and Dyson LJ in *Leigh v Michelin Tyre plc* [2003] EWCA Civ 1766 at §[19]–[21]. It is sufficient for present purposes to say that a practice direction has no legislative force. Practice directions provide invaluable guidance to matters of practice in the civil courts, but in so far as they contain statements of the law which are wrong they carry no authority at all.'

1.44 In *Secretary of State for Communities and Local Government v Bovale Ltd and anor*[53] Waller and Dyson LJJ gave a joint judgment. Where a judge had put forward his own practice guidance which also differed from what the court guide on the subject (judicial review and planning cases) said, the two lords justice, set themselves the following questions for their judgment to deal with:

> '[9] In considering any of the arguments in this case the starting point is an understanding of the legal force of the rules, the legal force of practice directions and to understand what are, and what are not, practice directions to which the [Constitutional Reform Act 2005] was intended to apply. To what extent can a judge or indeed any court vary the rules? To what extent are practice directions binding on a court? Who has the power to issue or vary practice directions? What are practice directions?'

1.45 Here we are mostly concerned with the extent to which practice directions are binding. The judges set out the statutory background (mostly from the *Civil Procedure Act 1997* and *Constitutional Reform Act 2005*) and to the history of practice directions in the context of CPR 1998 set out in Hale LJ's judgment in *Re*

48 See further 9.50.

49 See Ch 6.

50 There are very few recent examples of this form of quasi-legislation, as Sir James Munby P did not trouble with formal Lord Chancellor approval but issued what are often treated as practice direction as 'President's Guidance' (see below).

51 Per Lord Woolf LCJ [2001] 1 WLR 1001.

52 Sub nom *KU (A Child) v Liverpool CC* [2005] EWCA Civ 475, [2005] 1 WLR 2657.

53 [2009] EWCA Civ 171, [2009] 1 WLR 2274.

C (Legal Aid: Preparation of Bill of Costs).[54] The court's conclusion (all three judges were agreed on the points considered here) was that where the practice direction has been made within the terms of the *Constitutional Reform Act 2005, s 5(1)* (as explained in *Re C*) the judge has no power to go outside the practice direction (save where he or she finds it to have been made 'per incuriam'[55]).[56]

1.46 The Court of Appeal concluded with thoughts on the difference between formal practice directions and 'guidance':[57]

> '[36] There is, in our view, a distinction between directions, and guidance as to the way in which rules and practice directions will be interpreted. We accept that one object of the practice directions which supplement the rules is to provide guidance to litigants but they also contain directions as to the procedure that should be followed.'

1.47 The court explained the difference between the statutory practice directions – that is, made according to the appropriate statutory formula (that is under the *Constitutional Reform Act 2005, s 5*) – and the non-statutory guidance:

> '[36] ...The nature of the Guides is, or should be, different. They do not, or should not, contain directions; they do, or should, explain inter alia how practice directions apply and are interpreted. Guidance as to how a court interprets and applies practice directions and rules are not in our view themselves practice directions and have rightly not been treated as such. Furthermore Guides as to how the rules and practice directions are operated by the court seem to us something with which the Lord Chancellor should not be concerned.... It follows that since Guides are not practice directions, judgments, in so far as they are providing guidance on how the rules and practice directions work, could not be said to be practice directions.'

Practice directions and the law

1.48 If a practice direction conflicts with the law, the law – common law, statute law and any delegated legislation – takes precedence. Over the past two years at least three practice directions have been found by the Supreme Court to be wrong;[58] and in *Re a Ward of Court*[59] Sir James Munby P pointed out that FPR 2010, *PD12D*, para 5 (which at §5.2 says that permission is needed for police to interview a ward) needs radical review; and this has now been done.[60]

54 [2001] 1 FLR 602.
55 Ie that the maker of the practice direction misdirected him- or herself as to the law.
56 §[29].
57 Considered further at 1.49.
58 See, eg, *Wyatt v Vince* [2015] UKSC 14, [2015] 1 FLR 972 to name but one.
59 [2017] EWHC 1022 (Fam), Sir James Munby P – the police and other statutory agencies do not need court permission to interview a ward.
60 The Ministry of Justice and Family Procedure Rules Committee responded promptly to Sir James's comments FPR 2010 PD12D para 5 has been amended with effect from 16 June 2017 www.justice.gov.uk/courts/procedure-rules/family/practice_directions/pd_part_12d.

Practice guidance, guidelines, notes and protocols

Guidance and other 'quasi-legislation'

1.49 The forms of practice guidance touched on here are not law; though they may be authoritative according to by whom they are issued. They may provide guidance as to how the President of the Family Division or another senior judge wants practice to be conducted. They are what has been called by Wade and Forsythe part of the 'jungle of quasi-legislation'[61] in which many areas of law abound. Where they conflict with the law they should not be followed.

1.50 If a child has to assert that, or even to understand that guidance is not law, it will prove a testing area for judges and the rule of law. The 'jungle' which Wade and Forsythe speak of must be daunting indeed for the mature self-represented child.

Family Justice Council

1.51 A fertile source of 'guidance' for family courts is the Family Justice Council. This is an example of a QANGO. It is non-statutory but advisory. Its website describes that 'its primary role ... is to promote an inter-disciplinary approach to family justice and to monitor the system'. It is chaired by the President of the Family Division and its role is to consider the operation of the family justice system and the working of the family courts. It is now part of the President's office.

1.52 It is not a formal statutory body and has no power to make law. That said, the Family Justice Council's guidances are authoritative; and they are often accepted as such by High Court judges. In this book the following *Guidelines* will make frequent appearances:

- A child's evidence in the proceedings: Guidelines in relation to children giving evidence in family proceedings of 2011,[62] and
- Hearing a child's views: Guidelines for judges meeting children who are subject to family proceedings of 2010,[63] (ie children giving views concerning the proceedings).

Guidelines *and children giving evidence*

1.53 In *Re E (A Child)(Evidence)*[64] and in relation to the subject of children giving evidence in family proceedings, McFarlane LJ explained the relevance of the *Guidelines*:[65]

61 *Administrative Law* (2014) Wade & Forsyth (11th Ed) at 732.
62 [2012] Fam Law 70.
63 [2010] 2 FLR 1872.
64 [2016] EWCA Civ 473, [2017] 1 FLR 1675.
65 Similar comments were made by Ryder LJ in *Re L (Case Management: Child's Evidence)* [2013] EWCA Civ 1778, [2014] 2 FLR 972 at §[8].

'[57] In any case where the issue of children giving oral evidence is raised it is necessary for the court to engage with the factors identified by Baroness Hale in *Re W*, together with any other factors that are relevant to the particular child or the individual case, before coming to a reasoned and considered conclusion on the issue....

[59] The court should also have regard to the Working Party of the Family Justice Council *Guidelines on the issue of Children Giving Evidence in Family Proceedings* issued in December 2011 [2012] Fam Law 79. The Guidelines, which were specifically developed to assist courts following the decision in *Re W*, contain a list of no less than 21 factors to which the court should have regard when determining whether a child should give oral evidence in the context of the principal objective of achieving a fair trial (para 9(a)–(v)). The Guidelines require the court to carry out a balancing exercise: 'between the following primary considerations: (i) the possible advantages that the child being called will bring to the determination of truth balanced against; (ii) the possible damage to the child's welfare from giving evidence ie the risk of harm to the child from giving evidence.'

[60] Whilst not all of the elements described by Baroness Hale in *Re W* or in para 9 of the Guidelines will be relevant in every case, it is plain that the court undertaking a *Re W* determination will need to engage in a relatively full and sophisticated evaluation of the relevant factors; simply paying lip-service to *Re W* is not acceptable. By "full" I do not wish to suggest that a lengthy judgment is required, but simply that the judge must consider each of the relevant points with that process recorded in short form in a judgment. Such a detailed process is in my view justified given the importance of the decision for the welfare of the child and for the fairness of hearing.'

Statutory guidance

1.54 As explained in **Chapter 8**[66] *Working Together* is statutory guidance issued under the *Children Act 2004*, s 11(4). But what is the role of that 'guidance'? Guidance is not a formal type of delegated legislation[67] – codes of practice, guidance and so forth – which have proliferated alongside more conventional and formal legislation (eg such as statutes, delegated legislation and practice directions). As the name makes clear, it is 'guidance' – albeit of high authority; and it cannot be any more.

1.55 As explained in **Chapter 8**, a real issue may yet arise for a mature child where – as happened in *Local Authority X v HI and Others*[68] – that older child has reposed confidences in (say) a social worker; and the child does not want that confidence to go any further or to be acted upon. As explained in **Chapter 8**, in *Gillick v West Norfolk and Wisbech AHA*[69] the law points one way; whilst the 'sharing'

66 See Ch 8, Part 6.
67 As explained at 1.49.
68 [2016] EWHC 1123 (Fam), [2017] 1 FLR 1362, Roberts J.
69 [1985] UKHL 7, [1986] 1 AC 112, [1986] 1 FLR 224.

principles in *Working Together* may point the social worker or the children's guardian or other statutory professional in the opposite – and, perhaps, unlawful – direction. The common law as set out in *Gillick* by the House of Lords takes priority, as law, over guidance, even though the guidance is statutory. An example of the conflict between a children's guardian's confidentiality duties and the duty – perhaps, the case report is not clear – of the solicitor to observe the child clients' right to legal professional privilege is provided by *Wolverhampton City Council v JA & Ors.*[70]

5 PRECEDENT, *STARE DECISIS* AND RATIO

Rules of precedent

Doctrine of precedent: hierarchy of judges

1.56 The rules of precedent developed by the English common law are based on the principle that to be fair the law must, as far as possible, be predictable. Common law rule defines when a judge may deviate from previously decided cases; and this includes judges in the Supreme Court. To form a precedent, however, it is not just a question of what the judge has said. It is also a question of whether what is said is part of the reasoning (ration decidendi) behind the judge's decision.

1.57 The hierarchy of judges was explained by Lord Neuberger in *Willers v Joyce & Anor (as executors of Albert Gubay deceased)*:[71]

> '[4] In a common law system, where the law is in some areas made, and the law is in virtually all areas developed, by judges, the doctrine of precedent, or as it is sometimes known *stare decisis*, is fundamental. Decisions on points of law by more senior courts have to be accepted by more junior courts. Otherwise, the law becomes anarchic, and it loses coherence clarity and predictability....
>
> [5] The doctrine is, of course, seen in its simplest and most familiar form when applied to the hierarchy of courts. On issues of law, (i) Circuit Judges are bound by decisions of High Court Judges, the Court of Appeal and the Supreme Court, (ii) High Court Judges are bound by decisions of the Court of Appeal and the Supreme Court, and (iii) the Court of Appeal is bound by decisions of the Supreme Court....'

Stare decisis: keep to earlier court decisions

1.58 The doctrine of precedent leads to the doctrine of *stare decisis*, that is to say the rule that courts of equivalent level should keep to earlier decisions of the

70 [2017] EWFC 62; considered further at 8.102.
71 [2016] UKSC 44, [2016] 3 WLR 534.

same court. This was explained by the Court of Appeal in *Young v Bristol Aeroplane Co Ltd.*[72] The Court's conclusion on the subject remains the law. Lord Greene MR said of '*stare decisis*' the following:[73]

> 'On a careful examination of the whole matter we have come to the clear conclusion that this court is bound to follow previous decisions of its own as well as those of courts of co-ordinate jurisdiction. The only exceptions to this rule [are]:
>
> (1) The court is entitled and bound to decide which of two conflicting decisions of its own it will follow.
>
> (2) The court is bound to refuse to follow a decision of its own which, though not expressly overruled, cannot, in its opinion, stand with a decision of the House of Lords.
>
> (3) The court is not bound to follow a decision of its own if it is satisfied that the decision was given "per incuriam".'

Inherent jurisdiction of the high court

Function of the jurisdiction

1.59 The inherent jurisdiction of the High Court has been described, in a text which is still treated as authoritative,[74] as being capable of being invoked:

> '… In an apparently inexhaustible variety of circumstances and may be exercised in different ways. This peculiar concept is indeed so amorphous and ubiquitous and so pervasive in its operation that it seems to defy challenge to determine its quality and establish its limits.'[75]

1.60 In *Birmingham City Council v Riaz & Ors*[76] Keehan J was dealing with a child (13 years old) who had been the subject of sexual exploitation by a number of men. The local authority applied for civil injunctions under the inherent jurisdiction of the High Court (ie not under any statute, since there was none) to prevent the respondents from having any association with the girl.

1.61 First the local authority needed permission from the Court to pursue any application at all[77] (ie on terms which went beyond *CA 1989*). Keehan J explained this in the following way:

> '[43] The use of the inherent jurisdiction has been substantially curtailed by the provisions of s 100 of the Children Act 1989. A local authority may not

72 [1944] KB 718.

73 At 730.

74 See, eg, *Birmingham City Council v Riaz & Ors* [2014] EWHC 4247 (Fam) Keehan J at §[42].

75 Jacob *The Inherent Jurisdiction of the Court* (1970) Current Legal Problems 23.

76 [2014] EWHC 4247 (Fam), [2015] 2 FLR 763.

77 *CA 1989, s 100(3).*

apply for any exercise of the court's inherent jurisdiction with respect to children without the leave of the court: s 100(3) of the Children Act 1989.'

1.62 Keehan J took the view that he could assume inherent jurisdiction in this case (and made the orders as requested by the local authority[78]) in the following terms and by reference to what was said by Waite LJ in *Mrs R v Central Independent Television plc:*[79]

'The prerogative jurisdiction has shown a striking versatility, throughout its long history, in adapting its powers to the protective needs of children, in all kinds of different situations. Although the jurisdiction is theoretically boundless, the courts have, nevertheless, found it necessary to set self-imposed limits upon its exercise for the sake of clarity and consistency, and of avoiding conflict between child welfare and other public advantages.'

1.63 So he said, to assume inherent jurisdiction in a case like this was exactly what the duty of the court to protect children – '*parens patriae*' (parent of the country) – was all about; and that it was for him to do what he could as a judge to protect children against sex abuse:

'[46] I am of the firm view that the use of the inherent jurisdiction to make injunctive orders to prevent CSE strikes at the heart of the "parens patriae" jurisdiction of the High Court. I am satisfied that none of the statutory or the 'self-imposed limits' [quoting from Waite LJ (above)] on the exercise of the jurisdiction prevent the court from making the orders sought by the local authority in this case.'

Limits to the jurisdiction

1.64 The Family Court, like the County Court and the Crown Court[80] (and as distinct from the High Court) has no inherent jurisdiction. However, where the High Court has power to make an order under its inherent jurisdiction (eg to grant an injunction), then the *Matrimonial and Family Proceedings Act 1984, s 31E(1)*[81] gives the same power to the Family Court.[82]

---

78 At a later hearing in this case, and also slightly controversially, he made a reporting restriction order in favour of AB (the girl who had suffered the abuse) so that her name could not be reported for the remainder of her life: *Birmingham City Council v Riaz, AB & Ors* [2015] EWHC 1857 (Fam), [2016] 1 FLR 797.

79 [1994] Fam 192, [1994] 2 FLR 151, at 207–208 and 166 respectively.

80 See discussion of *R (Trinity Mirror) v Croydon Crown Court* [2008] EWCA Crim 50, [2008] QB 770 at 13.33.

81 In that part of *MFPA 1984* which introduced the Family Court.

82 Derived from the same provision in *County Courts Act 1981, s 38.*

6 STRAWS IN THE WIND

Vulnerable witnesses and children

Vulnerable Witnesses and Children Working Group

1.65 A Vulnerable Witnesses and Children Working Group (VWCWG), set up by Sir James Munby P in the summer of 2014, submitted a final report in February 2015.[83] Its recommendations have led to a set of draft amendment regulations (Family Procedure (Amendment X) Rules 2015[84] put out for consultation by the FPRC in August 2015. The report and draft rules derive a number of their ideas and terminology from the *Youth Justice and Criminal Evidence Act 1999* (*YJCEA 1999*). Like the 1999 Act the Amendment X rules deal with the evidence of children and of vulnerable witnesses. However, it is reasonable to argue that in terms of witnesses in a criminal trial this makes sense; but that in family proceedings there are in reality three separate subjects under consideration:

- A child's evidence;
- The question of a child meeting with a judge or otherwise having his or her views taken into account;[85]
- The evidence of a witness whose evidence is diminished by the factors referred to in the report (ie in line with the ideas in *YJCEA 1999*).

1.66 The authors of the report have not yet been persuaded to distinguish clearly between the three different areas of family proceedings involved; and, as far as is known, the report and recommendations remain becalmed in the Ministry of Justice. There will undoubtedly be resources issues in relation to some of the proposed 'special measures'.[86] If provisions akin to Youth Justice and Criminal Evidence Act 1999 *Pt 2* are to be incorporated into family proceedings then primary legislation will be needed.

Complainants as to alleged domestic abuse

'Courts bill': cross-examination of complainant witnesses

1.67 One of the casualties of the 2016/17 legislative session which was lost when the June 2017 general election was called was a passage in the proposed Prisons and Courts bill which was to have moved towards a resolution of the issues which confront a complainant of domestic abuse when she is proposed to be cross-examined by her – it is usually a woman, but it could also be a child, and

83 *Report of the Vulnerable Witnesses & Children Working Group February 2015* (Judiciary of England and Wales: the report is actually dated March 2015; www.judiciary.gov.uk/wp-content/uploads/2015/03/vwcwg-report-march-2015.pdf).

84 See https://consult.justice.gov.uk/digital-communications/draft-amendments-to-family-procedure-rules/supporting_documents/annexachildrenvulnerablewitnessesfprcdraftrule.pdf.

85 In the three ways emphasised by Lady Hale: see 4.41.

86 Explained further in Ch 3.

occasionally a man – alleged abuser. A Ministry of Justice press release explained the legislative plan as follows:

> 'The government is giving courts the power to put an end to domestic violence victims being quizzed by their attackers in the family courts, calling time on what the Justice Secretary has described as a "humiliating and appalling" practice. This follows an urgent review she commissioned last month.'

1.68 The 2017 Queen's Speech included: 'Legislation will be brought forward to protect the victims of domestic violence and abuse'. This seems likely, on the government's own background briefing[87] to convert[88] to a Courts Bill which is intended to include:

> 'To put an end to the direct cross examination of domestic violence victims by their alleged perpetrators in the family courts and extend the use of virtual hearings, which will allow victims to participate in trials without having to meet their alleged assailant face-to-face.'

1.69 The content of the bill is not known at the time of going to press. The previous bill (clause 47) inserted a number of amendments into the *Matrimonial and Family Proceedings Act 1984*, as proposed sections 31Q–31X. What follows is a summary of the previous bill, which is likely to form the basis of any new legislation.

Reform for alleged victims of abuse

1.70 The aim of the reforms is to deal with the cross-examination of a domestic violence complainant (A) by an unrepresented defendant (B). In law, if A makes allegations against him (mostly B is male, but not always), B has the right to cross-examine A about what she has told the court about him. In these circumstances, there are many in A's position who find that they are re-living the abusive situation; and this is precisely what the court hearing is designed to get her away from.

1.71 Exactly the same concerns arise if A is a child who is required to give evidence, where at present provision for special measures in family proceedings are limited. The provisions in any Courts Bill will, it must be hoped, reflect the needs also of alleged abused adolescent or young children.[89]

---

87 See www.gov.uk/government/uploads/system/uploads/attachment_data/file/620838/Queens_speech_2017_background_notes.pdf.

88 At page 40.

89 See, eg, the child witness K, whose evidence was not called in *Re S (Care Proceedings: Case Management)* [2016] EWCA Civ 83, [2017] 1 FLR 1476; see at 3.70.

Youth Justice and Criminal Evidence Act 1999

1.72 The 2017 bill had many similarities with the existing provisions of *YJCEA 1999*; though any reference to *YJCEA 1999* involves taking account of qualifications which apply to criminal proceedings but not to family cases:

- A is a witness, and always has a prosecution legal representative dealing with the case; whereas in family proceedings she is both party – the person bringing the application – and a main (perhaps the only) witness;
- The standard of proof against B is beyond reasonable doubt, whereas in family proceedings it is to the civil – more probable than not – standard, and
- In a criminal case there is a variety of 'special measures' available to the court (*YJCEA 1999, Pt 2*), which are not available in the same way to family courts and are not referred to in this bill.

1.73 Cross examination under the previous set of provisions – and perhaps under any future set of provisions – will require their own procedural rules to be incorporated into FPR 2010 (presumably). From the point of view of the parties to proceedings the important provisions of this bill are:

- The provisions for exclusion of cross-examination of A by B acting in person (*Matrimonial and Family Proceedings Act 1984* (*MFPA 1984*) *ss 31R, 31S* and *31T*).
- Alternatives to cross-examination by B in person which the court can order (s 31V(5): akin to *YJCEA 1999, s 38(4)*: appointment of an advocate to cross-examine for the court).
- Funding for s 31V cross-examination at s 31V(6).

A putative Courts Bill

1.74 The proposed reforms in the Prison and Courts Bill, cl 47 started with two provisions – s 31R which prevents a person in B's position, who has been prosecuted for a serious offence against A – the specific offences are yet to be defined – may not cross-examine a victim of that offence (s 31R(1)), balanced against a prohibition on a victim cross-examining B (s 31R(2)). Similar prohibitions apply in relation to an injunction order which has been made by the court and on notice to B (s 31S(1) and (2)).

1.75 The proposed amendment ss 31R and 31S applied where the court was able to take action because another court has previously made findings against B – in criminal or injunction proceedings – so another judge need not re-invent that wheel. Another judge or a jury have made findings against B by which the second court is bound; that is in effect a form of statutory issue estoppel.

1.76 *MFPA 1984, s 31T* was the central section of the reform proposals. It grappled with the question of what happens in relation to a witness whose evidence may be affected by their 'significant distress' at being cross-examined by B. Section

31T enabled 'a party to the proceedings' to apply for a direction, or on the court suggesting that such a direction should be considered (s 31T(1)) so that B does not cross-examine A directly. The conditions for an application depended on the court considering either that a witness's evidence would have been 'diminished' (s 31T(3)) or that that witness would be significantly distressed (s 31T(4)). In both cases the court was to decide whether, if the direction is given, then the 'quality [of a witness's] evidence' is likely to be improved.

Avoidance of cross-examination of a complainant by defendant in person

1.77 The proposed s 31V dealt with 'alternatives to cross-examination in person': that is where orders under ss 31R, 31S or 31T apply; and where the court considered there was no satisfactory alternative to cross-examination by B (s 31V(2)). In provisions which precisely replicate *YJCEA 1999, s 38* the court must invite B to appoint an advocate (for which he will only rarely have legal aid). If B cannot appoint his own advocate the court must consider whether it should do so (s 31V(5): exactly as in *YJCEA 1999, s 38(4)*).[90]

1.78 The court advocate (C) appointed 'represents the interests' of B, but – according to s 31V(7) (as with *YJCEA 1999, s 38(5)*) – C 'is not responsible to' B. In *YJCEA 1999, s 40*, payment for such advocate is guaranteed by statute. Payment for C under the previous bill was left to regulations (to be made under the proposed s 31X); though if that remains the Ministry of Justice plan, it will be recalled that regulations can be changed or revoked much more easily that a statute (ie the *YJCEA 1999* protection for the child witness is much more robust).

The present position

1.79 In the meantime, as explained in **Chapter 6**, the Court of Appeal has told judges they must do their best within the terms of *MFPA 1984, s 31G(6)*;[91] whilst Hayden J has said firmly that he will not again 'hear a case in this way' and permit cross-examination in the circumstances of *A (A Minor: Fact Finding; Unrepresented Party)*.[92] His judgment on the point bears full repetition. The case concerned a child arrangements order (a father's application for contact and residence).

1.80 What is described below could as easily have happened to a child witness (or an otherwise vulnerable young witness[93]) who is cross-examined by an allegedly abusive parent or other party to family proceedings. In *A (A Minor: Fact Finding; Unrepresented Party)* (above) Hayden J said:

> '[57] As I have made clear above it was necessary, in this case, to permit F to conduct cross examination of M directly. A number of points need to be

90 And as contemplated by the Court of Appeal in *Re K & H (Children)* [2015] EWCA Civ 543 sub nom *K and H (Private Law: Public Funding)* [2016] 1 FLR 754.

91 *Re K & H (Children)* (above).

92 [2017] EWHC 1195 (Fam), Hayden J.

93 See, eg, X in *Re A (Sexual Abuse: Disclosure)* [2012] UKSC 60, [2013] 1 FLR 948.

highlighted. Firstly, F was not present in the Courtroom but cross examined by video link. Secondly, M requested and I granted permission for her to have her back to the video screen in order that she did not have to engage face to face with F. Thirdly, F barely engaged with M's allegations of violence, choosing to conduct a case which concentrated on undermining M's credibility (which as emerges above was largely unsuccessful).

[58] Despite these features of the case, I have found it extremely disturbing to have been required to watch this woman cross examined about a period of her life that has been so obviously unhappy and by a man who was the direct cause of her unhappiness. M is articulate, educated and highly motivated to provide a decent life for herself and her son. She was represented at this hearing by leading and junior counsel and was prepared to submit to cross examination by her husband in order that the case could be concluded. She was faced with an invidious choice.

[59] Nothing of what I have said above has masked the impact that this ordeal has had on her. She has at times looked both exhausted and extremely distressed. M was desperate to have the case concluded in order that she and A could effect some closure on this period of their lives and leave behind the anxiety of what has been protracted litigation.

[60] It is a stain on the reputation of our Family Justice system that a Judge can still not prevent a victim being cross examined by an alleged perpetrator. This may not have been the worst or most extreme example but it serves only to underscore that the process is inherently and profoundly unfair. I would go further it is, in itself, abusive. For my part, I am simply not prepared to hear a case in this way again. I cannot regard it as consistent with my judicial oath and my responsibility to ensure fairness between the parties.'

1.81 Hayden J then went on to consider case law going back over ten years and more; though he does not seem to have been referred to *Re K & H*:[94]

'[61] The iniquity of the situation was first highlighted 11 years ago by Roderick Wood J in *H v L and R* [2006] EWHC 3099 (Fam) [2007] 2 FLR 162 Roderic Wood J. It was reiterated in *Re B (a child) (private law fact finding-unrepresented father), DVK* [2014] EWHC (Fam). Cross examination by a perpetrator is prohibited by statute in the Crown Court, in recognition of its impact on victims and in order to facilitate fairness to both prosecution and defence. In Wood J's case he called for "urgent attention" to be given to the issue. This call was volubly repeated by Sir James Munby, President of the Family Division in *Q v Q; Re B (a child); Re C (a child)* [2014] EWFC 31 …

[63] I understand that there is a real will to address this issue but it has taken too long. No victim of abuse should ever again be required to be cross examined by their abuser in any Court, let alone in a Family Court where protection of children and the vulnerable is central to its ethos.'

94 See n 96 above.

1.82 After that it might be thought impertinent to say that a party, such as the father in this case, is entitled by one fair means or another – hence the idea of special measures[95] – to cross-examine a witness or party in this mother's position. It can only be hoped that the one-time promised reforms are still brought forward by the present government.

European union withdrawal

EU Withdrawal Bill

1.83 As this book goes to press, the European Union (Withdrawal) Bill starts its passage through Parliament. Only a very short summary of relevant aspects can be offered here. Such consideration will mostly be limited to such European legislation as Brussels IIA[96] in mind and which impact directly on the family lawyer. Clause 4 of the bill deals with those parts of EU law that now have effect in the UK as a result of the *European Communities Act 1972, s 2(1)*, but which are not covered by clause 3.

1.84 Clause 3 extends to Parliament's efforts to preserve rights arising under directly effective provisions of the EU Treaties; but what is not clear is how the bill envisages that retained Treaty rights would have any real legal effect in the absence of reciprocal recognition by other EU states. For example, Parliament can say that clause 4 causes free movement rights to be retained; but if the UK is no longer a member of the EU, then the 'rights' of UK citizens, supposedly created by clause 4 are meaningless. Other EU states will have no legal obligation to acknowledge, still less to act upon, such 'rights' which Parliament believes it has created. The same will go for the reciprocal arrangements for recognition and enforcement of family law orders and other arrangements (under eg Brussels IIA).

1.85 Clause 5(4) sets out that from 'exit day' the Charter of Fundamental Rights of the European Union (2000/C 364/01)[97] ceases be part of domestic law. For the rights of children, this otherwise regrettable provision, may be of limited effect. European Convention 1950 – for now – remains; and the rights which the Charter protects for children are in any event replicated, more or less, in domestic law[98] and under United Nations Convention on the Rights of the Child 1989.[99]

Delegated powers and Henry VIII clauses

1.86 The powers delegated to government ministers by Clause 7 of the bill are substantial; and they constitute extensive Henry VIII powers (as explained below). For instance, Clause 7(1) provides almost unlimited powers to ministers by administrative direction to alter substantive EU law:

---

95 As explained in Ch 3, Part 7.

96 *Council Regulation (EC) No 2201/2003 of 27 November 2003 Concerning Jurisdiction and the Recognition and Enforcement of Judgments in Matrimonial Matters and in Matters of Parental Responsibility.*

97 See Ch 5.

98 *Re D (A Child) (International Recognition)* [2016] EWCA Civ 12, [2016] 1 WLR 2469, [2016] 2 FLR 347.

99 See Ch 5.

'(1) A Minister of the Crown may by regulations make such provision as the Minister considers appropriate to prevent, remedy or mitigate —

(a) any failure of retained EU law to operate effectively, or

(b) any other deficiency in retained EU law,

arising from the withdrawal of the United Kingdom from the EU.'

1.87 However, oppressive use of such powers as in Clause 7(1) – if it becomes law – can render a minister open to judicial review as happened recently in *R (The Public Law Project) v Lord Chancellor.*[100] This case suggests that if powers are exceeded by ministers the courts may review such ministerial action. In the *Public Law Project* case Lord Neuberger, who delivered the only judgment, referred to the tension between Henry VIII powers and parliamentary sovereignty:

'[23] Subordinate legislation will be held by a court to be invalid if it has an effect, or is made for a purpose, which is *ultra vires*, that is, outside the scope of the statutory power pursuant to which it was purportedly made. In declaring subordinate legislation to be invalid in such a case, the court is upholding the supremacy of Parliament over the Executive. That is because the court is preventing a member of the Executive from making an order which is outside the scope of the power which Parliament has given him or her by means of the statute concerned. Accordingly, when, as in this case, it is contended that actual or intended subordinate legislation is *ultra vires,* it is necessary for a court to determine the scope of the statutorily conferred power to make that legislation.'

1.88 Lord Neuberger cited *Craies on Legislation* (10th ed (2015)), edited by Daniel Greenberg) at §1.3.9: 'The term "Henry VIII power" is commonly used to describe a delegated power under which subordinate legislation is enabled to amend primary legislation'. He then continued:

'[25] ... When a court is considering the validity of a statutory instrument made under a Henry VIII power, its role in upholding Parliamentary supremacy is particularly striking, as the statutory instrument will be purporting to vary primary legislation passed into law by Parliament.

[26] The interpretation of the statutory provision conferring a power to make secondary legislation is, of course, to be effected in accordance with normal principles of statutory construction. However, in the case of an "amendment that is permitted under a Henry VIII power", to quote again from *Craies* (*op cit*) §1.3.11: "as with all delegated powers the only rule for construction is to test each proposed exercise by reference to whether or not it is within the class of action that Parliament must have contemplated when delegating. Although Henry VIII powers are often cast in very wide terms, the more general the words by Parliament to delegate a power, the more likely it is that an exercise within the literal meaning of the words will nevertheless be outside the legislature's contemplation".'

100 [2016] UKSC 39, [2016] 1 AC 1531, [2016] 3 WLR 387.

1.89 Extensive Administrative Court litigation is likely if this bill is enacted. Whether any of it will affect children law remains to be seen. Whether it does or not, there is no doubt that extensive delegated legislation affecting all areas of law – and family law will not be immune – will follow the passing into law of the EU Withdrawal Bill.

2

MEANING OF 'CHILD': LAW AND REALITY

1 INTRODUCTION

'Child': meaning and a child's role in proceedings

2.1 The meaning of 'child' in statute law and the reality of the child's development and the consequent operation of the law on that child raise two separate questions: the formal position and the gradation of a child's understanding and views as he or she approaches adulthood. The purpose of this chapter is to explain first the formal terminology for 'child' and then to contrast that with the reality of a child's understanding and the significance of this for the child's entitlement to confidentiality.

2.2 This chapter considers the subject as follows:

- **Part 2** deals with the law as it defines a child's age and the consequences of this in legal proceedings.
- **Part 3** explains the role a mature child may take in children proceedings, and the procedural constraints on this (and links up with the subject of children as parties to proceedings and their representation in **Chapter 6**).
- **Part 4** summarises the main aspects of the landmark *Gillick* case, and explains its continuing relevance today in terms of the role of adolescent under 18-year-olds in their own proceedings, in being heard by the court and their entitlement to confidentiality.
- **Part 5** links up with 'confidentiality' in **Chapter 8**, and – in the context especially of a child's understanding and *Gillick* – introduces medical practice and guidance in relation to mature children.

2 ACTUAL AGE

Child's biological age

2.3 Statute defines various ages at which for the purposes of this book a child's age will affect how he or she is treated by the court; and how that child's rights will be defined. By contrast, throughout any consideration of a child's role in proceedings that child's developmental age will be important; and this may have very little to do with the child's biological age.

2.4 By the *Family Law Reform Act 1969, s 1(1)* an individual attains majority at 18 (lowered by s 1(1) to that age with effect from 1 January 1970). Under the *Children Act 1989* a child remains a child – the term 'minor' was intended to go with the 1989 Act, but creeps in still in various places (eg in rules relating to wardship).

2.5 Under the *Children Act 1989, s 105(1)* a child is 'a person under the age of eighteen'; but the extent to which provisions of the Act can be adapted for use by a child – with or without permission of the court – is amongst the factors with which this book is concerned.

2.6 A sixteen-year-old can consent to medical and other treatment as if 'of full age'.

> '**8 Consent by persons over 16 to surgical, medical and dental treatment**
>
> (1) The consent of a minor who has attained the age of sixteen years to any surgical, medical or dental treatment which, in the absence of consent, would constitute a trespass to his person, shall be as effective as it would be if he were of full age; and where a minor has by virtue of this section given an effective consent to any treatment it shall not be necessary to obtain any consent for it from his parent or guardian.'

2.7 It was what should happen to the consent of a child of sixteen and under that age which was in issue in *Gillick v West Norfolk and Wisbech AHA*[1] (*Gillick*) as will be considered fully in **Part 4**.

Age and maturity

2.8 The variants of 'understanding and intelligence',[2] 'views of the child [to be] given due weight',[3] 'ascertainable wishes and feelings' and 'age and understanding',[4] 'views [of a child taken into account] accordance with their age and maturity'[5] will be important features of what follows in this book. Here the emphasis is on what was said by the House of Lords in *Gillick* where the term used was 'age and understanding'. It is an introduction to that case and its terminology which now follows.

---

1 [1985] UKHL 7, [1986] 1 AC 112, [1986] 1 FLR 224.
2 *Gillick* eg per Lord Scarman at [1986] 1 FLR 224 at 253; and see 2.21.
3 United Nations Convention on the Rights of the Child 1989, Art 12 (below).
4 *CA 1989, s 1(3)(a)*.
5 Charter of Fundamental Rights of the European Union (2000/C 364/01) Art 24.1 (below).

2.9 The context in which these terms arise will be explained especially in **Chapters 4**, **5** and **6**. In summary, in addition to *Gillick*, the most prominent examples of are:

Children Act 1989 s 1(3)(a)

(3) [On considering an application under CA 1989] a court shall have regard in particular to – (a) the ascertainable wishes and feelings of the child concerned (considered in the light of his age and understanding);...

United Nations Convention on the Rights of the Child 1989 Art 12

1. States Parties shall assure to the child who is capable of forming his or her own views the right to express those views freely in all matters affecting the child, the views of the child being given due weight in accordance with the age and maturity of the child.

Charter of Fundamental Rights of the European Union (2000/C 364/01) Art 24.1

The rights of the child

1. Children... may express their views freely. Such views shall be taken into consideration on matters which concern them in accordance with their age and maturity.

2.10 The extent to which these terms apply in children proceedings and are reflected in judicial decision-making will be introduced in **Part 4** and explained more fully, especially in **Chapter 6**.

3 CHILD'S ROLE IN PROCEEDINGS

Participation and evidence in proceedings

2.11 The role of a child (in the sense of a person under 18) in proceedings will vary according to whether the child is a party, a witness or neither of these but the subject of the proceedings (eg in child arrangements order proceedings under *Children's Act 1989* (*CA 1989*), *s 8*). The child's status or participation in the proceedings may be:

- as the applicant – the person who starts proceedings;[6]
- as a child who is subject to proceedings,[7] or

6 See, eg, *Re CT (A Minor) (Wardship: Representation)* [1993] 2 FLR 278 CA and other more recent cases at 6.71.

7 See, eg, *Re D (Abduction: Rights of Custody)* [2006] UKHL 51, [2007] 1 FLR 961 considered at 4.6.

- as a subject of the proceedings, who applies formally to be joined to express a view or give evidence.[8]

2.12 In any of these three categories of involvement in proceedings the child may be required to give evidence. This may be as a party (eg in care proceedings) or solely as a witness of fact.[9] This role of the child is dealt with in judicial guidelines[10] and is explained fully in **Chapter 3**.

2.13 Alternatively, or in addition, the child may wish to, and may be entitled to, tell the court of his or her views as to the outcome of proceedings.[11] As will be seen in **Chapter 4**, and as touched on below, this question is the subject of rights provision in UN and EU law; and is the subject of judicial guidance[12] in English proceedings. The extent to which a child must seek permission to express a view or should expect to do so as a matter of right will be considered in **Chapter 4**.

Party to proceedings and legal representation

2.14 According to a court's perception of a child's understanding of the application in question[13] a child may be permitted by a court to issue proceedings in the child's own right; or, by direction of the court, to join in proceedings which concern the child as a party.[14] In either case the child may be represented; though this may depend on the availability of legal aid.[15] In care proceedings the child will be represented as of right and regardless of the child's means or the merits of his or her case.

2.15 Legal representation in most care cases (ie under *CA 1989, Pts 4* and *5*) will be a matter for the court[16] and will be preceded by the fact that the court will appoint a children's guardian to represent the interests of the child.[17] Throughout the continuance of the care proceedings the guardian will remain responsible for the child; though the child gives instructions to the solicitor which conflict with the views of the guardian. As explained further in **Chapter 6** the solicitor will continue the proceedings acting on behalf of the child alone.

---

8 See, eg, *Mabon v Mabon* [2005] EWCA Civ 634, [2005] Fam 366, [2005] 2 FLR 1011 considered at 6.80.

9 The 14-year-old in *Re S (Care Proceedings: Case Management)* [2016] EWCA Civ 83, [2017] 1 FLR 1476 was a witness, and permitted by the judge not to be called to give evidence (see 3.32).

10 *Guidelines in relation to children giving evidence in family proceedings of December 2011* [2012] Fam Law 70; fully considered in Ch 3.

11 See, eg, *Mabon v Mabon* [2005] EWCA Civ 634, [2005] Fam 366, [2005] 2 FLR 1011 considered at 4.25.

12 *Guidelines on Judges Meeting Children who are subject to Family Proceedings April 2010* [2010] 2 FLR 1872; fully considered at Ch 4.

13 See especially *CA 1989, s 10(8)* at 6.67.

14 See, eg, *Mabon* and *Ciccone v Ritchie (No 1)* (above).

15 See Ch 6, Part 6.

16 *CA 1989, s 41(3)*; and see 6.58.

17 *CA 1989, s 41(2)*. These terms, and especially the concept of a child's 'interests' will be explained at 6.46.

2.16 In private law proceedings commenced by a child, or where a child is joined as a party (whether on the application of the child or of a parent)[18] it will generally be a matter for any lawyer instructed to decide whether the child has sufficient understanding to give instructions[19] subject to oversight of the lawyer's assessment by the court in cases of doubt.[20] As in any civil proceedings, the starting point for private law children proceedings is that a child must proceed with any application by a guardian or litigation friend.[21] Alternatively a child may be permitted to proceed without a guardian or litigation friend;[22] or, in principle, to proceed without representation of a guardian or a lawyer.

2.17 As will be explained in the next Part, and as discussed further in **Chapter 6**, the outcome of the children applications respectively under *CA 1989, s 10(8)* (applications in private law proceedings) and s 41 (representation in care proceedings) and under FPR 2010, r 16.6 (child proceeding without guardian, mostly with a lawyer) will depend on the court's assessment of the child's understanding at different levels of what is involved in the proceedings with which the child is concerned.

4 AGE AND UNDERSTANDING

The reality of the child's views, human development and social change

2.18 The extent to which *Gillick* remains important in modern law will be explained at different times in this book. Here it will be considered in outline. It has two main aspects:

(1) It defines the development of a child's understanding and intelligence and the extent to which the child may therefore be involved in decision-making which concerns them, and

(2) It defines the extent to which a child may be treated as being entitled to their own confidences (or, to break or otherwise publicise those confidences).

2.19 *Re Roddy (A Child) (Identification: Restriction on Publication)*[23] shows the extent to which these two aspect of *Gillick* can combine in one case. As more fully developed in **Chapter 5**, in *Roddy* Munby J (later Sir James Munby P) explained the importance of *Gillick* in the context of his order that reporting restrictions should not apply to a mother who was also a child; though nearly 17 at the date of the judgment. In particular he quoted Lord Fraser:[24]

18 FPR 2010, r 16.6(1); and see 6.54.
19 FPR 2010, r 16.6(3).
20 *Re CT (A Minor) (Wardship: Representation)* [1993] 2 FLR 278 (above).
21 FPR 2010, r 16.6
22 FPR 2010, r 16.6(5); and see 6.56.
23 [2003] EWHC 2927, [2004] 2 FLR 949 at §[56]; considered at 5.67.
24 At §[50].

'"... the degree of parental control actually exercised over a particular child does in practice vary considerably according to his understanding and intelligence and it would, in my opinion, be unrealistic for the courts not to recognise these facts. Social customs change, and the law ought to, and does in fact, have regard to such changes when they are of major importance."...'

2.20 Munby J concluded that aspect of Angela Roddy's case, that 'courts must face reality [and] be sensitive to human development and social change'. This was a development which the House of Lords, especially Lords Fraser and Scarman had begun with the *Gillick* case.

Gillick: consent to contraceptive advice for child under 16

2.21 In *Gillick v West Norfolk and Wisbech AHA*[25] Mrs Gillick raised the hypothetical question: what should the doctor of any of her five daughters do – if the question arose – were one of them, when still under 16, to seek contraceptive advice from that doctor? Could the doctor's advice only be given with parental consent? Alternatively, could the doctor proceed as if the daughter had, on her own behalf, given valid consent? (It was not suggested that any of the Gillick daughters was in need of contraceptive advice, nor expected were they expected to be.)

2.22 The then Department of Health ('DHSS'), in 1974, had issued guidance to health authorities which included particular reference to counselling and treatment for girls under 16 seeking contraceptive advice.[26] It emphasised the need for doctors 'not to undermine parental responsibility and family stability'. The guidance went on to say: 'that it would be most unusual to provide advice about contraception without parental consent'.

2.23 The 1974 guidance emphasised the importance of confidentiality as between doctor and patient. There may arise instances when a doctor is treating a child who does not want to involve her parents, that clinical judgment may – or must – override or ignore parental consent (see italicised passage in the guidance below); even though to treat a child 'without parental consent would be most unusual'. The DHSS guidance explained the question of clinical judgment as follows:

'It is, however, widely accepted that consultations between doctors and patients are confidential; and the department recognizes the importance which doctors and patients attach to this principle. It is a principle which applies also to the other professions concerned. To abandon this principle for children under 16 might cause some not to seek professional advice at all. They could then be exposed to the immediate risks of pregnancy and of sexually-transmitted diseases, as well as other long-term physical, psychological and emotional consequences which are equally a threat to stable family life. This

25 [1985] UKHL 7, [1986] 1 AC 112, [1986] 1 FLR 224.

26 The guidance is set out in full in Lord Fraser's opinion at [1986] 1 FLR 224 at 229.

would apply particularly to young people whose parents are, for example, unconcerned, entirely unresponsive,...

The Department realizes that in such exceptional cases the nature of any counselling must be a matter for the doctor or other professional worker concerned and that *the decision whether or not to prescribe contraception must be for the clinical judgment of a doctor*' (italics added).

2.24 So what does this passage mean to a doctor who is consulted by a girl under 16? Lord Fraser's view was:

'... in my view, it is perfectly clear that [the guidance] would convey to any doctor... that the decision whether or not to prescribe contraception for a girl under 16 was in the last resort a matter for the clinical judgment of a doctor, even if the girl's parents had not been informed that she had consulted the doctor, and even if they had expressed disapproval of contraception being prescribed for her.'

2.25 Mrs Gillick objected to this guidance. She asked the High Court for declarations in respect of it as follows:

(1) That it has 'no authority in law and gives advice which is unlawful and wrong'; and that therefore

(2) No doctor should give contraceptive advice without parental or guardian's consent.

2.26 At first instance Woolf J refused the declaration. On appeal, a declaration was granted by the Court of Appeal. On appeal to the House of Lords (on a majority of three Lords to two) the decision of Woolf J was upheld. It is the opinions of Lords Fraser and Scarman who gave the main speeches for the majority, which guide the law, medical practice and GMC guidance[27] today.

Contraceptive advice to a child under 16: whose judgment?

2.27 Lord Fraser set out the question which Mrs Gillick posed to the House as follows:[28]

'The central issue in the appeal is whether a doctor can ever, in any circumstances, lawfully give contraceptive advice or treatment to a girl under the age of 16 without her parents' consent.'

2.28 He resolved his response to this question into two 'strands of argument':

(1) Does a girl of under 16 have the legal capacity to give valid consent to contraceptive advice and treatment; and

27 See 2.83.
28 [1986] 1 FLR 224 at 231.

(2) If such advice is given, without parental consent, does this infringe a parent's rights?

2.29 Statute law prescribed then, as now – see *Family Law Reform Act 1969, s 8(1)* – that at 16 a child can consent to 'medical treatment' as if of full age.[29] But what of the law for a child under that age? Statute law was silent. The common law – judge-made law – must fill the gap. *Gillick* was concerned with how the common law should deal with the issue (as Lord Fraser's definition of the questions he must answer show); or as Lord Scarman explained:[30]

> 'Although statute has intervened in respect of a child's capacity to consent to medical treatment from the age of 16 onwards, neither statute nor the case law has ruled on the extent and duration of parental right in respect of children under the age of 16. More specifically, there is no rule yet applied to contraceptive treatment, which has special problems of its own and is a late-comer in medical practice. It is open, therefore, to the House to formulate a rule.'

Parental control against child's independence

2.30 Lord Fraser reflected on the extent to which parental authority increasingly gives way to the rights of children (this passage explains the approach of the three law lords in the Lords' majority):[31]

> '... It is, in my view, contrary to the ordinary experience of mankind, at least in Western Europe in the present century, to say that a child or a young person remains in fact under the complete control of his parents until he attains the definite age of majority, now 18 in the United Kingdom, and that on attaining that age he suddenly acquires independence. In practice most wise parents relax their control gradually as the child develops and encourage him or her to become increasingly independent.'

2.31 Lord Scarman developed the theme of the importance of the law taking account of modern values. Legal principle must try 'to keep the law abreast of the society in which [the judges] live and work'.[32] This case demanded a response from the common law in a field where the law might find itself having to deal with a conflict 'parental right and a doctor's duty':[33]

> 'The law has, therefore, to be found by a search in the judge-made law for the true principle. The legal difficulty is that in our search we find ourselves in a field of medical practice where parental right and a doctor's duty may point us in different directions. This is not surprising. Three features have

29 Set out in full at 2.6.
30 [1986] 1 FLR 224 at 250.
31 [1986] 1 FLR 224 at 236.
32 [1986] 1 FLR 224 at 248.
33 [1986] 1 FLR 224 at 247.

emerged in today's society which were not known to our predecessors: (1) contraception as a subject for medical advice and treatment; (2) the increasing independence of young people; and (3) the changed status of women.'

'Understanding and intelligence'

2.32 So, said Lord Scarman, the law which explains the balance as between parent and child is concerned with development of the 'human personality':[34]

> 'If the law should impose upon the process of "growing up" fixed limits where nature knows only a continuous process, the price would be artificiality and a lack of realism in an area where the law must be sensitive to human development and social change.... Unless and until Parliament should think fit to intervene, the courts should establish a principle flexible enough to enable justice to be achieved by its application to the particular circumstances proved by the evidence placed before them.'

2.33 This flexibility proposed by the House of Lords, it might be said, was preserved by parliament in *CA 1989, s 1(3)(a)*,[35] and has been maintained by practitioners since. For instance, in *R (Axon) v The Secretary of State for Health and anor*[36] Silber J treated them as the explanation for parents' dwindling rights over children.[37] Lord Scarman's words on the subject of a child's 'understanding and intelligence' and termination of parental rights in *Gillick* remain the common law position. As Silber J explained in *Axon*, the common law as explained in *Gillick* still represents the law, despite the later passing of *CA 1989*. Indeed, it can be said it illuminates certain aspects of *CA 1989*, especially s 1(3)(a).

2.34 Lord Scarman explained the significance of a mature child's 'understanding and intelligence':[38]

> '... I would hold that as a matter of law the parental right to determine whether or not their minor child below the age of 16 will have medical treatment terminates if and when the child achieves a *sufficient understanding*

---

34 [1986] 1 FLR 224 at 253.

35 *CA 1989, s 1(3)(a)* requires that 'a court shall have regard in particular to – (a) the ascertainable wishes and feelings of the child concerned (considered in the light of his age and understanding)' when considering an order in respect of a child. See further at 2.9.

36 [2006] EWHC 37 (Admin), [2006] 2 FLR 206, Silber J [Family Planning Association were joined as parties].

37 At [94]: '... the majority decision [of the House of Lords] is based on an analysis of the parental right to determine whether or not their minor child below the age of 16 will have medical treatment, which according to Lord Scarman: 'terminates if and when the child achieves a sufficient understanding and intelligence to enable him or her to fully understand what is proposed'. Lord Fraser also regarded the parents' authority as being a 'dwindling right' and 'that once the rule of the parents' absolute authority over minority children is abandoned, the solution to the problem in the appeal can no longer be found by referring to rigid parental rights at any particular age. The solution depends on what is best for the welfare of the particular child'.

38 [1986] 1 FLR 224 at 253.

> *and intelligence* to enable him or her to understand fully what is proposed. It will be a question of fact whether a child seeking advice has sufficient understanding of what is involved to give a consent valid in law. Until the child achieves the capacity to consent, the parental right to make the decision continues save only in exceptional circumstances. Emergency, parental neglect, abandonment of the child, or inability to find the parent are examples of exceptional situations justifying the doctor proceeding to treat the child without parental knowledge and consent: but there will arise, no doubt, other exceptional situations in which it will be reasonable for the doctor to proceed without the parent's consent.'

Gillick and confidentiality

2.35 In the final analysis parental right yields to what the welfare, or benefit, of the child demands. Lord Fraser expressed this as:[39]

> 'It was, I think, accepted both by Mrs Gillick and by the DHSS, and in any event I hold, that parental rights to control a child do not exist for the benefit of the parent. They exist for the benefit of the child and they are justified only in so far as they enable the parent to perform his duties towards the child, and towards other children in the family.'

2.36 Lord Fraser traced this idea – of a parent having a duty to, not rights over, a child – to early nineteenth century legal thinking and to the latter guardianship legislation which ultimately was absorbed into and replaced by the welfare principles set out in *CA 1989, s 1*:

> 'If necessary, this proposition can be supported by reference to *Blackstone's Commentaries*, 17th edn (1830), vol. 1, p. 452, where he wrote: "The power of parents over their children is derived from…their duty." The proposition is also consistent with the provisions of the Guardianship of Minors Act 1971, s. 1 (as amended) as follows:
>
> "Where in any proceedings before any court:…
>
> (a) the legal custody or upbringing of a minor… is in question, the court, in deciding that question, shall regard the welfare of the minor as the first and paramount consideration, and shall not take into consideration whether from any other point of view the claim of the father, in respect of such legal custody, upbringing, administration or application is superior to that of the mother, or the claim of the mother is superior to that of the father."'

2.37 Thus, says Lord Scarman, the underlying principle of the modern law – which he had set himself to find – is that parental right yields to a child's right to decide when the child is of 'sufficient understanding and intelligence':

39 [1986] 1 FLR 224 at 235.

> 'The underlying principle of the law was exposed by Blackstone and can be seen to have been acknowledged in the case law. It is that parental right yields to the child's right to make his own decisions when he reaches a sufficient understanding and intelligence to be capable of making up his own mind on the matter requiring decision.'

5 CONFIDENTIALITY AND CONSENT

Medical guidance

2.38 Medical practice associates confidentiality closely with patient trust;[40] and there is no reason why any professional (especially in the private field) should not take the same view of his/her duty of confidentiality. Lord Scarman was clear on this. He considered that the right of the parent to 'custody'[41] could be overridden in exceptional circumstances, where a doctor's judgment is that it should be overridden:[42]

> 'In my judgment the guidance clearly implies that in exceptional cases the parental right to make decisions as to the care of their children, which derives from their right of custody, can lawfully be overridden, and that in such cases the doctor may without parental consultation or consent prescribe contraceptive treatment in the exercise of his clinical judgment. And the guidance reminds the doctor that in such cases *he owes the duty of confidentiality to his patient, by which is meant that the doctor would be in breach of his duty to her if he did communicate with her parents.*' (italics added)

2.39 The passage in italics summarises the outcome of the case – an outcome which is born out by medical guidance on the subject. It also says starkly where confidentiality is owed, that if the doctor did not follow the guidance – or any similar guidance on confidentiality and children – s/he 'would be in breach of his/her duty of confidentiality'. There is no reason in law why the same duty of confidentiality should not be observed in respect of children by other professionals working in the private field.

---

40 *Good Medical Practice* issued by GMC for all medical practitioners (www.gmc-uk.org/guidance/ethical_guidance/children_guidance_index.asp). '42. Respecting patient confidentiality is an essential part of good care; this applies when the patient is a child or young person as well as when the patient is an adult. Without the trust that confidentiality brings, children and young people might not seek medical care and advice, or they might not tell you all the facts needed to provide good care' (www.gmc-uk.org/guidance/ethical_guidance/children_guidance_42_43_principles_of_confidentiality.asp). This is considered fully in Ch 8.

41 'Custody' is a term which disappeared – or should have disappeared: some lay people including journalists retain it – with *CA 1989, s 8*. It was replaced with the term 'residence' which has itself been replaced by the elusive 'child arrangements) concept by *Children and Families Act 2014*.

42 [1986] 1 FLR 224 at 245–6

Communication by doctor with parents

2.40 Lord Fraser concluded the section of his speech on 'The parents' rights and duties in respect of medical treatment of their child' by urging doctors to persuade a child to tell her parents of the treatment she was seeking; or to persuade her that the doctor should speak with the parents. Failing that, said Lord Fraser,[43] in cases:

> '... Where the girl refuses either to tell the parents herself or to permit the doctor to do so and in such cases, the doctor will, in my opinion, be justified in proceedings without the parents' consent or even knowledge provided he is satisfied on the following matters:
>
> (1) that the girl (although under 16 years of age) will understand his advice;
>
> (2) that he cannot persuade her to inform her parents or to allow him to inform the parents that she is seeking contraceptive advice;
>
> (3) that she is very likely to begin or to continue having sexual inter-course with or without contraceptive treatment;
>
> (4) that unless she receives contraceptive advice or treatment her physical or mental health or both are likely to suffer;
>
> (5) that her best interest require him to give her contraceptive advice, treatment or both without the parental consent.'

2.41 Translated into modern practice as regulated by the current GMC Guidance[44] this is updated under the heading '0-18 years guidance: Contraception, abortion and sexually transmitted infections (STIs)' as (addressed to the doctor):

> '70 You can provide contraceptive, abortion and STI advice and treatment, without parental knowledge or consent, to young people under 16 provided that:
>
> (a) they understand all aspects of the advice and its implications
>
> (b) you cannot persuade the young person to tell their parents or to allow you to tell them
>
> (c) in relation to contraception and STIs, the young person is very likely to have sex with or without such treatment
>
> (d) their physical or mental health is likely to suffer unless they receive such advice or treatment, and
>
> (e) it is in the best interests of the young person to receive the advice and treatment without parental knowledge or consent.'

2.42 *Gillick* and *Axon* (below) are still – and correctly – treated by the GMC Guidance as authority for the propositions set out in §70 above.

---

43 At [1986] 1 FLR 239 to 240.

44 See www.gmc-uk.org/guidance/ethical_guidance/children_guidance_70_71_contraception.asp; as considered more fully in Ch 8.

Child confidentiality and 2004 medical guidance

2.43 By 2004 further guidance had been issued by the Department of Health. This was challenged in *Axon* (above)[45] as being outside what was intended by *Gillick*. By the time of the *Axon* case there had been two important statutory developments. First, *CA 1989* defined 'parental responsibility'. The eclipse of parental rights by parental responsibility had been an important part of the reasoning of the House of Lords, but remained then part of the common law. Silber J affirmed the statutory source, at *CA 1989, s 3(1)*:

> '(1) In this Act "parental responsibility" means all the rights, duties, powers, responsibilities and authority which by law a parent of a child has in relation to the child and his property.'

2.44 Secondly, the *Human Rights Act 1998* had made the European Convention 1950 part of English law; and as will be seen he considered the modern requirement of guidance of the type considered in *Gillick* in the light of Art 8 of the Convention (right to respect for family life).

2.45 Silber J held as had the House of Lords in *Gillick*: that '.... the medical professional is entitled to provide medical advice and treatment on sexual matters without the parents' knowledge or consent' subject to the following factors:

(1) that the young person although under 16 years of age understands all aspects of the advice. In the light of Lord Scarman's comments in *Gillick* at 189C and 253 respectively set out in para [13](v), above, he or she must 'have sufficient maturity to understand what is involved' that understanding includes all relevant matters and it is not limited to family and moral aspects as well as all possible adverse consequences which might follow from the advice;

(2) that the medical professional cannot persuade the young person to inform his or her parents or to allow the medical professional to inform the parents that their child is seeking advice and/or treatment on sexual matters. [As stated in the 2004 Guidance, where the young person cannot be persuaded to involve a parent, every effort should be made to persuade the young person to help find another adult (such as another family member or a specialist youth worker) to provide support to the young person];

(3) that (in any case in which the issue is whether the medical professional should advise on or treat in respect of contraception and sexually transmissible illnesses) the young person is very likely to begin or to continue having sexual intercourse with or without contraceptive treatment or treatment for a sexually transmissible illness;

45 See n 36 above. Family Planning Association were joined as parties. The claimant was a divorced single parent with five children, the younger two of whom were daughters aged 12 and 15. She had had an abortion and she still regrets it. She hoped that neither of her daughters would have to undergo such an experience without her – their mother – being present. She considered that the 2004 Guidance undermined her role as a parent. In her view, said the judge, the prospect of her daughters receiving contraception or having an abortion without even her knowledge is horrifying (at [15] to [17]).

(4) that unless the young person receives advice and treatment on the relevant sexual matters, his or her physical or mental health or both are likely to suffer. [In considering this requirement, the medical professional must take into account all aspects of the young person's health]; and

(5) that the best interests of the young person require him or her to receive advice and treatment on sexual matters without parental consent or notification.

2.46 In all this it will be appreciated that the best interests or welfare test in terms of treatment, and any decision to override a child's confidentiality, remains with the doctor. *Gillick* remains a sound expression of the common law, despite the passage of time, the redrafting of the medical guidance and the passage of the *Children Act 1989* and other more recent children legislation (eg the *Children Act 2004*).

GMC Guidance 2017

2.47 Under the heading '0-18 years guidance: Assessing capacity to consent' the GMC Guidance[46] to all doctors in England, Wales and Scotland is helpful. It proposes as follows:

> '24 You[47] must decide whether a young person is able to understand the nature, purpose and possible consequences of investigations or treatments you propose, as well as the consequences of not having treatment. Only if they are able to understand, retain, use and weigh this information, and communicate their decision to others can they consent to that investigation or treatment. That means you must make sure that all relevant information has been provided and thoroughly discussed before deciding whether or not a child or young person has the capacity to consent.
>
> 25 The capacity to consent depends more on young people's ability to understand and weigh up options than on age. When assessing a young person's capacity to consent, you should bear in mind that:
>
> (a) at 16 a young person can be presumed to have the capacity to consent (see paragraphs 30 to 33);
>
> (b) a young person under 16 may have the capacity to consent, depending on their maturity and ability to understand what is involved.[48]
>
> 26 It is important that you assess maturity and understanding on an individual basis and with regard to the complexity and importance of

46 See www.gmc-uk.org/guidance/ethical_guidance/children_guidance_24_26_assessing_capacity.asp

47 The Guidance uses 'you' in the terminology of modern professional guidances to refer to the individual doctor who it seems to anticipate is its only reader

48 As a footnote for this reference the Guidance gives: 'Family Law Reform Act 1969; Age of Majority Act 1969 (Northern Ireland); Age of Legal Capacity (Scotland) Act 1991; Adults with Incapacity (Scotland) Act 2000; Mental Capacity Act 2005; *Gillick v West Norfolk and Wisbech AHA* [1986] AC 112'.

> the decision to be made. You should remember that a young person who has the capacity to consent to straightforward, relatively risk-free treatment may not necessarily have the capacity to consent to complex treatment involving high risks or serious consequences. The capacity to consent can also be affected by their physical and emotional development and by changes in their health and treatment.'

2.48 This Guidance and its relevance to a child's confidentiality is considered further in **Chapter 8.**

3

CHILD'S EVIDENCE

1 INTRODUCTION

Children giving evidence in family proceedings

3.1 **Chapter 4** considers a child's views on a case in which the child is a participant including as to its outcome. This chapter looks at the separate question of circumstances in which a child may give evidence in a children case. This will include:

(1) Where the child is a party. Plainly the child's evidence may have an influence on the outcome of the case; and

(2) Where the child may be called to give evidence for a party to proceedings in relation to facts which are relevant to questions in issue between the parties.

3.2 Two sets of guidelines have been issued by Family Justice Council. One deals with the hearing of a child's evidence of fact (the subject of this chapter) and the other with circumstances of a judge meeting with a child, or otherwise hearing that child's views (**Chapter 4**). In certain circumstances, a child may be called upon to give evidence in a case (as explained in this chapter). Separately or alongside that – or perhaps in a completely different format (eg speaking to a CAFCASS officer or social worker) – to express a view as to the outcome of the proceedings.

3.3 The guidelines are that – no more. They are not a statement of the law. There are two sets of guidelines, which in themselves make clear the difference between the two forms of what may be heard from children: their evidence and what may be said in a meeting with the judge:

- Evidence: *Guidelines in relation to children giving evidence in family proceedings* of 2011 (*'Guidelines on children's evidence'*),[1] and

1 [2012] Fam Law 70 (www.judiciary.gov.uk/wp-content/uploads/JCO/Documents/FJC/Publications/Children+Giving+Evidence+Guidelines+-+Final+Version.pdf); set out in the Appendix to this chapter.

- Hearing a child's views: *Guidelines for judges meeting children who are subject to family proceedings* of 2010 (*'Guidelines on meeting children'*).[2]

Children's evidence

3.4 This chapter deals with children's evidence in family proceedings and with the circumstances in which it may be put before the court. Other chapters deal with more general aspects of evidence in children proceedings:

- Disclosure in children proceedings (**Chapter 9**);
- Withholding production of evidence (**Chapter 10**) and public interest immunity (**Chapter 12**),
- Closed material procedures (**Chapter 11**).

3.5 This chapter proceeds as follows:

- **Part 2** explains the context in which children's evidence may be heard and introduces the legal issues which impact on it being adduced in court.
- **Part 3** considers children's evidence in criminal proceedings: their eligibility for assistance under *Youth Justice and Criminal Evidence Act 1999* ('YJCEA 1999') to contrast how their evidence is dealt with in such proceedings; special measures under the 1999 Act for children and their operation in the proceedings. This part finishes with a review of special measure in family proceedings.
- **Part 4** concentrates on the child as a witness of fact in family proceedings and by reference to the Supreme Court judgment in *Re W (Children) (Abuse: Oral Evidence)* (below); to case management of their evidence; their evidence at trial; and finally a review of the *Guidelines on children's evidence* (already referred to) which were issued after *Re W*.
- **Part 5** concentrates on the process of children giving evidence in practice.
- **Part 6** explains the operation of the Achieving Best Evidence (ABE) scheme and its usefulness in preparing child evidence.
- **Part 7** deals with the extent to which special measures are in operation in family proceedings; with the controversial area of a child being questioned by an alleged abuser acting in person and the extent to which such questioning may be required to be done by the judge.

2 CHILD'S EVIDENCE IN PROCEEDINGS

Evidence from a child

3.6 In English criminal and civil proceedings facts must be proved by oral evidence given on oath before the court. This evidence can then be tested by cross-

2 [2010] 2 FLR 1872, https://fnf.org.uk/phocadownload/downloads/guidelines_for_judges_meeting_children.pdf.

examination of the witness by the party not calling the evidence. These principles apply as much in family as in any other proceedings; and, subject to what is said in this chapter, they apply as much to children's evidence in family proceedings as to evidence from any other witness.

3.7 Evidence is the means whereby a party establishes his or her case. This was explained by Lord Nicholls in the House of Lords in *Re H (Minors) (Sexual Abuse: Standard of Proof)*:[3]

> 'The starting-point here is that courts act on evidence. They reach their decisions on the basis of the evidence before them. When considering whether an applicant for a care order has shown that the child is suffering harm or is likely to do so, a court will have regard to the undisputed evidence. The judge will attach to that evidence such weight, or importance, as he considers appropriate. Likewise with regard to disputed evidence which the judge accepts as reliable. None of that is controversial....'

3.8 He continued that 'evidence is the means by which relevant facts are proved'. What is relevant depends on what is at issue before the court. Where evidence is contested the judge must decide whether or not it is proved. Lord Hoffman explained this in *Re B (Children)*:[4]

> '[2] If a legal rule requires a fact to be proved (a 'fact in issue'), a judge or jury must decide whether or not it happened. There is no room for a finding that it might have happened. The law operates a binary system in which the only values are 0 and 1. The fact either happened or it did not. If the tribunal is left in doubt, the doubt is resolved by a rule that one party or the other carries the burden of proof. If the party who bears the burden of proof fails to discharge it, a value of 0 is returned and the fact is treated as not having happened. If he does discharge it, a value of 1 is returned and the fact is treated as having happened.'

3.9 As Lord Hoffman went on to explain,[5] proof of such facts is to the civil standard. Proof must be on the balance of probabilities ('preponderance of probability') – which he related back to what Lord Nicholls in *Re H and R* where Lord Nicholls had said:[6]

> 'Where the matters in issue are facts the standard of proof required in non-criminal proceedings is the preponderance of probability, usually referred to as the balance of probability. This is the established general principle.'

3.10 Lord Nicholls continued:[7]

---

3 [1996] AC 563 sub nom *Re H and R (Child Sexual Abuse: Standard of Proof)* [1996] 1 FLR 80 at 98 and 99.

4 [2008] UKHL 35 [2009] 1 AC 11, sub nom *Re B (Care Proceedings: Standard of Proof)* [2008] 2 FLR 141.

5 Especially at [5] and [13].

6 [1996] AC 563 sub nom *Re H and R (Child Sexual Abuse: Standard of Proof)* [1996] 1 FLR 80 at 95; and see 3.7.

7 [1996] AC 563 sub nom *Re H and R (Child Sexual Abuse: Standard of Proof)* [1996] 1 FLR 80 at 96.

> 'The balance of probability standard means that a court is satisfied an event occurred if the court considers that, on the evidence, the occurrence of the event was more likely than not. When assessing the probabilities the court will have in mind as a factor, to whatever extent is appropriate in the particular case, that the more serious the allegation the less likely it is that the event occurred and, hence, the stronger should be the evidence before the court concludes that the allegation is established on the balance of probability.... Deliberate physical injury is usually less likely than accidental physical injury. A stepfather is usually less likely to have repeatedly raped and had non-consensual oral sex with his under-age stepdaughter than on some occasion to have lost his temper and slapped her. Built into the preponderance of probability standard is a serious degree of flexibility in respect of the seriousness of the allegation.'

Evidence in children proceedings; evidence of children

3.11 Certain special rules apply to the evidence of children, and to evidence in children proceedings generally. For example, such hearsay rules as survive the *Civil Evidence Act 1995* are dispensed with;[8] and there are special rules in relation to self-incrimination privilege.[9]

3.12 Since the coming into operation of the *Children Act 1989 (CA 1989), s 96* sets out the position in relation to evidence from children:[10]

> **'96 Evidence given by, or with respect to, children**
>
> (1) Subsection (2) applies in any civil proceedings[11] where a child who is called as a witness in any civil proceedings does not, in the opinion of the court, understand the nature of an oath.
>
> (2) The child's evidence may be heard by the court if, in its opinion –
>
> (a) he understands that it is his duty to speak the truth; and
>
> (b) he has sufficient understanding to justify his evidence being heard.'

3.13 The effect of this is that a child may give unsworn evidence in any civil proceedings, even if he does not understand the nature of an oath, provided that he understands, first, that it is his/her duty to tell the truth and, secondly, that he or she has sufficient understanding in general to justify his or her evidence being heard by the court. In this way, *CA 1989, ss 96(1)* and *(2)* deals with the content of the child's evidence and of its admissibility.

---

8 Children (Admissibility of Hearsay Evidence) Order 1993.

9 See 9.19.

10 A child is defined as a person under 18: *CA 1989, s 105.*

11 'civil proceedings' is defined for this context by *CA 1989, s 96(7)* as 'civil proceedings, before any tribunal, in relation to which the strict rules of evidence apply, whether as a matter of law or by agreement of the parties, and references to "the court" shall be construed accordingly';

3.14 However, s 96 does not deal with the way in which the child's evidence is given to the court. This is a matter for procedure on which, as the rules now stand, FPR 2010 is not specific or always clear. There are proposals prepared by Vulnerable Witnesses and Children Working Group (VWCWG), considered in outline in the Introduction (**Chapter 1**). Some of the proposals from that Group may be capable of being brought into operation in existing children proceedings as explained in **Part 7**; and as foreshadowed, for example, by Lady Hale in the Supreme Court *Re W (Children) (Abuse: Oral Evidence)*[12] and as discussed shortly.

Evidence of child witness; competence

3.15 In *Re W (Abuse: Oral Evidence)* the Supreme Court was dealing with the question of the evidence of a child in care proceedings. Lady Hale explained that in criminal proceedings *YJCEA 1999, Pt 2* sets out a number of 'special measures'[13] to assist children to give evidence. These special measures include screens, live television links, using video recordings as evidence-in-chief, and providing aids to communication and examining the witness through an approved intermediary.

3.16 *YJCEA 1999, Pt 2* applies to criminal proceedings only. It permits witnesses of any age to give evidence in criminal proceedings, unless it appears to the court that they are unable to understand the questions put or that they are unable to give intelligible answers:

> **'53 Competence of witnesses to give evidence**
>
> (1) At every stage in criminal proceedings all persons are (whatever their age) competent to give evidence[; but]
>
> (3) A person is not competent to give evidence in criminal proceedings if it appears to the court that he is not a person who is able to—
>
> (a) understand questions put to him as a witness, and
>
> (b) give answers to them which can be understood.'

3.17 In *Re W (Abuse: Oral Evidence)* Lady Hale contrasted the position of child witnesses in criminal proceedings under *YJCEA 1999* with the procedural position in relation to children's evidence in family proceedings:

> *'[10] Family proceedings are typically very different from criminal proceedings. There is often a mass of documentary evidence, much of it hearsay, from which a picture can be built up or inferences drawn. A child may reveal what has happened to her in many different ways.... One consequence has been that video-recordings of 'Achieving Best Evidence' (ABE)*[14] *interviews are routinely used in care proceedings if they are available. The near-contemporaneous account, given in response to open-ended questioning, in relaxed and comfortable surroundings, is considered inherently more likely*

12 [2010] UKSC 12, [2010] 1 FLR 1485; and see 3.50.

13 As defined and explained at 3.26.

14 For further consideration of ABE interviews, see 3.87.

to be reliable than an account elicited by formal questioning in the stressful surroundings of a court room months if not years after the event.'

3.18 Lady Hale continued that 'unlike criminal proceedings... it is rare for a child to be called for cross-examination in family proceedings' (the question in issue in *Re W (Abuse: Oral Evidence)* (as explained later[15])). However, she suggested a way in which a court which is dealing with children proceedings can proceed:

> '[28] The family court will have to be realistic in evaluating how effective it can be in maximising the advantage while minimising the harm. There are things that the court can do but they are not things that it is used to doing at present. It is not limited by the usual courtroom procedures or to applying the special measures by analogy. The important thing is that the questions which challenge the child's account are fairly put to the child so that she can answer them, not that counsel should be able to question her directly. One possibility is an early video'd cross examination as proposed by Pigot.[16] Another is cross-examination via video link. But another is putting the required questions to her through an intermediary. This could be the court itself, as would be common in continental Europe and used to be much more common than it is now in the courts of this country.'

3.19 In the next part the way in which a child's evidence is dealt with in criminal proceedings under *YJCEA 1999, Pt 2* is explained.

3 CHILD'S EVIDENCE IN CRIMINAL PROCEEDINGS

Eligibility for assistance

Youth Justice and Criminal Evidence Act 1999 Part 2: eligibility for assistance

3.20 The aim of *YJCEA 1999, Pt 2* is to maximise the quality of the evidence which a child witness (as defined in the next paragraph) can give. This was explained by Lady Hale in *R (D (a minor)) v Camberwell Green Youth Court*[17] as:[18]

> '[19] .... The aim of the special measures is to assist vulnerable or intimidated witnesses who might otherwise be unwilling to come forward at all or unable to give the best evidence of which they are capable.'

15 See 3.50.

16 *Report of the Advisory Group on Video Evidence* (the Pigot Report, 1989), which recommended that both the evidence-in-chief and cross-examination of child witnesses should be video-recorded, and that the recording should stand as their evidence at trial. *YJCEA 1999* adopted the first part of these recommendations.

17 [2005] UKHL 4, [2005] 1 WLR 393.

18 As briefly explained in Ch 1, much of the terminology used, and many of the recommendations outlined, in the VWCWG reports are derived from *YJCEA 1999, Pt 2*.

3.21 A witness is 'eligible for assistance' if under the age of 17 at the time of the hearing.[19] (Meanwhile s 16(1)(b) and s 17[20] deal with witnesses who are otherwise eligible for assistance (ie what amounts to a 'vulnerable witness'[21]).) *YJCEA 1999, ss 16* (age and incapacity) and *17* (fear or distress about testifying) create three categories of witness who may be eligible for assistance by special measures under Pt 2. Thus s 16(1)(a) defines a witness in criminal proceedings as 'eligible for assistance' in the following circumstances:

> **'16 Witnesses eligible for assistance on grounds of age or incapacity**
>
> (1) For the purposes of this Chapter a witness in criminal proceedings (other than the accused) is eligible for assistance by virtue of this section—
>
> (a) if under the age of 17 at the time of the hearing; or
>
> (b) if the court considers that the quality of evidence given by the witness is likely to be diminished by reason of any circumstances falling within subsection (2)....'

Camberwell Green Youth Court case

3.22 The evidence of children aged under the age of 17 (ie not under 18 per *CA 1989, s 105*) qualifies for assistance automatically. The child witness becomes eligible for assistance in the form of one or more of the special measures directions set out in *YJCEA 1999, ss 23–30;*[22,23] for as already mentioned regardless of age a child witness is compellable.[24] In *R (ota D (a minor) v Camberwell Green Youth Court*[25] Lady Hale explained the working of *YJCEA 1999, Pt 2, s 21* in relation to a child's evidence and to that particular case.[26] In particular, the House of Lords had to examine the extent to which certain provisions in the then relatively new Act were compatible with a defendant's right to a fair trial (European Convention 1950, Art 6). She explained this issue first:

> '[18] The issue before us is whether the new scheme providing for how child witnesses are to give their evidence in criminal cases is compatible with the right of the defendant to a fair trial under article 6 of the European Convention on Human Rights, in particular when that defendant is also a child. The question certified for us by the Divisional Court was this:

---

19 'Time of hearing' is defined by s 16(3) as the date on which the court determines (under *YJCEA 1999, s 19(2)*) whether a child witness is eligible for assistance under the Act.

20 *YJCEA 1999, s 17(1)* defines as eligible for assistance a witness where: '... the court is satisfied that the quality of evidence given by the witness is likely to be diminished by reason of fear or distress on the part of the witness in connection with testifying in the proceedings.'

21 See further 3.26.

22 *YJCEA 1999, s 18(1).*

23 A witness who comes within the terms of s 17(1) is not entitled to benefit from an intermediary (s 29) or other assistance with communication (s 30): s 18(1)(b).

24 *YJCEA 1999, s 53(1).*

25 [2005] UKHL 4, [2005] 1 WLR 393.

26 See 3.38.

> "Are the provisions of YJCEA 1999 s 21(5) compliant with European Convention Art 6 insofar as they prevent individualised consideration of the necessity for a special measures direction at the stage at which the direction is made?"'

3.23 Having defined the Convention issue, Lady Hale then summarised the way in which the special measures provisions for child witness's evidence, alongside that of vulnerable and intimidated witnesses, worked in *YJCEA 1999, Pt 2*:

> '[19] It is necessary, therefore, to explain how s 21(5) fits into the scheme for "special measures directions in the case of vulnerable and intimidated witnesses", set up by Chapter I of Part II to the Youth Justice and Criminal Evidence Act 1999. This followed from *Speaking Up for Justice, Report of the Interdepartmental Working Group on the treatment of Vulnerable or Intimidated Witnesses in the Criminal Justice System* (Home Office, 1998). This is turn followed a Council of Europe Recommendation No R (97)13, *Intimidation of witnesses and the rights of the defence,* adopted on 10 September 1997. The new scheme built upon and expanded earlier tentative steps taken both by the common law and statute to enable children to give evidence in criminal trials: removing the accused from the sight though not the hearing of a witness (*R v Smellie* (1919) 14 Cr App R 128); setting up screens to prevent the witness seeing or being seen from the dock (*R v X, Y and Z* (1990) 91 Cr App R 36); allowing a child to give evidence by live television link (Criminal Justice Act 1988, s 32); and admitting a video recorded interview as the child's evidence in chief (Criminal Justice Act 1988, section 32A, inserted by the Criminal Justice Act 1991, s 54)....'

3.24 As can be seen, the aim of *YJCEA 1999, Pt 2* was to bring together earlier common law and statutory developments to enable a child to provide the 'best evidence of which a [child] was capable for the court'. Lady Hale concluded the above passage:

> '[19] ... The aim of the special measures is to assist vulnerable or intimidated witnesses who might otherwise be unwilling to come forward at all or unable to give the best evidence of which they are capable.'

3.25 *YJCEA 1999, Pt 2* does not guarantee the accused an opportunity of face-to-face questioning – cross-examination – of a defence witness. It was therefore necessary for the House of Lords, in the *Camberwell Green Youth Court* case, to consider whether in the denial of a right to cross-examination, the Act was compliant with the European Convention 1950, Art 6(3)(d).[27] The House held that the Convention does not guarantee face-to-face questioning, in the sense urged by the defendants; that in the respect that *YJCEA 1999* was before the court the Act was Convention compliant; and the appeals were dismissed.

---

27 Set out in full at 5.16.

Special measures directions

3.26 The effect of *YJCEA 1999, ss 19* to *21* is to define the witnesses to whom special measures[28] may be applied. In the case of 'child witnesses' (ie children under 17) s 21 sets out particular provisions which apply to them. Section 19 defines how application can be made for a special measures direction; or that a judge may make a direction on the court's own initiative. Section 20 deals with the effect and duration of the direction. Section 21 sets out a number of 'special provisions' for special measure directions for children; and it refers in particular to s 35(3) which exempts children altogether from being required to give live evidence and be cross-examined in the case of particular offences, that is for children requiring 'special protection' (ie if the offence being tried is a sexual offence, kidnapping, child abduction or cruelty as defined by s 35(3)).[29,30]

3.27 If a special measures direction is made, the measures themselves are set out in ss 23–30:

- preventing a witness from seeing a party, by 'screen or other arrangement' (s 23);
- allowing a witness to give evidence by live link (s 24; ie video-link or other means for a witness, absent from the hearing room, to give evidence: s 24(8));
- hearing a witness' evidence to the exclusion of others (ie in private, which is normally the case in children proceedings) (s 25);

---

28 The special measures directions provisions of *YJCEA 1999* are supported by Criminal Procedure Rules 2015, (CPR 2015) Pt 18; and Pt 18 is supported by three practice directions.

29 *YJCEA 1999, s 21(5).*

30 **35 Child complainants and other child witnesses**

(1) No person charged with an offence to which this section applies may in any criminal proceedings cross-examine in person a protected witness, either—
  (a) in connection with that offence, or
  (b) in connection with any other offence (of whatever nature) with which that person is charged in the proceedings.

(2) For the purposes of subsection (1) a "protected witness" is a witness who—
  (a) either is the complainant or is alleged to have been a witness to the commission of the offence to which this section applies, and (b) either is a child or falls to be cross-examined after giving evidence in chief (whether wholly or in part)— (i) by means of a video recording made (for the purposes of section 27) at a time when the witness was a child, or (ii) in any other way at any such time.

(3) The offences to which this section applies are—
  (a) any offence under—
    (i) the M1 Sexual Offences Act 1956,
    (ii) the M2 Indecency with Children Act 1960,
    (iii) the M3 Sexual Offences Act 1967,
    (iv) section 54 of the M4 Criminal Law Act 1977, or
    (v) the M5 Protection of Children Act 1978;
  (b) kidnapping, false imprisonment or an offence under section 1 or 2 of the M6Child Abduction Act 1984;
  (c) any offence under section 1 of the M7Children and Young Persons Act 1933;
  (d) any offence (not within any of the preceding paragraphs) which involves an assault on, or injury or a threat of injury to, any person.

(4) In this section "child" means—
  (a) where the offence falls within subsection (3)(a), a person under the age of 17; or
  (b) where the offence falls within subsection (3)(b), (c) or (d), a person under the age of 14.

- that advocates should be relieved from wearing wigs and gowns[31] (s 26);
- admitting video recorded evidence or cross-examination (ss 27 and 28);
- questioning a witness through an intermediary (s 29);
- using a device to help a witness communicate (s 30).

Special measures direction

3.28 Though the making of a special measures direction applies to all protected parties (as set out in *YJCEA 1999, ss 16* and *17*[32]), in this chapter the emphasis will be on children's evidence. If following an application or decision under *YJCEA 1999, s 19* the court decides that a witness 'is eligible for assistance'[33] the next step is for the court to decide whether any of the available measures would 'be likely to improve the quality of evidence given by the witness'[34]; and give a direction accordingly.[35]

> '(2) Where the court determines that [a child] the witness is eligible for assistance…, the court must then—
>
> (a) determine whether any of the special measures available in relation to the witness (or any combination of them) would, in its opinion, be likely to improve the quality of evidence given by the witness; and
>
> (b) if so—
>
> (i) determine which of those measures (or combination of them) would, in its opinion, be likely to maximise so far as practicable the quality of such evidence; and
>
> (ii) give a direction under this section providing for the measure or measures so determined to apply to evidence given by the witness.'

3.29 In making any such special measure direction:[36]

> '… the court must consider all the circumstances of the case, including in particular—
>
> (a) any views expressed by the witness; and
>
> (b) whether the measure or measures might tend to inhibit such evidence being effectively tested by a party to the proceedings.'

31 A 'direction may provide for the wearing of wigs or gowns to be dispensed with during the giving of the witness's evidence'.
32 See 3.21.
33 *YJCEA 1999, s 19(2).*
34 *YJCEA 1999, s 19(2)(a).*
35 *YJCEA 1999, s 19(2)(b).*
36 *YJCEA 1999, s 19(3).*

3.30 An important distinction between criminal and civil and family proceedings is that in the former as far as *YJCEA 1999* is concerned the child will only be a witness. The court's focus is on the accused who is the main subject of the court proceedings. In family proceedings, the child may also be a party, either as respondent (eg in care proceedings); a third party (in his or her parents' private law proceedings); or as applicant in his or her own right. The child witness may also be both a witness, a party and the subject of the application.

3.31 In their joint judgment in *Re W (Children) (Abuse: Oral Evidence)*[37] (the case which lead to the Supreme Court appeal in *Re W (Abuse: Oral Evidence)*[38] Wall and Wilson LJJ said on the question of a child's evidence in criminal trials as witness, and as subject in care proceedings:

> '[31] In presenting his appeal Mr Geekie urged upon us a comparison with criminal proceedings in which a complainant of C's age would be required – indeed C herself will be required – to attend for cross-examination whether by video-link or otherwise. There are major differences between criminal proceedings and care proceedings. In the former the focus is upon the defendant, namely that if he is innocent he should be acquitted and, subject thereto, that if he is guilty he should be convicted.... In the latter the focus is upon the child, namely whether the state is required to intervene in order to protect him or her. Although the child's welfare is not the paramount consideration in determining whether he or she should give oral evidence in care proceedings, that different focus will affect the determination....'

3.32 This states the distinctions in stark terms. As the approach of the VWCWG reports show, an approach by the courts akin to *YJCEA 1999* for children evidence in children proceedings however the child may be called upon to give evidence.[39] In *Re S (Care Proceedings: Case Management),*[40] the putative witness, K, may have been a child, but she was not the subject of the care proceedings as Wall and Wilson LJJ anticipated in their above comments. As the main witness for the case against the father she was in a position precisely parallel to the child witness provided for by *YJCEA 1999, s 21*.

Special provisions for child witnesses

Provision for child witnesses

3.33 *YJCEA 1999, s 21* makes 'Special provisions relating to child witnesses', namely witnesses under 17, amongst the witnesses eligible for protection under Pt 2. In addition, s 21 identifies child witnesses who are in need of 'special protection' under *YJCEA 1999, s 21(1)* as a result of the types of offence in connection with which they are required to provide evidence, as follows:

37 [2010] EWCA Civ 57.
38 [2010] UKSC 12, [2010] 1 FLR 1485.
39 See, eg, *Re S (Care Proceedings: Case Management)* [2016] EWCA Civ 83, [2017] 1 FLR 1476..
40 [2016] EWCA Civ 83, [2017] 1 FLR 1476.

'(b) a child witness is 'in need of special protection' if the offence (or any of the offences) to which the proceedings relate is—

(i) an offence falling within section 35(3)(a) (sexual offences etc.), or

(ii) an offence falling within section 35(3)(b), (c) or (d) (kidnapping, assaults etc.);...'

3.34 Where the court is considering whether to make a special measures direction under *YJCEA 1999, s 19* (as above) in respect of a child witness the court must first take into account the factors set out in *YJCEA 1999, s 21(3)* to *(7)* and, only once that list has been considered, does the court go to the factors in s 19(2) above.[41]

3.35 Accordingly, s 21(3) sets out a 'primary rule', namely that:

'(3) The primary rule in the case of a child witness is that the court must give a special measures direction in relation to the witness which complies with the following requirements—

(a) it must provide for any relevant recording to be admitted under section 27 (video recorded evidence in chief); and

(b) it must provide for any evidence given by the witness in the proceedings which is not given by means of a video recording (whether in chief or otherwise) to be given by means of a live link in accordance with section 24.'

3.36 The primary rule is subject to 'limitations' set out in s 21(4):

- That suitable recording or other equipment is available;
- That evidence provided by video recording or other means is fair to the party against who it is given in accordance with YJCEA 1999 s 27(2);[42] and
- A direction will only be made if 'the court is satisfied that compliance with it would not be likely to maximise the quality of the witness's evidence'[43] save where 'a child witness in need of special protection'.[44]

3.37 The rules in s 21 can be disapplied if it is thought they might work against the interests of justice; save that disapplication is not permitted in the case of children requiring 'special protection' (ie if the offence being tried is a sexual

41 *YJCEA 1999, s 21(2).*

42 *YJCEA 1999, s 27(2)* provides: A special measures direction may, however, not provide for a video recording, or a part of such a recording, to be admitted under this section if the court is of the opinion, having regard to all the circumstances of the case, that in the interests of justice the recording, or that part of it, should not be so admitted.

43 *YJCEA 1999, s 21(4)(c).*

44 *YJCEA 1999, s 21(5).*

offence, kidnapping, child abduction or cruelty as defined by s 35(3)).[45] In the *Camberwell Green Youth Justice* case[46] Lady Hale explained *YJCEA 1999, s 21(4)(c)*:

> '[28] ...In cases where the child is in need of special protection, however, the court has no power to disapply the rule for that reason (section 21(5)). The irrebuttable presumption is that in all proceedings for offences of a sexual or violent nature, giving evidence in this way is likely to enable the child to give her best quality evidence.'

Child's evidence in chief

3.38 In the *Camberwell Green Youth Justice* case, Lady Hale explained the working of *YJCEA 1999, Pt 2* in relation to a child's evidence. In doing so, she distinguished between the main body of child's evidence and the child's evidence where the child is entitled to special protection:

> '[24] Thus the presumption is that all child witnesses give their evidence in chief by means of a video-recorded interview (which has been conducted for that purpose, see section 21(1)(c)), if there is one. The court does, however, have a discretion to refuse to admit the video or part of it under section 27(2). This reads:
>
> "(2) A special measures direction may, however, not provide for a video recording, or a part of such a recording, to be admitted under this section if the court is of the opinion, having regard to all the circumstances of the case, that in the interests of justice the recording, or that part of it, should not be so admitted."'

3.39 It is generally intended that a child will give the majority, or all, of his/her evidence by live link; though other than in cases where 'special protection' applies the court may override this rule:

> '[26] The presumption also is that all child witnesses will give the rest or the whole of their evidence by live link, if it is available (section 21(4)(a)). This is not subject to a discretion comparable to that in section 27(2). This is not surprising, as the only difference between giving evidence by live link and giving evidence in the normal way is that the witness is not physically present in the court room. She can still be seen and heard, often at closer range than in many courtrooms....
>
> [28] In cases where the child is not "in need of special protection", that is where the offences do not involve sex, kidnapping, cruelty or violence, the court may also disapply the rule in favour of video recording and live link, if it is satisfied that it "would not be likely to maximise the quality of the [child's] evidence" (section 21(4)(c)).'

45 *YJCEA 1999, s 21(5)*.

46 *R (D (a minor)) v Camberwell Green Youth Court* [2005] UKHL 4, [2005] 1 WLR 393.

Special measures in family proceedings

Child witnesses in family proceedings

3.40 Under *YJCEA 1999* Parliament has statutorily defined special measures for children in criminal proceedings. Any extension, modification or cancellation can only be provided by the Secretary of State for Justice by order.[47]

3.41 Comments of Lady Hale in the Supreme Court can be referred to in support of the proposition that, to a degree, the common law already provides in family proceedings for a number of the measures available for criminal proceedings under *YJCEA 1999, Pt 2*. In *Re W* she made reference to 'special measures by analogy';[48] and in *Re A (Sexual Abuse: Disclosure)*[49] she explained how the common law already provides family proceedings with the means to protect child witnesses:[50]

> '[36] It does not follow, however, that X will have to give evidence in person in these proceedings.... If any party wishes to call X to give oral evidence, up to date medical evidence can be obtained to discover whether she is fit to do so. There are many ways in which her evidence could be received without recourse to the normal method of courtroom confrontation. Family proceedings have long been more flexible than other proceedings in this respect. The court has power to receive and act upon hearsay evidence. It is commonplace for children to give their accounts in videotaped conversations with specially trained police officers or social workers. Such arrangements might be extended to other vulnerable witnesses such as X. These could include the facility to have specific questions put to the witness at the request of the parties. If she is too unwell to cope with oral questioning, the court may have to do its best with her recorded allegations.... On the other hand, oral questioning could be arranged in ways which did not involve face to face confrontation. It is not a requirement that the father be able to see her face. It is, to say the least, unlikely that the court would ever allow direct questioning by the father, should he still (other than in this court) be acting in person. The court's only concern in family proceedings is to get at the truth. The object of the procedure is to enable witnesses to give their evidence in the way which best enables the court to assess its reliability. It is certainly not to compound any abuse which may have been suffered.'

3.42 When it comes to family proceedings, in *Re W (Abuse: Oral Evidence)* the comparisons between criminal and family proceedings were specifically discussed

---

47 *YJCEA 1999, s 18(5)*.

48 *Re W (Children) (Abuse: Oral Evidence)* [2010] UKSC 12, [2010] 1 FLR 1485 at [29].

49 [2012] UKSC 60, [2013] 1 FLR 948.

50 *Re A* involved disclosure of the statements made by a vulnerable young adult witness ('X') to social workers about the child A; and the likely later calling of X to give evidence during A's fathers claim for contact with A.

in the Supreme Court.[51] In *Re A*,[52] though the Supreme Court does not comment specifically on *YJCEA 1999, Pt 2* or on the *Camberwell Green Youth Court* case, there are reminders aplenty of the measures available under the 1999 Act in the above paragraph. In the *Camberwell Green Youth Court* case Lady Hale summarises some of the earlier common law and statutory steps which were taken to deal with children's evidence in criminal proceedings. To the extent that protection for child witnesses is part of the common law, family courts can adapt its procedures to the courts' requirements for children within the terms of what the common law can permit.

4 CHILD AS WITNESS OF FACT IN CHILDREN PROCEEDINGS

Introduction

Evidence from children: how far

3.43 The special measures provisions of *YJCEA 1999, Pt 2* explained earlier in this chapter provide a version which works out how the hearing of children's evidence can be dealt with in court. The subject must now be looked at from the starting-point of the decision of the Supreme Court in *Re W (Abuse: Oral Evidence)*[53] (especially what was said by Lady Hale); of the *Guidelines on children's evidence* which followed that case; and then of the approach which judges have adopted to children – as parties and as witnesses – who may be required to give evidence in children proceedings.

3.44 In May 2016, in *Re E (A Child)(Evidence)*[54] McFarlane LJ quoted 'key passages' from the judgment[55] of Lady Hale's judgment in *Re W (Abuse: Oral Evidence)*[56] and then went on:

> '[48] I make no apology for quoting so extensively from Baroness Hale's judgment, which would seem to have gone unheeded in the 5 or more years since it was given. The need to give appropriate consideration to a child giving evidence in a case where that issue arises will soon be given further endorsement by amendments to the Family Procedure Rules 2010 and Practice Directions in accordance with recommendations from the President's working group on children and other vulnerable witnesses.[57] In the meantime the decision in this case should serve as

51 As explained at 3.38.

52 And see, eg, *H v L and R* [2006] EWHC 3099 (Fam) [2007] 2 FLR 162 Roderic Wood J; *Q v Q; Re B (A Child); Re C (A Child) (Practice Note)* [2014] EWFC 31, sub nom *Q v A; Re B; Re C (Private Law: Public Funding)* [2015] 1 FLR 324, Sir James Munby P.

53 *Re W (Children) (Abuse: Oral Evidence)* [2010] UKSC 12, [2010] 1 FLR 1485.

54 [2016] EWCA Civ 473, [2017] 1 FLR 1675.

55 At §[47]; passages quoted: §§[22], [24]–[28].

56 Considered further at 3.31.

57 On this point McFarlane LJ's enthusiasm may be premature, as explained at 1.65.

a firm reminder to the judiciary and to the profession of the need to engage fully with all that is required by Re W and the Guidelines.'

3.45 Meanwhile, in *Re S (Care Proceedings: Case Management)*[58] Black LJ concluded that it was not intended to 'become routine for children to give evidence in family cases'.[59] The extra-judicial comments of Lady Hale and of King LJ are touched on in **Chapter 1**. As an introduction to the subject in this part of this Chapter the views of Black LJ and McFarlane LJ will be summarised.

Case management and a child's evidence

3.46 In *Re F (Children)* [2016] EWCA Civ 546 Sir James Munby P drew attention to the importance of the *Guidelines on children's evidence* in assessing whether a child should be called on to give evidence 'in the context of the principal objective of achieving a fair trial'.[60] Yet in a number of cases the decision as to whether a child should give evidence is described as a matter of case management.

3.47 The facts of *Re S (Care Proceedings: Case Management)*[61] are provided later.[62] That case, on appeal to the Court of Appeal, saw a fifteen-year-old (X) being relieved of being asked questions about allegations she had made, which resulted in a child being said to be suffering significant harm and a father prevented from having other than supervised contact with his child. The decision as to that evidence was described as one of 'case management'. The term used to describe the decision only matters because case management decisions are generally treated as matters of the court's discretion; whereas a decision to rely on a child's evidence – especially where it is not to be challenged, would normally be a matter of law (with different appeal rights and different stringency as to the judge's reasoning).

3.48 Case management or not, perhaps the following passage from Black LJ's judgement, read alongside Sir James Munby P's comments in *Re F* (above) are sufficient to establish that the decision is in fact one of law:

> '[41] When considering whether a particular child should be called as a witness, the court has to weigh two considerations, namely the advantages that calling the child will bring to the determination of the truth and the damage it may do to the welfare of this or any other child (*Re W*... at [24]). On both sides of the equation, the court must take

58 [2016] EWCA Civ 83, [2017] 1 FLR 1476.

59 §[21].

60 '[59] The court should also have regard to the [*Guidelines on children's evidence*]. The *Guidelines*, which were specifically developed to assist courts following the decision in *Re W*, contain a list of no less than 21 factors to which the court should have regard when determining whether a child should give oral evidence in the context of the principal objective of achieving a fair trial [paragraph 9(a) to (v)]. The *Guidelines* require the court to carry out a balancing exercise 'between the following primary considerations: i) the possible advantages that the child being called will bring to the determination of truth balanced against; ii) the possible damage to the child's welfare from giving evidence i.e. the risk of harm to the child from giving evidence.'

61 [2016] EWCA Civ 83, [2017] 1 FLR 1476.

62 See 3.70.

account of what steps can be taken to improve the quality of the child's evidence and at the same time to decrease the risk of harm to the child (para [27] ibid).

[42] All sorts of factors will enter into the court's deliberation, as can be seen from paras [25] and [26] of *Re W*, the precise mix depending on the facts of the individual case. In the context of this case, it might be worth noting specifically that in para [26] Baroness Hale said: "We endorse the view that an unwilling child should rarely, if ever, be obliged to give evidence". I would also note that she went on to say later in that paragraph that in taking the risk of harm into account, as it must always do, the court does not need expert evidence.

[43] In the passage which I have quoted above from para [22], Baroness Hale forecast that the result of striking the balance may well be that the child should not be called to give evidence in the great majority of cases. In para [30], having observed that the "essential test is whether justice can be done to all the parties without further questioning of the child", she predicted that the consequence of the balancing exercise that has to be done by the court "will usually be that the additional benefits to the court's task in calling the child do not outweigh the additional harm that it will do to the child". And in para [31], she stressed that although the issue of the child giving evidence should be addressed, that was not "an invitation to elaborate consideration of what will usually be a non-issue". It was perhaps with these observations as to the comparative "rarity" (a word used in para [30]) of children giving evidence in mind, that at para [23], Baroness Hale observed that the court "cannot ignore relevant evidence just because other evidence might have been better" but "will have to do the best it can on what it has".'

3.49 Perhaps the final word – for now – on this subject, can go to McFarlane LJ in *Re E (A Child) (Evidence)*[63] who again speaks of the 'relatively full and sophisticated evaluation' required to decide whether a child should give evidence:

'[59] The court should also have regard to the Working Party of the Family Justice Council *Guidelines on the issue of Children Giving Evidence in Family Proceedings* issued in December 2011 [2012] Fam Law 79. The Guidelines, which were specifically developed to assist courts following the decision in *Re W*, contain a list of no less than 21 factors to which the court should have regard when determining whether a child should give oral evidence in the context of the principal objective of achieving a fair trial (para 9(a)–(v)). The Guidelines require the court to carry out a balancing exercise:

"between the following primary considerations:

(i) the possible advantages that the child being called will bring to the determination of truth balanced against;

63 [2016] EWCA Civ 473, [2017] 1 FLR 1675.

(ii) the possible damage to the child's welfare from giving evidence ie the risk of harm to the child from giving evidence."

[60] Whilst not all of the elements described by Baroness Hale in *Re W* or in para 9 of the Guidelines will be relevant in every case, it is plain that the court undertaking a *Re W* determination will need to engage in a relatively full and sophisticated evaluation of the relevant factors; simply paying lip-service to *Re W* is not acceptable. By "full" I do not wish to suggest that a lengthy judgment is required, but simply that the judge must consider each of the relevant points with that process recorded in short form in a judgment. Such a detailed process is in my view justified given the importance of the decision for the welfare of the child and for the fairness of hearing.'

Child's evidence and a fair trial

Background to Re W

3.50 In *Re W (Abuse: Oral Evidence)*[64] there were five children: a 14-year-old ('Charlotte') and her four half-siblings. The appellant ('F') was father of the younger children but not of Charlotte. He was treated as de facto step-father of Charlotte and is referred to as 'the father'. The proceedings started when Charlotte made allegations at school – as she had to others before – that F had sexually abused her on a number of occasions. She had also made allegations against F to friends and other adults, from whom the police had statements. Charlotte was ABE interviewed and medically examined. F was charged with 13 criminal offences against Charlotte. H was on bail awaiting trial.

3.51 The local authority decided not to call Charlotte in her care proceedings; but F applied for her to be called. The judge refused this application. The Court of Appeal dismissed the father's appeal. In a joint judgement Wall and Wilson LJJ adhered to the practice as laid down in the previous decisions of that court; but wondered whether the time had now come for a wider consideration of the question of child evidence.

Calling of child's evidence: a matter for the common law

3.52 As the law stood then in relation to children being called to give evidence (subject to any special measures direction) Lady Hale said that it was a matter for the common law to resolve whether a child could or should be called. The Court of Appeal had held that as a matter of law – they plainly did not consider the issue of calling a witness a matter of discretion and of case management[65] – precedent bound them from requiring the child's evidence to be put before the court. However, in their joint judgment Wall and Wilson LJJ said:

64 *Re W (Children) (Abuse: Oral Evidence)* [2010] UKSC 12, [2010] 1 FLR 1485.
65 See 3.48.

'[27] ... Because of their age [and also] of the difficulties exemplified by the facts of the present case, we believe that the time has come for a wider consideration of the issue of [children's evidence] in relation to family proceedings than is possible in the light of the doctrine of precedent, as reflected in the proposal which we make in [30] below.'

3.53 Rimer LJ agreed with them. He emphasised the different approaches between family lawyers and other litigation disciplines (as he saw it), by adding:

'[40] In light of the authorities to which [Wall and Wilson LJJ] have referred (in particular, *LM (by her Guardian) v. Medway Council, RM and YM* (below) and *Re W (Care Order: Sexual Abuse)* [2009] EWCA Civ 644; [2009] 2 FLR 1106, per Wall LJ at [55] to [57]), the judge's decision to re-open the question of the calling of C as a witness was, if I may say so, a thoughtful and correct one. The outcome does, however, strike me as profoundly worrying. For a judge to have to decide factual issues as serious as allegations of child rape without the alleged perpetrator having the right to test by cross-examination the primary evidence given against him by his 14-year old accuser may not cause a child and adolescent psychiatrist to lose a moment's sleep. It may not cause a family lawyer to do so either. But I consider that it would cause surprise to most litigation lawyers experienced in different disciplines.'

Child's evidence: issue before the Supreme Court in Re W

3.54 Lady Hale summarised the position for the individual judge in relation to the calling of evidence and the issue before the Supreme Court was 'a question of law' for the Supreme Court.[66] The prevailing judicial view in relation to children giving live evidence was best expressed by the *Medway Council* case,[67] as Lady Hale explained:

'[1] .... The current approach was stated by Smith LJ in [*LM v Medway Council*[68]]: "The correct starting point ... is that it is undesirable that a child should have to give evidence in care proceedings and that particular justification will be required before that course is taken. There will be some cases in which it will be right to make an order. In my view they will be rare."'[69]

3.55 In *Re W (Abuse: Oral Evidence)* it was argued for F that in the case of a child, such as Charlotte, for her to give evidence need not be regarded as rare. The test defined by the *Medway Council* and the judges in the Court of Appeal should

66 §[16].

67 *LM v Medway Council, RM and YM* [2007] EWCA Civ 9, [2007] 1 FLR 1698.

68 See above at §[44].

69 This approach, said Lady Hale (at para [2]) was based on such earlier cases as *R v B County Council, ex parte P* [1991] 1 WLR 221, *Re P (Witness Summons)* [1997] 2 FLR 447 and *SW v Portsmouth City Council; Re W (children: concurrent care and criminal proceedings)* [2009] EWCA 644, [2009] 3 FCR 1; and had been followed by Wall and Wilson LJJ in *Re W* in the Court of Appeal ([2010] EWCA Civ 57).

be reconsidered. Giving of evidence by a child might engage the child's and other party's Convention and other common law rights:

> '[3] … placing the burden upon the person wishing to cross-examine a child to show some "particular justification" for doing so, gives insufficient weight to the Convention rights of all concerned. All the parties in care proceedings are entitled to a fair hearing in the determination of their civil rights and obligations – the parents who stand to lose their children if allegations of abuse are made out, the children who stand to lose their parents if allegations of abuse are made out, but also stand to suffer abuse or further abuse if they are left at home because those allegations cannot be proved. And it is not only their article 6 rights which are in play. The civil rights in issue are also Convention rights in themselves – the right to respect for the family lives of the parents and their children but also the right to respect for the private lives of the children, which include their rights to be protected from attacks upon their physical and psychological integrity.'

Convention rights: fairness and a child giving evidence

3.56 Lady Hale summarised her conclusion on the balance to be drawn where a judge is called on to decide whether a child should give evidence:

> '[22] … The existing law erects a presumption against a child giving evidence which requires to be rebutted by anyone seeking to put questions to the child. That cannot be reconciled with the approach of the European Court of Human Rights, which always aims to strike a fair balance between competing Convention rights. Article 6 requires that the proceedings overall be fair and this normally entails an opportunity to challenge the evidence presented by the other side. But even in criminal proceedings account must be taken of the article 8 rights of the perceived victim: see *SN v Sweden,* App no 34209/96, 2 July 2002, BAILII: [2002] ECHR 551. Striking that balance in care proceedings may well mean that the child should not be called to give evidence in the great majority of cases, but that is a result and not a presumption or even a starting point.'

3.57 In Charlotte's case, Lady Hale concluded that the issue of whether she should give evidence should be returned to the care proceedings judge in the light of what the Supreme Court had said. In general terms, a court must do what it can to 'improve the quality of the child's evidence', and to minimise any harm to the child caused by giving evidence, said the Supreme Court.[70] 'An unwilling child should rarely, if ever, be obliged to give evidence' she said.[71]

3.58 In her ALC speech in 2015 Lady Hale reviewed *Re W (Abuse: Oral Evidence)*. There was a need for fairness as much to the child witness as to the alleged abuser:

70 §[25].
71 §[26].

> 'My view in *Re W* was that it was simply not fair either to the child or to the alleged abuser to presume that the child should not give evidence. The child's evidence might well be rejected on the basis of an inadequate ABE interview when it would have been so much more powerful if given live. But the child's evidence may not have been adequately tested in that ABE interview and there have to be mechanisms for ensuring that it is. Testing the evidence, if done in the right way, may well strengthen it.'

Child in private law proceedings

3.59 Lady Hale considered the related question of the child giving evidence in private law proceedings, and the possible 'specific risks' which this might involve (there being no independent local authority as intermediary). In *Re W (Abuse: Oral Evidence)* she said:

> '[29] In principle, the approach in private family proceedings between parents should be the same as the approach in care proceedings. However, there are specific risks to which the court must be alive. Allegations of abuse are not being made by a neutral and expert local authority which has nothing to gain by making them, but by a parent who is seeking to gain an advantage in the battle against the other parent. This does not mean that they are false but it does increase the risk of misinterpretation, exaggeration or downright fabrication. On the other hand, the child will not routinely have the protection and support of a Cafcass guardian. There are also many more litigants in person in private proceedings. So if the court does reach the conclusion that justice cannot be done unless the child gives evidence, it will have to take very careful precautions to ensure that the child is not harmed by this.'

3.60 In *Re B (Private Law Proceedings: Child Evidence)*[72] the question – 'a rudimentary foundation for [an] argument'[73] – arose as to whether the *Re W* approach should apply to the evidence of a child who was not a party.[74] Black LJ short-circuited any possible argument. She saw no reason why a similar approach should not be adopted to such a child witness as the approach in *Re W (Abuse: Oral Evidence)*:

> '[19] However, not only do I not think there is any reason in principle why this variation (or indeed the fact that the child has not yet given an account of events) should render the *Re W* approach inapplicable [to a non-party witness], in fact this court has very recently treated it as applicable in the case of a child who was not the subject of the proceedings in *Re B (A Child) (Wrongful Removal: Orders against Non-Parties)* [2014] EWCA Civ 843, [2015] 2 WLR 392, sub nom *Re B (A Child:*

---

72 [2014] EWCA Civ 1015, [2015] 1 FLR 1381.

73 §[18].

74 The same non-party witness factor was present in *Re S (Care Proceedings: Case Management)* [2016] EWCA Civ 83, [2017] 1 FLR 1476 but though *Re B* is cited, the issue of the non-party child witness did not arise.

Evidence: Passport Order) [2015] 1 FLR 871, which concerned the question of whether a 16-year-old boy should have been required to give evidence against his mother in wardship proceedings about his sister.'

Guidelines on child's evidence

Children's evidence after Re W

3.61 Following the Supreme Court decision in *Re W (Abuse: Oral Evidence)* the Family Justice Council issued *Guidelines in relation to children giving evidence in family proceedings*[75] (*Guidelines on children's evidence*). These were intended to provide anyone involved in family proceedings with 'advice as to what matters should be taken into account' where a child may be proposed to give evidence.[76]

3.62 McFarlane LJ has mentioned his concerns as to whether family courts are yet taking *Re W (Abuse: Oral Evidence)* sufficiently into account. In *Re E*[77] he commented – in 'acid remarks' as they were described by Sir James Munby P in *Re F (Children)*[78] – as follows:

> '[59] The court should also have regard to the [*Guidelines on children's evidence*]. The *Guidelines*, which were specifically developed to assist courts following the decision in *Re W*, contain a list of no less than 21 factors to which the court should have regard when determining whether a child should give oral evidence in the context of the principal objective of achieving a fair trial [paragraph 9(a) to (v)]. The *Guidelines* require the court to carry out a balancing exercise "between the following primary considerations:
>
> i) the possible advantages that the child being called will bring to the determination of truth balanced against;
>
> ii) the possible damage to the child's welfare from giving evidence i.e. the risk of harm to the child from giving evidence."'

3.63 In *Re L (Case Management: Child's Evidence)*[79] Ryder LJ treats the *Guidelines* as an aid to understanding of what was said in *Re W (Abuse: Oral Evidence)*, which was essential for the judge for evaluation of the relevant evidence. *Re W (Abuse: Oral Evidence)*, he says, sets out the law. The guidelines can only help to explain it:

> '[8] Everyone agrees that in the absence of a transcript of that interview, a viewing of the DVD was essential. The judge could not do justice to the

75 *Guidelines in relation to children giving evidence in family proceedings* (www.judiciary.gov.uk/wp-content/uploads/JCO/Documents/FJC/Publications/Children+Giving+Evidence+Guidelines+-+Final+Version.pdf) [2012] Fam Law 79.

76 *Guidelines* at para 5.

77 *Re E (A Child)(Evidence)* [2016] EWCA Civ 473, [2017] 1 FLR 1675; and see 3.70.

78 [2016] EWCA Civ 546.

79 [2013] EWCA Civ 1778, [2014] 2 FLR 972 (the judge dealt with a care application where he said he had not had time or the appropriate IT equipment to consider a child's ABE interview).

interests of L and have regard to the interests of A...without viewing the DVD. Furthermore, without a consideration of that material, the judge could not apply the guidance given in *Re W (Children) (Family Proceedings: Evidence)* [2010] UKSC 12, [2010] 1 WLR 701, sub nom *Re W (Children) (Abuse: Oral Evidence)* [2010] 1 FLR 1485, which is helpfully expanded by the Family Justice Council in the [*Guidelines*].'

5 CHILDREN'S EVIDENCE IN COURT PROCEEDINGS

Child witnesses and fairness

Youth Justice and Criminal Evidence Act 1999, evidence and the common law

3.64 In *R v Barker*[80] Lord Judge LCJ (who was sitting in the Court of Criminal Appeal with Hallett LJ and Macur J; as extensively referred to in the Vulnerable Witnesses and Children Working Group 2015 report[81]) commented:

> '[42] The trial process must, of course, and increasingly has, catered for the needs of child witnesses, as indeed it has increasingly catered for the use of adult witnesses whose evidence in former years would not have been heard, by, for example, the now well understood and valuable use of intermediaries. In short, the competency test is not failed because the forensic techniques of the advocate (in particular in relation to cross-examination) or the processes of the court (for example, in relation to the patient expenditure of time) have to be adapted to enable the child to give the best evidence of which he or she is capable. *At the same time the right of the defendant to a fair trial must be undiminished* (emphasis supplied).'

3.65 So how does English law deal with fairness, and deal with facts which, in criminal and family proceedings, are the same? This question can be considered by a comparison of *R v Lubemba, R v JP*[82] (for criminal proceedings) and the cases of *Re S (Care Proceedings: Case Management)*[83] and *Re E (A Child)(Evidence)*[84] (for children proceedings). All cases were heard in the Court of Appeal.

Lubemba *and a child's evidence*

3.66 The *Lubemba* case consisted of two appeals, the second of which was the appeal of JP in *R v JP*. It is that second case which is of concern here. JP had been convicted of three counts of sexual assault on an eight-year old (C). Special

80 [2010] EWCA Crim 4 at [42].
81 Discussed at 1.65.
82 *R v Lubemba & Ors, R v JP* [2014] EWCA (Crim) 2064, [2015] 1 WLR 157 (also referred to in the VW-CWG report).
83 [2016] EWCA Civ 83, [2017] 1 FLR 1476 considered at 3.70.
84 [2016] EWCA Civ 473, [2017] 1 FLR 1675.

measures directions had been given[85] to deal with C's evidence. Hallett LJ described the special measures as follows:

> '[9] ... The child's video interview, in which she gave a clear and concise account, was to be played as her evidence-in-chief and she was to be cross-examined by defence counsel, Mr Bennett, using the live link. He undertook to limit his questioning and to conduct his cross-examination in accordance with the Advocate's Gateway Toolkit. All parties agreed that [C], described as an intelligent and capable witness, was willing and able to attend court to be examined and that the services of an intermediary were not required.'

3.67 On the day of the hearing, C attended court to be cross-examined over the live-link.[86] The prosecuting barrister took defence counsel – both, it can be assumed, without wigs and gowns[87] – to meet C. She was with her parents. Both barristers believed she was willing to be asked questions in the way already agreed. On his own the judge then went to see C. She was shown her video evidence. She received another visit from the judge, who was alone again. Next, the judge stated that he was not willing for C to be asked questions. He proceeded with the case as follows:

> '[13] .... [He] returned to court and announced, with no warning, that the complainant was "not even managing to communicate in monosyllables on ... neutral subjects". In his opinion the child could not participate in cross-examination, however sensitively done. Both counsel... urged the judge to let [defence counsel] at least try and ask a few questions to see whether the witness [C] could communicate. Unfortunately, perhaps because they were both somewhat taken aback by events, neither of them referred the judge to the law (other than Article 6) and in particular the relevant statutory provisions that permit the playing of a recorded interview as the child's evidence in chief.
>
> [14] The judge would not be moved. He informed defence counsel he would not permit any questioning of the child, but indicated that the defence would be allowed the rest of the day to prepare a document to be placed before the jury, containing any points the defence would have wished to have made to the witness.'

3.68 The video was played as C's only evidence at the hearing. She could not be asked any questions by the defence barrister. Her parents gave evidence. The jury were permitted by the judge to see the video evidence for a second time and during their deliberations on sentence, at which point the judge reminded them of the defence document with points they would have liked to be able to put to the witness.

---

85 In accordance with what would now be CPR 2015, Pt 18.

86 *YJCEA 1999, ss 18(1)* and *24*.

87 In accordance with *YJCEA 1999, s 26*.

Procedural fairness

3.69 JP appealed on one ground only: that the judge was wrong to have prevented any questions of C. He had not had a fair trial, he said. The prosecution accepted that there had been a number of procedural errors by the judge. First, if a recording is to be admitted 'the witness must be called by the party tendering [the recording] in evidence'[88] subject to conditions neither of which applied. Secondly, the judge failed to consider the rule[89] that in criminal proceedings 'all persons are (whatever their age) competent to give evidence' unless unable to understand questions and specifically to determine the question of the competence of C to answer questions.[90] Finally the judge did not consider whether further special measures, such as an intermediary, might assist; nor did he seek expert assistance to assess the child's ability to answer questions. Because the procedural questions which applied under *YJCEA 1999* were not tested by the judge JP's appeal was allowed.

Child witnesses and children proceedings

Family proceedings: child's evidence and Re S

3.70 In *Re S (Care Proceedings: Case Management)*[91] the Court of Appeal looked at whether a 15-year-old child, K, who had alleged serious sexual abuse by her brother, B, since she was six, should give oral evidence. Her evidence was relevant in care proceedings relating to B's two children (now aged four and two). K was considered to be competent to give evidence; but she varied as to whether she was willing, or not, to come to court. The issue was whether she could be asked questions on behalf of B, or not. Already her evidence had been treated as insufficiently reliable, that the police had decided to abandon their prosecution of B.

3.71 The question for the judge was: should K be required by the court to give evidence and be asked questions by B (her brother's) advocate. The judge decided that the evidence of what K had said to a social worker and the child's guardian was sufficient and could be treated as her evidence in chief. Further, she held that that 'evidence' could not be challenged by any form of questioning of K by or on behalf of B. It would not therefore be open in any way for the father (K's brother B) directly to challenge her evidence.

3.72 Gloster LJ would have allowed the appeal. In her list of features of the case[92] she included the following about the detail of the evidence and its presentation:

88 *YJCEA 1999, s 27(5)(a)*; para [20].
89 *YJCEA 1999, s 53(1)*; para [22].
90 *YJCEA 1999, s 54*; para [23].
91 [2016] EWCA Civ 83, [2017] 1 FLR 1476.
92 §[59].

'(v) The ABE video interviews of K, upon which the judge heavily relied in reaching her conclusions, had taken place in March and April 2013, at a time well before K had started to attempt to halt the criminal process (July 2013) or had begun, albeit somewhat equivocally, to retract her allegations in their entirety.... So those interviews contained no evidence about the reasons for her retractions.

(vi) K frequently changed her mind as to whether she was prepared to give evidence [further detail is added]....

(vii) In deciding whether K should give evidence, the judge relied upon the opinion of K's guardian and the social worker to the effect that: "I do not feel that [K] is able to recognise any links to her self-reported frustration and anger with the coping strategies she may have adopted to deal with how she was feeling with her experiences of the current situation. I feel that she seeks to display a certain persona in order to ease her emotions while having built up a barrier up to others to cover how she is feeling.... I would not be in support of [K] giving direct evidence at the fact-finding hearing due to the concerns outlined above. I do not feel that she is emotionally able to deal with the impact that this could have on her. I feel [K] would struggle to manage in-depth questioning on the basis that giving direct evidence is to have her say and [inaudible]."'

3.73 Of her criticisms of the social worker's and guardian's evidence Gloster LJ concluded:

(viii)On any basis, the evidence of K's guardian and the social worker as to K's wish or ability to give evidence at trial was highly unsatisfactory and vague opinion evidence. It could not replace an assessment of K's evidence by the judge.

3.74 The judge's determination, on the evidence available to the court, was that the children should stay with their mother under a supervision order (ie she found 'significant harm' under *CA 1989, s 31(2)*), and that B should have limited supervised contact.

No opportunity to cross-examine

3.75 Black LJ (with whom Voss LJ agreed, but over the dissent of Gloster LJ) dealt with the lack of an opportunity to cross-examine, and disposal of the appeal, as follows:

'[55] It was submitted that the judge was wrong to make [her] findings on the basis of the untested evidence which she had. The appellant submitted that she had not given sufficient weight to the fact that the father had no opportunity for cross-examination, for example when evaluating the cogency of the ABE interviews which she found to be compelling. The mention that the judge made of the lack of opportunity for cross-examination at the end of paragraph 5 of her judgment was criticised as insufficient. I do not accept that.'

3.76 In her dissenting judgement – 'this case has left me with a deep sense of unease'[93] – Gloster LJ questioned the fairness to the father, of the way the case was dealt. She doubted that the balance required by the Supreme Court in *Re W (Abuse: Oral Evidence)*[94] – between the need to establish the truth as against the possible detriment to the welfare of the child – had been struck in a way which was fair:

> '[60] In my judgment HHJ Moir's case management decision dated 15 October 2014, in which she decided that K should not be called as a witness, failed in any adequate way to weigh up the two relevant considerations set out in *Re W (Children)* [2010] UKSC 12 namely: the advantages that a child giving evidence will bring to the determination of the truth; and the damage which it might do to the welfare of the child witness. In my judgment, there was no adequate medical, or indeed other, evidence, apart from the vague and dubious views of K's guardian and the social worker, to support the conclusion that it would be so harmful for K to give evidence that she should not be asked to do so. Nor was there any adequate analysis by the judge as to why those concerns trumped the entitlement of the Appellant to question why she had retracted, or, at the least, to some extent resiled from, her previous allegations.'

3.77 She regarded the views of the guardian and social worker as 'dubious' in terms of establishing that it would be harmful for K to give evidence.[95] K was 'a mature young person' who had made serious allegations; and there was 'no psychiatric or psychological evidence to support the idea' that it would be damaging to her to give evidence.[96] She set out a number of 'critical features' of the case, the first three of which were:[97]

> 'i) The single issue was whether the Appellant had abused K.
>
> ii) The case against the Appellant depended entirely on the veracity of K's allegations.
>
> iii) The burden of proof at all times was on the Local Authority to establish on the balance of probabilities that the abuse had occurred....'

Opportunity for use of special measures

3.78 She went on to examine options for the judge in terms of measures available to the court. She places the duty on the judge to explore options: that is

93 §[58].
94 [2010] UKSC 12, [2010] 1 FLR 1485.
95 Gloster LJ was on the constitution in *Re E (A Child)* [2016] EWCA Civ 473. Of this aspect of a judge's consideration in the latter case McFarlane LJ said: '[61] Where such advice is based upon the consideration of harm alone, it is unlikely to be of great assistance to the court which is required to consider not only 'harm' but also the other side of the balance described in the *Guidelines*, namely the possible advantages that the child's testimony will bring to the determination of truth.
96 §[61].
97 §[59].

to say, she held that it was not for the parties only to propose measures. As a matter of case management law this is likely to be correct (see eg Family Procedure Rules 2010, rr 1.4(2) and 22.1(1)(c)); and it will be recalled that *YJCEA 1999, s 19(1)(b),* in criminal proceedings, gives the power to the judge, of his/her own initiative, to initiate measures to protect witnesses.[98]

3.79 In a passage which may have been written with *YJCEA 1999* in mind, Gloster LJ said:

> '[63] In my view the judge was also wrong not to explore other ways in which K could have given evidence, apart from being subjected to cross-examination in open court in front of the Appellant and others… This was a case that cried out for special measures so as to ensure that the judge received direct evidence from K in relation to the allegations, and, in particular, her retraction of them, and was not forced to rely on the very unsatisfactory secondary evidence of the social worker and the Guardian as to their interpretation of K's evidence. In my judgment some sort of measure should have been in place to ensure that the judge heard directly from K on the fact-finding hearing.'

3.80 It is tempting to ask, had provisions equivalent to *YJCEA 1999, Pt 2* formally applied to family proceedings, whether the answer, in terms of K giving evidence in *Re S*, would have been the same; and, in particular, whether the court would have regarded as the same its priorities in terms of the rights of B as against the welfare of the 15-year-old K. (It must also be recalled that the children in the case, the subject of the proceedings, and their mother had Art 8, and perhaps Art 6, rights.[99]) If – as the comments of Lady Hale in *Re W (Abuse: Oral Evidence)*[100] and *Re A (Sexual Abuse: Disclosure)* [101] suggest – the special measures summarised in *YJCEA 1999* apply by analogy in family proceedings it could be said that the court has a duty to consider what measures it may adopt to ensure as fair an outcome as possible. The balance in *Re W (Abuse: Oral Evidence)* can be struck with the comments of Gloster LJ, and perhaps European Convention 1950, Art 6(3)(d), in mind.

3.81 Finally it may perhaps be recalled that K was not in the position of the child whom Wall and Wilson LJJ had in mind in their comments when the *Re W (Abuse: Oral Evidence)* case was in the Court of Appeal.[102] In *Re S,* K may have been a child, but she was not the subject of the care proceedings as Wall and Wilson LJJ anticipated in their comments on the position of child witness's giving evidence. As the main witness for the case against the father she was in a position precisely parallel to the witness provided for by *YJCEA 1999.*

---

98 See 3.28.

99 Amongst Gloster LJ 'critical features in the case at §[59] was: '(x) The case was one of huge importance for the future life of the appellant and his relationship with his two infant sons and his partner, their mother. It clearly raised serious issues, so far as he was concerned, in relation to his rights under Art 6 of the European Convention to a fair trial, and, so far as he, and his children were concerned, in relation to his rights under Art 8 to a family life.'

100 *Re W (Children) (Abuse: Oral Evidence)* [2010] UKSC 12, [2010] 1 FLR 1485.

101 [2012] UKSC 60, [2013] 1 FLR 948.

102 *Re W (Children) (Abuse: Oral Evidence)* [2010] EWCA Civ 57.

6 ACHIEVING BEST EVIDENCE

Achieving best evidence: Guidance

3.82 *Achieving Best Evidence in Criminal Proceedings Guidance on interviewing victims and witnesses, and guidance on using special measures* (Ministry of Justice, March 2011)[103] ('*ABE Guidance*') is guidance for those conducting interviews of children and vulnerable witnesses, primarily in relation to possible criminal proceedings. As will be seen from references in the *ABE Guidance* itself and the cases considered in this part, it is regarded as entirely appropriate also for interview material which may be used in children proceedings, care and private law.[104]

3.83 The *Guidance* describes its scope as being to prepare interviewers for interviews with witnesses and for decisions as to whether to conduct an interview, and if so in what form:

> '1.3 ... It covers the interviewing of witnesses both for the purposes of making a video-recorded statement and also for taking a written statement, their preparation for court and the subsequent court appearance. It... is intended for all persons involved in relevant investigations, including the police, adults and children's social care workers, and members of the legal profession.'

3.84 It stresses its status as guidance, but also its significance in terms of court proceedings and administration of justice as follows:[105]

> '1.1 This document describes good practice in interviewing victims and witnesses, and in preparing them to give their best evidence in court. While it is advisory and does not constitute a legally enforceable code of conduct,[106] practitioners should bear in mind that significant departures from the good practice advocated in it may have to be justified in the courts.[107]
>
> 1.2 The guidance is generic; it cannot cater for every possible set of circumstances that might arise. Each witness is unique and the manner in which they are interviewed and subsequently prepared for their court appearance must be tailored to their particular needs and circumstances.'

103 See www.cps.gov.uk/publications/docs/best_evidence_in_criminal_proceedings.pdf.

104 For a private law example, see, eg, *AS v TH (False Allegations of Abuse)* [2016] EWHC 532 Fam, MacDonald J.

105 Page 16 paras 1.8 and 1.9.

106 As emphasised by Cobb J in *GD and BD* §[86] (referred to below).

107 Failings of the police and local authorities concerned in their conduct of ABE interviews were included in the reasons for Cobb J's findings in *GD and BD (Children) and ors v Wakefield MDC and West Yorks Police* (below) at §[120] that, in that case 'There is now no dispute that the [European Convention 1950] *Article 6* and *Article 8* rights of these Claimants were breached by these public authorities in a number of significant respects during the course of this joint investigation. These Claimants were in my judgement subjected to a largely inexcusable failure of professional good practice, with serious consequences for them all.'

3.85 The *Guidance* was described by Cobb J in *GD and BD (Children) and ors v Wakefield MDC and West Yorks Police*[108] J as:

> '[86] ABE interviews should always be conducted with reference to the March 2011 Guidance: "Achieving Best Evidence in Criminal Proceedings: Guidance on interviewing victims and witnesses, and guidance on using special measures". Although this guidance is advisory, and is not a legally enforceable code of conduct, as the Guide makes clear "practitioners should bear in mind that significant departures from the good practice advocated in it may have to be justified in the courts" (see §1.1). This is not the place for a detailed examination of the guidance, but it is essential reading for any professional conducting such an interview, and for those engaged in the preparation of a case which depends upon interview.'

3.86 Of the ABE interviewing done in *GD and BD* (above) Cobb J said:

> '[131] (xiii) ABE interviewing is a skilled exercise, which should only be conducted by trained professionals. It is not acceptable under any circumstances to provide false or misleading information to a child; after all, there is a high expectation that the child will be encouraged to provide accurate information to the interviewers.'

The ABE Guidance and child interviews

3.87 The *Guidance* is geared towards interviewing of child witnesses for criminal proceedings; but as case law references in this part show,[109] it is regarded as entirely apt for interviews for children in family proceedings. It provides[110] a definition of vulnerable and intimidated witnesses within the terms of *YJCEA 1999, s 16*; and recalls in particular that all children under 18 who appear as defence or prosecution witnesses in criminal proceedings, eligible for special measures to assist them to give their evidence in court (the same provisions are not yet fully available in family proceedings[111]).

3.88 Paras 2.17–2.40 deals in particular with interviews with children and with child protection issues. It stresses that any video-recorded interview of the child will serve two primary purposes:[112]

- Evidence gathering for use in the investigation and in criminal proceedings; and
- The evidence-in-chief of the witness.

> '2.18 ... In addition [says the *Guidance*], any relevant information gained during the interview can also be used to inform enquiries regarding

108 [2016] EWHC 3312 (Fam), [2017] Fam Law 283.
109 See, eg, at 3.85.
110 At paras 1.5–1.6.
111 As explained at 3.20.
112 Para 2.18.

significant harm under [CA 1989 s 47[113]] of the Children Act 1989 and any subsequent actions to safeguard and promote the child's welfare, and in some cases, the welfare of other children.

2.19 Some information may be common to both purposes, but there will be issues specific to each to be considered at the planning stage. A video-recorded interview may additionally serve a useful purpose in informing any subsequent civil childcare proceedings, or in disciplinary proceedings against adult carers (e.g. in residential institutions), and its potential value for these too should not be overlooked.'

3.89 The *Guidance* stresses that '2.23 Enquiries should be carried out in such a way as to minimise distress to the child and to ensure that families are treated sympathetically and with respect'; and that prior to interview inquiries about others who may know the child should be undertaken.

Special measures

3.90 The *ABE Guidance* advises consideration at this early stage – by interviewers, and (as appropriate) with the child and carers – of special measures:[114]

'2.28 Consideration should be given to holding a discussion between the investigating officer and the CPS where necessary to discuss what Special Measures might be needed to assist the witness before and during the trial....'

3.91 However, says the *Guidance*

'2.36 It is not uncommon for a child witness to change their views about giving evidence using particular Special Measures. Therefore, Special Measures discussions should be ongoing and discussed at the police interview stage, before submission of a Special Measures application and reviewed again after a pre-court familiarisation visit.'

3.92 More detail and information on special measures is provided in the *Guidance* in **Part 5** (Witnesses in court) and Appendix B; and see **Part 3** of this chapter. At the stage of the initial interviews of a child the *Guidance* advises how helping the child to give their best evidence in court as follows:

'2.33 The child should be advised that, should the case proceed, whether a video-recording is made or not, they may be required to attend court to answer further questions directly (e.g. cross-examination). A live

113 *CA 1989, s 47*: local authority's duty to investigate (eg where a child is in police protection (s 47(1)(a)(ii)) where a child may be in harm etc. The *Guidance* describes (at paras 2.21–2.22) how inquiries should proceed in co-operation with the local authority and other professionals involved, such as '2.22 ... Having responsibility for the criminal investigation does not mean that the police should always take the lead in the investigative interview. Provided both the police officer and social worker have been adequately trained to interview child witnesses in accordance with the guidance set out in this document, there is no reason why either should not lead the interview....'.

114 Special measures are explained further at 3.26.

link facility will normally be available to enable the witness to give best evidence at court. There is a presumption that this aid will normally be required by the child. The existence of a video-recorded interview does not by itself guarantee that it will be used.

2.34 If a child wishes to opt out of video-recorded evidence-in-chief, they may give all their evidence by live link from outside the courtroom, if the court agrees. The child may also opt out of live link evidence, if the court agrees but the law presumes that they will give evidence in the court room behind a screen. Should they not wish to use a screen, they may also be allowed to opt out of using it. Ultimately this is a matter for the court to decide but the court must take the witness' views into account when making its decision on whether to approve an opt out request.'

Consent of child and parents

3.93 Under the heading 'Consent'[115] the *ABE Guidance* stresses the need to 'consider each child as an individual', and to consider their 'individual needs' and their 'confidence and developmental level. In particular, 'when considering the needs of child witnesses' an interviewer:

'2.30 … should NOT:

- Assume that an older child will necessarily be more confident than a younger one;
- Assume that an older child will always want to give evidence live in the court room;
- Make assumptions based on the child's demeanour (for example, some children may behave with a degree of bravado even though they are actually experiencing a great deal of angst at the prospect of giving evidence).'

3.94 Parents of a child[116] should normally be 'informed of any interview before it takes place'; but:

'2.40 … In exceptional circumstances, however, it may be necessary to interview a suspected child victim without the knowledge of the parent or carer. Such circumstances include the possibility that a child would be threatened or otherwise coerced into silence; a strong likelihood that important evidence would be destroyed; or that the child in question did

115 Paras 2.29–2.30.

116 It is not necessary for the consent of the court to be obtained for a ward to be interviewed by the police: *Re a Ward of Court* [2017] EWHC 1022 (Fam), Sir James Munby P. Sir James considered the extent to which wardship did not, as a matter of law, constrain dealings with a ward (*A v Liverpool City Council and anor* [1982] AC 363 [1981] 2 WLR 948; *Re F (orse A) (a Minor) (Publication of Information)* [1977] Fam 58, [1976] 3 WLR 813, CA). He pointed out that FPR 2010 *PD12D* para 5 (which at §5.2 says that such permission is needed) needs radical review. *PD12D* has now been redrafted (effective from 16 June 2017) so that a new para 5 replaces the former version criticised by Sir James.

> not wish the parent to be involved at that stage, and is competent to take that decision (*see Working Together to Safeguard Children (Department for Children, Schools and Families, March 2010* [*sic*])…. Proceeding with the interview in the absence of parental knowledge needs to be carefully managed in interventions with the family by the local children's services authority, but may be necessary for example where children are at risk of honour-based violence or forced marriage.'

7 SPECIAL MEASURES AND CHILDREN PROCEEDINGS

CHILD'S EVIDENCE AND EXISTING PROCEDURE

Practice and the child's evidence: 'special measures by analogy'

3.95 In *Re W (Children) (Abuse: Oral Evidence)* (see below) the Supreme Court looked at how the adducing of a child's evidence might work in practice. Lady Hale drew attention to two particular ways in which the quality of the child's evidence be improved:

> '[27]…But on both sides of the equation, the court must factor in what steps can be taken to improve the quality of the child's evidence and at the same time to decrease the risk of harm to the child. These two aims are not in opposition to one another. The whole premise of *Achieving Best Evidence* and the special measures in criminal cases is that this will improve rather than diminish the quality of the evidence to the court.'

3.96 Secondly, procedures must operate so that questions which test the child's evidence are put to him or her fairly; and not necessarily that she can be cross-examined face-to-face:

> '[29]…There are things that the court can do but they are not things that it is used to doing at present. It is not limited by the usual courtroom procedures or to applying the special measures by analogy. The important thing is that the questions which challenge the child's account are fairly put to the child so that she can answer them, not that counsel should be able to question her directly. One possibility is an early videoed cross examination…. Another is cross-examination via video link. But another is putting the required questions to her through an intermediary. This could be the court itself, as would be common in continental Europe and used to be much more common than it is now in the courts of this country.'

3.97 The question returns: is a person against whom allegations are made in a family court – a parent respondent in care proceedings, for example – entitled to the same level of fairness to that to which an accused, on the same allegations, is entitled in a criminal trial? Asked that question in the Supreme Court or the Court of Appeal (Rimer and Gloster LJJ) respectively in *Re W (Children) (Abuse: Oral*

Evidence)[117] and *Re S (Care Proceedings: Case Management)*[118] are likely to say: yes, they should have the same level of fairness (save that proof need be only to the civil standard). As mentioned above, Gloster LJ doubted[119] that the balance required by the Supreme Court in *Re W (Children) (Abuse: Oral Evidence)*[120] – between the need to establish the truth as against the possible detriment to the welfare of the child – had been struck in a way which was fair to the father:

3.98 After what was said by the Supreme Court in *Re W (Abuse: Oral Evidence)*, and with such special measures as are available in the family courts and under Family Procedure Rules 2010 it must be possible for family justice to approach that which can be achieved in criminal proceedings.

'Special' measures and Re S

3.99 That said, it remains the case that no special measures for dealing with K's evidence were considered by the first instance judge in *Re S (Children)*,[121] though they were explored in oral submissions by the Court of Appeal. Thus, Black LJ:

> '[45] ... Much was made during the appellant's oral submissions of other ways in which the court might have investigated K's allegations with her. Amongst the possible methods were said to be using an intermediary or other special measures, pre-recording cross-examination in which questions were put which had been approved in advance by the court, or arranging for K to have a meeting with the judge (possibly not at court but in the presence of the advocates) at which the judge put questions covering pre-planned topics....'

3.100 In *Re W (Abuse: Oral Evidence)*[122] Lady Hale said of special measures: there are 'things that the [family] court can do but they are not things that it is used to doing at present'; and that these things go beyond 'applying special measures by analogy'. It is not necessarily a question only of cross-examination but that 'questions which challenge the child's account are fairly put to the child so that she can answer them': ie that the questioning of a child recognises his/her age and understanding and what will best enable the child to give the best evidence. For example, Lady Hale proposed[123] in particular the following:

(a) Early videoed cross examination;

(b) Cross-examination via video link;

(c) Putting cross-examination questions to a child witness through an intermediary. 'This could be the court itself'[124] said Lady Hale.

117 [2010] EWCA 57 at [40] (see 3.50).
118 [2016] EWCA Civ 83, [2017] 1 FLR 1476 at [58] *et seq* (see 3.70).
119 Para [60].
120 [2010] UKSC 12, [2010] 1 FLR 1485.
121 [2016] EWCA Civ 83.
122 [2010] UKSC 12, [2010] 1 FLR 1485.
123 At [28].
124 See questions from the court at 4.37.

QUESTIONS BY THE JUDGE

Court's options for questions to a child

3.101 A particular issue arises, mostly in private law proceedings, where a respondent is not represented but he (it will generally, though not invariably be a man) wishes to exercise his right to cross-examine – or ask questions of – a child witness. At present the *Matrimonial and Family Proceedings Act 1984, s 31G(6)* deals with the question of where a court is able in family proceedings to take over cross-examination of a witness for an unrepresented party. Section 31G(6) provides as follows:

> '(6) Where in any proceedings in the family court it appears to the court that any party to the proceedings who is not legally represented is unable to examine or cross-examine a witness effectively, the court is to –
>
> (a) ascertain from that party the matters about which the witness may be able to depose or on which the witness ought to be cross-examined, and
>
> (b) put, or cause to be put, to the witness such questions in the interests of that party as may appear to the court to be proper.'

3.102 The last government had plans to make provision to assist allegedly abused victims of domestic abuse (equivalent to that in *YJCEA 1999, s 38(4)*); but this was not extended specifically to children. The proposal was that a court appointed advocate should be appointed by the court to ask questions of an allegedly violent defendant; but this would not necessarily be the same as for (say) the father who is said – as in the case of K and Re S, for example – to have abused the proposed witness.

3.103 As discussed in **Part 2** this is considered already in the special measures available in criminal proceedings under *YJCEA 1999, Pt 2*. Similar means of cross-examination of an unrepresented defendant are not guaranteed in family proceedings (especially if video-link equipment is not available to the court). So, says the Court of Appeal in *Re K & H (Children)*.[125] The conclusion of the court was that, save in exceptional circumstances, a judge will be expected to deal with questions of the child alleged victim, without assistance from, for example, an advocate to the court.

3.104 In *K & H* the Court of Appeal had rejected the judge's proposal that he had power to require the Lord Chancellor to pay for an advocate to ask questions of an unrepresented parent in private law contact proceedings. The children in the case were six and four, and they had an older half-sister (S) who alleged that their father (F) had sexually abused her when she was 15. The judge decided that there should be a fact-finding hearing to determine the truthfulness of her allegations, and that S should give evidence. F was outside of scope for legal aid on his means.

---

125 [2015] EWCA Civ 543 sub nom *K and H (Private Law: Public Funding)* [2016] 1 FLR 754 (Lord Dyson MR, Black and McFarlane LJJ).

The judge held that he should not cross-examine S, his accuser and that a legal representative should be appointed to conduct the cross-examination at the expense of Her Majesty's Court & Tribunal Service (HMCTS). The Lord Chancellor appealed against this and the Court of Appeal allowed the appeal.

Judge's questions for the defendant

3.105 Lord Dyson MR held that the judge could himself ask questions of the witness:

> '[60] In a simple straightforward case, questioning by the judge is likely to be the preferred option and it should present no difficulties. The judge will know what the unrepresented party's case is. It may be helpful for the judge to ask him or her to prepare written questions for the court to consider in advance. Sometimes, unexpected answers may be given to the judge. These may require the judge to ask the unrepresented party to comment on the unexpected answers and to suggest supplementary questions for the judge's consideration.'

3.106 Lord Dyson MR accepted that there might be more difficult cases; but offered no basis on which these cases could be resolved under s 31G(6). In such cases of difficulty, the 'lack of legal representation [might] result in the proceedings not being conducted in compliance with Arts 6 or 8 of the European Convention'.[126] If such problems arose the solution of the Master of the Rolls was that consideration should be given to further statutory provision (ie no immediate relief that he could suggest was available at law):

> 'In order to avoid the risk of a breach of the European Convention, consideration should be given to the enactment of a statutory provision for (i) the appointment of a legal representative to conduct the cross-examination and (ii) the payment out of central funds of such sums as appear to be reasonably necessary to cover the cost of the legal representative, ie a provision in civil proceedings analogous to s 38(4) of the Youth Justice and Criminal Evidence Act 1999 and s 19(3)(e) of the Prosecution of Offenders Act 1985.'

3.107 And this reference to *YJCEA 1999, s 38(4)* brings the subject full circle; for that is the provision in *YJCEA 1999* which enable an independent advocate to be appointed by the court and for that advocate to be paid for out of public funds.[127] If the accused – in the case of criminal proceedings – has no legal representative *YJCEA 1999, s 38(3)* requires the court to 'consider whether it is necessary in the

126 '[62] I acknowledge that there may be cases where the position is different. I have in mind, for example, a case where the oral evidence which needs to be tested by questioning is complicated. It may be complex medical or other expert evidence. Or it may be complex and/or confused factual evidence, say, from a vulnerable witness. It may be that in such cases, none of the options to which I have referred can make up for the absence of a legal representative able to conduct the cross-examination....'

127 *YJCEA 1999, s 40.*

interests of justice for the witness to be cross-examined by a legal representative appointed to represent the interests of the accused'. *YJCEA 1999, s 38(4)* continues with the requirement that an advocate be appointed to cross-examine 'in the interests' but not necessarily on the instructions of, the accused:

> '(4) If the court decides that it is necessary in the interests of justice for the witness to be so cross-examined, the court must appoint a qualified legal representative (chosen by the court) to cross-examine the witness in the interests of the accused.'

3.108 If the legislation proposed by the government in the Queen's Speech does indeed revive the proposal in the Prison and Courts Bill on cross-examination of complainants in domestic abuse cases,[128] then there would seem to be no reason why a similar provision should not be included for child witnesses where the quality of their evidence might be diminished by cross-examination by a parent or other party acting in person.

---

128 Considered fully at 1.67.

APPENDIX

Working Party of the Family Justice Council Guidelines December 2011

These guidelines on the issue of children giving evidence in family proceedings, have been produced by the Family Justice Council Working Party on Children Giving Evidence, chaired by the Rt Hon. Lord Justice Thorpe. They have been approved by the Council and I wish to add my endorsement.

The working party was set up following a referral from the Court of Appeal in *Re W* [2010] EWCA Civ 57. The Supreme Court in *Re W* [2010] UKSC 12 subsequently held that there was no longer a presumption or even a starting point against children giving evidence in such cases.

I am sure that these guidelines will be of benefit to members of the judiciary, lawyers and professionals, who have to deal with applications for children to give evidence in family proceedings.

May I take this opportunity to express my gratitude to all the members of the working party, and in particular to Alex Verdan QC, for the final version of these guidelines.

Sir Nicholas Wall President of the Family Division

Children Giving Evidence in Family Proceedings

1 These Guidelines have been produced by Lord Justice Thorpe's Working Party.

2 This Working Party was set up following a request to the President of the Family Division by the Court of Appeal in *Re W* [2010] EWCA Civ 57, a case which considered the issue of children giving evidence in family proceedings.

3 That same case then went to the Supreme Court and is reported as *Re W* [2010] UKSC 12. It is now the leading authority on this issue. The Supreme Court held that there was no longer a presumption or even a starting point against children giving evidence in such cases.

4 Enquiries by this Working Party suggests that the number of applications for children giving evidence since this decision may be increasing.

5 The aim of these Guidelines is to provide those involved in family proceedings with advice as to what matters should be taken into account in such situations.

6 Hearsay evidence is of course admissible in family proceedings: Children (Admissibility of Hearsay Evidence) Order 1993, SI 1993/621.

7 The issue of whether a child should be further questioned or give evidence in family proceedings should be considered at the earliest possible opportunity by the court and all the parties and not left to the party intending to so apply.

Legal considerations

8 In light of Re W, in deciding whether a child should give evidence, the court's principal objective should be achieving a fair trial.

9 With that objective the court should carry out a balancing exercise between the following primary considerations:

(i) the possible advantages that the child being called will bring to the determination of truth balanced against;

(ii) the possible damage to the child's welfare from giving evidence i.e. the risk of harm to the child from giving evidence;

having regard to:

(a) the child's wishes and feelings, in particular their willingness to give evidence, as an unwilling child should rarely if ever be obliged to give evidence;

(b) the child's particular needs and abilities;

(c) the issues that need to be determined;

(d) the nature and gravity of the allegations;

(e) the source of the allegations;

(f) whether the case depends on the child's allegations alone;

(g) corroborative evidence;

(h) the quality and reliability of the existing evidence;

(i) the quality and reliability of any ABE interview;

(j) whether the child has retracted allegations;

(k) the nature of any challenge a party wishes to make;

(l) the age of the child; generally the older the child the better;

(m) the maturity, vulnerability and understanding, capacity and competence of the child; this may be apparent from the ABE or from professionals' discussions with the child;

(n) the length of time since the events in question;

(o) the support or lack of support the child has;

(p) the quality and importance of the child's evidence;

(q) the right to challenge evidence;

(r) whether justice can be done without further questioning;

(s) the risk of further delay;

(t) the views of the guardian who is expected to have discussed the issue with the child concerned if appropriate and those with parental responsibility;

(u) specific risks arising from the possibility of the child giving evidence twice in criminal or other and family proceedings taking into account that normally the family proceedings will be heard before the criminal; and

(v) the serious consequences of the allegations i.e. whether the findings impact upon care and contact decisions.

10 The Court must always take into account the risk of harm which giving evidence may do to children and how to minimise that harm, although that may vary from case to case but the Court does not necessarily need expert evidence in order to assess the risk.

11 Where there are concurrent or linked criminal proceedings there should be close liaison between the respective parties and the allocated judges and ideally linked directions hearings. The Police/CPS should be informed of any proposal that a child give evidence in family proceedings and their views obtained before any such decision is made.

Alternatives to child giving live evidence at a hearing

12 The Court needs to consider seriously the possibility of further questions being put to the child on an occasion distinct from the substantive hearing so as to avoid oral examination. This option would have significant advantages to the child and should be considered at the earliest opportunity and in any event before that substantive hearing. Such further questioning should be carried out as soon as possible after the incident in question.

The Court will need to take into account practical and procedural issues including:

(a) giving the child the opportunity to refresh his memory;

(b) the appropriate identity of the questioner;

(c) matching the skills of the questioner to the communication needs of the child;

(d) where the questioning should take place;

(e) the type and nature of the questions;

(f) advance judicial approval of any questions proposed to be put to the child;

(g) the need for ground rules to be discussed ahead of time by the judge, lawyers (and intermediary, if applicable) about the examination; and

(h) how the interview should be recorded.

Practical considerations pre-hearing

13 Once a decision has been made that a child should give evidence at a hearing and be questioned at court, the Court must factor in steps to improve the quality of the child's evidence and minimise the risk of harm to the child.

14 At the earliest opportunity and in any event before the hearing at which the child's evidence is taken, the following matters need to be considered:

(a) if 'live' cross examination is appropriate, the need for and use of a registered intermediary (subject to their availability) or other communication specialist to facilitate the communication of others with the child or relay questions directly, if indicated by the needs of the child;

(b) the use of other 'special measures' in particular live video link and screens;

(c) the full range of special measures in light of the child's wishes and needs;

(d) advance judicial approval of any questions proposed to be put to the child;

(e) the need for ground rules to be discussed ahead of time by the judge, lawyers (and intermediary, if applicable) about the examination;

(f) information about the child's communication skills, length of concentration span and level of understanding e.g. from an expert or an intermediary or other communication specialist;

(g) the need for breaks;

(h) the involvement and identity of a supporter for the child;

(i) the timetable for children's evidence to minimise time at court and give them a fresh clear start in the morning;

(j) the child's dates to avoid attending court;

(k) the length of any ABE recording, the best time for the child and the Court to view it (the best time for the child may not be when the recording is viewed by the court);

(l) admissions of as much of the child's evidence as possible in advance; including locations, times, and lay-outs;

(m) save in exceptional circumstances, agreement as to (i) the proper form and limit of questioning and (ii) the identity of the questioner.

15 If a child is to give oral evidence at the hearing the following should occur:

(a) a familiarisation visit by the child to the court before the hearing with a demonstration of special measures, so that the child can make an informed view about their use;

(b) the child should be accompanied and have a known neutral supporter, not directly involved in the case, present during their evidence;

(c) the child should see their ABE interview and/or their existing evidence before giving evidence for the purpose of memory refreshing;

(d) consideration of the child's secure access to the building and suitability of waiting/eating areas so as to ensure there is no possibility of any confrontation with anyone which might cause distress to the child (where facilities are inadequate, use of a remote link from another court or non-court location);

(e) identification of where the child will be located at court and the need for privacy.

16 Where possible the children's solicitor/Cafcass should be deputed to organise these matters.

17 A child should never be questioned directly by a litigant in person who is an alleged perpetrator.

Practical considerations at hearing

18 If the decision has been made that the child should give oral evidence at the hearing the following should occur:

(a) advocates should introduce themselves to the child;

(b) judges and magistrates should ask if the child would like to meet them, to help to establish rapport and reinforce advice;

(c) children should be encouraged to let the court know if they have a problem or want a break but cannot be relied upon to do so;

(d) professionals should be vigilant to identify potential miscommunication;

(e) the child should be told how the live video link works and who can see who;

(f) a check should be made (before the child is seated in the TV link room) to ensure that the equipment is working, recordings can be played and that camera angles will not permit the witness to see the Respondents;

(g) the parties should agree which documents the child will be referred to and ensure they are in the room where the child is situated for ease of access.

Examination of children

19 If the Court decides a child should give oral evidence, the Court and all parties should take into account the Good Practice Guidance in managing young witness cases and questioning children (part of the NSPCC/Nuffield Foundation research 'Measuring Up' July 2009 by Joyce Plotnikoff and Richard Woolfson) and the subsequent Progress Report which Guidance has been endorsed by the Judicial Studies Board, the Director of Public Prosecutions, the Criminal Bar Association and the Law Society: http://www.nspcc.org.uk/Inform/research/findings/measuring_up_guidance_wdf66581.pdf.

20 Examination of the child should take into account the Court of Appeal judgment in *R v Barker* [2010] EWCA Crim 4, para [42], which called for the advocacy to be adapted 'to enable the child to give the best evidence of which he or she is capable› and which questioning should:

(a) be at the child's pace and consistent with their understanding;

(b) use simple common words and phrases;

(c) repeat names and places frequently;

(d) ask one short question (one idea) at a time;

(e) let the child know the subject of the question;

(f) follow a structured approach, signposting the subject;

(g) avoid negatives;

(h) avoid repetition;

(i) avoid suggestion or leading, including 'tag' questions;

(j) avoid a criminal or 'Old Bailey' style cross examination;

(k) avoid 'do you remember' questions;

(l) avoid restricted choice questions;

(m) be slow and allow enough time to answer;

(n) check child's understanding;

(o) test the evidence not trick the witness;

(p) take into account and check the child's level of understanding;

(q) not assume the child understands;

(r) be alert to literal interpretation;

(s) take care with times, numbers and frequency;

(t) avoid asking the child to demonstrate intimate touching on his or her own body (if such a question is essential, an alternative method, such as pointing to a body outline, should be agreed beforehand).

Court's overriding duty

21 All advocates have a responsibility to manage the questioning of a child witness fairly. However, the ultimate responsibility for ensuring that the child gives the best possible evidence in order to inform the court's decision rests with the tribunal. It should set out its expectations of the advocates and make it clear to the child witness that they can indicate to the court if they feel they are not saying what they want to say or do not understand what is being said to them.

The court must be scrupulous in the attention it gives to the case management and control of the questioning process and should be prepared to intervene if the questioning is inappropriate or unnecessary.

22 These Guidelines will be reviewed periodically. Those involved in family proceedings are invited to contact the Family Justice Council with any relevant comments.

Working Party of the Family Justice Council

4

CHILD'S VIEWS

1 INTRODUCTION

Children meeting with judges

4.1 This chapter considers one of the two subjects which are central to this book: the appropriateness of, and circumstances for, a child meeting with the judge in a case which concerns them. That is to say, a child may express an often unchallenged view of his or her role in the proceedings and of the child's view of his or her future.

4.2 **Chapter 3** has dealt with a child's evidence (as distinct from views). This chapter proceeds as follows:

- **Part 2** looks at the child's 'age and understanding' and its origins in terms of child law reform and of a child's rights.
- **Part 3** considers a child's age and understanding: that the child's views is a 'fundamental principle'[1] of English child law; and in particular how this applies in child abduction cases.
- Finally **Part 4** provides an assessment of the modern law on judge's meeting with children and how

Child's views, child's evidence

4.3 As with the entirety of this book the difference must be clear between a child who gives evidence in a family case;[2] and of a child expressing a view about that child's role in the case[3] – in particular about their future – to a judge, or to a court officer or other professional for passing on to the court. The first is a role

1 *Re D (A Child) (International Recognition)* [2016] EWCA Civ 12, [2016] 1 WLR 2469, [2016] 2 FLR 347.

2 *Guidelines in relation to children giving evidence in family proceedings of December 2011* [2012] Fam Law 70 (www.judiciary.gov.uk/wp-content/uploads/2014/10/fjc_guidelines_-in_relation_children_-giving_evidence_-in_-family_-proceedings_dec2011.pdf) ('Guidelines on children's evidence').

3 *Guidelines on Judges Meeting Children who are subject to Family Proceedings April 2010* [2010] 2 FLR 1872 – https://fnf.org.uk/phocadownload/downloads/guidelines_for_judges_meeting_children.pdf ('Guidelines to meeting children') set out in the Appendix to this Ch.

in the course of proceedings which might be carried out by any individual with relevant evidence, including the child. The second is the view of a child, where appropriate, who is the subject of the case. The distinction was emphasised by the Court of Appeal in *Re KP (Abduction: Child's Objections)*:[4]

> '[50]… the *Guidelines* [for a judge meeting with the child] indicate that there is a firm line to be drawn between a process in which the judge and a young person simply encounter each other and communicate in a manner which is not for the purpose of evidence gathering, and a process in which one of the aims of the meeting is to gather evidence. In so stating the Guidelines are not at odds with any of the reported cases to which reference has already been made.'

4.4 Though the two forms of information may be provided by the same child, and sometimes in, or as part of, the same hearing, the separate functions are emphasised by the fact of different sets of guidelines having been issued. In *Re KP* the Court of Appeal stressed the need for care 'to be taken in distinguishing the two processes' and for the need to respect the Convention rights, especially Art 6, of all parties if a child is in fact providing evidence to the court.[5]

'Opportunity to be heard'

4.5 Throughout this chapter it is the case that what is considered is the right of the child to be heard, the 'opportunity to be heard', the availability of the court to hear views. It is a voluntary matter, unlike for example, the requirement to give evidence which might be imposed on a child witness. Indeed, as will be seen,[6] the Court of Appeal has been critical of a judge who overstepped her role in seeing the child as between the child providing evidence for the court and expressing only a view.

4.6 There may be many cases where a child has no wish to express a view. The point of this chapter is to stress the rights a child has if that child wants to express a view. As Lady Hale points out in *Re D (Abduction: Rights of Custody)*:[7] 'It is the child more than anyone else who will have to live with what the court decides'. Art 12 guarantees that they have the right, if they want to, to have a say to the court.

Proposals for reform

4.7 The work of the Vulnerable Witnesses and Children Working Group (VWCWG) relating to hearing children is considered briefly in the Introduction to

4 [2014] EWCA Civ 554, [2014] 2 FLR 660; see further discussion of this case and of the Guidelines on children's evidence at 3.55 and 4.44.
5 §51; and see 4.50.
6 *Re KP (Abduction: Child's Objections)* [2014] EWCA Civ 554, [2014] 2 FLR 660.
7 [2006] UKHL 51, [2007] 1 FLR 961.

this book. The current published draft rule 3B.2 proposes to impose of the court a duty 'to consider how a child can participate in proceedings'.

4.8 Given the informal nature of the present *Guidelines* for judges meeting children it is disappointing that the content of guidelines may not be adopted by the new rules and given quasi-statutory force, at least by being adopted as part of the practice direction.[8] There is a clear recognition that a child's views 'about participating in proceedings' must be considered.[9] There is no mention of how this is to be done; nor (if this is the intent) that this consideration must be according to the child's age and maturity.

4.9 The Ministry of Justice, in drafting rules for children and their evidence, do not seem to have picked up Black LJ's comment that nothing is said in any enactment – she mentioned specifically the rules – as to how age and 'the precise nature of the understanding' of a child[10] is intended to be assessed. That said, the court's mind is directed to deal with matters of right, such as a child's representation and meeting with the judge.

2 CHILD'S AGE, MATURITY AND UNDERSTANDING

Child's views: a 'sea-change' in judicial attitudes

4.10 A starting point for considering the role of children's views in cases about them is the comments of Sir James Munby P in *Re F (Children)*[11] (a child abduction case concerning children aged fourteen, seven and four[12]). He explained the recent history:

> '[43] It is apparent that in relation to [children being heard] there has been a sea-change in attitudes over the last decade and more, even if on occasion practitioners and the courts have been and still are too slow to recognise the need for change or to acknowledge the pace of change. Moreover, and I wish to emphasise this, the process of change continues apace.
>
> [42] In April 2010, [*Guidelines on Judges Meeting Children*] were issued by the Family Justice Council with the approval of Sir Nicholas Wall P. In December 2011, and following the decision of the Supreme Court in *Re W*, the Family Justice Council issued [*Guidelines in relation to children giving evidence*].'

---

8 *PD3AA* as at present drafted.

9 Draft r 3B.2(4).

10 *Re W (A Child) (Care Proceedings: Child's Representation) Practice Note* [2016] EWCA Civ 1051, [2017] 1 WLR 1027: [21] There is no assistance to be found in the rules as to the precise nature of the understanding that will be required of a child before he or she is considered able to give instructions. There is some assistance to be found in the authorities, in particular in the case of *Mabon v Mabon* [2005] EWCA Civ 634, [2005] 2 FLR 1011....'; and see further consideration at 6.81.

11 [2016] EWCA Civ 546.

12 Considered further at 7.33.

4.11 Sir James went on to explain briefly the work of the VWCWG,[13] and concluded:

> '[43] One thing is quite clear: that proper adherence to the principles laid down in *Re W*[14] will see ever increasing numbers of children giving evidence in family proceedings.'

4.12 *Re W* [2010] concerned a child's evidence, and has been considered in **Chapter 3**. *Re F* was about children's views. There may have been a 'sea change' in attitudes of judges and practitioners as Sir James says in §41 above; but the case of *Re F* shows that the law is still not entirely clear as to how it operates and is operated by the courts.

Rights of a child

4.13 The United Nations Convention on the Rights of the Child 1989, Art 12 provides the following:

> '*Article 12*
>
> 1. States Parties shall assure to the child who is capable of forming his or her own views the right to express those views freely in all matters affecting the child, the views of the child being given due weight in accordance with the age and maturity of the child.
> 2. For this purpose, the child shall in particular be provided the opportunity to be heard in any judicial and administrative proceedings affecting the child, either directly, or through a representative or an appropriate body, in a manner consistent with the procedural rules of national law.'

4.14 It is submitted that this is the law as to how a child should be heard in relation to matters which affect the child. Similar provisions appear in the Charter of Fundamental Rights of the European Union (2000/C 364/01), Art 24.1.

> '*Article 24*
>
> **The rights of the child**
>
> 1. Children… may express their views freely. Such views shall be taken into consideration on matters which concern them in accordance with their age and maturity.

4.15 Provisions as to a child's 'opportunity to be heard' recur in Brussels IIA,[15] for example, at Art 11(2):

---

13 See Ch 1.

14 *Re W (Children) (Abuse: Oral Evidence)* [2010] UKSC 12, [2010] 1 FLR 1485.

15 Council Regulation (EC) No 2201/2003 of 27 November 2003 Concerning Jurisdiction and the Recognition and Enforcement of Judgments in Matrimonial Matters and in Matters of Parental Responsibility; see also, eg, Art 23(b) at 4.32.

2 When applying Articles 12 and 13 of the 1980 Hague Convention, it shall be ensured that the child is given the opportunity to be heard during the proceedings unless this appears inappropriate having regard to his or her age or degree of maturity.'

4.16 Art 12 with the remaining references (subject as explained in **Chapter 5**[16]) must be the starting-point for a family court dealing with an issue which concerns a child. The question is, how far is this done in English courts?[17] And how far by judges who have a tendency to see Charter rights such as this through eyes accustomed mostly to following English common law and statute.

4.17 Though the definition of 'child' includes all individuals under 18, statute law accords adulthood to 'children' who are 16 and over in questions of consent to medical treatment. The *Family Law Reform Act 1969, s 8* is as follows:

'8 Consent by persons over 16 to surgical, medical and dental treatment

(1) The consent of a minor who has attained the age of sixteen years to any surgical, medical or dental treatment which, in the absence of consent, would constitute a trespass to his person, shall be as effective as it would be if he were of full age; and where a minor has by virtue of this section given an effective consent to any treatment it shall not be necessary to obtain any consent for it from his parent or guardian….'

4.18 The question for the House of Lords in *Gillick v West Norfolk and Wisbech AHA*[18] was to what extent the common law could extend the principle of consent for children below 16; and if so to what extent and on what terms could they do so?[19]

4.19 Starting from Art 12, the following questions will be asked in this and the following parts of this chapter on child's views:

- Assessment of age and maturity.
- How a child's views should be heard.
- Should the child be represented?
- What should the judge tell the parties.
- What weight should be given to a child's views.

Child's age and understanding: Gillick

4.20 The background to the law on a child being heard starts with *Gillick* (above). The question for the House of Lords was whether or not confidential

16 See especially 5.67.
17 *Re P-S* [2013] EWCA Civ 223, [2014] 2 FLR 27 per Sir Alan Ward.
18 [1985] UKHL 7, [1986] 1 AC 112, [1986] 1 FLR 224.
19 See Ch 5, Part 2.

information provided by a child under 16 to her general practitioner should automatically be passed to the child's parent. However, the speeches of their lordships ranged over consent to, and understanding of, not only medical treatment but also all questions for a child's consideration in relation to that child's future: that is any view of a child relevant to the issue as to their future, that is to say the court's 'decision-making process about [a child's] own future'.[20]

4.21 The law had prescribed the position on medical treatment for a child of 16 and 17.[21] But what of a child under that age? Given the gap in the law – statute law and common law – as Lord Scarman saw it:[22] 'It is open [to the House of Lords] to formulate a rule'. Legal principle, he said, must try 'to keep the law abreast of the society in which [the judges] live and work':[23]

> 'If the law should impose upon the process of "growing up" fixed limits where nature knows only a continuous process, the price would be artificiality and a lack of realism in an area where the law must be sensitive to human development and social change.... Unless and until Parliament should think fit to intervene, the courts should establish a principle flexible enough to enable justice to be achieved by its application to the particular circumstances proved by the evidence placed before them.'

4.22 'Age and maturity of the child' is the terminology used by Art 12. 'Understanding and intelligence' is Lord Scarman's term. 'Age and understanding' is used in *Children's Act 1989* (*CA 1989*), *s 1(3)(a)*. All have the same connotation which Lord Scarman explained as he said:[24]

> '... I would hold that as a matter of law the parental right to determine whether or not their minor child below the age of 16 will have medical treatment terminates if and when the child achieves a *sufficient understanding and intelligence* to enable him or her to understand fully what is proposed. It will be a question of fact whether a child seeking advice has sufficient understanding of what is involved to give a consent valid in law.'

4.23 In principle, the same approach applies to a child's views under *CA 1989, s 1(3)(a)*. A child's views may not decide the issue, but those views must be fully considered by the court. Hayden J explained this distinction in *An NHS Foundation Trust v A and Others*:[25]

> '[12] Accordingly it is right that I should give thought to A's own wishes and feelings on her treatment.... I start from the premise that a competent young person under the age of 16 years, who is able to understand all the

20 Per Lady Hale in ALC speech 2015: see 1.7.
21 *Family Law Reform Act 1969, s 8* (above).
22 At [1986] 1 FLR 224 at 250.
23 At [1986] 1 FLR 224 at 248.
24 At [1986] 1 FLR 224 at 253.
25 [2014] EWHC 920 (Fam), [2015] 1 FLR 503: A was a 15-year-old who was not eating, and whose mother opposed an application by a hospital, in effect, to force feed her.

> relevant advice and the consequences of that advice, is to be treated as an autonomous individual and respected as such.'

That of course would not mean her views would be determinative, but they would be given great weight: *R (Axon) v Secretary of State for Health*[[26]]; *Gillick v West Norfolk and Wisbech AHA* [(above)].

Law Commission and Children Act 1989

4.24 *Gillick* coincided with a wide-ranging review of children's law in the 1980s and in particular with the work of the Law Commission lead by Brenda Hoggett (now Lady Hale in the Supreme Court). The Commission's work lead (via the recommendations of Cleveland Report[27]) to *CA 1989*. From introduction of CA 1989 the court was formally to 'have regard to… the wishes and feelings' of a child. *CA 1989, s 1(3)(a)*[28] is as follows:

> '(3) [Where the court is considering whether to make a private law order in civil proceedings], a court shall have regard in particular to – (a) the ascertainable wishes and feelings of the child concerned (considered in the light of his age and understanding);…'

4.25 As will be seen, it is s 1(3)(a) and the cases and procedures under it which represents the modern law.[29] Section 1(3)(a) must now be reviewed in the light of a number of child abduction cases; then in the light of recent domestic cases. Article 12 and case law references to the *Guidelines on meeting children* provides an indication as to the present state of children law. Historical developments can be looked at on this basis starting from a similar time point – 2005/2006 – with *Mabon v Mabon*[30] and *Re D (A Child) (Abduction: Custody Rights)* (below).

4.26 A starting point for this review of cases over the past twelve years can be the comment of Lady Hale in *Re D (A Child) (Abduction: Custody Rights)* (below), as to the importance of a child's views:

---

26 [2006] EWHC 37 (Admin), [2006] 2 FLR 206, Silber J.

27 *Report of the inquiry into child abuse in Cleveland 1987* Cm 412 London: Her Majesty's Stationery Office; the inquiry was chaired by Dame Elizabeth Butler-Sloss P (as she became).

28 Section 1(3) lists a number of factors amongst which wishes and feelings is one:
'(a) the ascertainable wishes and feelings of the child concerned (considered in the light of his age and understanding);
(b) his physical, emotional and educational needs;
(c) the likely effect on him of any change in his circumstances;
(d) his age, sex, background and any characteristics of his which the court considers relevant;
(e) any harm which he has suffered or is at risk of suffering;
(f) how capable each of his parents, and any other person in relation to whom the court considers the question to be relevant, is of meeting his needs;
(g) the range of powers available to the court under this Act in the proceedings in question.'

29 See, eg, *Re D (A Child) (International Recognition)* [2016] EWCA Civ 12, [2016] 1 WLR 2469, [2016] 2 FLR 347 considered at 4.29 and in Ch 7.

30 [2005] EWCA Civ 634, [2005] Fam 366, [2005] 2 FLR 1011.

> '[57] ... As any parent who has ever asked a child what he wants for tea knows, there is a large difference between taking account of a child's views and doing what he wants. Especially in Hague Convention cases, the relevance of the child's views to the issues in the case may be limited. But there is now a growing understanding of the importance of listening to the children involved in children's cases. It is the child, more than anyone else, who will have to live with what the court decides. Those who do listen to children understand that they often have a point of view which is quite distinct from that of the person looking after them. They are quite capable of being moral actors in their own right. Just as the adults may have to do what the court decides whether they like it or not, so may the child. But that is no more a reason for failing to hear what the child has to say than it is for refusing to hear the parents' views.'

4.27 As will be shown in this chapter the principles of hearing a child's views are the same across the full spectrum of children proceedings where those views are relevant and whether in Hague Convention cases or otherwise (as explained by Ryder LJ in *Re D (International Recognition)*, considered below).

3 CHILD'S VIEWS ACCORDING TO AGE AND MATURITY

Child's views: a 'fundamental principle'

UN Convention on the Rights of the Child

4.28 The United Nations Convention on the Rights of the Child 1989, Art 12[31] is in similar terms to Art 24 of the Charter as to a child's right to be heard in 'judicial proceedings': that is 'to express... views freely'; and for them to be 'given due weight [according to the child's] age and maturity' (Art 12.1).[32]

4.29 In *Re D (A Child) (International Recognition)*[33]Art 24 of the Charter was considered by Ryder LJ in the Court of Appeal, with whose judgment Moore-Bick and Briggs LJJ agreed. One of the two bases (the second related to service of documents) on which the court proceeded with the appeal was whether the child, David, was given an opportunity to be heard 'in violation of the fundamental principles of procedure in [an English] jurisdiction'.[34] The court was concerned with a Romanian court order, and the question of whether this should be enforced in the UK where a child was not given 'an opportunity to be heard' on parental responsibility (ie in where he was to live). The child (aged 7 when the decision

31 See www.ohchr.org/EN/ProfessionalInterest/Pages/CRC.aspx – by which the UK will still be bound, so far as its provisions are enforceable.

32 UNCRC Art 12 and Charter of Fundamental Rights of the European Union (2000/C 364/01) Art 24 are set out and explained in Ch 7, 5.37 and 5.25 respectively.

33 [2016] EWCA Civ 12, [2016] 2 FLR 347.

34 §6.

appealed against was made) had not been given this opportunity in Romania, as required by Brussels IIA Art 23(b), so his father could not enforce the order in this country.[35]

4.30 Article 23(b) deals with whether or not a Member State of the EU must recognise a judgment or order of another Member State for purposes of its enforcement, and is as follows:

> '*Article 23*
>
> **Grounds of non-recognition for judgments relating to parental responsibility**
>
> A judgment relating to parental responsibility shall not be recognised:...
>
> (b) if it was given, except in case of urgency, without the child having been given an opportunity to be heard, in violation of fundamental principles of procedure of the Member State in which recognition is sought;'

4.31 The question for the Court of Appeal was how to deal with the opportunity to be heard as a 'fundamental principle of procedure' in English procedural law. Ryder LJ dealt with this first by setting out 'general principles'. Parental responsibility[36] is dealt with in Arts 8 to 15; and specific reference is made by Recital (33) not only of the EU Charter, but also of Art 24 and the rights of the child:

> '(33) This Regulation recognises the fundamental rights and observes the principles of the Charter of Fundamental Rights of the European Union. In particular, it seeks to ensure respect for the fundamental rights of the child as set out in Article 24 of the Charter of Fundamental Rights of the European Union.'

Fundamental principle

4.32 Ryder LJ cites Art 24 in full. It followed from Art 23(b), and from the English court's interpretation of EU rules in Brussels IIA in a way which accords with 'mutual trust',[37] that the Court of Appeal must now seek to define what is intended in English law by the reference to 'fundamental principle' in Art 23(b). It is this analysis which must be taken to represent the most authoritative analysis of the law on the child's views.

---

35 Incidentally, the decision in David's case depended on reciprocal arrangements between the English and Romanian courts. This cannot necessarily be expected to survive EU withdrawal in the same form (as explained at 1.83).

36 'parental responsibility' is defined by Art.2.7 as '7 the term 'parental responsibility' shall mean all rights and duties relating to the person or the property of a child which are given to a natural or legal person by judgment, by operation of law or by an agreement having legal effect. The term shall include rights of custody and rights of access;...'

37 See Brussels IIA Recital 21; and see *Re Rinau* [2008] 2 FLR 1495.

4.33 In the search for 'fundamental principles' Ryder LJ started[38] with the *Children Act 1989* especially the check-list of factors for considering court-ordered arrangements for children in s 1(3) which says:

> '(3) [When the court is considering making an order about a child it] shall have regard in particular to –
>
> (a) the ascertainable wishes and feelings of the child concerned (considered in the light of his age and understanding);'

4.34 Section 1(3)(a) was a 'fundamental principle' on which the court's discretion is founded and which no 'parent can seek to avoid'.[39] It therefore goes further than 'a check-list factor'. It is, said Ryder LJ, 'plainly an example of domestic jurisdiction giving force to a fundamental principle of procedure'.[40] So, said the judge:

> '[41]... In every case, the court is required to ensure that the child is given the opportunity to be heard. That means asking the questions, "whether and if so how is the child to be heard". There are a range of answers, many of which were foreshadowed in *Re D*.[41] It is not the answer that is key to the question before this court but the fact that the question must be asked.... Furthermore, the provisions of Art 24 of the Charter of Fundamental Rights and Freedoms of the European Union are directly applicable (see above) with the consequence that the court is required to ask the question I have identified.'

4.35 The child's right to an opportunity to be heard is a 'child-centred issue' said the judge. It 'ensures that the child is engaged in the process and is accorded due respect in that process'.[42] It is thus part of the rule of law in England and Wales that a child has the right to participate in the process about the child (emphasis added):

> '[44] That is rightly an acceptance that the rule of law in England and Wales includes the right of the child to participate in the process that is about him or her. That is the fundamental principle that is reflected in our legislation, our rules and practice directions and our jurisprudence. *At its most basic level it involves asking at an early stage in family proceedings whether and how that child is going to be given the opportunity to be heard.* The qualification in s 1(3)(a) of the CA 1989 like that in Art 12(1) of the UNCRC 1989 relates to the weight to be put upon a child's wishes and feelings, not their participation.'

---

38 At §36.
39 §38.
40 §40.
41 *Re D (A Child)* [2006] UKHL 51 sub nom *Re D (Abduction: Rights of Custody)* [2007] 1 FLR 961.
42 §43.

Child abduction

Child's views in child abduction proceedings

4.36 Starting from *Re D (A Child) (Abduction: Custody Rights)*[43] in the recent period, there are important cases on children expressing their views on the outcome of their case, many in the area of child abduction. However, as Ryder LJ stresses in *Re D (International Recognition)*[44] the same 'fundamental principle' applies to all children proceedings – child abduction and private and public law – in relation to Art 24 and to the hearing of children. *Re D (Abduction: Custody Rights)* can therefore be taken as a watershed in judicial thinking for assessing children's views.

4.37 In *Re D (Abduction: Custody Rights)*, the House of Lords considered the importance of children's views in child abduction proceedings[45] and how those views could, or should, be ascertained by or for the court. In a case which Lady Hale described as 'on any view extraordinary' in respect of procedures adopted in Romania and the consequent delays, a Romanian child (A), aged nearly 8 when the first instance case was heard, had been unlawfully removed by his mother.[46] The judge in Hague Convention proceedings in England ordered his return to Romania, when the case was finally heard. The Court of Appeal refused the mother's appeal.

4.38 In the House of Lords, Lady Hale summarised the issue for the court on A's views, after she had explained the court's duties in respect of findings of wrongful removal, as follows:

> '[23]... If the conclusion is that the removal was wrongful, two further questions arise. Is the court entitled to refuse to return the child under Art 13 – either because there is a grave risk that his return would place him in an intolerable situation or because he objects to his return and is of an age and maturity where it would be appropriate to take account of his views? Finally, we are asked to consider the ways in which the point of view of a child in A's situation should be placed before the court in Hague Convention proceedings.'

4.39 The child applied to be made party to the abduction proceedings. This application was refused by the Court of Appeal, though the court directed a report from a CAFCASS officer. This report made it clear that A was adamantly opposed to returning to Romania. Lady Hale gave the most extensive of the opinions. Under the heading 'The child himself' she said, of the CAFCASS report:

> '[57] ... Until the case reached this House, no defence based on the child's objections was raised. This is not surprising. A was only four and a half when

43 [2006] UKHL 51, [2007] 1 AC 619, [2007] 1 FLR 961.

44 Considered at 4.32.

45 Convention on the Civil Aspects of International Child Abduction 1980 ('Hague Convention') per *Child Abduction and Custody Act 1985*.

46 §§20–22.

> these proceedings were begun. At that age few courts would accept that he has "attained an age and degree of maturity at which it is appropriate to take account of its views".[47] But he is now more than eight years old and he was more than seven and a half when these proceedings were heard by the trial judge.'

4.40 However, the next question was: once the case arrived with the judge (when A was more than seven-and-a-half) should the judge have seen A, or in some way have received information and his views from him? Lady Hale continued with the passage quoted above;[48] and then went on in particular to consider the provisions of Brussels II (then in force). She pointed out that Brussels IIA, Art 11.2 had reversed the obligation on the court to hear the child and positively requires that the child to have the opportunity be heard.[49]

Receiving the child's views

4.41 It follows from Brussels IIA, Art 11.2 'that children should be heard far more frequently in Hague Convention cases than has been the practice hitherto', said Lady Hale;[50] but how should this be done? She suggested three possible ways.

(1) 'Full scale legal representation of the child';

(2) Report of an independent CAFCASS officer or other professional (which she expected to be the most common means of obtaining views), or

(3) Meeting with the judge.

4.42 The first and third of these means of the child's views will be considered after the meeting with the child has taken place.[51] Lady Hale described the CAFCASS officer's report as the 'most common method' of obtaining a child's views (as was done with A); and that in the High Court in London where the officers were aware of the 'limited compass' within which the child's views might be relevant in child abduction cases.

4.43 The *Guidelines* for judges meeting children[52] have been published since the *Re D (Abduction: Custody Rights)* case. *Re KP (Abduction: Child's Objections)*[53] provided the Court of Appeal[54] with an opportunity to review that guidance

47 Hague Convention Art 13 (below).
48 At 4.26.
49 As explained further at 7.77.
50 *Re D (Abduction: Custody Rights)* §59.
51 Of legal representation Lady Hale said: '[60]... Only in a few cases will full scale legal representation be necessary. But whenever it seems likely that the child's views and interests may not be properly presented to the court, and in particular where there are legal arguments which the adult parties are not putting forward, then the child should be separately represented...)' and see, eg, *Re KP (Abduction: Child's Objections)* [2014] EWCA Civ 554, [2014] 2 FLR 660.
52 *Guidelines on Judges Meeting Children who are subject to Family Proceedings April 2010* [2010] 2 FLR 1872 https://fnf.org.uk/phocadownload/downloads/guidelines_for_judges_meeting_children.pdf.
53 [2014] EWCA Civ 554, [2014] 2 FLR 660.
54 Moore-Bick LJ gave the judgement of the court with Black and McFarlane LJJ.

especially in the context of child abduction proceedings and following on from *Re D (A Child) (Abduction: Custody Rights)*.

4.44 In *Re KP* a 13-year-old Maltese girl was wrongfully brought to the UK by her mother. When her father applied for her return the girl was seen by the High Court judge for over an hour. The mother appealed against the judge's order that her daughter K should be returned to Malta, and in particular that 'the judge conducted an extensive meeting with the child during the hearing'.[55] The Court of Appeal allowed the appeal and remitted the case to another High Court judge.

4.45 The case came back before Mostyn J with the child – now 'Kate' – a party (as she had been before the Court of Appeal).[56] He refused a return to Europe. Kate had discussed her views with a CAFCASS officer. Mostyn J held that she had 'maintained her objection to return reasonably'. It could be many months before the court in Malta might conclude proceedings concerning her; and in the meantime her education here would suffer. She had, said Mostyn J, expressed 'a sound, reasoned and mature objection to being returned to her homeland'.[57] He considered her position in the light of her objections to return:

> '[20]... As the words of Art 13(2) of the Hague Convention 1980[58] require, Kate must be of a sufficient age and maturity to voice an objection that is capable of being taken into account. That she is of sufficient age and maturity is accepted by ... the father. Beyond that she must express, as I stated in *B v B* [2014] EWHC 1804 (Fam), (unreported) 21 May 2014, at [4], "a sound, reasoned and mature objection to being returned to her homeland for the sole limited purpose of enabling the court of that country to determine her long-term future".... It has yet even to be started. It could be many months, perhaps over a year, before a final resolution [of the father's case in Malta]. In such circumstances Kate is well justified, in my judgment, in objecting to a return for what may be a prolonged period where her whole present life including, most importantly, her education would be turned upside down.'

4.46 He continued, in relation to the respective Convention rights of Kate and her father:

> '[22] ... I consider that a return would violate Kate's right to family life under Art 6 of the European Convention (and Art 7 of the Charter of Fundamental Rights of the European Union (2000) OJ 64/1), and that therefore a defence under Art 20 of the Hague Convention 1980 is established also. Kate's family life extends to her direct family, her new home, her society of friends and her education. All this would be considerably disturbed by a return for a prolonged period, as [the CAFCASS officer's] report and his oral testimony so

55 §3.

56 *SP v EB* and KP [2014] EWHC 3964 (Fam), [2016] 1 FLR 228, Mostyn J (rehearing after *Re KP (Abduction: Child's Objections)* [2014] EWCA Civ 554, [2014] 2 FLR 660 (above)).

57 §20.

58 Art 13.2 reads: 'The judicial or administrative authority may also refuse to order the return of the child if it finds that the child objects to being returned and has attained an age and degree of maturity at which it is appropriate to take account of its views.'

vividly prove. Certainly the non-return of Kate violates, or potentially violates, the father's equivalent right to an aspect of family life namely the society of his daughter, but it is well established that if the same family rights of a parent and child are in competition the child's rights will prevail (see *Yousef v The Netherlands* [2002] ECHR 716, (2003) 36 EHRR 20, [2003] 1 FLR 210[59]).'

4.47 In *Re KP* in the Court of Appeal the *Guidelines for judge's meeting children*, and in particular the passage in the pre-amble which stresses that the judge's interview is 'not for the purpose of gathering evidence'.[60] This passage, said the Court of Appeal, went no further than any of the reported cases they had cited. From these themes the Court of Appeal concluded that the judge's dealing with the case – by 'probing' the child's position – caused her to fall on the wrong side of a spectrum: between hearing the child's views and providing information at one end of the spectrum, or of gathering evidence at the other.[61]

4 CHILD'S VIEWS: THE MODERN LAW

A right to be heard

4.48 The modern law on hearing children's views has three statutory or rights-based foundations:

- *Children Act 1989, s 1(3)(a).*
- United Nations Convention on the Rights of the Child 1989, Art 12.
- Charter of Fundamental Rights of the European Union (2000/C 364/01), Art 24.

4.49 The second and third of these are clear in the extent to which they give a child rights. The first is permissive in the sense that the court must take the wishes and feelings of a child into account when called upon to make a discretionary decision, but on its own it gives the child no enforceable right.

4.50 In *Re KP (Abduction: Child's Objections)*[62] the Court of Appeal considered two judgments of Thorpe LJ in the Court of Appeal in which he stressed the fundamental importance of considering the views of mature children and, in the

59 For a consideration of European Convention 1950, Art 8 and *Yousef* and the parent-child balance of rights see 5.40.

60 §§36 and 50. Of this case Lady Hale commented in her November 2015 ALC speech: '... the Court of Appeal stated very firmly that a meeting between the judge and a child involved in abduction proceedings should not be used for the purpose of obtaining evidence. When listening to what the child has to say (as opposed to explaining the nature of the court process) the judge should largely be a passive recipient and should certainly not seek to probe or test what the child says. We refused permission to appeal to the Supreme Court in that case. Having seen a transcript of the judge's exchanges with the child, I can quite understand why the court said what it did. The judge in question was a formidable cross-examiner when she was at the Bar and entered into the task with gusto. It cannot have been a pleasant experience for the child.

61 §56.

62 [2014] EWCA Civ 554, [2014] 2 FLR 660.

second cases, of being strongly influenced by those views.[63] In *Re J (Abduction: Children's Objections)*[64] the Court of Appeal was dealing with children aged 15, 13 and 10 in Hague Convention proceedings where they had been wrongfully removed from their home in Poland by their mother. The primary issue in the case was whether a child's objection exception under Art 13 of the Hague Convention was established and, if so, whether a return order should be made. At first instance evidence of the children's strong wish to remain in England came from an interview conducted by a specialist CAFCASS officer. The judge doubted that the children's position was sufficient for an exception under Art 13. In any event he would exercise his discretion to say that the children should return to Poland.

4.51 The children were treated as interveners in the Court of Appeal, but their evidence there was in the mother's statement and a CAFCASS officer's report.[65] On appeal, the children's counsel argued that the facts required the judge to have seen the children. It was, he said, 'simply unacceptable for the judge to impose on the children the return that they dreaded without engaging them in the process'.

The voice of the child at trial

4.52 Thorpe LJ agreed. He considered the submission of the children's counsel in the context of things he had said in *Re G (Abduction: Children's Objections)*[66] and then in relation to the *Guidelines for meeting children*. In *Re G* Thorpe LJ had said, of a judge's failure to meet with a child aged 13 or to hear or receive her views:

> '[21] Courts of trial and appellate courts have to consider the implementation of a judgment for return. A court needs to be alive to the difficulty of implementing a return order, where the subject of the return order is an articulate, naturally determined and courageous adolescent. E is such a child. I also was impressed by the cogency of her reasoning for rejecting Canada as a future for her, as a country where she could complete her education with the necessary sense of security and peace of mind. Everything which she said about the challenge of her education in her present secondary school, everything that she said about her reliance on the wider family and friends in Middlesbrough, drove me to the conclusion that the judge might well have refused return had he had the advantage which we have had today. It is highly unusual for this court to meet a child before deciding an appeal. It is the first time I have ever had that experience, but I believe that it was justified and necessary in this case, given the fact that the judge did not himself meet E and did not seemingly attach much weight to the letter that she had written to him as decision-maker.'

63 §31.
64 [2011] EWCA Civ 1448, [2012] 1 FLR 457 (judgment 22 September 2011).
65 See §[20]–[24].
66 [2010] EWCA Civ 1232, [2011] 1 FLR 1645.

4.53 In *Re G* Thorpe LJ went on to emphasise the value of a judicial meeting in Hague Convention cases.[67] This assertion applies as strongly in all children cases, where a child wishes to speak to the court; or to have his or her views communicated to the judge:

> '[40] In these cases an option open to the judge is a meeting at which practicalities, consequences and reassurances can be ventilated. The judge sits above the family turmoil. The judge's authority can be an influence for acceptance. Importantly a meeting gives the judge an opportunity directly to assess where the return order will lead if enforcement will be resisted.'

Courts feeling their way

4.54 In *Re KP (Abduction: Child's Objections)*[68] the Court of Appeal commented on what Thorpe LJ had stressed in *Re J* that the *Guidelines for judge's meeting children* applied as much to Hague Convention proceedings. They quoted[69] the following paragraphs from *Re J* in which Thorpe LJ lists the types of factors which children are entitled to understand about the proceedings in which they are involved:

> '[39] These children understandably felt themselves to be vulnerable and lost in a complex legal landscape. They needed to understand that the proceedings in this jurisdiction were brought under an international instrument and were essentially summary in character. They needed to understand that they were habitually resident in Poland and that accordingly the Polish court had primary jurisdiction under Article 8 of Brussels IIA. They needed to understand that any profound investigation of their future would be determined by the paramount consideration of their welfare and that the task of assessing that was for the Polish Judge. They needed to understand that their mother had initiated that process during the course of the summer holiday. They needed to understand that a summary return order might be a transient order dependent on the outcome of the mother's application for custody and relocation. They needed to be informed of the fundamental shift in their mother's case elicited by the judge's questions.'

67 In *Re J* Thorpe LJ also took the opportunity to assert that in his view *The Guidelines* applied equally in Hague Convention as in any other proceedings with a 'significant impact on a child's future: '[38] The Practice Note (Guidelines for Judges Meeting Children Who Are Subject to Family Proceedings) should be taken to apply to all proceedings in which the decision of the court will have a significant impact on the future life of the child. Further if the Practice Note has as yet had no effect that is a matter of concern. Practice guidance from the President is not, like most of today's news, safely forgotten tomorrow. Practitioners and judges have the responsibility to consider in what way and to what extent the guidance applies during preparations for trial and at the trial itself.'

68 [2014] EWCA Civ 554, [2014] 2 FLR 660.

69 At §[31].

The Guidelines and how a child should be heard

4.55 In *Re KP (Abduction: Child's Objections)*[70] the Court of Appeal emphasised that the *Guidelines* were 'no more than they purport to be, namely guidelines'. They were, they said, feeling their way forward'. They went on, in the same paragraph:

> '[52] … In like manner nothing that we may say in this judgment should be taken as more than a description of the approach to hearing the voice of a child in such cases that is currently endorsed by judicial authority. Our collective understanding of these matters and how best to 'hear' a young person within the court setting, is developing and is still, to an extent, in its infancy. It is not our aim to say anything that may set current practice in concrete or otherwise prevent discussion, thought and the further development of good practice.'

4.56 How the child should be heard, they said, would 'differ from case to case':

> '[52] … What is, or is not, the appropriate channel through which a child is heard will differ from case to case, and the manner in which the task is undertaken will depend upon the developing skill and understanding of the judge and the other professionals involved. It is therefore right that the Guidelines are no more than they purport to be, namely guidelines….'

4.57 The court's judgment[71] in *Re KP (Abduction: Child's Objections)*[72] drew together a number of the themes which are common to the authorities they had been reviewing. The court's discussion of its conclusions[73] took as its starting point the *Guidelines*, and their relevance as a means of:

> '[50] In stating that "it cannot be stressed too often that the child's meeting with the judge is not for the purpose of gathering evidence" the Guidelines indicate that there is a firm line to be drawn between a process in which the judge and a young person simply encounter each other and communicate in a manner which is not for the purpose of evidence gathering, and a process in which one of the aims of the meeting is to gather evidence. In so stating the Guidelines are not at odds with any of the reported cases to which reference has already been made.'

4.58 The principles which the Court of Appeal extracted from the authorities they had reviewed were as follows:

70 [2014] EWCA Civ 554, [2014] 2 FLR 660.

71 It will be recalled that *Re KP* was a judgment of the court consisting of Moore-Bick, Black and McFarlane LJJ.

72 [2014] EWCA Civ 554, [2014] 2 FLR 660.

73 At §§[50]–[55].

(a) There is a presumption that a child will be heard during Hague Convention proceedings, unless this appears inappropriate (*Re D* (above); and see Brussels IIA Art 11.2[74]);

(b) In this context, 'hearing' the child involves listening to the child's point of view and hearing what they have to say (*Re D* at §57; *JPC v SLW and SMW* at §47[75]);

(c) The means of conveying a child's views to the court must be independent of the parent (*Re D* at §59);

(d) There are three possible channels through which a child may be heard (*Re D* §60[76]; and in their list the court sets out what Lady Hale says in *Re D* (above));

(e) Where a meeting takes place it is an opportunity (*JPC v SLW*, §47; *De L v H*[77] §45[78]; *Re J (Abduction: Children's Objections)* (above) §31–40):

  (i) for the judge to hear what the child may wish to say; and

  (ii) for the child to hear the judge explain the nature of the process and, in particular, why, despite hearing what the child may say, the court's order may direct a different outcome;

(f) A meeting between judge and child may be appropriate when the child is asking to meet the judge, but there will also be cases where the judge of his or her own motion should attempt to engage the child in the process (*Re J* [2011] §31).

Guidelines for judges meeting children

4.59 The *Guidelines on meeting children*[79] must be seen through the prism of the four sets of source material set out at the beginning of this part: *CA 1989, s 1(3)(a);*

74 Set out in full at 7.34.

75 [2007] EWHC 1349 (Fam), [2007] 2 FLR 900 where Sir Mark Potter P said at: '[47] I have already set out the firmness and clarity of S's objections. In addition to reading her evidence and hearing the submissions of counsel on her behalf, I saw her in my room for some 15 to 20 minutes, in accordance with Art 11(2) of Brussels II Revised. I did so in the presence of her solicitor and the mother's solicitors as note-takers, having explained to the parties that I did not consider their presence appropriate in the light of the inhibitions it might place upon my conversation my with S, which position was accepted by the mother and father. Apart from hearing anything which S wished to tell me, I was concerned to explain to her the nature of my task and why, in the face of her objections, I might nonetheless feel obliged to order her return in the light of the nature of the Hague Convention jurisdiction. I was impressed by her articulacy and her understanding in relation to those matters as explained to her. She did not rein back upon any of the views she had expressed in her evidence....'

76 Set out at 4.41.

77 [2009] EWHC 3074 (Fam), [2010] 1 FLR 1229, Sir Mark Potter P.

78 And see para [74]: '... in the face of R [the child]'s rationally advanced objections and strong feelings which appear to me soundly based, I propose in my discretion to refuse an order for return. While it is not the function of this court on an application of this kind to conduct or decide welfare issues as such, when deciding whether or not to exercise its discretion to refuse an order for return, which involves an examination of the rationale of those objections, it cannot avoid taking into account what will be the plain effect upon a child of making [a return] order [namely] the disruption of R's schooling and contented home life in England, the distress and feelings of disillusion which I have no doubt he will experience at being forced to return and await the uncertain outcome of the Portuguese proceedings, and the unhappy home conditions to which he will be returning...'.

79 The *Guidelines* are set out in full in the Appendix to this Chapter.

UN Charter, Art 12; EU Charter, 24 and Brussels IIA, Art 11.2. Section 1(3)(a) can be seen as defined by Ryder LJ in *Re D (A Child) (International Recognition)*[80] as a 'fundamental principle' (though that assertion cannot make it a right).

4.60 The extent to which and with what consequences the English courts are bound by EU law is considered in **Chapter 7**.[81] Here it will be assumed that English courts are bound by the provisions of the Charter of Fundamental Rights of the European Union (2000/C 364/01), Art 24 and the United Nations Convention on the Rights of the Child 1989, Art 12; and specifically in child abduction cases by Brussels IIA. But so too are the courts bound by the European Convention 1950 rights. Many cases include reference to the European Convention 1950 – especially Arts 6, 8 and 10, in family proceedings.

4.61 The *Guidance* will be reviewed in the light of the above statutory and Charter authorities; and, alongside those, in the light of such cases as *Re D (A Child)*[82] where the House of Lords (especially Lady Hale) considered how the courts should deal with objections from children in child abduction cases.

Purpose of the Guidelines

4.62 The 'purpose' of the *Guidelines* is set out in an introductory section, and is described as 'to encourage judges to enable children to feel more involved' etc. There is no reference to either Art 12 or Art 24, still less to the fact that – if the child is of age and maturity – they are entitled to be 'involved' (as the *Guidelines* put it). If they are regarded by the judge as sufficiently mature then their right to give the court their views does not depend on the decision of the judge.

4.63 The right to be heard is not the same as a right to have a child's views accepted and followed. Lady Hale concluded her oft-quoted passage in *Re D (A Child)*[83] on asking a child what she 'wants for tea' by stressing that, of the answer, 'there is a large difference between' taking account of views and 'doing what [the child] wants':

> '[57] It is the child, more than anyone else, who will have to live with what the court decides. Those who do listen to children understand that they often have a point of view which is quite distinct from that of the person looking after them. They are quite capable of being moral actors in their own right. Just as the adults may have to do what the court decides whether they like it or not, so may the child. But that is no more a reason for failing to hear what the child has to say than it is for refusing to hear the parents' views.'

80 [2016] EWCA Civ 12, [2016] 1 WLR 2469, [2016] 2 FLR 347; and see full discussion of this case at 4.29.
81 See especially Pt 2.
82 [2006] UKHL 51 sub nom *Re D (Abduction: Rights of Custody)* [2007] 1 FLR 961.
83 [2006] UKHL 51 sub nom *Re D (Abduction: Rights of Custody)* [2007] 1 FLR 961 at §57.

APPENDIX

Guidelines — Judges meeting children subject to family proceedings

SIR NICHOLAS WALL P

These guidelines are produced by the Family Justice Council and approved by the President of the Family Division.

In these guidelines:

- All references to 'child' or 'children' are intended to include a young person or young people the subject of proceedings under the Children Act 1989.
- 'Family proceedings' includes both public and private law cases.
- 'Judge' includes magistrates.
- Cafcass includes CAFCASS CYMRU.

Purpose

The purpose of these guidelines is to encourage judges to enable children to feel more involved and connected with proceedings in which important decisions are made in their lives and to give them an opportunity to satisfy themselves that the judge has understood their wishes and feelings and to understand the nature of the judge's task.

Preamble

- In England and Wales in most cases a child's needs, wishes and feelings are brought to the court in written form by a Cafcass officer. Nothing in this guidance document is intended to replace or undermine that responsibility.
- It is Cafcass practice to discuss with a child in a manner appropriate to their developmental understanding whether their participation in the process includes a wish to meet the judge. If the child does not wish to meet the judge discussions can centre on other ways of enabling the child to feel a part of the process. If the child wishes to meet the judge, that wish should be conveyed to the judge where appropriate.
- The primary purpose of the meeting is to benefit the child. However, it may also benefit the judge and other family members.

Guidelines

[1] The judge is entitled to expect the lawyer for the child and/or the Cafcass officer:

(i) to advise whether the child wishes to meet the judge;

(ii) if so, to explain from the child's perspective, the purpose of the meeting;

(iii) to advise whether it accords with the welfare interests of the child for such a meeting take place; and

(iv) to identify the purpose of the proposed meeting as perceived by the child's professional representative/s.

[2] The other parties shall be entitled to make representations as to any proposed meeting with the judge before the judge decides whether or not it shall take place.

[3] In deciding whether or not a meeting shall take place and, if so, in what circumstances, the child's chronological age is relevant but not determinative. Some children of 7 or even younger have a clear understanding of their circumstances and very clear views which they may wish to express.

[4] If the child wishes to meet the judge but the judge decides that a meeting would be inappropriate, the judge should consider providing a brief explanation in writing for the child.

[5] If a judge decides to meet a child, it is a matter for the discretion of the judge, having considered representations from the parties:

(i) the purpose and proposed content of the meeting;

(ii) at what stage during the proceedings, or after they have concluded, the meeting should take place;

(iii) where the meeting will take place;

(iv) who will bring the child to the meeting;

(v) who will prepare the child for the meeting (this should usually be the Cafcass officer);

(vi) who shall attend during the meeting – although a judge should never see a child alone;

(vii) by whom a minute of the meeting shall be taken, how that minute is to be approved by the judge, and how it is to be communicated to the other parties.

It cannot be stressed too often that the child's meeting with the judge is not for the purpose of gathering evidence. That is the responsibility of the Cafcass officer. The purpose is to enable the child to gain some understanding of what is going on, and to be reassured that the judge has understood him/her.

[6] If the meeting takes place prior to the conclusion of the proceedings:

(i) The judge should explain to the child at an early stage that a judge cannot hold secrets. What is said by the child will, other than in exceptional circumstances, be communicated to his/her parents and other parties.

(ii) The judge should also explain that decisions in the case are the responsibility of the judge, who will have to weigh a number of factors, and that the outcome is never the responsibility of the child.

(iii) The judge should discuss with the child how his or her decisions will be communicated to the child.

(iv) The parties or their representatives shall have the opportunity to respond to the content of the meeting, whether by way of oral evidence or submissions.

The Family Justice Council

Sir Nicholas Wall President of the Family Division and Head of Family Justice

5

HUMAN RIGHTS AND THE CHILD

1 INTRODUCTION

Human rights and English law

5.1 This chapter deals with European Convention for the Protection of Human Rights and Fundamental Freedoms 1950 ('the Convention') and English human rights legislation and case law in relation to children, their participation in court proceedings and their confidentiality; especially in relation to court proceedings in which they are participants – or in which they might be expected to be participating.

5.2 Two issues predominate. The first is the extent to which the courts might now restrict publicity as against the risk of identifying a child indirectly involved in court proceedings.[1] How far are the interests of a child a factor than which nothing 'must be given greater weight'[2] – if this be the case? Secondly is the importance of the principle of respecting a mature child's decision, as in the case of Angela Roddy.[3] These issues, in particular, are considered in the contexts of freedom of media expression (**Part 3**) and of the rights of a child to seek her own publicity (**Parts 4** and **7**).

5.3 The chapter proceeds as follows:

- **Part 2** looks at the European Convention 1950 and the *Human Rights Act 1998* (*HRA 1998*): the background to the Convention; and an outline of the 1998 Act and how it works.
- **Part 3** sets out the Articles most often engaged in children proceedings: right to a fair trial (Art 6); right to respect for family life (Art 8); freedom of expression

1 See contrast between *Re S (Identification: Restrictions on Publication)* [2004] UKHL 47, [2005] 1 AC 593, [2005] 1 FLR 591 in the House of Lords and, twelve years later, *PJS v News Group Newspapers Ltd* [2016] UKSC 26, [2016] AC 1081, [2016] 2 FLR 251, [2016] 2 WLR 1253 in the Supreme Court. These cases are considered at 5.85 and 5.29 respectively.

2 Per Lord Kerr in *H(H) v Deputy Prosecutor of the Italian Republic, Genoa (Official Solicitor intervening)* [2012] UKSC 25, [2013] 1 AC 338 considered at 5.111.

3 *Re Roddy (A Child) (Identification: Restriction on Publication)* [2003] EWHC 2927, [2004] 2 FLR 949 Munby J.

(Art 10). In the context of freedom of expression and the grant of restraint orders, *HRA 1998, s 12* is explained especially in the light of *PJS*.[4]

- **Part 4** concentrates on the European Convention for the Protection of Human Rights and Fundamental Freedoms 1950 and children's rights.
- **Part 5** deals with freedom of expression, restraint orders and factors under the *HRA 1988, s 12*. Freedom of expression and why it should be is explored alongside the rights of a parent to publicity.
- **Part 6** summarises a child's rights and freedom of expression. It centres on Angela Roddy's case[5] and the way in which Munby J dealt with a mature child's freedom of expression: what are the rights of a *Gillick*-competent child; and how, 'in reality' and in legal principle should those rights be dealt with?
- **Part 7** summarises and explains the Convention 'ultimate balancing test'[6] and its operation in recent case law.
- **Part 8** looks at a number of aspects of Convention rights in relation to the mature child, and at how these are dealt with by the courts.
- **Part 9** asks to what extent, in a Convention rights balance, do the best interests of a child take primary position? Or are their rights 'paramount'; or is it that no-one's rights 'should rank higher' than those of a child.[7]

2 HUMAN RIGHTS ACT 1998 AND EUROPEAN CONVENTION

Protection of human rights

Justification for a Convention on human rights

5.4 This part looks at the framework of *Human Rights Act 1998* and the Convention. First it is necessary to summarise the Convention's basic aims. These were explained by the Privy Council in *Brown v Stott (Procurator Fiscal, Dunfermline) and another*[8] early in the life of the 1998 Act. In what he described as 'the first real test of the Human Rights Act 1998' Lord Steyn said of the Convention:

> '... It is opportune to stand back and consider what the basic aims of the Convention are. One finds the explanation in the very words of the preambles of the Convention. There were two principal objectives. The first was to maintain and further realise human rights and fundamental freedoms. The framers of the Convention recognised that it was not only morally right

4 *PJS* at n 1 (above).
5 See n 3 above.
6 *Re S (Identification: Restrictions on Publication)* [2004] UKHL 47, [2005] 1 AC 593, [2005] 1 FLR 591.
7 Per Lord Kerr in *H(H) v Deputy Prosecutor of the Italian Republic, Genoa (Official Solicitor intervening)* [2012] UKSC 25, [2013] 1 AC 338 as explained at 5.111.
8 [2000] UKPC D3, [2003] 1 AC 681 at 707.

to promote the observance of human rights but that it was also the best way of achieving pluralistic and just societies in which all can peaceably go about their lives. The second aim was to foster effective political democracy….'

5.5 One individual right protected by the Convention might, in certain circumstances, conflict with another. A common example of this – considered further later in this chapter[9] – is the right to respect for privacy and family life (Art 8: 'privacy') balanced against the right of the press and others to freedom of expression and reporting of legal proceedings (Art 10: 'freedom of speech'). So, said Lord Steyn:[10]

> '… from time to time the fundamental right of one individual may conflict with the human right of another. Thus the principles of free speech and privacy may collide. They also realised only too well that a single-minded concentration on the pursuit of fundamental rights of individuals to the exclusion of the interests of the wider public might be subversive of the ideal of tolerant European liberal democracies. The fundamental rights of individuals are of supreme importance but those rights are not unlimited: we live in communities of individuals who also have rights. …'

Convention rights: the balance

5.6 In this position, a balance must be struck between the Convention rights of each party involved. Under the Convention system, it is an independent judiciary which is required to resolve this balance and to secure and enforce the rights under it:[11]

> 'The European Convention requires that where difficult questions arise a balance must be struck. Subject to a limited number of absolute guarantees, the scheme and structure of the Convention reflects this balanced approach. It differs in material respects from other constitutional systems but as a European nation it represents our Bill of Rights. We must be guided by it. And it is a basic premise of the Convention system that only an entirely neutral, impartial, and independent judiciary can carry out the primary task of securing and enforcing Convention rights….'

5.7 The three Convention Articles referred to in **Part 1** – Arts 6, 8 and 10 – are set out in **Part 3** of this chapter. The way in which the rights protected by these Articles relate to one another and the means whereby they are balanced when they come into conflict was explained by Lord Steyn in *Re S (Identification: Restrictions on Publication)*.[12] The way in which this human rights balance works is explained later in this part, after which the individual Articles and their operation

---

9 See 5.85; and in particular see references to *Re S (Identification: Restrictions on Publication)* [2004] UKHL 47, [2005] 1 AC 593, [2005] 1 FLR 591.
10 [2000] UKPC D3, [2003] 1 AC 681 at 707.
11 [2000] UKPC D3, [2003] 1 AC 681 at 708.
12 [2004] UKHL 47, [2005] 1 FLR 591.

will be considered in the next part. Before that the framework of the 1998 Act, in which the Articles in operation in English law are set out in Schedule 1, will be summarised.

Human rights act 1998

Human Rights Act 1998: effect to the European Convention 1950

5.8 *HRA 1998, s 1(2)* gives 'effect' to the majority of the Convention[13] rights set out in *HRA 1998, s 1(1)*, which includes those specifically referred to in this chapter and, in particular, those described as 'in play' later in this part. The 'Convention rights' referred to in s 1(1), and thus those which are in operation in English law, are set out in the Act's Sch 1. As English law now stands the Convention, its significance and operation in English proceedings and the role of its courts, will not be affected by the UK withdrawal from the European Union.[14]

5.9 By *HRA 1989, s 2*, an English court dealing with a case must 'take into account' decisions and judgements of the European Court of Human Rights and Commission ('European Court') opinions and decisions.[15] The duty is to 'take into account' rather than invariably and precisely to follow decisions. As Lord Bingham explained in *Kay and others v Lambeth London Borough Council*[16] it is generally the duty of English courts 'to give practical recognition to the principles laid down by the Strasbourg court as governing the Convention rights' specified by *HRA 1998, s 1(1)*, save where 'primary domestic legislation' points in another direction.

5.10 This explanation was affirmed by Lord Neuberger in *Manchester City Council v Pinnock* .[17] On the question of whether or not English courts must follow European Court jurisprudence, Lord Neuberger said:

> '[48]: ... Where, however, there is a clear and constant line of decisions whose effect is not inconsistent with some fundamental substantive or procedural aspect of our law, and whose reasoning does not appear to overlook or

---

13 The 'Convention' is defined by *HRA 1998, s 21(1)* as: '... the Convention for the Protection of Human Rights and Fundamental Freedoms, agreed by the Council of Europe at Rome on 4 November 1950 as it has effect for the time being in relation to the United Kingdom;...'.

14 The effects on children proceedings of UK withdrawal from European Union is considered in Ch 7.

15 *HRA 1998, s 2(1).*

16 [2006] UKHL 10, [2006] 2 AC 465 at §[28]: The mandatory duty imposed on domestic courts by [*HRA 1998, s 2*] is to take into account any judgment of the Strasbourg court and any opinion of the commission. Thus they are not strictly required to follow Strasbourg rulings, as they are bound by [*ECA 1972, s 3(1)*] and as they are bound by the rulings of superior courts in the domestic curial hierarchy. But by HRA 1998 s 6] it is unlawful for domestic courts, as public authorities, to act in a way which is incompatible with a Convention right such as a right arising under article 8. There are isolated occasions... when a domestic court may challenge the application by the Strasbourg court of the principles it has expounded to the detailed facts of a particular class of case peculiarly within the knowledge of national authorities. The 1998 Act gives it scope to do so. But it is ordinarily the clear duty of our domestic courts, save where and so far as constrained by primary domestic legislation, to give practical recognition to the principles laid down by the Strasbourg court as governing the Convention rights specified in [*HRA 1998, s 1(1)*].

17 [2010] UKSC 45; [2011] 2 AC 104.

> misunderstand some argument or point of principle, we consider that it would be wrong for this court not to follow that line.'

Primary legislation: given effect in a way compatible with Convention rights

5.11 *HRA 1998, s 3* provides that English courts should 'read and give effect' to 'primary and secondary legislation'[18] and, so as far possible, 'in a way which is compatible with the Convention rights'.[19] For example, in *Re S (Minors) (Care Order: Implementation of Care Plan)*,[20] the House of Lords was dealing with care orders where two local authorities had not complied with their own care plan. The parents appealed against the care orders. The House of Lords was asked to confirm the view of the Court of Appeal that unless the interpretation and operation of the *Children's Act 1989* (*CA 1989*) were modified, it was incompatible with the Convention. The Court of Appeal had declared that to avoid breaching Convention rights that, first, judges should have a wider discretion to make interim care orders, rather than final care orders; and, secondly, that the essential milestones of any care plan for children in care proceedings, should be identified at trial. The local authority appealed against the proposed 'adjustments' to the statute implied by these findings.

5.12 Lord Nicholls, with whom the other four law lords agreed, said that courts were not entitled to find legislation incompatible with UK legislation as a disguised way of amending primary legislation. Any declaration of incompatibility with the European Convention 1950 should be seen as compared with primary UK legislation. The reach of *HRA 1989, s 3* 'is not unlimited'. It is 'concerned with interpretation', said Lord Nicholls:

> '[38] .... This is apparent from the opening words of s 3(1): "so far as it is possible to do so". The side heading of the section is "Interpretation of legislation". Section 4 (power to make a declaration of incompatibility) and, indeed, s 3(2)(b) presuppose that not all provisions in primary legislation can be rendered Convention compliant by the application of s 3(1). The existence of this limit on the scope of s 3(1) has already been the subject of judicial confirmation, more than once [citations from 2001 case law added].
>
> [39] In applying s 3 courts must be ever mindful of this outer limit. The Human Rights Act 1998 reserves the amendment of primary legislation to Parliament. By this means the Act seeks to preserve parliamentary sovereignty. The Act maintains the constitutional boundary. Interpretation of statutes is

---

18 *HRA 1998, s 3(2)* explains what is meant by legislation in this context:
(2) This section –
(a) applies to primary legislation and subordinate legislation whenever enacted;
(b) does not affect the validity, continuing operation or enforcement of any incompatible primary legislation; and
(c) does not affect the validity, continuing operation or enforcement of any incompatible subordinate legislation if (disregarding any possibility of revocation) primary legislation prevents removal of the incompatibility.

19 *HRA 1998, s 3(1).*

20 [2002] UKHL 10, [2002] 2 AC291, [2002] 1 FLR 815.

a matter for the courts; the enactment of statutes, and the amendment of statutes, are matters for Parliament.'

5.13 In the case of operation of care orders, Parliament had set out its clear intention in *CA 1989*. Once a care order had been made, the responsibility for the child's care thereafter lay with the authority, not with the court; and the courts were not permitted to intervene as Parliament intended *CA 1989* to work. This division of responsibility, between courts and local authority, was a fundamental principle of the Act. *HRA 1998, s 3* required primary legislation to be read and given effect in a way compatible with Convention rights, so far as was possible. The judicial innovation of starred milestones under review in *Re S* passed beyond the boundary of interpretation, and constituted what amounted to statutory amendment.

5.14 *HRA 1989* proceeds, at s 4, to deal with the consequences of incompatibility (if found); to provide remedies for victims of unlawful action by public authorities (ss 6–9); to make particular provision in respect of freedom of expression (s 12; and see Art 10[21]). Save for s 12 (considered further below) these provisions are mostly outside the scope of this book.

3 EUROPEAN CONVENTION ARTICLES AND CHILDREN LAW

Right to a fair trial

Article 6

5.15 Article 6 provides for an individual's right to a fair trial. Art 6.1 is concerned with all court proceedings – both in civil and in criminal courts. Arts 6.2 and 6.3 are concerned only with criminal proceedings, but their provisions may be of relevance in committal proceedings in family cases[22] and in child care proceedings where allegations amount to criminal claims[23] (or which may result in criminal proceedings):

> '*Article 6*
>
> **Right to a fair trial**
>
> 1 In the determination of his civil rights and obligations or of any criminal charge against him, everyone is entitled to a fair and public hearing within a reasonable time by an independent and impartial tribunal established by law. Judgment shall be pronounced publicly but the press

21 Considered further at 5.24.

22 See *Engel and Others v The Netherlands (No 1)* (1979) 1 EHRR 647, at 677 §§[80] and [81] concerning Art 6(3)(c).

23 See, eg, *Re W (A Child) (Care Proceedings: Child's Representation) Practice Note* [2016] EWCA Civ 1051, [2017] 1 WLR 1027.

and public may be excluded from all or part of the trial in the interest of morals, public order or national security in a democratic society, where the interests of juveniles or the protection of the private life of the parties so require, or to the extent strictly necessary in the opinion of the court in special circumstances where publicity would prejudice the interests of justice.'

5.16 The sections of Art 6 which apply only to 'criminal' proceedings are:

'2 Everyone charged with a criminal offence shall be presumed innocent until proved guilty according to law.

3 Everyone charged with a criminal offence has the following minimum rights –

(a) to be informed promptly, in a language which he understands and in detail, of the nature and cause of the accusation against him;

(b) to have adequate time and facilities for the preparation of his defence;

(c) to defend himself in person or through legal assistance of his own choosing or, if he has not sufficient means to pay for legal assistance, to be given it free when the interests of justice so require;

(d) to examine or have examined witnesses against him and to obtain the attendance and examination of witnesses on his behalf under the same conditions as witnesses against him;

(e) to have the free assistance of an interpreter if he cannot understand or speak the language used in court.'

'Concept of a fair trial'

5.17 The right to a fair trial under Art 6 is absolute. The right does not permit a balance to be weighed as between what may and may not be fair. However, the component rights within Art 6 – 'in respect of what the concept of a fair trial entails'[24] – may be balanced against other rights and may be subject to a proportionality test. That test requires the court to consider: does any restriction of the right by operation of another right (such as to respect for private life: Art 8[25]) justify restriction of a component aspect of free trial rights. Does the end sought to be achieved by any restriction of the aspect of the Art 6 right justify the means proposed by the court to achieve it?

5.18 The operation of the principle of proportionality in this context was explained by Lord Steyn in *Regina v A (No 2)*.[26] The House of Lords were considering whether a defendant should be permitted to cross-examine a complainant as to their sexual relationship in a rape trial within the terms of *Youth Justice and Criminal*

24 Per Lord Steyn in *Regina v A (No 2)* (below).
25 See, eg, *Re B (Disclosure to Other Parties)* [2001] 2 FLR 1017, Munby J considered further at 13.20.
26 [2001] UKHL 25, [2002] 1 AC 45.

Evidence Act 1999, s 41. Did any restriction in s 41 restrict the defendant's rights to a fair trial? Of the defendant's right to a fair trial in the light of Art 6, Lord Steyn said:

> '[38] It is well established that the guarantee of a fair trial under article 6 is absolute: a conviction obtained in breach of it cannot stand.... The only balancing permitted is in respect of what the concept of a fair trial entails: here account may be taken of the familiar triangulation of interests of the accused, the victim and society.'

Proportionality and restriction of a right

5.19 What is a fair trial in this context? Any restriction on a defendant's rights, and in this case, any of the defendant's right to a fair trial must be proportionate to the end sought to be achieved by the restriction. That is to say (and as explained further in **Chapter 10**[27]) the means must justify the ends. Lord Steyn continued:

> '[38] ... In this context proportionality has a role to play. The criteria for determining the test of proportionality have been analysed in similar terms in the case law of the European Court of Justice and the European Court of Human Rights. It is not necessary for us to re-invent the wheel. In *de Freitas v Permanent Secretary of Ministry of Agriculture, Fisheries, Lands and Housing* [1999] 1 AC 69 Lord Clyde adopted a precise and concrete analysis of the criteria. In determining whether a limitation is arbitrary or excessive a court should ask itself: "whether: (i) the legislative objective is sufficiently important to justify limiting a fundamental right; (ii) the measures designed to meet the legislative objective are rationally connected to it; and (iii) the means used to impair the right or freedom are no more than is necessary to accomplish the objective." The critical matter is the third criterion. Given the centrality of the right of a fair trial in the scheme of the Convention, and giving due weight to the important legislative goal of countering the twin myths,[28] the question is whether [YJCEA 1999 s] 41 makes an excessive inroad into the guarantee of a fair trial.'

5.20 Proceedings governed by FPR 2010 are mostly in private as a wide exception to the right to a public hearing generally guaranteed by Art 6 and as discussed in **Chapter 13**. Publicity (and limitations on publication) for judgments is dealt with also in the same chapter.

---

27 See especially Ch 10, Pt 3.

28 By 'twin myths', Lord Steyn meant: '[27] ... Discriminatory stereotypes which depict women as sexually available have been exposed as an affront to their fundamental rights. Nevertheless, it has to be acknowledged that in the criminal courts of our country, as in others, outmoded beliefs about women and sexual matters lingered on. In recent Canadian jurisprudence they have been described as the discredited twin myths, viz "that unchaste women were more likely to consent to intercourse and in any event, were less worthy of belief": *R v Seaboyer* (1991) 83 DLR (4th), per McLachlin J.

Right to respect for private and family life

Article 8

5.21 Art 8 represents a right which is qualified by the reservations in Art 8.2. Thus, where engaged, the right may still be interfered with where it is held to be (1) in accordance with the law; (2) necessary in a democratic society (in relation to the factors set out in Art 8.2); and (3) the degree of interference is proportionate to the objective sought to be achieved by the state.

> '*Article 8*
>
> **Right to respect for private and family life**
>
> 1 Everyone has the right to respect for his private and family life, his home and his correspondence.
>
> 2 There shall be no interference by a public authority with the exercise of this right except such as is in accordance with the law and is necessary in a democratic society in the interests of national security, public safety or the economic well-being of the country, for the prevention of disorder or crime, for the protection of health or morals, or for the protection of the rights and freedoms of others.'

5.22 Article 8.1 covers four elements of the rights it aims to protect:

(1) Private life;

(2) Family life;

(3) An individual's home or other personal space, and

(4) That individual's correspondence.

5.23 Where the rights of parents as against those of a child are balanced one against the other under Art 8 it is 'the child's rights [which are] the paramount consideration' as explained in *Yousef v The Netherlands*:[29]

> '[73] The court reiterates that in judicial decisions where the rights under Art 8 of parents and those of a child are at stake, the child's rights must be the paramount consideration. If any balancing of interests is necessary, the interests of the child must prevail (see *Elsholz v Germany* (2002) 34 EHRR 58, [2000] 2 FLR 486, para 52 and *TP and KM v United Kingdom* (2002) 34 EHRR 2, [2001] 2 FLR 549, para 72).'

29 *Yousef v The Netherlands (Application No 33711/96)* (2003) 36 EHRR 20, [2003] 1 FLR 210, ECtHR.

Freedom of expression

Article 10

5.24 The subject of freedom of expression – which applies mostly to the press and media, but can also apply, for example to a child or parents who seeks publicity – is dealt with in two sections: here Art 10 is summarised; and then later the additional provision of s 12 in *HRA 1998* to deal with 'Freedom of expression' and the reasoning behind the subject is explained.

5.25 The extent to which the rights of children to their own confidentiality and privacy must be balanced against the rights of freedom of expression of the media is also explained in this chapter; as is the extent to which this is a developing subject in law affecting children as participants in the family litigation, and as non-parties affected by their parents' litigation.[30]

5.26 Article 10 is as follows:

> '*Article 10*
>
> **Freedom of expression**
>
> 1 Everyone has the right to freedom of expression. This right shall include freedom to hold opinions and to receive and impart information and ideas without interference by public authority and regardless of frontiers. This Article shall not prevent States from requiring the licensing of broadcasting, television or cinema enterprises.
>
> 2 The exercise of these freedoms, since it carries with it duties and responsibilities, may be subject to such formalities, conditions, restrictions or penalties as are prescribed by law and are necessary in a democratic society, in the interests of national security, territorial integrity or public safety, for the prevention of disorder or crime, for the protection of health or morals, for the protection of the reputation or rights of others, for preventing the disclosure of information received in confidence, or for maintaining the authority and impartiality of the judiciary.'

Human Rights Act 1998, s 12

5.27 The Act makes particular provision, for the benefit of those entitled to freedom of expression and for factors the court must take into account where the press or others seeking freedom of expression are concerned. Thus *HRA 1989, s 12* provides as follows:

30 See especially *PJS v News Group Newspapers Ltd* [2016] UKSC 26, [2016] AC 1081, [2016] 2 FLR 251, [2016] 2 WLR 1253 considered at 5.29.

'12 Freedom of expression

(1) This section applies if a court is considering whether to grant any relief which, if granted, might affect the exercise of the Convention right to freedom of expression.

(2) If the person against whom the application for relief is made ("the respondent") is neither present nor represented, no such relief is to be granted unless the court is satisfied –

(a) that the applicant has taken all practicable steps to notify the respondent; or

(b) that there are compelling reasons why the respondent should not be notified.

(3) No such relief is to be granted so as to restrain publication before trial unless the court is satisfied that the applicant is likely to establish that publication should not be allowed.

(4) The court must have particular regard to the importance of the Convention right to freedom of expression and, where the proceedings relate to material which the respondent claims, or which appears to the court, to be journalistic, literary or artistic material (or to conduct connected with such material), to –

(a) the extent to which –

(i) the material has, or is about to, become available to the public; or

(ii) it is, or would be, in the public interest for the material to be published;

(b) any relevant privacy code.'

Human rights act 1998, s 12 and success at trial

Interim publicity restraint orders and PJS

5.28 The context and the rationale for s 12, especially s 12(4), was considered by the Supreme Court in *PJS v News Group Newspapers Ltd*.[31] PJS, said Lord Mance, is 'in the entertainment business and is married to YMA, a well-known individual in the same business'.[32] They have young children. PJS met AB with whom he had sex occasionally. AB had a partner, CD. By text message on 15 December 2011, the claimant asked if CD was 'up for a three-way'. AB said he was. The three then had a three-way sexual encounter, after which the sexual relationship between PJS and AB ended.

31 [2016] UKSC 26, [2016] AC 1081, [2016] 2 FLR 251, [2016] 2 WLR 1253.

32 Said Lord Mance at §[4].

5.29 At around the end of January 2016, AB and CD approached the editor of *The Sun on Sunday*, and told him about their earlier sexual encounters with PJS. The editor notified PJS that he proposed to publish the story. Lord Mance summarised PJS's case as 'that publication would breach confidence and invade privacy'. He 'applied for an interim injunction to restrain the proposed publication'.[33] Cranston J refused an interim injunction on 15 January 2016, but the Court of Appeal (Jackson and King LJJ) on 22 January 2016 allowed an appeal and restrained publication of the relevant names and of details of their relationship. The story was published abroad, leading *The Times*, amongst others, to complain of their own inability to publish material which was available on the internet.

5.30 Lord Mance pointed out that s 12(4) creates a test, in press freedom cases, that reporting should not be restricted 'unless the court is satisfied that the applicant is likely to establish [at trial] that publication should not be allowed'. As Lord Nicholls (cited by Lord Mance) explained, of s 12(3), in *Cream Holdings Ltd and ors v Banerjee and Another*,[34] success at trial was the criterion for whether or not to impose reporting restrictions, or otherwise to prevent publication. Said Lord Nicholls:

> '[22] ... [HRA 1998 s] 12(3) makes the likelihood of success at the trial an essential element in the court's consideration of whether to make an interim order. But in order to achieve the necessary flexibility the degree of likelihood of success at the trial needed to satisfy section 12(3) must depend on the circumstances. There can be no single, rigid standard governing all applications for interim restraint orders. Rather, on its proper construction the effect of section 12(3) is that the court is not to make an interim restraint order unless satisfied the applicant's prospects of success at the trial are sufficiently favourable to justify such an order being made in the particular circumstances of the case.'

5.31 The degree of likelihood depended on the courts being 'slow to make interim restraint orders' unless an applicant court satisfy the court that he or she – PJS in the eponymous case – 'will probably succeed at trial' with his application for a breach of confidence or privacy order (a reporting restrictions order in children law terms). Lord Nicholls continued:

> '[22] ... As to what degree of likelihood makes the prospects of success "sufficiently favourable", the general approach should be that courts will be exceedingly slow to make interim restraint orders where the applicant has not satisfied the court he will probably ("more likely than not") succeed at the trial. In general, that should be the threshold an applicant must cross before the court embarks on exercising its discretion, duly taking into account the relevant jurisprudence on Art 10 and any countervailing Convention rights. But there will be cases where it is necessary for a court to depart from this general approach and a lesser degree of likelihood will suffice as a prerequisite. Circumstances where this may be so include those

---

33 §[5].

34 [2004] UKHL 44, [2005] 1 AC 253.

mentioned above: where the potential adverse consequences of disclosure are particularly grave, or where a short-lived injunction is needed to enable the court to hear and give proper consideration to an application for interim relief pending the trial or any relevant appeal.'

Balance of human rights factors

5.32 However, said Lord Mance, even – perhaps especially – at the interim stage, consideration of the factors in *Re S (Identification: Restrictions on Publication)*[35] was as important as ever. The Court of Appeal had failed to take this fully into account. Thus:

> '[20] ... Even at the interlocutory stage: (i) neither Article has preference over the other; (ii) where their values are in conflict, what is necessary is an intense focus on the comparative importance of the rights being claimed in the individual case; (iii) the justifications for interfering with or restricting each right must be taken into account; and (iv) the proportionality test must be applied: see eg *Re S (A Child) (Identification: Restrictions on Publication)* [(above)] at [17], per Lord Steyn, with whom all other members of the House agreed; *McKennitt v Ash* [2006] EWCA Civ 1714, [2008] QB 73, at [47], per Buxton LJ, with whom the other members of the court agreed; and *Mosley v News Group Newspapers Ltd* [2008] EWHC 687 (QB), [2008] All ER (D) 135 (Apr), at [28], per Eady J, describing this as a "very well established" methodology...'.

5.33 Every case must be decided on its own facts; but there is no presumption that there is a public interest in publication of private facts:

> '[32] ... Every case must be considered on its particular facts. But the starting point is that: (i) there is not, without more, any public interest in a legal sense in the disclosure or publication of purely private sexual encounters, even though they involve adultery or more than one person at the same time; (ii) any such disclosure or publication will on the face of it constitute the tort of invasion of privacy; (iii) repetition of such a disclosure or publication on further occasions is capable of constituting a further tort of invasion of privacy, even in relation to persons to whom disclosure or publication was previously made – especially if it occurs in a different medium....'

5.34 In a decision as to whether a restraint order should be made, 'particular regard must be had to the importance of Art 10 and to s 12(4)';[36] but, in the light of what he had already said (at §§[19]–20] (above) Art 10 rights have 'no necessary claim to priority over the need to have due regard to any Art 8 privacy right which the applicant for an injunction enjoys'.[37]

35 [2004] UKHL 47, [2005] 1 AC 593, [2005] 1 FLR 591 per Lord Steyn at [17].
36 Set out at 5.27.
37 §[33].

Children's rights and the operation of Human Rights Act 1998, s 12

5.35 In relation to press involvement in children proceedings and the operation of s 12, in *Bristol City Council v NGN Ltd and Others*[38] Baker J dealt with the section amongst the legal principles he was concerned with in relation to involvement of the press with which he was concerned in that case.[39] In §[12] of his judgment he explained that the general rule was that children hearings be in private. He explained the basis on which the court considered what rights were engaged in a case and how these interrelated. In the *Bristol City Council* case he could identify that Art 8 and 10 were engaged. When Art 10 is engaged, s 12 and especially s 12(4) must be considered.[40]

5.36 At para [22](9) in his list of principles, Baker J explained as follows:

> '(9) [HRA 1998 s] 12(4)(a)(ii) reiterates the principle that amongst the matters to be taken into account when determining where the balance lies in each case is the extent to which the information is already in the public domain. "Once [information] has entered what is usually called the public domain (which means no more than the information in question is so generally accessible that, in all the circumstances, it cannot be regarded as confidential) then, as a general rule, the principle of confidentiality can have no application to it" (per Lord Goff in *Attorney-General v Guardian Newspapers Ltd (No 2)* [1990] 1 AC 109, [1988] 3 WLR 776 at 282 and 806–807 respectively).'[41]

5.37 Section 12(4)(a)(ii) involves recalling that decisions on what is of interest to the public is a matter for newspaper editors not judges.[42] And, in relation to any 'relevant privacy code' referred to in s 12(4)(b), Baker J explained the importance of the IPSO Code:[43]

> '(11) The Press Complaints Commission Editors' Code of Practice is a "relevant privacy code" within the meaning of s 12(4)(b). The following clauses of the code are relevant to this case.
>
> (a) "The press must take care not to publish inaccurate, misleading or distorted information …" (cl 1(i)).
>
> (b) "In cases involving personal grief or shock, inquiries and approaches must be made with sympathy and discretion, and publication handled sensitively. This should not restrict the right to report legal proceedings such as inquests" (cl 5(i)).
>
> (c) "The public interest includes, but is not confined to, (i) detecting or exposing crime or serious impropriety, (ii) protecting public health

---

38 [2012] EWHC 3748 (Fam), [2013] 1 FLR 1205.

39 The background to *Bristol City Council v NGN* is summarised at 5.87.

40 Bake J at §[12](8).

41 Other applications of this passage are explained at 8.7.

42 And see, eg, *Re J (Reporting Restriction: Internet: Video)* [2013] EWHC 2694 (Fam), [2014] 1 FLR 523, Sir James Munby P.

43 See www.editorscode.org.uk/downloads/codebook/codebook-2016.pdf ie as referred to by Lady Hale in *PJS* at §[72].

and safety, (iii) preventing the public from being misled by an action or statement of an individual or organisation" (section headed "The Public Interest", cl 1).

(d) In cases involving children under 16, editors must demonstrate "an exceptional public interest to override the normally paramount interests of the child' (section headed "The Public Interest", cl 5).'[44]

5.38 Baker J concludes this passage of his judgement (§[12](12)) by referring to the 'balancing exercise' list in *Re S* [2004] at §[17] which he cites in full; and, it will be recalled.

5.39 The importance of the rights of children in relation to these findings is considered in **Part 4**, and in the light of Lady Hale's short judgement in *PJS*, concurring in the result with Lord Mance. An example of rights in children proceedings will suffice here.

4 CHILDREN'S RIGHTS AND THE CONVENTION

Children's rights and the interests of the child

Yousef *and rights of children*

5.40 The importance of press freedom in the context of family proceedings must always be balanced against the interests and welfare of children. The importance of the welfare of a child, was asserted by the European Court in *Yousef v The Netherlands*[45] (in a decision handed down on 5 November 2002) in very clear terms:

> '[66] ... If there was any clash of Art 8 rights between a child and its father, the interests of the child should always prevail.
>
> [73] The court reiterates that in judicial decisions where the rights under Art 8 of parents and those of a child are at stake, the child's rights must be the paramount consideration. If any balancing of interests is necessary, the interests of the child must prevail (see *Elsholz v Germany* (2002) 34 EHRR 58, [2000] 2 FLR 486, para 52 and *TP and KM v United Kingdom* (2002) 34 EHRR 2, [2001] 2 FLR 549, para 72).'

5.41 This statement and the decision on which it is based is referred to frequently in children cases (see, for example, by Roberts J in *Local Authority X v HI and Others*[46]). The legal principles on which *Re S (Identification: Restrictions on*

44 Still clause 5 under 'Public interest' in the Code: '5 In cases involving children under 16, editors must demonstrate an exceptional public interest to over-ride the normally paramount interest of the child.' http://editorscode.org.uk/downloads/the_code/archive/Code_1_page_A4_1-2014.pdf.

45 *Yousef v The Netherlands (Application No 33711/96)* (2003) 36 EHRR 20, [2003] 1 FLR 210, ECtHR.

46 [2016] EWHC 1123 (Fam), [2017] 1 FLR 1362, Roberts J, especially at §§[57]–[59].

Publication)[47] was decided remain as important as ever.[48] In the field of children law it is permissible to ask whether, in the light of subsequent developments in the common law: would *Re S* be decided in the same way now?

5.42 In *Yousef v Netherlands* the Dutch mother and Egyptian father (Y) lived together, before his return to the Middle east when their daughter (L) was 18 months old. On Y's return to the Netherlands two years later he had contact; but the mother (M) refused to give permission to Y to 'recognise' L legally, which would have resulted in a change to L's surname. M became terminally ill. She made a will naming her brother as guardian of L. Y brought proceedings for an order that M give him permission to recognise L as his son (which would give L his surname). The court refused to make such an order, considering that M had not abused her right to withhold permission, since the change of surname would not be in L's best interests. After M's death, Y brought proceedings to have his 'recognition' of L registered, and in separate proceedings to have his contact increased. In successive Dutch courts his application for recognition was refused: whatever family life there might have been between Y and L had been broken: and, even if there was a family life between them, L's interests should be the foremost consideration. It was in L's best interests to grow up in the family she knew. After further court applications, Y complained that his right to respect for his private and family life (Art 8) had been violated.

5.43 The European Court of Human Rights held that there had been no violation. On L's rights, they held that in court decisions where Art 8 rights of a parent and of a child were in issue, the child's rights were the paramount consideration. If any balancing of interests were necessary, the interests of the child must prevail (see reference to §§[66] and [73] above). The refusal of Y to 'recognise' L was an interference with his right to respect for his family life, but was in accordance with Dutch law. It pursued a legitimate aim (ie of protecting the rights and freedoms of L), and was necessary in a democratic society, in that it was considered to be in L's best interests.

5.44 The Court explained their view in the following way:

> '[53] The denial [by one of the right of another] to recognition where family life exists, such as occurred in the present case, constitutes an "interference" with the right to respect for family life. It will constitute a violation of Art 8 of the Convention unless the requirements of the second paragraph of that Article were met.'

---

47 [2004] UKHL 47, [2005] 1 AC 593, [2005] 1 FLR 591.

48 See, eg, in *PJS v News Group Newspapers Ltd* (see below) Lord Mance, speaking of the basis on which the court of appeal had wrongly directed itself on any precedence of the Convention Articles, referred to Lord Steyn's opinion: '[20] The Court of Appeal's initial self-direction is however contrary to considerable authority, including authority at the highest level, which establishes that, even at the interlocutory stage: (i) neither Article has preference over the other; (ii) where their values are in conflict, what is necessary is an intense focus on the comparative importance of the rights being claimed in the individual case; (iii) the justifications for interfering with or restricting each right must be taken into account; and (iv) the proportionality test must be applied: see, eg, *Re S (A Child) (Identification: Restrictions on Publication)*....'.

5.45 So, said the Court, it must consider whether the interference in this case was 'in accordance with the law' as required by the Convention, Art 8.2.[49] Because of the consequences, in Dutch law, of recognition of L after her mother's death, the Dutch court considered that it must 'balance the interests of [Y] in having his paternity recognised against the rights of [L] protected by Art 8'. This, said the European Court was a matter for the domestic authorities, especially the court, to deal with in accordance with domestic law, in the light of the Convention. This had been done. It follows, said the European Court, 'that the interference complained of was 'in accordance with the law' for the purposes of Art 8, para 2 of the Convention'.[50]

Press freedom balanced against rights of children: House of Lords and Re S

5.46 It must be open to question whether on the subject of the child's Art 8 rights and in the light of subsequent case law the decision on the facts of *Re S* [2004] would necessarily have gone the same way in 2017.[51] Lady Hale, then Hale LJ, was in the minority in the decision appealed from,[52] unsuccessfully, in *Re S (Identification: Restrictions on Publication)*.[53] Lord Steyn (ie disagreeing with the minority view of Hale LJ) explained this:

> '[30] Dealing with the relative importance of the freedom of the press to report the proceedings in a criminal trial Hale LJ drew a distinction. She observed (at §[56]): "The court must consider what restriction, if any, is needed to meet the legitimate aim of protecting the rights of CS. If prohibiting publication of the family name and photographs is needed, the court must consider how great an impact that will in fact have upon the freedom protected by Art 10.... These considerations are also relevant to the extent of the interference with CS's rights."'

5.47 In *Re S* [2004] Lord Steyn said that he was not willing to 'accept these observations without substantial qualification'. He continued the paragraph quoted above:

> '[30] ... A criminal trial is a public event. The principle of open justice puts, as has often been said, the judge and all who participate in the trial under intense scrutiny.[54] The glare of contemporaneous publicity ensures that trials are properly conducted. It is a valuable check on the criminal process....'

---

49 Art 8 is set out in full at 5.21.

50 §§[56]–[57].

51 See Lady Hale in *PJS* (below at 5.49), and eg Peter Jackson J decision on Art 8 and reporting restrictions in *A Council v M and Others (No 3) (Reporting Restriction Order; Adoption; Artificial Insemination)* [2012] EWHC 2038 (Fam), [2013] 2 FLR 1270.

52 *Re S (Identification: Restrictions on Publication)* [2003] EWCA Civ 963, [2004] Fam 43, [2003] 2 FLR 1253 (judgment 10 July 2003).

53 [2004] UKHL 47, [2005] 1 AC 593, [2005] 1 FLR 591 (opinions handed down on 28 October 2004).

54 See especially Jeremy Bentham quoted at 5.55.

Children and press freedom

Primacy of children's interests

5.48 *Yousef v The Netherlands (Application No 33711/96)*[55] was not cited in *Re S* in the House of Lords (nor had it been cited in the Court of Appeal). As can be seen from such recent cases as *Local Authority X v HI and Others*[56] and *Leicester City Council v T*,[57] the principle enunciated in *Yousef* remains very much the basis on which the balancing of Art 8 rights as between parents and children are now decided. This is emphasised still further by the Supreme Court approach to *PJS*.

5.49 In *PJS v News Group Newspapers Ltd*,[58] a decision over 12 years after *Re S* [2004] in the House of Lords, Lady Hale in the Supreme Court said of a child's Art 8 rights and the importance of the court's close attention to such rights:

> '[72] I agree that this appeal should be allowed and the interim injunction restored for the reasons given by Lord Mance. I wish only to add a few words about the interests of the two children whom PJS has with YMA. It is simply not good enough to dismiss the interests of any children who are likely to be affected by the publication of private information about their parents with the bland statement that "these cannot be a trump card".[59] Of course they cannot always rule the day. But they deserve closer attention than they have so far received in this case, for two main reasons. First, not only are the children's interests likely to be affected by a breach of the privacy interests of their parents, but the children have independent privacy interests of their own. They also have a right to respect for their family life with their parents. Secondly, by s 12(4)(b) of the HRA 1998, any court considering whether to grant either an interim or a permanent injunction has to have "particular regard" to "any relevant privacy code". It is not disputed that the IPSO Code, which came into force in January, is a relevant Code for this purpose. This, as Lord Mance has explained, provides that "editors must demonstrate an exceptional public interest to override the normally paramount interests of [children under 16]".'

---

55 (2003) 36 EHRR 20, [2003] 1 FLR 210, ECtHR.

56 [2016] EWHC 1123 (Fam), [2017] 1 FLR 1362, Roberts J.

57 [2016] EWFC 20, [2017] 1 FLR 1585 (judgment 28 January 2016) where Keehan J said: '[7] In considering making care orders I have close regard to the Art 6 and Art 8 European Convention rights of the mother and of the children, but I remind myself that where there is tension between the Art 8 rights of the parent, on the one hand, and of the children, on the other, the rights of the children prevail: *Yousef v The Netherlands* (2003) 36 EHRR 20, [2003] 1 FLR 210.'

58 [2016] UKSC 26, [2016] AC 1081, [2016] 2 FLR 251, [2016] 2 WLR 1253.

59 As Lord Mance explained at §[18] the Court of Appeal had adopted the first instance judge's reference to the children not being 'trump cards' in the following terms: '[48] I turn next to the position of YMA and the children. As explained in para [39] of my previous judgment, the interests of other family members, in particular children, are a significant consideration, but they cannot be a trump card. Paragraph [61] of the redacted judgment (para [63] of the full judgment) referred to the likelihood that, in the absence of an injunction, the children would in the future learn about these matters from school friends or the Internet. That is now a less material consideration. In my view, whether or not the court grants an injunction, it is inevitable that the two children will in due course learn about these matters.'

5.50 In both *Re S* [2004] and *PJS* the children concerned were not parties to the proceedings where reporting restrictions were applied for. The fact of the child's non-party status was a factor which was emphasised by Lord Steyn in *Re S* [2004]: 'There is no decision of the Strasbourg court granting injunctive relief to non-parties, juvenile or adult, in respect of publication of criminal proceedings'.[60]

5.51 Lord Steyn continued by pursuing the point by reference and in contrast to UNCRC 1989 (which, as he pointed out, came into force in the UK on 2 September 1990) 'protects the privacy of children' but only where they are 'directly involved in criminal proceedings'. (It will be recalled that alongside *Re S* [2004]: nor was L (the young child) in *Yousef v Netherlands* [61] a party to the proceedings; yet it was her rights which determined the outcome of the case in the European Court.)

5.52 Both sets of proceedings – though respectively criminal (*Re S*) and civil (*PJS*) – would have been heard in open court in accordance with common law and Art 6 principles, subject to any direction to the contrary (eg in the case of *PJS*, in accordance with *CPR 1998, r 39.2*[62]). The rights of the children, who were not parties to the injunction application – it was their father (PJS) who was the applicant – were as set out by Lady Hale, in §[72] above.

5 THE CONVENTION AND FREEDOM OF EXPRESSION

Freedom of expression and the interests of justice

Importance of press freedom

5.53 So why press freedom? Why the right – and, perhaps, the need – for open justice? Why is press freedom so important, especially in a jurisdiction – children proceedings – where most cases are heard privately, no documents are published and judgments are mostly anonymised?

5.54 Reasons for freedom of expression were judicially explained by Lord Steyn in *R v Secretary of State for the Home Department, exp Simms*:[63]

> 'Freedom of expression is, of course, intrinsically important: it is valued for its own sake. But it is well recognised that it is also instrumentally important. It serves a number of broad objectives. First, it promotes the self-fulfilment of individuals in society. Secondly, in the famous words of Holmes J (echoing John Stuart Mill) "the best test of truth is the power of the thought to get itself accepted in the competition of the market": *Abrams v. United States* (1919) 250 US 616, 630, per Holmes J (dissenting). Thirdly, freedom of speech is the lifeblood of democracy. The free flow of information and ideas informs political debate. It is a safety valve: people are more ready to accept

60 At §[26].

61 Discussed with outline of facts at 5.40.

62 *CPR 1998, r 39.2* is set out and discussed at 13.8.

63 [1999] UKHL 33, [2000] 2 AC 115 at 126, [1999] 3 WLR 328.

decisions that go against them if they can in principle seek to influence them. It acts as a brake on the abuse of power by public officials....'[64]

5.55 Of publicity and the need for it in the court system Jeremy Bentham said, in a frequently quoted passage:[65]

'Publicity is the very soul of justice. It is the keenest spur to exertion and the surest of all guards against improbity. It keeps the judge himself while trying under trial.'

5.56 The same point was made by Lord Woolf MR in *R v Legal Aid Board (exp Kiam Todner (a firm))*:[66]

'... It is so important not to forget why proceedings are required to be subjected to the full glare of a public hearing. It is necessary because the public nature of the proceedings deters inappropriate behaviour on the part of the court. It also maintains the public's confidence in the administration of justice. It enables the public to know that justice is being administered impartially....'

Media in children proceedings

5.57 Shortly after the original rule change (Family Proceedings Rules 1991, r 10.28(4)[67]) in *Re Child X (Residence and Contact: Rights of Media Attendance: FPR Rule 10.28(4))*[68] Sir Mark Potter P commented on the ability of the media to come into court:

'[47] The net result of all this is that, while the press are entitled to report on the nature of the dispute in the proceedings, and to identify the issues in the case and the identity of the participating witnesses (save those whose published identity would reveal the identity of the child in the case), they are not entitled to set out the content of the evidence or the details of matters investigated by the Court. Thus the position has been created that, whereas the media are now enabled to exercise a role of "watchdog" on the part of the public at large and to observe family justice at work for the purpose of informed comment upon its workings and the behaviour of its judges, they are unable to report in their newspapers or programmes the identity of the

64 This passage was cited by Sir James Munby P in *Re J* (considered further below at 5.61) in support of his emphasis on the need for transparency in family courts: '[31] The compelling need for transparency in the family justice system is demanded as a matter of both principle and pragmatism. So far as concerns principle I can do no better than repeat what Lord Steyn said in [*exp Simms* (above)].... "freedom of speech is the lifeblood of democracy. The free flow of information and ideas informs political debate. ... It facilitates the exposure of errors in the ... administration of justice of the country".'

65 Including by Lord Shaw in *Scott v Scott* [1913] AC 417 at 477.

66 [1999] QB 966 at 977, [1998] 3 WLR 925, CA.

67 As explained at 13.10.

68 [2009] EWHC 1728 (Fam), [2009] 2 FLR 1467.

parties or the details of the evidence which are likely to catch the eye and engage the interest of the average reader or viewer.

5.58 Finally, the particular importance of the media was stressed by Lord Bingham in *McCartan Turkington Breen v Times Newspapers Ltd*.[69] The House of Lords hearing started the day after the coming into force of *HRA 1998*. Lord Bingham said why he believed the freedom of the press was fundamental. Any restriction should be fully justified:

> '... The majority [of people] cannot participate in the public life of their society... if they are not alerted to and informed about matters which call or may call for consideration and action. It is very largely through the media, including of course the press, that they will be so alerted and informed. The proper functioning of a modern participatory democracy requires that the media be free, active, professional and inquiring. For this reason the courts, here and elsewhere, have recognised the cardinal importance of press freedom and the need for any restriction on that freedom to be proportionate and no more than is necessary to promote the legitimate object of the restriction.'

Judge, not editor

5.59 And of the quality of what is published? In *Re J (Reporting Restriction: Internet: Video)*[70] Sir James Munby P pointed out that 'Freedom of speech is not something to be awarded to those who are thought deserving and denied to those who are thought undeserving'. He quoted Lord Oliver's comment in *Attorney-General v Guardian Newspapers Ltd*:[71]

> '... the liberty of the press is essential to the nature of a free state. The price that we pay is that that liberty may be and sometimes is harnessed to the carriage of liars and charlatans, but that cannot be avoided if the liberty is to be preserved.'

5.60 In *Re Roddy (A child) (Identification: Restriction on Publication)*,[72] where Sir James (as Munby J) had pointed out that it was not for judges to decide what should be published or in what form (in the absence of defamation or of a crime being committed):

> '... judges are not arbiters of taste or decency ... It is not the function of the judges to legitimise "responsible" reporting whilst censoring what some are pleased to call "irresponsible" reporting ... And as the Strasbourg jurisprudence establishes... the freedom of expression secured by Art 10 is

69 [2001] 2 AC 277 at 290–291, [2003] 3 WLR 1670 at 1679–1680; the concerned the question of whether a meeting to which the press was called was public and therefore whether a report of it could be libellous.
70 [2013] EWHC 2694 (Fam), [2014] 1 FLR 523 at §[40].
71 [1987] 1 WLR 1248, at 1320.
72 [2003] EWHC 2927 (Fam), [2004] 2 FLR 949 at para [89].

applicable not only to information or ideas that are favourably received, or regarded as inoffensive, but also to those that offend, shock or disturb the state or any section of the community.... It is not for the court to substitute its own views for those of the press as to what technique of reporting should be adopted by journalists....'

Private individuals and freedom of expression

The balance and private rights

5.61 Under the headline: 'Let "glare of publicity" into family courts, says Munby' the *Law Society's Gazette*[73] reported on *Re J (Reporting Restriction: Internet: Video)*,[74] a case in which it said Sir James Munby P 'has defended the right of individuals aggrieved by the family courts process to post their grievances on the internet, even when expressed in "vigorous, trenchant or outspoken terms".'

5.62 In *Re J* Sir James Munby P reviewed the basis on which, as he saw it, *Re S*[75] was being applied in the courts, especially in the light of 'what it has become conventional to call transparency',[76] tested in the light of what parents should be allowed to say publicly about children proceedings. He stressed the balance which must be struck between the necessary respect for privacy for children, as against the right of their parents and the press to give publicity to family cases.

'Need for more transparency' in family proceedings

5.63 There was a need, he said, for more transparency in family proceedings; and this was even more so given the consequences for parents and a child which might flow from a care order:

'[26] ... There is a pressing need for more transparency, indeed for much more transparency, in the family justice system. There are a number of aspects to this.

[27] One is the right of the public to know, the need for the public to be confronted with, what is being done in its name. Nowhere is this more necessary than in relation to care and adoption cases. Such cases, by definition, involve interference, intrusion, by the State, by local authorities and by the court, into family life....

[28] I have said this many times in the past but it must never be forgotten that, with the State's abandonment of the right to impose capital sentences, orders of the kind which family judges are typically invited to make in

73 10 September 2013, online.
74 [2013] EWHC 2694 (Fam), [2014] 1 FLR 523.
75 *Re S (Identification: Restrictions on Publication)* [2004] UKHL 47, [2005] 1 FLR 591.
76 §[26].

public law proceedings are amongst the most drastic that any judge in any jurisdiction is ever empowered to make....'

5.64 In *Re J* Sir James set out the legislative restrictions on publicity and then explained the importance to the family justice system that it should receive publicity. He starts by pointing out the 'automatic constraints' on publicity. The *Children Act 1989, s 97* (prohibits publication, but only until the conclusion of proceedings[77]). *Administration of Justice Act 1960 (AJA 1960), s 12(1)*[78] relates to 'proceedings in private', including family proceedings, but narrows those proceedings to those in relation to children and only to 'proceedings before any court'; and it does not apply to 'anyone involved in the proceedings' (eg expert witnesses, social workers, the local authority etc).

5.65 The court may by order extend or reduce the automatic constraints publicity; but to do so it must conduct a balancing exercise within the European Convention 1950 as described in *Re S (Identification: Restrictions on Publication)*,[79] said Sir James. It is 'necessary to measure the nature of the impact ... on the child' of what is in prospect, Lord Steyn had said in that case. However, since *ZH (Tanzania) v Secretary of State for the Home Department*[80] the interests of the child must be a primary – though not a paramount – consideration for the court.[81] The balance must be drawn between respect for the child's private life (Art 8) and the right of the press and a parent or others who might want (as was the case in *Re J*) to publicise information (Article 10).

5.66 From this it followed that the views of parents 'caught up in' the court system should be discussed publicly. They must be able, if they wished, to publicise their views of the failings of judges or the system or their criticisms of local authorities. It was not for the judge to exercise editorial control of such publicity:

6 CHILD'S RIGHT TO FREEDOM OF EXPRESSION

Child's right to freedom of expression

Roddy: *Convention rights engaged*

5.67 The case of *Re Roddy (A Child) (Identification: Restriction on Publication)*[82] emphasises the importance of looking at the other side of the publicity coin, namely the wish of a mature child to publish her story. This is the immediate outcome of

77 *Clayton v Clayton* [2006] EWCA Civ 878, [2006] 1 FLR 11.

78 Section 12(1) is set out in full at 13.19.

79 [2004] UKHL 47, [2005] 1 FLR 591 per Lord Steyn at para [17].

80 [2011] UKSC 4 at para [33]; and see *Yousef v The Netherlands (Application No 33711/96)* (2003) 36 EHRR 20, [2003] 1 FLR 210, ECtHR discussed at 5.40.

81 Explained further at Part 9.

82 [2003] EWHC 2927, [2004] 2 FLR 949 (judgment 2 December 2003); and see consideration of this case in Ch 8 (*Yousef* is not referred to by Munby J).

the case. However, *Roddy* shows an experienced family judge looking more deeply at a number of issues relating to a mature child, including:

- In reality, what were the rights of a 16-year-old to make up her own mind?
- How should these rights be balanced against the rights of others in the case, such as Angela's (now adopted) child and her family; and of the father of Angela's child?
- How should Angela's rights must be regarded by the courts in the light of *Gillick v West Norfolk and Wisbech AHA*[83] in late 2003 (and now?).

5.68 In *Roddy* Munby J was confronted by a 'child', Angela Roddy, who wanted to tell her own story. She was born on 4 December 1986. Munby J's judgment was given on 3 December 2003[84] (when she was nearly 17). As a 12-year-old Angela – for so Munby J calls her – had become pregnant and was taken into care. It was reported in the press that the Roman Catholic Church had given money to Angela to persuade her against an abortion. The local authority was granted an order protecting her identity and that of the father ('X'), a boy of similar age. Once the child ('Y') was born, the local authority began care proceedings. Angela remained in foster care. Angela was opposed to adoption, but her consent was dispensed with and Y was adopted. Associated Newspapers Ltd ('ANL') applied to vary the terms of the order protecting the identities of the parents. The order was discharged and replaced with another, operative until Angela's eighteenth birthday, intended to protect her and X. Angela's care order was later discharged and she returned to live with her parents.

5.69 Angela approached *The Mail on Sunday*, saying that she was happy to be named and photographed for any ensuing article. ANL, owners of *The Mail on Sunday*, sought a variation of the reporting restrictions order which then prohibited identification of Angela and of X, to enable it to publish Angela's story, but without identifying X or Y. The local authority was prepared to agree to the proposed variation, but sought a further order explicitly protecting the identity of Y.

5.70 Munby J held that Convention articles were engaged in *Roddy* as follows:

> '[38] I approach the present case on the footing that neither X nor Y (nor their parents on their behalf) wish to waive their privacy. And both have a family life which, I imagine, they and their parents are anxious to preserve and protect. Angela, on the other hand, not merely wishes to waive her privacy: she is anxious to communicate her story to the whole world. She is, however, still a child. It can, therefore, be seen that the following European Convention rights are or may be engaged:

83 [1985] UKHL 7, [1986] 1 AC 112, [1986] 1 FLR 224; considered fully in Ch 2, Part 4.

84 As is clear from §§[16]–[22] the hearing and delivery of judgment took place between judgment in the Court of Appeal and its upholding in the House of Lords in *Re S (Identification: Restrictions on Publication)* [2004] UKHL 47, [2005] 1 AC 593, [2005] 1 FLR 591.

(i) X's rights under Art 8 (a) to keep his private life private and (b) to preserve and protect the family life he enjoys with his parents and other members of his family;

(ii) Y's rights under Art 8 (a) to keep her private life private and (b) to preserve and protect the family life she is now enjoying with her adoptive parents;

(iii) Angela's rights under Arts 8 and 10, as she wishes to assert them, to tell her story to the world through the medium of *The Mail on Sunday*;

(iv) Angela's rights under Art 8, as Angela's parents or the court might wish to assert them on her behalf, (a) to keep her private life private and (b) to preserve and protect the family life she enjoys with her parents and other members of her family;

(v) ANL's [(for *Mail on Sunday*)] rights under Art 10 (a) to obtain the story that Angela wishes to tell and (b) to publish Angela's story in *The Mail on Sunday.*'

Confidentiality and rights of a mature child

5.71 At the time of the hearing Angela's own position was set out in her solicitor's statement for the hearing:[85]

> 'Angela has emphasised to me that she wishes to tell her own story about her experiences of being a teenage mother in care and that this is her primary motivation for approaching the newspaper. Angela is a mature and articulate young person who states that she has given very careful consideration to this course of action and has decided that it is something she definitely wishes to take forward. In these circumstances the application for discharge of the existing order and the substitution of a variation order in the proposed terms of the draft order would seem to be appropriate.'

5.72 Munby J treated Angela as competent to take her own decisions on her own confidentiality. The same principles, he said, applied to her for herself, in this context, as for any other decision-making by a mature, or *Gillick*-competent, child both in respect of freedom of expression (Art 10) and for her to waive her right to privacy under Art 8. The court must recognise the child's integrity as a human being and acknowledge that, in order to respect the child's rights under the European Convention, the child must be allowed to make his or her own decision.[86]

5.73 Munby J started the part of his judgement which dealt with Angela's Convention rights as follows:

---

85 Set out in §[12] of the judgment.
86 §§[50]–[58].

> '[45] In a sense there might be thought to be no issue [as to Angela's right to freedom of expression]. As we have seen, Angela wishes to tell her story. ANL obviously wants her to. Her parents do not object. Subject only to safeguarding Y's position, the local authority does not oppose what is being proposed. Angela's solicitor, B, has expressed the view that the proposed variation of my order is appropriate. But the fact is that – in law – Angela is a child and that as recently as July 2000 I thought it necessary to protect her by the very injunction which she now seeks to have discharged.'

Children's rights taken 'seriously'

5.74 Munby J treated the issue – so far as it was an issue – before him as one which must be resolved either in a *parens patriae* mode (ie by looking in an objective way, from an adult stand-point, at what was in the best interests of Angela); or should the court face 'reality'[87] and accept that decision-making in relation to a child of Angela's age was a matter for her, and for Angela to make her own choices? These options are summarised in the passage italicised below.

> '[46] There is in fact a very important point of principle lurking behind all this. Are children of Angela's age to be allowed to exercise for themselves the rights they have under the European Convention – here the vitally important rights under Arts 8 and 10? Are we to recognise that Angela should in relation to her European Convention rights enjoy the same autonomy, the same decision-making power, as she will undoubtedly have when she reaches the age of 18 in just one year's time?... *Are we, in other words, to take children's rights seriously and as our children see them? Or are we to treat children as little more than the largely passive objects of more or less paternalistic parental or judicial decision-making?*' (emphasis added)

5.75 Angela, he said was seeking 'to tell her story to the world – a right, and it is nothing less, securely founded in Arts 8 and 10'.[88] So what were Angela's rights and on what jurisprudence were they based? First Munby J considered the question of Angela's competence, in *Gillick* terms, to make a decision. Unless the court found that she was *Gillick*-competent there must remain a question as to whether the court could hold that she was in a position to exercise any rights.

87 See references by Munby J to 'reality' at §[56].
88 §[47].

Competence: Gillick and Convention rights

5.76 Munby J explained what he was being asked about in the context of *Gillick*,[89] and of what Lord Fraser[90] and Lord Scarman had said in that case. He cited Lord Scarman[91] as follows:

> 'The law relating to parent and child is concerned with the problems of the growth and maturity of the human personality. If the law should impose upon the process of "growing up" fixed limits where nature knows only a continuous process, the price would be artificiality and a lack of realism in an area where the law must be sensitive to human development and social change ... The underlying principle of the law ... is that parental right yields to the child's right to make his own decisions when he reaches a sufficient understanding and intelligence to be capable of making up his own mind on the matter requiring decision.'

5.77 The approach, said Munby J, was the same as in cases on medical treatment for mature children. For example, in *Re W (A Minor) (Medical Treatment: Court's Jurisdiction)*,[92] Balcombe LJ said:

89 *Gillick v West Norfolk and Wisbech AHA* [1985] UKHL 7, [1986] 1 AC 112, [1986] 1 FLR 224, discussed at 8.16.

90 [1986] AC 112, [1986] 1 FLR 224 at 171 and 236 respectively: 'It is, in my view, contrary to the ordinary experience of mankind, at least in Western Europe in the present century, to say that a child or a young person remains in fact under the complete control of his parents until he attains the definite age of majority, now 18 in the UK, and that on attaining that age he suddenly acquires independence. In practice most wise parents' relax their control gradually as the child develops and encourage him or her to become increasingly independent. Moreover, the degree of parental control actually exercised over a particular child does in practice vary considerably according to his understanding and intelligence and it would, in my opinion, be unrealistic for the courts not to recognise these facts. Social customs change, and the law ought to, and does in fact, have regard to such changes when they are of major importance.'

91 In *Roddy* at §[51], in *Gillick* [1986] AC 112, [1986] 1 FLR 224 at 186 and 250 respectively.

92 [1993] Fam 64 at 88, [1993] 1 FLR 1 at 19; in which James Munby QC and Roderic Wood assisted the court as *amici curiae*. In *Re W (A Minor) (Medical Treatment: Court's Jurisdiction)*, as Nolan LJ pointed out at [1993] 1 FLR 23–24: '... It is essential to bear in mind that [in *Gillick* the House of Lords was] concerned with the extent of parental rights over the welfare of the child. They were not concerned with the jurisdiction of the court. It is of the essence of that jurisdiction that the court has the power and the responsibility in appropriate cases to override the views of both the child and the parent in determining what is in the child's best interests. Authoritative and instructive as they are, the speeches in *Gillick* do not deal with the principles which should govern the exercise of this court›s jurisdiction in the present case. In my judgment, those principles are to be found in s 1 of the Children Act 1989. The child›s welfare is to be the paramount consideration: see s 1(1). In giving effect to that consideration, the court is to have particular regard to the factors set out in s 1(3).' The Court of Appeal held that they had power to override W's wishes and consent to treatment for her; for, said Nolan LJ: '... I would emphasise that the only aspect of J's welfare with which we are concerned in the present case in her refusal to undergo a particular form of treatment for anorexia. So far in this judgment I have been principally concerned to explain why, as it seems to me, the court has not only the power but the inescapable responsibility of deciding, in that specific context, what is to be done in the interests of her welfare. I am very far from asserting any general rule that the court should prefer its own view as to what is in the best interests of the child to those of the child itself.'

> 'Accordingly the older the child concerned the greater the weight the court should give to [the child's] wishes, certainly in the field of medical treatment. In a sense this is merely one aspect of the application of the test that the welfare of the child is the paramount consideration. It will normally be in the best interests of a child of sufficient age and understanding to make an informed decision that the court should respect its integrity as a human being and not lightly override its decision on such a personal matter as medical treatment, all the more so if that treatment is invasive. In my judgment, therefore, the court exercising the inherent jurisdiction in relation to a 16- or 17-year-old child who is not mentally incompetent will, as a matter of course, ascertain the wishes of the child and will approach its decision with a strong predilection to give effect to the child's wishes.'

Rights and legal principle

'Reality': Angela Roddy, rights and legal principle

5.78 So said Munby J (and of a decision as to publicity, he can be seen saying the same, in effect, in *Re J* (above)[93]) that 'The courts must face reality [and] be sensitive to human development and social change'.

> '[56] The courts must face reality. We must, as Lord Scarman said [in *Gillick*],[94] be sensitive to human development and social change. Angela may not yet be quite 17 years old but she is a young woman with a mind of her own and, as her solicitor B has said, a mature and articulate young person. We no longer treat our 17-year-old daughters as our Victorian ancestors did, and if we try to do so it is at our – and their – peril. Angela, in my judgment, is of an age, and has sufficient understanding and maturity, to decide for herself whether that which is private, personal and intimate should remain private or whether it should be shared with the whole world.... She is, to use the language of Woolf J (as he then was) in *Gillick v West Norfolk and Wisbech Area Health Authority* [1984] QB 581 at 596, 'capable of making a reasonable assessment of the advantages and disadvantages' of what is proposed.'

5.79 Though Angela was not quite yet 17, Munby J went on:

> '[56] ... We no longer treat our 17-year-old daughters as our Victorian ancestors did, and if we try to do so it is at our – and their – peril. Angela, in my judgment, is of an age, and has sufficient understanding and maturity, to decide for herself whether that which is private, personal and intimate should remain private or whether it should be shared with the whole world.'

---

93 See 5.61.
94 Set out in 5.76.

Defence of the right of a child

5.80 As a matter of practical reality, and of legal principle, the courts must look to a child's rights. A little earlier in his judgment, Munby J had cited Nolan LJ in *Re W (A Minor) (Medical Treatment: Court's Jurisdiction)*:[95]

> 'In considering the welfare of the child, the court must not only recognise but if necessary defend the right of the child, having sufficient understanding to take an informed decision, to make his or her own choice. In most areas of life it would be not only wrong in principle but also futile and counter-productive for the court to adopt any different approach…'

5.81 In *Roddy*, Munby J asserted – as Nolan LJ had done in *Re W* – the right generally of a child like Angela Roddy, that is as 'a child of sufficient understanding to make an informed decision, to make his or her own choice'; and the 'duty of the court' to recognise such right:

> '[57] In my judgment (and I wish to emphasise this) it is the responsibility – it is the duty – of the court not merely to recognise but, as Nolan LJ said, to defend what, if I may respectfully say so, he correctly described as the right of the child who has sufficient understanding to make an informed decision, to make his or her own choice.'[96]

5.82 Further, as Nolan LJ had pointed out, this was a matter of legal principle, and a matter of Angela's integrity as a human being; and unless this was not recognised, society failed to recognise her Convention rights under Art 8 and 10. Angela must be entitled to make her own choice:

> '[57] … For, as Balcombe LJ recognised, the court must recognise the child's integrity as a human being. And we do not recognise Angela's dignity and integrity as a human being – we do not respect her rights under Arts 8 and 10 – unless we acknowledge that it is for her to make her own choice, and not for her parents or a judge or any other public authority to seek to make the choice on her behalf.'

5.83 But for his need to consider also the possible consequences for her daughter, Y, Munby J said he 'would have not the slightest hesitation in granting Angela and' the newspapers what they were asking for:[97]

---

95 [1993] Fam 64 at 93, [1993] 1 FLR 1 at 24.

96 Baker J expressed the same point in *Bristol City Council v NGN Ltd and Others* [2012] EWHC 3748 (Fam), [2013] 1 FLR 1205 at [12]… 'Art 8 … embraces both the right to maintain one's privacy and, if this is what one prefers, not merely the right to waive that privacy but also the right to share what would otherwise be private with others or, indeed, with the world at large. So the right to communicate one's story to one's fellow beings is protected not merely by Art 10 but also by Art 8' (per Munby J in *Re Roddy (A Child) (Identification: Restriction on Publication); Torbay Borough Council v News Group Newspapers* [(above)].'

97 §[60].

'[60] … Angela a week before her seventeenth birthday should be freed from the fetters of the injunction that was necessary to protect her at a time when, at the age of only 13½, she was not able to decide for herself where her best interests lay…'

5.84 Having considered the arguments for Y for preventing Angela from publishing her story, Munby J concluded:

'[85] … I reject the local authority's assertion that the proper safeguarding of Y's interests requires that the media be restrained not merely from soliciting information about Y from Angela and her parents, and for that matter also from X, but moreover that the media be restrained from publishing Angela's story…. Even if the local authority was able to make good the factual assertion for which it contends – the risk to the stability of the adoptive placement – the balance in all probability would still come down in favour of Angela and ANL.'

7 THE CONVENTION BALANCING TEST: RIGHTS OF EQUAL FORCE

Interplay between rights

5.85 The interplay between Articles was explained authoritatively in *Re S (Identification: Restrictions on Publication)*[98] (in that case the interplay was between Arts 8 and 10):

'[17] The interplay between Arts 8 and 10 has been illuminated by the opinions in the House of Lords in *Campbell v MGN Ltd* [2004] UKHL 22, [2004] 2 WLR 1232, [2004] UKHRR 648. For present purposes the decision of the House on the facts of *Campbell v MGN Ltd* and the differences between the majority and the minority are not material. What does, however, emerge clearly from the opinions are four propositions. First, neither Article has *as such* precedence over the other. Secondly, where the values under the two Articles are in conflict, an intense focus on the comparative importance of the specific rights being claimed in the individual case is necessary. Thirdly, the justifications for interfering with or restricting each right must be taken into account. Finally, the proportionality test must be applied to each. For convenience I will call this the ultimate balancing test. This is how I will approach the present case.'

5.86 The importance of this statement of the law has been repeated by the courts since then, as for example by Lord Mance in *PJS* mentioned above;[99] especially in relation to Lord Steyn's emphasis on articles under the Convention not having 'precedence' one over another. For example, in relation to whether or not

98 [2004] UKHL 47, [2005] 1 AC 593, [2005] 1 FLR 591.
99 §[20] quoted in full at 5.32.

his judgment in a case concerning the son of Madonna and whether his judgment should be anonymised *Ciccone v Ritchie (No 1)*,[100] MacDonald J said of the Arts 8 and 10 balancing exercise:

> '[57]... (iv)When conducting a balancing exercise between Art 8 and Art 10, the court applies the four propositions identified by Lord Steyn in *Re S (Identification: Restrictions on Publication)* [(above)] at §[17]. In applying what Lord Steyn described as the 'ultimate balancing test' of proportionality, it is important that the court considers carefully whether the order that is being sought is proportionate having regard to the end that the order seeks to achieve.'

5.87 In *Bristol City Council v NGN Ltd and Others*[101] Baker J considered the principles applicable, and in particular the Convention rights engaged, in a decision as to whether the media should be permitted to attend a children case, where the magistrates' court and county court had earlier imposed a reporting restriction order in relation to care proceedings. He held that the correct approach for the Family Court to imposing a reporting restriction – listed amongst the 'legal principles' he identified for making such an order[102] – was the following:

> '(4) Since the implementation of the Human Rights Act 1998 passed by Parliament to incorporate the European Convention for the Protection of Human Rights and Fundamental Freedoms 1950 (European Convention) into English law, the foundation of the jurisdiction to restrain publicity is now derived from the European Convention. Applications for reporting restriction orders are determined by analysing and balancing the competing rights under the European Convention: *Campbell v MGN Ltd* [2004] UKHL 22, [2004] 2 AC 457, [2004] 2 WLR 1232, [2004] UKHRR 648, *Re S (Identification: Restrictions on Publication)*'[(above)].

Rights and the media

5.88 In *A Council v M and Others (No 3) (Reporting Restriction Order; Adoption; Artificial Insemination)*[103] Peter Jackson J was dealing with a case in which the issue was whether a mother should be named in the reporting of criminal proceedings which arose from her causing her 16-year-old daughter to be artificially inseminated to give her another child to adopt. Peter Jackson J made a reporting restriction order. In so doing he set out *HRA 1998, s 12(4)* and then explained the jurisdiction of the High Court to restrain publicity:

> '[25] There is no dispute that the High Court has jurisdiction to make an order restraining publicity. The definitive statement of principle about how these issues should be approached is found in the decision in *Re S (Identification:*

100 [2016] EWHC 608, [2017] 1 FLR 795 and see further at 5.98.
101 [2012] EWHC 3748 (Fam), [2013] 1 FLR 1205.
102 At §[12].
103 [2012] EWHC 2038 (Fam), [2013] 2 FLR 1270; this case has an Annex 1 in which Peter Jackson J sets out the then 'relevant authorities' on restriction of publication.

> *Restrictions on Publication*) [2004] UKHL 47, [2005] 1 AC 593, [2004] 3 WLR 1129, [2005] 1 FLR 591, [2005] UKHRR 129. As is well known, the House of Lords held that an intense focus on the comparative importance of the competing European Convention rights under Arts 8 and 10 was required, with neither Article having presumptive weight over the other and with the proportionality test to be applied to each.'

5.89 However, in this case, he said that the exceptional course of Art 8 rights serving to restrict Art 10 rights was 'not beyond contemplation'.

> '[27] Since *Re S (Identification: Restrictions on Publication)* was decided, its analysis has been applied to all applications of this kind. Consequently, a conclusion that the Art 8 rights of individuals should prevail over the Art 10 rights of the public so as to restrict the reporting of criminal proceedings will be highly exceptional, though not beyond contemplation.'

5.90 Peter Jackson J stressed that decisions in cases like this were fact specific. He made a reporting restrictions order until the grandchild (D) was 18 in respect of the mother, her three adopted children and D. He stressed that there was no hierarchy of rights in the Convention, and balanced the private rights of the individuals concerned against with those of the media for freedom of expression, as follows:

> '[83] Rights arising under Art 8 on the one hand and Art 10 on the other are different in quality. Art 8 rights are by their nature of crucial importance to a few, while Art 10 rights are typically of general importance to many. The decided cases, together with s 12(4) HRA, act as a strong reminder that the rights of the many should not be undervalued and incrementally eroded in response to a series of hard cases of individual misfortune.
>
> [84] On the other hand, there is no hierarchy of rights in this context and there are cases where individual rights must prevail. In highly exceptional cases this can even include making inroads into the fundamental right to report criminal proceedings, but only where that is absolutely necessary.
>
> [85] I have concluded that this is such a case. In such unique circumstances, the claims of Art 10 are very strong, but those of Art 8 are even stronger. The risks to private and family life are exceptional and the injunction sought is nothing less than an absolute necessity. While there is no evidence of a risk to life and limb, if M [the adoptive mother] is publicly identified the probable consequences for the younger family members would at best be harmful and at worst disastrous. The wellbeing of A [M's first, now 18-year-old, adopted child] is inseparable from the wellbeing of D [A's child]. A's sisters, the fortunes of A, B and C are also interlinked and any harm to one will be felt by the others. If these youngsters are identified, the effect on them would be long-lasting and profound.'

5.91 In this way the judge dealt with the Art 8 rights. The result was that the Art 10 infringement was only partial (though restriction on reporting included the mother who was on trial). The reporting restrictions order did not prevent reporting of the trial or of the wider issues which it raised:

> '[86] In contrast, the proposed infringement of Art 10 is partial, not absolute. While an order preventing the identification of a criminal defendant will deprive the story of the personal details that are so potent if it is to attract the widest audience, it will not prevent the reporting of the trial itself or of the wider issues that arise. The events can be reported in a way that is not at the expense of young people who have already been direct victims of behaviour that takes the case outside the normal run of child cruelty cases. These children are at an age and stage where the impact of being identified would be particularly heavy.'

8 RIGHTS AND THE CHILD MATURE CHILD

Confidentiality rights and the Convention

5.92 *Local Authority X v HI and Others*[104] was a case about a child's right to confidentiality.[105] Roberts J dealt with a preliminary issue as to production of information which the 15-year-old, HI, had given, in confidence, to local authority professionals. This information, it was thought, might be relevant – and therefore it should be disclosed (ie its existence stated[106]) – in his care proceedings; but the question was whether it should be produced? HI did not want it to be released, or produced, to his father and step mother ('parents'). Roberts J concluded that HI (whom she called 'I') and the local authority were permitted not to produce the confidential information in the care proceedings.

5.93 The judge considered the parties' Convention rights – in this case Arts 6 and 8[107] – engaged by the application to withhold production:

> '[56] … The final step is to weigh the interests of the [parents] in having the opportunity to see and respond to the material. This involves a rigorous consideration of the engagement of their Art 6 and Art 8 European Convention rights.
>
> [57] … These rights, whilst engaged, cannot take precedence over I's Art 8 rights and he is clearly expressing a wish for no communication with his father or stepmother at the present time. As *Yousef* makes clear,[108] the child's rights are the paramount consideration in any balancing of competing Art 8 rights.'

---

104 [2016] EWHC 1123 (Fam), [2017] 1 FLR 1362.
105 Considered more fully at 10.58.
106 FPR 2010, r 21.1; and see Ch 10.
107 As further explained at 10.60.
108 *Yousef v The Netherlands (Application No 33711/96)* (2003) 36 EHRR 20, [2003] 1 FLR 210, ECtHR; and see 5.23.

5.94 HI's rights to confidentiality (ie confidentiality is the right at issue in this context; or, in Convention terms, HI's Art 8 rights) took precedence over the rights of his parents, in any balancing exercise.[109] But what of any Art 6 rights, especially in relation to HI's parents' right to a fair trial with all relevant material before the court?

> '[58] As to the respondents' Art 6 European Convention rights, the relevance of the information to outcome has already been addressed.[110]... The respondents' rights to a fair trial are, of course, absolute but, as Hale LJ acknowledged in *Re X*,[111] in deciding how to conduct a fair trial, it is perfectly reasonable to take account of the facts and circumstances of the particular case with which the court is dealing. The concept of a fair trial is inviolable but the *content* (including the evidence) which is placed before the court is flexible and depends upon context and the issues with which the court is dealing....'

5.95 Roberts J concluded that to deprive the parents of an opportunity to have this information produced to them 'will not deny to any of them a fair trial. Disclosure would, however, be a breach of [HI's] Art 8 European Convention rights'.[112]

Rights and the child with a view

5.96 In *Re D (A Child) (International Recognition)*[113] the Court of Appeal considered the importance in the context of the Hague Convention of a child, David, having 'an opportunity to be heard' in proceedings concerning his future. Ryder LJ explained David's Art 8 rights as follows:[114]

> '[48] The involvement in proceedings of children whose interests are affected was specifically highlighted by Baroness Hale in *Re D* (above) and in *ZH (Tanzania) v Secretary of State for the Home Department* [2011] UKSC 4, [2011] 2 AC 166, [2011] 1 FLR 2170. These dicta were brought together by Sir James Munby P in *Cambra v Jones* [2014] EWHC 913 (Fam), [2015] 1 FLR 263. [He said] "[18] ... If and to the extent that [the child's] Article 8

109 *Yousef v The Netherlands* (above).

110 The judge had already held that any relevance of the evidence was at most 'tangential' (see 10.49).

111 See further at 10.24. Of Convention Art 6 and *Re X (Adoption: Confidential Procedure)* [2002] EWCA Civ 828, [2002] 2 FLR 476 Hale LJ said: '[13] Unlike the right to respect for family and private life in Art 8, the right to a fair trial in Art 6 is absolute and unqualified. But the content of a fair trial in any particular case is more flexible and depends upon the context: as Lord Bingham of Cornhill said in *Brown v Stott (Procurator Fiscal, Dunfermline) and Another* [2001] 2 WLR 817, at 824:'What a fair trial requires cannot, however, be the subject of a single unvarying rule or collection of rules. It is proper to take account of the facts and circumstances of particular cases, as the European Court has consistently done.' Departures from the usual requirements of an adversarial trial must, of course, be for a legitimate aim and proportionate to that aim. Protecting the welfare of these very vulnerable children is undoubtedly a legitimate aim.'

112 §[59].

113 [2016] EWCA Civ 12, [2016] 1 WLR 2469, [2016] 2 FLR 347; and see full consideration at 4.36.

114 Explained further in Ch 4, Part 3.

> rights are engaged, then that will carry with it the important procedural right to be involved in the decision-making process, seen as a whole, to a degree sufficient to provide [her] with the requisite protection of [her] interests" see *W v United Kingdom* (1988) 10 EHRR 29, para 64.'

5.97 Of the Art 6 rights of David's parents' in the same case, Ryder LJ said:

'*Human rights*

> [63] Two human rights issues have been canvassed before us. First are the Art 8 of the European Convention for the Protection of Human Rights and Fundamental Freedoms 1950 (the European Convention) rights of all the parties to this case to respect for their family life. Second is the Art 6 right of the mother to a fair trial of the issue between her and the father. On the one hand, the plaintiff in a Hague Convention case has the benefit of automatic legal aid, without merits or means test, enhanced by the services of the specialist practitioners to whom these cases are referred by the central authority. On the other hand, the defendant is only entitled to legal aid on the usual means and merits tests, and may well not find his or her way to a specialist solicitor in the early days when crucial decisions have to be taken and affidavits filed. This, it is argued, it not the 'equality of arms' which is inherent in the concept of a fair trial.

Mature child and publication of judgment

5.98 In *Ciccone v Ritchie (No 1)*[115] MacDonald J determined the application of Rocco John Ritchie (then aged 15 years 4 months: R) to be joined as a party in the proceedings of his parents, Madonna Ciccone (the singer 'Madonna': M) and Guy Ritchie (G). M sought his summary return to New York State. She said G had wrongfully retained R in the UK. The judge granted R's application to be made a party.[116]

5.99 The question next arose as to whether the *(No 1)* judgement should be published. This was dealt with in *Ciccone v Ritchie (No 2)*.[117]

5.100 McDonald J referred to his own judgment in *H v A (No 2)*[118] for a definition of the principles which guide publication of judgements. These principles can be summarised as follows:[119]

- The public has a legitimate interest in knowing how the family courts exercise their jurisdiction.
- In making a decision a judge must balance parties' Art 8 and 10 rights.

115 [2016] EWHC 608, [2017] 1 FLR 795.
116 This aspect of Rocco's case is considered at 5.86.
117 [2016] EWHC 616 (Fam), [2017] 1 FLR 812.
118 [2015] EWHC 2630 (Fam).
119 See §[57].

- This is a 'simple case management decision[120] to be taken at the conclusion of the judgment and following a broad consideration of the applicable principles with basic reasons'.
- The judge 'applies the four propositions identified' in *Re S (Identification: Restrictions on Publication)* (above). In applying the 'ultimate balancing test' in *Re S*, it is important to consider carefully whether the order that is being sought is proportionate having regard to the end that the order seeks to achieve.

5.101 McDonald J concluded his list by referring to the best interests of the child or children concerned; though he does not specifically mention their views.[121] On behalf on any child concerned he does make the following points:

> '[57] ... The child's best interests are not paramount but rather are a primary consideration. Those best interests must accordingly be considered first, although they can be outweighed by the cumulative effect of other considerations.'

5.102 His conclusion was that the report should be published:

> '[77] Balancing the competing Art 8 and Art 10 European Convention rights, I am satisfied that my judgment of 3 February 2016 following the hearing on 21 December 2015 and this judgment should be published. I am further satisfied that, in the exceptional circumstances of this case and subject to some limited redaction, the judgments should be published without anonymisation.'

9 CHILD'S INTERESTS A PRIMARY CONSIDERATION

Child's rights and the European Convention

5.103 In *Yousef v The Netherlands (Application No 33711/96)*[122] the European Court says that:[123]

> '[73] ... where the rights under Art 8 of parents and those of a child are at stake, the child's rights must be the paramount consideration. If any balancing of interests is necessary, the interests of the child must prevail...'

5.104 MacDonald J concluded his guide to factors for publication of children proceedings judgements in *Ciccone v Ritchie (No 2)*[124] with the comments that

120 It may perhaps be said that the length of judgment in this case (87 paragraphs) does slightly belie the 'case management' aspect of his decision; though the judge does mention the 'exceptional facts of the case' and its effect on the decision involved.

121 See, eg, United Nations Convention on the Rights of the Child 1989 Art 12 and Charter of Fundamental Rights of the European Union (2000/C 364/01) Art 24 considered at in Ch 7.

122 (2003) 36 EHRR 20, [2003] 1 FLR 210, ECtHR.

123 This passage is quoted more fully at 5.40.

124 §[57].

'child's best interests are not paramount but rather are a primary consideration'. 'Paramount' or 'primary': is there a difference which matters? And does use of the term 'best interests' of a child alter the meaning and significance of a child's rights?

5.105 A starting-point could be Lady Hale in *H (H)* (below) where she set out three bases on which to consider the rights of children; and, it will be seen, she suggests that there are four factors which she identifies as determining children's rights: that their best interests come first; that they 'need a family life'; that there is a strong public interest in children being 'properly brought up'; and that effects of court decisions (eg as in *H(H)* on the effects of extradition) on children are likely to be more severe than on adults. Of the first of these she said:

> '[33] The family rights of children are of a different order from those of adults, for several reasons. In the first place, as *Neulinger*[125] and *ZH (Tanzania)* have explained, article 8 has to be interpreted in such a way that their best interests are a primary consideration, although not always the only primary consideration and not necessarily the paramount consideration. This gives them an importance which the family rights of other people... may not have....'

Child's best interests

5.106 A definition of a 'child's interests' is provided by the European Court (and explained in the context of the Hague Convention) by *Neulinger* and *Shuruk v Switzerland Application No 41615/07*.[126] In that case the Court said:

> '[136] The child's interest comprises two limbs. On the one hand, it dictates that the child's ties with its family must be maintained, except in cases where the family has proved particularly unfit.... On the other hand, it is clearly also in the child's interest to ensure its development in a sound environment, and a parent cannot be entitled under Art 8 to have such measures taken as would harm the child's health and development (see, among many other authorities, *Elsholz v Germany* (Application No 25735/94) (2002) 34 EHRR 58, [2000] 2 FLR 486, para 50....
>
> [137] The same philosophy is inherent in the Hague Convention, which in principle requires the prompt return of the abducted child unless there is a grave risk that the child's return would expose it to physical or psychological harm or otherwise place it in an intolerable situation (Art 13(b)). In other words, the concept of the child's best interests is also an underlying principle of the Hague Convention.'

5.107 A child's best interests, specifically in the context of the Convention, were explained in the Supreme Court in *ZH (Tanzania) v Secretary of State for the Home*

125 *Neulinger* and *Shuruk v Switzerland Application No 41615/07* (2010) 54 EHRR 1087, [2011] 1 FLR 122, ECtHR.

126 (2010) 54 EHRR 1087, [2011] 1 FLR 122, ECtHR (child of Swiss-Jewish mother and ultra-orthodox Jewish father, taken from Israel to Switzerland.

Department[127] ('*ZH*') and *H(H) v Deputy Prosecutor of the Italian Republic, Genoa (Official Solicitor intervening)*[128] ('*HH*'). Both cases involved the balancing of public interests against the parties' Art 8 rights; and both involved consideration of the rights of children in each of the families. In the first case, the issue was enforcement of an immigration deportation decision. In the second case (consisting of two sets of proceedings), the balance was between the children and support for international extradition treaties.

5.108 Both cases explained how children's welfare should be treated in the balancing of rights. As Lord Judge CJ explained in *H(H)*, the two cases involved different considerations for the court of the outcome for the children of the adult appellants. The finality of a deportation decision might create different issues for the court to consider in relation to a family, as distinct from what may be a temporary removal:

> '[123] For these reasons, in my judgment, assuming for the sake of argument that the child or children are in identical family situations, it follows that an extradition order for one or both parents may be appropriate when deportation or removal would not. In other words, because distinct issues are involved, the same facts, involving the same interests of and the same potential or likely damage to the child or children, may produce a different outcome when the court is deciding whether to remove foreign citizens from this country or extraditing convicted or suspected criminals (including citizens of this country) to serve their sentences or stand trial for crimes committed abroad.'

Children: 'a primary consideration'

5.109 In both cases, the Court brought into the balance in their decisions, the right to respect for the applicant's family life. And this involved an assessment of the rights of their respective children under Art 8. The main issue in each case was whether or not adults with children should be sent away from the UK.

5.110 In *ZH*, the earlier case, Lady Hale described what to her represented the 'best interests of the child' in an assessment of proportionality under Art 8(2). She equated this with the 'the well-being of the child'[129] which she defined in terms of where the child was to live and how much the child's living arrangements would be interrupted by any order.

5.111 Lord Kerr reflected further on the best interests of children. They are more than just a factor which weighs in the balance, he said (see italicised passage in para [46] below). If the best interests of children favour a particular course, that course should be chosen unless opposing reasons displace it; or as he put it in the

127 [2011] UKSC 4, [2011] 2 AC 166, [2011] 1 FLR 2170.
128 [2012] UKSC 25, [2013] 1 AC 338.
129 §[29].

later *H(H)* (para [143], below): 'no factor must be given greater weight than the interests of the child'. In *ZH* he said:

> '[46] It is a universal theme of the various international and domestic instruments to which Baroness Hale JSC has referred that, in reaching decisions that will affect a child, a primacy of importance must be accorded to his or her best interests. This is not, it is agreed, a factor of limitless importance in the sense that it will prevail over all other considerations. *It is a factor, however, that must rank higher than any other.* It is not merely one consideration that weighs in the balance alongside other competing factors....'

Children's interests: no factor given greater weight

5.112 In *H(H)* Lord Kerr adopted the simple proposition that no factor should be given greater weight that the interests of children:

> '[145] Baroness Hale JSC (in para 14 above) has correctly described my statement in para 46 of [*ZH*] as expressing more strongly than other members of the court the importance that should be attached to their best interests in reaching decisions that will affect children. In suggesting that these should be given a primacy of importance, I did not intend to stoke the debate about the distinction between "a factor of primary importance" and "the factor of primary importance". What I was seeking to say was that, in common with the opinion of the High Court of Australia in *Wan* (*Wan v Minister for Immigration and Multicultural Affairs* (2001) 107 FCR 133[130]), no factor must be given greater weight than the interests of the child.'

5.113 But how should the children's Art 8 rights be identified; for unquestionably such rights are in issue? Once they are defined, how should any relevant interference be categorised and justified? In *H(H)* Lord Kerr suggests a 'sequencing' of assessment of the infringement of a child's rights:

> '[144] ... This calls for a sequencing of, first, consideration of the importance to be attached to the children's rights (by obtaining a clear-sighted understanding of their nature), then an assessment of the degree of interference and finally addressing the question whether extradition justifies the interference....'

---

130 In *Wan* the Australian court had said: 'Provided that the tribunal did not treat any other consideration as inherently more significant than the best interests of Mr Wan's children, it was entitled to conclude, after a proper consideration of the evidence and other material before it, that the strength of other considerations outweighed the best interests of the children. However, it was required to identify what the best interests of Mr Wan's children required with respect to the exercise of its discretion and then to assess whether the strength of any other consideration, or the cumulative effect of other considerations, outweighed the consideration of the best interests of the children understood as a primary consideration.'

'Sequencing' of children's rights

5.114 Lord Kerr therefore proposed that, once the child or children concerned have been identified by the court or other process, as relevant to the court's decision, assessment a child's rights (including those to privacy and confidentiality) should be dealt with in a 'logical progression':

> '[144] … As a matter of logical progression, therefore, one must first recognise the interference and then consider whether the interference is justified. This calls for a sequencing of, first, consideration of the importance to be attached to the children's rights (by obtaining a clear-sighted understanding of their nature), then an assessment of the degree of interference and finally addressing the question whether extradition justifies the interference. This is not merely a mechanistic or slavishly technical approach to the order in which the various considerations require to be evaluated. It accords proper prominence to the matter of the children's interests. It also ensures a structured approach to the application of article 8.'

5.115 This provides a structured approach to the application of Art 8 to a child's rights, and proceeds as follows:

(1) First, the court must ask the question: has there been (or is there proposed to be) any interference with the Art 8 rights of the child?

(2) If so, what is the nature of the child's rights engaged?

(3) What is the importance of those rights, relative to other rights engaged by the particular proceedings?

(4) What is the degree of interference with the child's Art 8 rights (and see per Lord Steyn pointed out in *Re S*, (at §[25]), it is 'necessary to measure the nature of the impact … on the child' of what is in prospect)?

(5) Whether the action proposed justifies interference with the rights engaged? In *H(H)* the proposal was that a parent should be extradited, and the court must consider in relation to a child, whether and to what extent the right to family life of the child was justifiably interfered with.

Paramountcy, primacy, or no right to rank higher

5.116 In *H(H)* Lady Hale says the 'best interests [of children] are a primary consideration, although not always the only primary consideration and not necessarily the paramount consideration'.[131] In the same case Lord Kerr says that children's rights were such that no rights should rank higher. Perhaps the last word should go to the European Court in *Yousef*: that in a conflict between a child's rights and those of his or parents 'the child's rights must be the paramount consideration. If any balancing of interests is necessary, the interests of the child must prevail'.[132]

131 §[33].

132 Quoted in full at 5.40.

6

THE CHILD AS A PARTY TO PROCEEDINGS

1 INTRODUCTION

Representation of children in civil proceedings

6.1 The general rule in civil proceedings is a child may only conduct proceedings through a litigation friend (as defined later); but the court may order that a child be permitted to conduct the proceedings alone. In family proceedings, especially in children proceedings, the position is more complex where the child is of understanding and treated by a lawyer or by the courts as of sufficient age to conduct the proceedings without a litigation friend.

6.2 This chapter seeks to explain the varying circumstance in which a child may be represented in children proceedings, and especially where the child is considered to be of 'understanding' and therefor or taking part with representation, or alone, in the case and its presentation. The chapter proceeds as follows:

- **Part 2** explains the structure of the law on child representation: what form that representation takes; the procedure by which representation is set up under *Children's Act 1989* (*CA 1989*) and Family Procedure Rules 2010 (FPR 2010); and the legal form which the representation takes and by whom (including the Official Solicitor) represents the child.
- **Part 3** looks in more detail at those who represent and the way in which FPR 2010 defines the way they operate: the children's guardian under FPR 2010, rr 16.3 and 16.20; the guardian under r 16.4; the role of the litigation friend; the solicitor for the child; and the solicitor in specified proceedings (ie *CA 1989*[1] public law proceedings).
- **Part 4** concentrates on assessment of a child's 'understanding' which can be a crucial component in deciding what part a child may take in proceedings; and at the procedural contexts in which 'understanding' may arise; the application by a mature child in proceedings; and a child's application to join in proceedings.
- **Part 5** considers briefly children in civil (ie non-family) proceedings.

1 *CA 1989, s 41(6)*, defined at 6.12.

- **Part 6** explains legal aid for children and its availability in various types of public law (including special *Children Act 1989* cases) and private law proceedings; with a worked example showing how the different types of legal aid and public law children proceedings and representation work.

Age, understanding and maturity

6.3 An important element in all this is the extent to which a child is of age and understanding,[2] or age and maturity;[3] and who, according to context, is responsible for assessing this. The question of age and maturity has been considered in the context of a child's views has been considered in **Chapter 3**.[4] Assessment of understanding where it is a matter of a child being represented will be explained in this chapter.

6.4 Though a child is defined as 'a person under 18' it will be recalled that a 'child' of 16 and 17 can consent to medical treatment.[5] This must surely provide a basis in the vast majority of cases for a child to be treated as entitled to proceed alone as a litigant in person (subject to the ability actually to undertake the work) or to instruct a lawyer, more or less as of right, in his/her own proceedings.

Representation of children under FPR 2010, Part 16

6.5 As explained in the introduction to this chapter[6] this part will break down the subject of the law on child representation into: procedure, the importance of a child's understanding in relation to the proceedings, who may represent and who are parties to the proceedings. The law in relation to representation of children in family proceedings is a mixture of common law, statute and rules (supported by practice direction and case law). Access to it, and its interpretation, is not straightforward.

6.6 For a litigant in person, especially where that litigant may be a child (as may prove to be the case, where legal aid is not always available[7]) – as will be seen – the law is confused; or 'complex' as it was termed by Black LJ in a 2016 case.[8] That said at least family law does not – as does Civil Procedure Rules 1998 (CPR 1998), Pt 21 – include in the same rule provisions for children and for protected parties (ie those under *Mental Capacity Act 2005* who lack capacity: those who lack capacity are dealt with in FPR 2010, Pt 15 (representation of protected parties)). Provisions for children stand alone in FPR 2010, Pt 16 (representation of children

2 *CA 1989, s 1(3)(a)*; FPR 2010, r 16.6(3)(b)(i).

3 United Nations Convention on the Rights of the Child 1989, Art 24; Charter of Fundamental Rights of the European Union (2000/C 364/01) Art 12.

4 See especially at Part 5.

5 *Family Law Reform Act 1969*, s 8, which is set out at 2.6.

6 See 6.2.

7 See Part 7. W in *Re W* (below) was only represented because her lawyers acted pro bono.

8 *Re W (A Child) (Care Proceedings: Child's Representation) Practice Note* [2016] EWCA Civ 1051, [2017] 1 WLR 1027 at §[18].

and reports in proceedings involving children). Part 16 aims to bring together the main procedural provisions for children acting alone or represented – by guardian, litigation friend or lawyer – in family proceedings.

2 STRUCTURE OF LAW ON CHILD REPRESENTATION

Representation of a child

Who may represent a child

6.7 The individuals who may represent a child are summarised in this part. Their role and how they act in relation to a child will be explained in **Part 3**. Representation of a child, whether as legal representation, by a court officer, or by others on behalf of the child, in family proceedings is by a variety of individuals. Their precise role may alter slightly according to the context in which they assist, 'safeguard his [or her] interests'[9] or represent the child entitled respectively.

6.8 The individuals who may represent a child, as defined by *CA 1989, s 41* and FPR 2010 (mostly Pt 16), are defined as follows:

- The term 'children's guardian' is defined by FPR 2010, r 2.3(1) by reference to the guardian's appointment under FPR 2010, rr 16.3 or 16.4.[10] The term is not defined by *CA 1989*; and it must not be confused with a 'guardian of a child' (*CA 1989, ss 5* and *105(1)*: ie a person who mostly takes on responsibility for a child following a parent's, or parents', death*). CA 1989, s 41(1)*[11] avoids use of the term 'guardian', but says that a child will have appointed to represent him/her[12] an 'officer of the Service[13] or a Welsh family proceedings officer[14]' in 'specified proceedings' (ie care and related public law proceedings[15]) and adoption proceedings.[16] More information as to the guardian's role can be found in rr 16.3 and 16.16, as explained below.[17]
- 'litigation friend' – is defined by FPR 2010, r 2.1(1); and, in relation to a child, 'has the meaning given... by Part 16', where it is not defined. This therefore still begs the question. Rule 16.5 requires a child to have a litigation friend to conduct proceedings (unless r 16.6[18] applies) and as set out in Ch 5 of Pt 16.[19] A 'litigation friend' need not have a professional standing, as will be explained below.[20]

9 *CA 1989, s 41(1).*
10 See further 6.37 and 6.46.
11 The form of words used in s 41(1) is repeated in FPR 2010, r 16.17.
12 See further 6.39.
13 As defined by *Criminal Justice and Court Services Act 2000* s 12 per *CA 1989, s 105(1)*; and see 6.39.
14 As defined by *Children Act 2004, s 35*: *CA 1989, s 105(1).*
15 As further explained at 6.12.
16 FPR 2010, r 16.3(1).
17 See further 6.37.
18 See 6.56.
19 See 6.54.
20 See 6.50.

- 'solicitor' – appointment is dealt with by *CA 1989, s 41(3)* (in public law proceedings) or r 16.6 (as explained in **Part 3**, below).
- Official Solicitor (explained more fully below[21]).

Procedure for representation under children act 1989

Representation in 'specified proceedings'

6.9 The only statutory provisions which deal with representation of children (as opposed to for the ordering of a welfare report[22]) is in public law (known as 'specified') proceedings. The provision for this is set out at the end of *CA 1989, Pt IV* (care and supervision order proceedings) in s 41.

6.10 *Children Act 1989, s 41(1)–(5)* provides:

> **'41 Representation of child and of his interests in certain proceedings**
>
> (1) For the purpose of any specified proceedings, the court shall appoint an officer of the Service or a Welsh family proceedings officer for the child concerned unless satisfied that it is not necessary to do so in order to safeguard his interests.
>
> (2) The officer of the Service or a Welsh family proceedings officer shall –
>
> (a) be appointed in accordance with rules of court; and
>
> (b) be under a duty to safeguard the interests of the child in the manner prescribed by such rules.
>
> (3) Where –
>
> (a) the child concerned is not represented by a solicitor; and
>
> (b) any of the conditions mentioned in subsection (4) is satisfied,
>
> the court may appoint a solicitor to represent him.
>
> (4) The conditions are that –
>
> (a) no officer of the Service or Welsh family proceedings officer has been appointed for the child;
>
> (b) the child has sufficient understanding to instruct a solicitor and wishes to do so;
>
> (c) it appears to the court that it would be in the child's best interests for him to be represented by a solicitor.

21 See 6.26.
22 *CA 1989, s 7.*

(5) Any solicitor appointed under or by virtue of this section shall be appointed, and shall represent the child, in accordance with rules of court.'

6.11 The scheme of *CA 1989, s 41* is to require that 'for any specified proceedings[23] the court shall appoint an officer' (s 41(1))[24]) who is to 'safeguard the interests of the child [as] prescribed by the rules' (s 41(2)(b)).[25] *CA 1989, s 41(6)* defines 'specified proceedings' for which representation is to be available *(CA 1989, ss 41(6)*[26] and *(6)(i)*[27]). The court has a duty to appoint a children's guardian[28] in such proceedings, 'unless satisfied that it is not necessary to do so in order to safeguard [the child's] interests'.[29] Not to appoint in specified proceedings will be rare.[30]

---

23 For definition of 'specified proceedings' see n 26.

24 As explained further in relation to FPR 2010, r 16.4 at 6.46.

25 The meaning of 'safeguard interests' in this context is explained at 6.42.

26 'specified proceedings' are defined as:

'(a) on an application for a care order or supervision order [under CA 1989 Pt 4];

(b) in which the court has given a direction under section 37(1) [investigation as to child's circumstances] and has made, or is considering whether to make, an interim care order;

(c) on an application for the discharge of a care order or the variation or discharge of a supervision order;

(d) on an application under section 39(4) [consideration of substitution of supervision for care order];

(e) in which the court is considering whether to make a child arrangements order with respect to the living arrangements of a child who is the subject of a care order;

(f) with respect to contact between a child who is the subject of a care order and any other person;

(g) under [CA 1989] Part V [protection of children, including emergency protection] ;

(h) on an appeal against –

(i) the making of, or refusal to make, a care order, supervision order or any order under section 34 [variation, discharge etc of order];

(ii) the making of, or refusal to make, a child arrangements order with respect to the living arrangements of a child who is the subject of a care order; or

(iii) the variation or discharge of, or refusal of an application to vary or discharge, an order of a kind mentioned in sub-paragraph (i) or (ii);

(iv) the refusal of an application under section 39(4);

(v)the making of, or refusal to make, an order under Part V;

(hh) on an application for the making or revocation of a placement order (within the meaning of section 21 of the Adoption and Children Act 2002); or...'.

27 *CA 1989, s 41(6)* provides that in addition proceedings may be '(i) ... specified for the time being, for the purposes of this section, by rules of court'. FPR 2010 r 12.27(1) adds the following as 'specified proceedings' for the purposes of s 41(6)(i):

'(1) Proceedings for an order under any of the following provisions of the 1989 Act –

(a) a secure accommodation order under section 25;

(b) an order giving permission to change a child's surname or remove a child from the United Kingdom under section 33(7);

(c) an order permitting the local authority to arrange for any child in its care to live outside England and Wales under paragraph 19(1) of Schedule 2;

(d) the extension or further extension of a supervision order under paragraph 6(3) of Schedule 3;

(e) appeals against the determination of proceedings of a kind set out in sub-paragraphs (a) to (d);...'

28 As defined at 6.8 above.

29 *CA 1989, s 41(1)*; and see FPR 2010, r 16.3(1) set out at 6.21.

30 But see, eg, *Re J (Change of Name)* [1993] 1 FLR 699 where Booth J felt it was unnecessary to appoint a guardian where the local authority sought a change of name for a child in care.

Specified proceedings

6.12 However, it is important to identify whether the proceedings in question are or are not specified proceedings under *CA 1989*; and thus to determine whether a child must have a children's guardian (in accordance with *CA 1989, s 41(1)*); or whether the child must proceed with a children's guardian at all (FPR 2010, r 16.6[31]). For example, in *Re W (A Child) (Care Proceedings: Child's Representation) Practice Note*[32] the proceedings which started the case, were probably[33] by application to a judge by the local authority for a recovery order under *CA 1989, s 50*. An application under s 50 is not specified proceedings.[34] That is to say it is not in the list in *CA 1989, s 41(6)*; and the child the subject of the application is not a party to the proceedings, in any event,[35] unless formally joined by order of the court.

6.13 FPR 2010, r 16.4(1) could not apply, unless the court made the child a party. Despite this, the s 50 application in *Re W* resulted 'in the appointment of a children's guardian' says Black LJ,[36] with whom the child (FW) had anyway fallen out when the care order was made.

6.14 FW made a parallel, but subsequent, application under *CA 1989, s 39* for discharge of the original care order, for which she was entitled to apply (s 39(1)(b). Proceedings under s 39 are 'specified'.[37] At that point the court was entitled to ask, surely: is appointment of a children's guardian (with whom FW has already fallen out) 'necessary… to safe guard her interests'. This question must be seen alongside that FW was entitled to legal aid and could proceed with her own solicitor appointed – it might be hoped – by the court under s 41(5) and FPR 2010, r 16.29(2). This will be explained later.[38]

6.15 The terms of *CA 1989, s 41(1)* make it clear that the question of whether a children's guardian is 'necessary' requires a judicial assessment and a reasoned reply. This does not seem to have been attempted by the first instance judge in *Re W* so far as can be deduced from the report.

---

31 See 6.54.

32 [2016] EWCA Civ 1051, [2017] 1 WLR 1027. The case turned on her entitlement to instruct her own lawyer: the Court of Appeal said the rules said she could; though Black LJ assumed (without considering the statutory scheme as does Part 6 of this Ch) that the court had power to consider whether she 'should be allowed to instruct her own solicitor' (§[37]). With respect, that the court has this power is not clear from the 1989 Act or rules under it.

33 Black LJ could not be entirely clear on the chronology (see §[11]).

34 It is a public law children case, but not a special *Children Act 1989* case, for legal aid and as will be explained in Part 6.

35 See table to FPR 2010, r 12.3(1) and its reference to 'recovery order' *CA 1989, s 50*.

36 §[12].

37 *CA 1989, s 41(6)(d)*.

38 See 6.88 and Part 6 of this chapter.

Representation under the rules

Structure of Family Procedure Rules 2010, Part 16

6.16 FPR 2010, Pt 16 is entitled 'Representation of children and reports in children proceedings'. Its supporting practice direction, *PD16A*, deals with 'Representation of children'. It is divided into 14 'Chapters'. The first eight of these will be deal with here. The remainder deal mostly with court reporting, and enforcement of certain orders (outside the scope of this book). This part of this chapter will concentrate on those parts of Pt 16 and its practice direction which deal with representation of children, both by reference to the rule and to its statutory and case law background.

6.17 A short introductory rule (Ch 1, FPR 2010, r 16.2) tells the reader that Pt 16 is designed to set out when a child may be made a party to proceedings and that is contains 'special provisions' in children proceedings. Chapter 2 (consisting only of r 16.2) sets out the principle where the court may make a child a party to proceedings.

6.18 Chapter 3 deals with three sets of circumstance: (1) when a children's guardian or litigation friend may be appointed (r 16.3); (2) when a guardian is required where a child is, as the rules put it, a party to proceedings other than those – particularly 'specified proceedings' – set out in r 16.3(1) (r 16.4); and (3) where a litigation friend is required. Chapter 5 deals with appointment of, and the responsibilities of, the litigation friend.

6.19 Chapter 4 (only r 16.6) deals with circumstances in which a child does not need a guardian or litigation friend. Chapters 6 and 7 deal with proceedings where a children's guardian is appointed: first in proceedings, mostly specified proceedings, under r 16.3; and then in cases covered by r 16.4. Chapter 8 deals with the duties of a solicitor who is appointed to act for a child' or who is approached by a child to act.

6.20 This part will deal with how all this looks from the point of view of a child; and of those who may represent that child.

Representatives

When a children's guardian will be appointed

6.21 FPR 2010, r 16.3 deals with the appointment of a children's guardian, in public law proceedings, mostly specified proceedings. Under the heading: 'Appointment of a children's guardian in specified proceedings or proceedings to which Part 14[39] applies' r 16.3(1) states:

---

39 Part 14 deals with adoption which is outside the intended scope of this book.

'(1) Unless it is satisfied that it is not necessary to do so to safeguard the interests of the child, the court must appoint a children's guardian for a child who is –

(a) the subject of; and

(b) a party to,

proceedings –

(i) which are specified proceedings; or

(ii) to which Part 14 applies.

(2) At any stage in the proceedings –

(a) a party may apply, without notice to the other parties unless the court directs otherwise, for the appointment of a children's guardian; or

(b) the court may of its own initiative appoint a children's guardian.'

6.22 Rule 16.3(1) restates *CA 1989, s 41(1)* for appointment in specified proceedings. Rule 16(2) adds to s 41(1) that a party can apply, in such proceedings, for appointment of a guardian; and that the court can on its own initiative appoint a guardian.

Children's guardian in other proceedings

6.23 A children's guardian must be appointed, other than in proceedings covered by r 16.3(1) (ie mostly specified proceedings), in the following proceedings (r 16.4(1)):

'16.4(1) … [40] Without prejudice to rule … 16.6[41] the court must appoint a children's guardian for a child who is the subject of proceedings, which are not proceedings of a type referred to in rule 16.3(1), if –

(a) the child is an applicant in the proceedings;

(b) a provision in these rules provides for the child to be a party to the proceedings; or

(c) the court has made the child a party in accordance with rule 16.2.'

6.24 The circumstances in which a child is applicant or a child is joined as a party are considered in this part; though in practice r 16.4(1) is likely to be subsumed by the extent to which a child wishes and is able to conduct proceedings in his or her own right (r 16.6). The main significance of r 16.4(1) is in the extent to which it may be used to apply in Hague Convention proceedings, as explained below.

---

40 The rule excludes proceedings for a declaration of parentage (*Family Law Act 1986, s 55A*) and for consent to marry or to register a civil partnership; and is expressed to be 'without prejudice to r 16.6' (below).

41 The effects of r 16.6 is explained at 6.54.

Requirement for a litigation friend

6.25 FPR 2010, r 16.5 provides that a child must have a litigation friend where the child is '(a) a party to proceedings; but (b) [the child is] not the subject of those proceedings'. It will be very unusual for this provision to apply. For example, a child may be a witness in domestic abuse or in proceedings concerning the care of another child, though that child may not be the subject of the proceedings.[42] This does not make the child witness a party so that r 16.5(1) applies.

Official Solicitor

6.26 The Official Solicitor (full title: Official Solicitor to the Senior Court) is a hybrid: part solicitor who takes instructions from a client (a child client, in this case); part reporter for the court who provides evidence and information (eg as to a child's views), and only a small part children's guardian as envisaged by the officers (ie mostly former social workers) who fulfil this role under eg *CA 1989, s 41(1)*. As a solicitor, the Official Solicitor has a duty to represent the child's wishes, as does any other solicitor;[43] but as reporter to the court and akin to a CAFCASS officer his role under the rules is different. The ability of a mature child to differ from the Official Solicitor or to refuse representation by him is considered below.[44]

6.27 This is not the place to explain exactly when and by what means the Official Solicitor is appointed; and it is likely only to be rare in family proceedings. A recent definition of when the Official Solicitor may be appointed in family proceedings is provided by a practice note: *The Official Solicitor to the Senior Courts: appointment in family proceedings and proceedings under the inherent jurisdiction in relation to adults.*[45] Its second paragraph confirms its aims, which include acting as a litigation friend for 'a child in family proceedings';[46] though in the next paragraph the practice note says that appointment of the Official Solicitor occurs in only 'very exceptional circumstances'.[47]

6.28 The likelihood is that the Official Solicitor, if he is to act at all, will only do so as a 'last resort' (as the practice note terms it):

42 See, eg, *Re S (A Child)* [2017] EWCA Civ 44 (though the child 'A' was the subject of the proceedings); *Re S (Care Proceedings: Case Management)* [2016] EWCA Civ 83, [2017] 1 FLR 1476.

43 As explained at 6.53.

44 See 6.58.

45 See www.familylaw.co.uk/system/froala_assets/documents/1414/January_2017__Practice_Note__Official_Solicitor__Appointment_in_Family_Proceedings.pdf.

46 The practice note (below) says that 'It concerns' (para 2(a)): 'the appointment of the Official Solicitor as "litigation friend" of a "protected party" or child in family proceedings, where the Family Division of the High Court is being invited to exercise its inherent jurisdiction in relation to a vulnerable adult1 or where proceedings in relation to a child aged 16 or 17 are transferred into the Court of Protection'. It probably makes more sense with numbering or semi-colons or both viz '(1) the appointment of the Official Solicitor as "litigation friend" of (i) a "protected party" or (ii) a child in family proceedings; (2) where the Family Division .... to a vulnerable adult; or (3) where proceedings...'. That is to say, it makes it clear that the Family Court proceedings are not only in respect of a 'vulnerable adult'.

47 Since 1 April 2001 the Official Solicitor has not represented a child who is the subject of family proceedings (other than in very exceptional circumstances).

> '17 The Official Solicitor is the litigation friend of last resort. No person, including the Official Solicitor, can be appointed to act as litigation friend without their consent. The Official Solicitor will not accept appointment where there is another person who is suitable and willing to act as litigation friend. The Official Solicitor's criteria for consenting to act as litigation friend [include that] (c) the case is a last resort case.'

6.29 The Official Solicitor anticipates that it is CAFCASS which will deal with the substantial majority of reports: '3 For the avoidance of doubt [CAFCASS] has responsibilities in relation to a child in family proceedings in which their welfare is or may be in question'; and in support of this point they cite the *Criminal Justice and Court Services Act 2000, s 12.*[48] In practice this is likely to leave r 16.24(1)(b) largely redundant.

6.30 What is clear, though it could be much clearer, is that at common law the mature child has a choice as to whether she or he either accepts that the Official Solicitor be instructed; or that, if the Official Solicitor is appointed by the court, that that appointment continues, where the child wishes to act alone and has instructed her or his own lawyer.[49] This will be subject to the overriding entitlement of the court to direct appointment of a children's guardian or litigation friend separate from the child's solicitor. Waite LJ explained this in *re CT*[50] as follows:

> '... [The rules] must in my view be taken to reserve to the court the ultimate right to decide whether a child who comes before it as a party without a next friend or guardian has the necessary ability, having regard to his understanding, to instruct his solicitor.
>
> I would hope and expect that instances where a challenge is directed to a solicitor's view of his minor client's ability to instruct him will be rare, and that cases where the court felt bound to question such ability of its own motion would be rarer still. If and when such instances do arise, I would expect them to be resolved by a swift, pragmatic inquiry conducted in a manner which involved the minimum delay and the least possible distress to the child concerned....'

Children's guardian in Hague Convention proceedings

6.31 The Convention on the Civil Aspects of International Child Abduction 1980 ('Hague Convention') Art 13 includes:

> 'The judicial or administrative authority may also refuse to order the return of the child if it finds that the child objects to being returned and has attained an age and degree of maturity at which it is appropriate to take account of its views.'

---

48 Set out, as to s 12(1), at 6.39.

49 *Re CT (A Minor) (Wardship: Representation)* [1993] 2 FLR 278, sub nom *Re T (A Minor) (Child: Representation)* [1994] Fam 49, [1993] 3 WLR 602, CA.

50 [1993] 2 FLR 278 at 289.

6.32 Brussels IIA, Art 11.2 provides:

> '2 When applying Articles 12 and 13 of the 1980 Hague Convention, it shall be ensured that the child is given the opportunity to be heard during the proceedings unless this appears inappropriate having regard to his or her age or degree of maturity.'

6.33 These provisions led Lady Hale, in *Re D (Abduction: Rights of Custody)*[51] to state her opinion that in the future (opinions were handed down in November 2006) children should be heard 'far more frequently'.

> '[59] It follows that children should be heard far more frequently in Hague Convention cases than has been the practice hitherto. The only question is how this should be done. It is plainly not good enough to say that the abducting parent, with whom the child is living, can present the child's views to the court. If those views coincide with the views of the abducting parent, the court will either assume that they are not authentically the child's own or give them very little independent weight. There has to be some means of conveying them to the court independently of the abducting parent.'

6.34 That children should be 'heard' was one thing. How this was to be done was another. Lady Hale explained that there were three ways of doing this:

- 'Full scale legal representation';
- CAFCASS report (ie in accordance with FPR 2010, r 16.4);
- Meeting with the judge.

> '[60] … The most common method [she suggested] is, therefore, an interview with a CAFCASS officer, who is not only skilled and experienced in talking with children but also, if practising in the High Court, aware of the limited compass within which the child's views are relevant in Hague Convention cases. In most cases, this should be enough. In others, and especially where the child has asked to see the judge, it may also be necessary for the judge to hear the child. Only in a few cases will full scale legal representation be necessary. But whenever it seems likely that the child's views and interests may not be properly presented to the court, and in particular where there are legal arguments which the adult parties are not putting forward, then the child should be separately represented.'

6.35 This led Ryder LJ to speak, in *Re D (A Child) (International Recognition)*[52] of the obligation, in Hague Convention proceedings, being separate from any specific defence being raised under the Convention and for children to be involved in the decision-making process.[53] This is considered in detail in **Chapter 4**.[54]

51 [2006] UKHL 51, [2007] 1 FLR 961, considered also at 4.36.
52 [2016] EWCA Civ 12, [2016] 1 WLR 2469, [2016] 2 FLR 347.
53 §§[46] and [48].
54 See especially 4.28.

6.36 In *Re M (Abduction: Child's Objections: Appeal)* [2014] EWCA Civ 1519, [2016] 1 FLR 296, Black LJ made the point that where a Hague Convention Art 13 defence is raised, based on a child's objections, then the court must as far as it can 'ascertain…the views of the child concerned'.[55] In that case, she said, it would be wrong to order a return of a 14-year-old child 'without knowing [his] views on a return to his country of habitual residence'.[56]

3 REPRESENTATION UNDER FAMILY PROCEDURE RULES

Guardian appointed under rule 16.3 and 16.20

Family Procedure Rules 2010, 16.3 and the children's guardian

6.37 Chapter 6 set out the rules for children's guardian's appointed under r 16.3. FPR 2010, rr 16.17–16.19 deal with who is to be appointed as a children's guardian and how long their appointment will last. Chapter 6 at r 16.20 deals with the guardian's duties and 16.21 sets out the duties of the guardian if their views conflict with those of the child, who then instructs the solicitor independently (r 16.29(2)). In what follows, Ch 6 will be considered primarily from the point of view of a mature child, whose views may or may not coincide with the guardian's views.

6.38 Rule 16.20 provides as follows

> **'16.20 Powers and duties of the children's guardian**
>
> (1) The children's guardian is to act on behalf of the child upon the hearing of any application in proceedings to which this Chapter applies with the duty of safeguarding the interests of the child.
>
> (2) The children's guardian must also provide the court with such other assistance as it may require.
>
> (3) The children's guardian, when carrying out duties in relation to specified proceedings, other than placement proceedings, must have regard to the principle set out in section 1(2) and the matters set out in section 1(3)(a) to (f) of the 1989 Act as if for the word "court" in that section there were substituted the words "children's guardian".
>
> (4) The children's guardian, when carrying out duties in relation to proceedings to which Part 14 applies, must have regard to the principle set out in section 1(3) and the matters set out in section 1(4)(a) to (f) of the 2002 Act as if for the word 'court' in that section there were substituted the words "children's guardian".

55 At §[54].
56 §§[54] and [55].

(5) The children's guardian's duties must be exercised in accordance with Practice Direction 16A.

(6) A report to the court by the children's guardian is confidential.'

6.39 *CA 1989, s 41(2)(b)* provides that the duty of the children's guardian is to 'safeguard the interests of the child' as prescribed by FPR 2010. This is supplemented for CAFCASS officers by *Criminal Justice and Court Services Act 2000, s 12,* which defines the principal functions of CAFCASS:

'**12 Principal functions of the Service.**

(1) In respect of family proceedings in which the welfare of children is or may be in question, it is a function of the Service to—

(a) safeguard and promote the welfare of the children,

(b) give advice to any court about any application made to it in such proceedings,

(c) make provision for the children to be represented in such proceedings,

(d) provide information, advice and other support for the children and their families.'

6.40 Rule 16.20 prescribes the general manner in which this duty should be performed; and in particular refers to *PD16A,* in this case to Part 4 (paras 6.1–6.10). The particular duties which relate directly to representation of the child by the guardian are paras 6.2 and 6.4 (the remainder of the practice direction deals with attendance at court; filing of reports and inspection of records):

'6.2 The children's guardian must –

(a) appoint a solicitor for the child unless a solicitor has already been appointed;

(b) give such advice to the child as is appropriate having regard to that child's understanding; and

(c) where appropriate instruct the solicitor representing the child on all matters relevant to the interests of the child arising in the course of proceedings, including possibilities for appeal....

6.4 Where rule 16.21 (Where the child instructs a solicitor or conducts proceedings on the child's own behalf) applies, the duties set out in paragraph 6.2(a) and (c) do not apply.'

6.41 Rule 16.20(6) asserts that the report is confidential; but it is not said to whom. Is something beyond the confidentiality of all family proceedings (FPR 2010, r 27.10) intended; or is this to take the report – if the guardian so applies – into the realms of the report kept confidential in *Re K (Infants)*[57] so that information can

57 [1965] AC 201, sub nom *Official Solicitor to Supreme Court v K* [1963] 3 WLR 408, (1963) FLR Rep 520.

be passed privately by the guardian to the court? The provision is not supported by statute, so its vires within the rules are not clear. If it is intended to put material beyond the reach of the parties then it must be read with *Re D (Minors) (Adoption Reports: Confidentiality)*,[58] subsequent case law and the necessary European Convention 1950 balancing exercise (especially in relation to Art 6) in mind.[59]

Safeguarding a child's interests

6.42 To safeguard interests is a more objective duty, with duties which may conflict with what the child seeks. It may differ from the concept of 'representation' which applies in the case of a lawyer. Rule 16.21 therefore makes provision for the steps to be taken by the children's guardian if the plans of the guardian and what the child seeks conflict. In that situation the solicitor for the child continues to act and the guardian seeks directions from the court under r 16.21(2).

6.43 Rule 16.21 therefore provides as follows:

> '**16.21 Where the child instructs a solicitor or conducts proceedings on the child's own behalf**
>
> (1) Where it appears to the children's guardian that the child –
>
> (a) is instructing a solicitor direct; or
>
> (b) intends to conduct and is capable of conducting the proceedings on that child's own behalf,
>
> the children's guardian must inform the court of that fact.
>
> (2) Where paragraph (1) applies the children's guardian –
>
> (a) must perform such additional duties as the court may direct;
>
> (b) must take such part in the proceedings as the court may direct; and
>
> (c) may, with the permission of the court, have legal representation in the conduct of those duties.'

6.44 *CA 1989, s 41(2)* says that the duty of the children's guardian is to 'safeguard the interests of the child', which implies a more objective role than that of the solicitor for the mature child. The solicitor's duty is to advise, but ultimately to act on a client's instructions, whatever view the solicitor personally may take of those instructions.

6.45 Those instructions may diverge from the children's guardian's view of the way forward. The guardian then has an independent function. This was explained by Waite LJ in *Re CT (A Minor) (Wardship: Representation)*[60] in the following way:

58 [1996] AC 593, sub nom *Re D (Adoption Reports: Confidentiality)* [1995] 2 FLR 687.
59 As explained in Ch 11.
60 [1994] Fam 49 at 58, [1993] 2 FLR 278 at 280–281.

'Family proceedings are in general subject to the ordinary rules of disability, applying to all civil proceedings, which prevent a minor from bringing or defending any proceedings except by a next friend[61] or guardian ad litem (as the case may be) – RSC Ord 80[62] and Family Proceedings Rules 1991 r 9.2.[63] A next friend or guardian does not in those circumstances act merely as the child's representative. He has an independent function to perform, and must act in what he believes to be the minor's best interests, even if that should involve acting in contravention of the wishes of a minor who is old enough to articulate views of his own...'

Guardian appointed under rule 16.4

Family Procedure Rules 2010, r 16.4

6.46 FPR 2010, r 16.4 deals with proceedings which are not specified proceedings, and links to r 16.24 in terms of the duties of the representatives appointed. Appointment under r 16.4 would include for child abduction proceedings, and would also apply if a young (under 16) mother – though not the subject of care proceedings herself – was a party as parent in care proceedings, where her child was the subject of the local authority application.

6.47 The following may be appointed by order of the court to act as children's guardian by the proceedings covered by r 16.4[64]:

- An 'officer of the Service or a Welsh family proceedings officer' which seems to be much the same in intent as *CA 1989, s 41(1)*;
- The Official Solicitor; or
- 'A person other than the Official Solicitor', if they consent.

6.48 Appointment is by the court on application,[65] or on the court's own initiative.[66] In a provision which precisely mirrors that for appointment of a litigation friend under r 16.9 r 16.24(5) sets out a condition on appointment which – though it does not say so – can only be intended to apply to the category of person (rarely to be appointed in practice, surely?) referred to in the third bullet point above. The sub-rule provides:

> '(5) The court may not appoint a children's guardian under this rule unless it is satisfied that that person –
>
> (a) can fairly and competently conduct proceedings on behalf of the child;

61 Now 'litigation friend': see 6.8.

62 Now see CPR 1998, r 21.2; see Part 5.

63 This provision is now in FPR 2010, r 16.3.

64 FPR 2010, r 16.24(1).

65 *PD16A* paras 7.13–7.16, the effect of which is to make it necessary for the 'person other than the Official Solicitor' in fact to provide evidence for their application (para 7.15).

66 FPR 2010, r 16.24(2).

(b) has no interest adverse to that of the child; and

(c) subject to paragraph (6), undertakes to pay any costs which the child may be ordered to pay in relation to the proceedings, subject to any right that person may have to be repaid from the assets of the child.'

6.49 The powers and duties of the children's guardian under r 16.4 are specifically set out in *PD16A* para 7.8 and in effect impose of the children's guardian if 'any person other than the Official Solicitor' to act as r 16.24(5) anticipates:

Appointment of a litigation friend

When a child must proceed by a litigation friend

6.50 Chapter 5 deals with circumstances in which a child must have a litigation friend. It bears many similarities to FPR 2010, rr 15.3–15.8 (litigation friend for a protected party). The provisions will be rarely applicable in practice; and where a mature child is represented by a solicitor there is unlikely to be any need also for a litigation friend.

6.51 The duties of a litigation friend to act for the benefit of the child and on the child's behalf are summarised by *PD16A* Pt 2 as follows:

> '2.1 It is the duty of a litigation friend fairly and competently to conduct proceedings on behalf of the child. The litigation friend must have no interest in the proceedings adverse to that of the child and all steps and decisions the litigation friend takes in the proceedings must be taken for the benefit of the child.'

6.52 To act without a court order, the litigation friend must file a certificate which is prescribed by *PD16A* para 3.1.

Solicitor acting for a child

Solicitor's role in private law proceedings

6.53 From the introduction of *CA 1989* solicitors – as representatives for the child, not necessarily as advocates – have been given a particular role.[67] This role is developed by FPR 2010, r 16.29 (Chapter 8 for 'specified proceedings'), and, by default (since the rule is concerned with a child acting without a children's guardian or litigation friend, exclusively in a variety of private law proceedings (other than adoption)), by r 16.6 (Chapter 4). (Little is said about solicitor's representation of a child in *PD16A* the practice direction to FPR 2010, Pt 16.)

67 *CA 1989, s 41(3)* (court appointment of a solicitor); FPR 2010, r 16.29.

6.54 Rule 16.6 applies to the following proceedings and where the conditions in r 16.6(3) applies to the following:

> **'16.6 Circumstances in which a child does not need a children's guardian or litigation friend**
>
> (1) ... a child may conduct proceedings without a children's guardian or litigation friend where the proceedings are proceedings –
>
> (a) under the 1989 Act;
>
> (b) to which Part 11 (applications under Part 4A of the Family Law Act 1996 or Part 1 of Schedule 2 to the Female Genital Mutilation Act 2003) or Part 14 (applications in adoption, placement and related proceedings) of these rules apply;
>
> (c) relating to the exercise of the court's inherent jurisdiction with respect to children; or
>
> (d) under section 55A of the 1986 Act,
>
> and one of the conditions set out in paragraph (3) is satisfied....
>
> (3) The conditions referred to in paragraph (1) are that either –
>
> (a) the child has obtained the court's permission;[68] or
>
> (b) a solicitor –
>
> (i) considers that the child is able, having regard to the child's understanding, to give instructions in relation to the proceedings; and
>
> (ii) has accepted instructions from that child to act for that child in the proceedings and, if the proceedings have begun, the solicitor is already acting.'

6.55 Part 16.6 does not apply 'where the child is the subject of and a party to proceedings' which are specified proceedings (public law proceedings, where a children's guardian will in any event generally have been appointed) or adoption proceedings. In those proceedings, a children's guardian will be appointed under separate provisions.

Proceedings where r 16.6 applies

6.56 The remainder of r 16.6 deals with three situations:

- That a child wishes act alone, and thus to dispense with the involvement of a children's guardian or litigation friend (r 16.6(5)–(7);
- The power of the court to restore a children's guardian or litigation friend to act (r 16.6(8) and (10);

68 A child may seek permission from the court without giving notice to anyone: r 16.6(4) – 'An application for permission under paragraph (3)(a) may be made by the child without notice.'

- Rule 16.6(9) imposes a duty on a solicitor to report to the court if that solicitor considers that the child is no longer 'able, having regard to the child's understanding, to give instructions in relation to the proceedings'.

The remainder of r 16.6 reads as follows:

'(5) Where a child –

(a) has a litigation friend or children's guardian in proceedings to which this rule applies; and

(b) wishes to conduct the remaining stages of the proceedings without the litigation friend or children's guardian,

the child may apply to the court, on notice to the litigation friend or children's guardian, for permission for that purpose and for the removal of the litigation friend or children's guardian.

(6) The court will grant an application under paragraph (3)(a) or (5) if it considers that the child has sufficient understanding to conduct the proceedings concerned or proposed without a litigation friend or children's guardian.

(7) In exercising its powers under paragraph (6) the court may require the litigation friend or children's guardian to take such part in the proceedings as the court directs.

(8) The court may revoke any permission granted under paragraph (3)(a) where it considers that the child does not have sufficient understanding to participate as a party in the proceedings concerned without a litigation friend or children's guardian.

(9) Where a solicitor is acting for a child in proceedings without a litigation friend or children's guardian by virtue of paragraph (3)(b) and either of the conditions specified in paragraph (3)(b)(i) or (ii) cease to be fulfilled, the solicitor must inform the court immediately.

(10) Where –

(a) the court revokes any permission under paragraph (8); or

(b) either of the conditions specified in paragraph (3)(b)(i) or (ii) is no longer fulfilled,

the court may, if it considers it necessary in order to protect the interests of the child concerned, appoint a person to be that child's litigation friend or children's guardian.'

6.57 The duty under r 16.6(9) said to be imposed by this sub-rule on solicitors is controversial. It imposes a duty on the solicitor to inform the court which is not backed by statutory provision; and which appears to go beyond the solicitor's duty of confidentiality[69] to his or her child client. To explain why a solicitor – not any

69 As explained further at 8.25.

other advocate who represents the child – takes a view of a child's 'understanding' in this context may also involve breach the client's right to advice privilege.[70]

Solicitor in specified proceedings

Solicitor representation on issue of public law proceedings

6.58 On issue of public law proceedings, a child may have a solicitor or the court may appoint one.[71] Nominally, r 16.29 deals only with court appointment or where the children's guardian appoints a child's lawyer; but the commentary here on r 16.29 and the duties of a child's solicitor are intended to include reference to solicitors on the court record for any child, however they were retained or appointed.

6.59 FPR 2010, Ch 8 is entitled: 'Duties of solicitor acting for the child'. It comprises of r 16.29 which deals with four main aspects of the public law procedural scheme where a solicitor is appointed by the court or by the children's guardian under *PD16A*:

- Where a solicitor acts in accordance with instructions form the children's guardian: r 16.29(1).
- Where a solicitor considers the child has the maturity to give instructions, acts on the child's instructions: r 16.29(2), (3) and (5).
- How a solicitor should proceed where no children's guardian has been appointed r 16.29(4).
- Termination on application by a child to the court of a solicitor's appointment (a) by the child r 16.29(7); and (b) by the children's guardian r 16.29(8).

6.60 FPR 2010, r 16.29 provides as follows.

> '**16.29 Solicitor for child**[72]
>
> (1) Subject to paragraphs (2) and (4), a solicitor appointed –
>
> (a) under section 41(3) of the 1989 Act; or
>
> (b) by the children's guardian in accordance with the Practice Direction 16A,
>
> must represent the child in accordance with instructions received from the children's guardian.
>
> (2) If a solicitor appointed as mentioned in paragraph (1) considers, having taken into account the matters referred to in paragraph (3), that the child –

---

70 For a summary of advice privilege see 9.15.

71 *CA 1989, s 41(3)*; and see 6.10 for the text of s 41.

72 Paras (6), (9) and (10) relate to administrative matters in relation to appointment and service of documents.

(a) wishes to give instructions which conflict with those of the children's guardian; and

(b) is able, having regard to the child's understanding, to give such instructions on the child's own behalf,

the solicitor must conduct the proceedings in accordance with instructions received from the child.

(3) The matters the solicitor must take into account for the purposes of paragraph (2) are –

(a) the views of the children's guardian; and

(b) any direction given by the court to the children's guardian concerning the part to be taken by the children's guardian in the proceedings.

(4) Where –

(a) no children's guardian has been appointed; and

(b) the condition in section 41(4)(b) of the 1989 Act is satisfied,

a solicitor appointed under section 41(3) of the 1989 Act must represent the child in accordance with instructions received from the child.

(5) Where a solicitor appointed as mentioned in paragraph (1) receives no instructions under paragraphs (1), (2) or (4), the solicitor must represent the child in furtherance of the best interests of the child....

(7) Where the child wishes an appointment of a solicitor –

(a) under section 41(3) of the 1989 Act; or

(b) by the children's guardian in accordance with the Practice Direction 16A,

to be terminated –

(i) the child may apply to the court for an order terminating the appointment; and

(ii) the solicitor and the children's guardian will be given an opportunity to make representations.

(8) Where the children's guardian wishes an appointment of a solicitor under section 41(3) of the 1989 Act to be terminated –

(a) the children's guardian may apply to the court for an order terminating the appointment; and

(b) the solicitor and, if of sufficient understanding, the child, will be given an opportunity to make representations.'

6.61 Rule 16.29(2) is central to the question of whether a child can instruct a lawyer separately in any case where a children's guardian has been appointed. It turns on what is meant by a solicitor's assessment of a child's understanding; and must be considered separately later in this chapter.

6.62 If the child's understanding is such that the solicitor takes the view he or she can continue to act, then the solicitor conducts the proceedings in accordance 'with instructions received from the child', and following such professional practice rules as may apply in the circumstances of the case (including as to confidentiality, duty to the court and so on).

4 CHILD'S UNDERSTANDING AND REPRESENTATION

Contexts of child's 'understanding'

Understanding and involvement in proceedings

6.63 The contexts in which a child's understanding is critical to their involvement in proceedings arise as follows:

(1) A child who wants to make a free-standing application, whether or not with representation (*CA 1989, s 10(8)*; eg *Re CT*[73]).

(2) A child who wants to join in proceedings: that is to make a separate application (with or without representation in existing proceedings) (eg *Cambra v Jones (Contempt Proceedings: Child Joined as Party)*[74]).

(3) Within existing private law proceedings, to dispense with a court-appointed guardian and proceed alone or represented by his/her own lawyer (eg *Mabon v Mabon*[75]).

(4) A child whose instructions to his or her instructed solicitor conflict with those of the children's guardian; and the child wants his or her part in the case to proceed on the child's instructions (FPR 2010, r 16.29(2)(a)).

(5) A child who wishes to pursue fresh applications alongside a care order made in earlier care proceedings and wants to instruct a solicitor where the child's views conflict, or are likely to conflict with the children's guardian (FPR 2010, r 16.29(2); *Re W (A Child) (Care Proceedings: Child's Representation) Practice Note* ('*Re W (Child's Representation)*').[76]

6.64 In each of these types of case the 'understanding' of the child determines whether he or she can instruct a lawyer who will proceed with the case on the child's instruction; or can apply to the court to proceed with a case as a party and in accordance with his or her wishes. Each instance starts from a relatively simple proposition – though one which is critical not just to the child's right to

73 *Re CT (A Minor) (Wardship: Representation)* [1993] 2 FLR 278, sub nom *Re T (A Minor) (Child: Representation)* [1994] Fam 49, [1993] 3 WLR 602, CA.
74 [2014] EWHC 913 (Fam), [2015] 1 FLR 263, Sir James Munby P; see further at 6.85.
75 [2005] EWCA Civ 634, [2005] Fam 366, [2005] 2 FLR 1011; see further at 6.81.
76 [2016] EWCA Civ 1051, [2017] 1 WLR 1027.

a fair trial, but in some instances, to whether the child has a trial at all (as in the case of *CA 1989, s 10(8)*): whether the child's understanding is such that a course of action should be available to the child. However, the rules which cover this are by no means as simple as they might be, as will be shown when *Re W (Child's Representation)* is considered.[77]

6.65 To illustrate the complexity which a child faces in knowing whether he or she may be represented or pursue a court application it is appropriate to quote from Black LJ on the 'complexity' of the representation scheme (see italicised passage below) in *Re W (Child's Representation)*, where she said:

> '[18] There was some divergence of view as to which precise part of [FPR 2010 Pt 16] should be the focus of the court's attention [to determine] whether or not FW was entitled to be separately represented. I should make clear that when I speak of FW being separately represented, this is a loose term not entirely reflecting *the complexity of the scheme under section 41 of the Children Act 1989 and [FPR 2010 Pt 16]*. What I seek to convey by it is a situation in which FW separates from the children's guardian appointed to represent her interests, and gives her own instructions to a solicitor, as occurred in the original care proceedings' (emphasis added)

Application for a child to issue proceedings

Child's application in family proceedings

6.66 From its introduction, *CA 1989* enabled a child, with permission ('leave') of the court,[78] to make a free-standing application for a private law order, and for a child to apply to be a party to proceedings which concern the child. *CA 1989, s 10(8)*, in the context of the powers of the court to make *CA 1989, s 8* orders (child arrangements orders) generally, provides as follows:

> '(8) Where the person applying for leave to make an application for a section 8 order is the child concerned, the court may only grant leave if it is satisfied that he has sufficient understanding to make the proposed application for the section 8 order.'

6.67 This section is accepted as meaning that a child may, in law, make an application for a private law order, as Waite LJ explained in *Re CT (A Minor) (Wardship: Representation)*:[79]

> 'An application for a residence order (or one of the other orders for which provision is made in s 8(1) of the Children Act) may be made by the child concerned himself, but only with the leave of the court. [CA 1989 s 10(8) set

77 At 6.88.

78 *CA 1989, s 10(8)*.

79 [1993] 2 FLR 278, sub nom *Re T (A Minor) (Child: Representation)* [1994] Fam 49, [1993] 3 WLR 602, CA at 58 and [1993] 2 FLR 280 respectively (Sir Thomas Bingham MR, Staughton and Waite LJJ).

out.] The court, in other words, must be judicially satisfied by appropriate evidence that the child has the necessary understanding....'

6.68 The grant of permission is dependant only on whether or not the court 'is satisfied that [the child] has sufficient understanding to make the proposed application'; but this requirement must be seen in the context of the logically prior provision (where it applies) set out in rules (ie with no express statutory basis). If a child is to proceed with an application, then it is necessary that one of the two conditions in FPR 2010, r 16.6(3)[80] apply:

'(3) ... that either –

(a) the child has obtained the court's permission;[81] or

(b) a solicitor –

(i) considers that the child is able, having regard to the child's understanding, to give instructions in relation to the proceedings; and

(ii) has accepted instructions from that child to act for that child in the proceedings and, if the proceedings have begun, the solicitor is already acting.'

6.69 In principle, at least, application for permission is to the High Court. *Practice Direction of 22 February 1993 (Children Act 1989 – Applications by Children)*[82] (which is assumed still to be in force) states:

'Under s10 of the Children Act 1989, the prior leave of the court is required in respect of applications by the child concerned for s8 orders (contact) prohibited steps, residence and specific issue orders).... Such applications raise issues which are more appropriate for determination in the High Court and should be transferred there for hearing.'

Assessment of understanding

6.70 FPR 2010, r 16.6(3)(b)(i) is not specific as to who is to assess a child's understanding and ability to give instructions; but this was considered by the Court of Appeal early on in the life of *CA 1989* in *Re CT*. The question was whether the 13-year-old, CT, could proceed with a free-standing application under *CA 1989, s 10(8)*; and whether the court could question her lawyer's understanding of her ability to give instructions.

6.71 Family Proceedings Rules 1991, r 9.2A was added to the then family proceedings rules, with effect from 1 April 1992.[83] *Re CT* was concerned with

80 The relevant paragraphs of FPR 2010, r 16.6 are set out at 6.54.

81 A child may seek permission from the court without giving notice to anyone: r 16.6(4) – 'An application for permission under paragraph (3)(a) may be made by the child without notice.'

82 [1993] 1 FLR 668.

83 Six months after the main rules came into operation.

r 9.2A(1) which enabled a child to pursue her own application or otherwise to be a party to proceedings in following terms exactly equivalent to r 16.6(3) (set out above).

6.72 Rule 9.2A(1)(a)(i) and its significance in relation to a solicitor acting for a child, was explained by the Court of Appeal in *Re CT*. CT, who was then 13, had been adopted in 1987. Problems arose and she was placed with a foster mother, at which point she re-established contact with her natural family. She wanted to live with them. She contacted a solicitor (DB) who considered her able to give instructions. She obtained leave to seek a residence order with her natural family without a litigation friend (as it would now be) per r 9.2A(1). Proceedings were transferred to the High Court. On the adoptive parents undertaking to apply for wardship, the Official Solicitor was given leave to appear on the child's behalf as her guardian ad litem, with leave to instruct a psychiatrist. CT's application was consolidated with the wardship proceedings. CT appealed: she wanted to be able to conduct her own proceedings, not through the Official Solicitor. Her appeal was allowed so that the Official Solicitor ceased to be instructed and DB's assessment of her understanding was treated as applicable to operation of r 9.2A(1).

Understanding of the child

6.73 Waite LJ explained that the normal way for a child to proceed would be by a guardian or next friend (now CPR 1998, r 21.2[84]); but that FPR 1991, r 9.2A had introduced an exception to that principle in certain specific instances.[85] He defined these as follows:

(1) Where the court has given leave at the outset for a minor to begin or defend proceedings without a next friend or guardian ad litem. Such leave is only to be granted if the court considers that 'the minor concerned has sufficient understanding to participate as a party in the proceedings… without a next friend or guardian ad litem' (r 9.2A(1)(a), (6)[86]).

(2) Where a minor has a next friend or guardian ad litem in proceedings that are already on foot and applies successfully for leave to prosecute or defend the remaining stages of the proceedings without a next friend or guardian ad litem. Leave for that purpose is only to be granted if the court reaches the same conclusion as in case (1) (r 9.2A(4),(6)[87]).

(3) Where a solicitor has accepted instructions from the minor to act in the proceedings, and where that solicitor 'considers that the minor is able, having regard to his understanding, to give instructions in relation to the proceedings' (r 9.2A(1)(b)(i),(ii)[88]).

---

84 Set out at 6.99.
85 [1993] 2 FLR 278 at 281.
86 Now FPR 2010, r 16.6(3)(a) and (6).
87 Now FPR 2010, r 16.6(5).
88 Now FPR 2010, r 16.6(3)(b).

6.74 Immediately after this categorisation of where a child might apply without children's guardian or litigation friend, Waite LJ explained the way in which 'understanding' applied in this and the context of *CA 1989, s 10(8)*:

> '3. *The child's 'understanding'*
>
> This is a factor expressly to be considered by the court when considering whether to grant leave to apply under s 10(8) of the Act, and also when considering whether to grant leave to initiate or continue proceedings without a next friend or guardian ad litem under cases (1) and (2) of 2 above. It is also a factor expressly to be construed by the solicitor in considering whether to accept instructions in case (3). No definition of "understanding" is attempted by the 1989 Act or the rules, but guidance was offered by this court in *Re S* (above)[89], where Sir Thomas Bingham MR said at p 444G: "Different children have differing levels of understanding at the same age. And understanding is not an absolute. It has to be assessed relatively to the issues in the proceedings. Where any sound judgment on these issues calls for insight and imagination which only maturity and experience can bring, both the court and the solicitor will be slow to conclude that the child's understanding is sufficient."...'

Court's assessment of understanding

6.75 Waite LJ concluded the previous passage by pointing out that one of the main issues in the *Re CT* appeal, was whether assessment of understanding 'is a matter for consideration by the court, or whether it is exclusively a matter for assessment by the solicitor who is deciding whether or not to accept instructions'.[90] The court had allowed CT's appeal to the extent of saying that she should not have been made a ward. But what of the judge's anxieties which had led to the wardship in the first place?

> 'The result of ruling out wardship is that the judge will be left, at any future hearings of the case, with the same anxieties that led him to explore means of imposing a guardian ad litem in the first place. I have stressed that there has not so far been any suggestion that Mr Burrows[91] is or may be incorrect in the view that he has formed, for the purpose of r 9.2A(1)(b)(i), that C is able, having regard to her understanding, to give instructions in relation to the proceedings. It seems to me, however, that it would be unhelpful to the judge – and for that matter to other judges who may find themselves confronted with a similar situation – simply to leave the matter there. A conclusion has to be reached on the question (to which I have already referred in passing) of who is to be the judge of the minor's ability to give instructions?'

---

89 *Re S (A Minor) (Independent Representation)* [1993] 2 FLR 437, CA.
90 [1993] 2 FLR 278 at 282.
91 Yes, 'DB' is the author.

6.76 The question on this aspect of the appeal was:

(1) Was it for the solicitor alone to define the child's understanding and thus to proceed alone; or

(2) Can the court on its own initiative 'or on the application of another party, to go behind the solicitor's view and examine for itself the state of the child's understanding and come to a conclusion which may differ from the view taken by the solicitor?'[92]

6.77 Waite LJ pointed out that the first course:

> '... would accord with the emancipated view taken by the law these days of children's rights of choice (exemplified by the decision in *Gillick v West Norfolk and Wisbech Area Health Authority* [1986] 1 AC 112, [1986] 1 FLR 224) to impute to the draftsman of FPR 1991 Rules a resolve to free from the constraints of representation involved in the appointment of a next friend or guardian ad litem any child who can satisfy a solicitor as to her ability and understanding.'

6.78 He preferred the second course; that in cases of doubt about a solicitor's assessment of a child's understanding the court would have 'the ultimate right to decide':[93]

> 'I would hope and expect that instances where a challenge is directed to a solicitor's view of his minor client's ability to instruct him will be rare, and that cases where the court felt bound to question such ability of its own motion would be rarer still. If and when such instances do arise, I would expect them to be resolved by a swift, pragmatic inquiry conducted in a manner which involved the minimum delay and the least possible distress to the child concerned. It would be very unsatisfactory if such issues themselves became the subject of detailed medical or other professional investigation....'

6.79 Sir Thomas Bingham based his conclusion, which was to the same effect as that of Waite LJ, on the duty of the court to promote a child's welfare:[94]

> '... That the solicitor's judgment is to be respected and given great weight, I do not doubt. Judges should be very slow to go behind or question the professional judgment of a responsible solicitor. But the judge's overriding duty is to promote the welfare of the child and if he is properly persuaded that it is necessary in order to protect the interests of the child that some proper person be appointed his or her next friend or guardian ad litem I do not think he is precluded from exercising his power under para (10) by the refusal of the child's solicitor to accept that the condition in para (1)(b)(i) is not, or is no longer, fulfilled. Cases must arise in which, for whatever reason,

---

92 [1993] 2 FLR 278 at 288.
93 [1993] 2 FLR 278 at 289.
94 [1993] 2 FLR 278 at 291.

solicitors will take an unsustainable view of a child's understanding, and in such a situation the judge should not be powerless.'

Child's application to join in children proceedings

Child joining in family proceedings

6.80 FPR 2010, r 12.3(3) enables the court to direct any person or body can be added or removed as a party. FPR 2010, r 12.12(2)(c) enables the court to deal with this as part of directions in children proceedings. Rule 12.3(3) is 'Subject to [FPR 2010 r] 16.2', which enables the court to make a child a party to proceedings 'if it considers it in the best interests of the child to do so';[95] though this provision does not apply to specified proceedings.[96]

6.81 In *Mabon v Mabon*[97] the Court of Appeal made an order in private law proceedings, that three children, whose views were not being independently represented by their children's guardian, be no longer represented by him. Parents of six children were engaged in residence order proceedings relating to the three older, boys aged 17, 15 and 13. A CAFCASS officer was appointed as the guardian of all six children, who were joined as parties. Following a fact-finding hearing the older children wanted to instruct a solicitor to represent them for the hearing to resolve where they should live. The judge refused to grant the application for separate representation (now under FPR 2010, r 16.6(5)).

6.82 Thorpe LJ explained how the courts must adapt and recognise a developing attitude to children's rights, their autonomy and to the court's obligations to comply with them:

> '[26] In my judgment, the rule is sufficiently widely framed to meet our obligations to comply with both Art 12 of the UN Convention and Art 8 of the European Convention, providing that judges correctly focus on the sufficiency of the child's understanding and, in measuring that sufficiency, reflect the extent to which, in the twenty-first century, there is a keener appreciation of the autonomy of the child and the child's consequential right to participate in decision-making processes that fundamentally affect his family life.'

6.83 In passages to which Black LJ drew particular attention in *Re W (A Child) (Care Proceedings: Child's Representation)*[98] Thorpe LJ continued by drawing attention to the need to balance the welfare of the child against the harm to a mature child which might arise 'from denying the child knowledge of and participation in the continuing proceedings'.[99] He concluded:

---

95 FPR 2010, r 16.2(1).
96 FPR 2010, r 16.2(2).
97 [2005] EWCA Civ 634, [2005] Fam 366, [2005] 2 FLR 1011 (Thorpe, Latham and Wall LJJ).
98 *Practice Note* [2016] EWCA Civ 1051, [2017] 1 WLR 1027, especially at [24] and [25].
99 §[29].

> '[32] In conclusion, this case provides a timely opportunity to recognise the growing acknowledgement of the autonomy and consequential rights of children, both nationally and internationally. The FPR are sufficiently robustly drawn to accommodate that shift. In individual cases, trial judges must equally acknowledge the shift when they make a proportionate judgment of the sufficiency of the child's understanding.'

6.84 In agreement with Thorpe LJ, Wall LJ commented that the guardian 'would be advancing to the judge' for the boys a case which was 'directly opposed to what the boys were actually saying'.[100] By refusing representation to the boys – including a 17-year-old – the first instance judge overlooked the need for them 'to emerge from the proceedings (whatever the result) with the knowledge that their position had been independently represented and their perspective fully advanced to the judge'.[101]

Child joined in proceedings

6.85 Joining of a child in committal proceedings arising from child abduction proceedings, of which the child J was the subject, was considered in *Cambra v Jones (Contempt Proceedings: Child Joined as Party)*[102] Sir James Munby P. Children had been abducted from Spain to Wales. The High Court required the mother (M) to return four of the children to Spain on a specific day, but two of them tried to run away on the day in question. They were found by the police, who contacted M. When she collected the children she told them they would not be returned to Spain. She did not return to Cardiff as the order required. Five days later M and the children were found by the police. Two of the children were returned to the father. He later made a further and more specific order, again requiring M to return the two older children to Spain. The deadline for compliance with that further order expired without either of the two children being returned. The father now sought the committal of M for breach of that order.

6.86 M denied that she was in contempt because, she argued, it had been impossible for her to compel the two older children to return to Spain. The eldest child (J) was now 16; the second child was 14. Shortly before the committal proceedings were due to be heard, J asked to be made a party to the committal proceedings; the committal hearing was therefore adjourned; and there was a hearing on this preliminary issue. The President joined the older child as a party to the committal proceedings. He held as follows:

> '[13] Jessica [the older girl] is, in the eyes of the law, a child, though she is, and no doubt sees herself as, a young woman. I must of course consider what is in her best interests. But I have to ask myself whether it can really be in her best interests to shut her out from participating in proceedings which, whether or not they engage her Art 8 European Convention rights,

100 Para [43].
101 Para [44].
102 [2014] EWHC 913 (Fam), [2015] 1 FLR 263.

> affect her very profoundly for all the reasons which she, and Mr Williams on her behalf, have articulated, and which she is so very anxious to be able to participate in....
>
> [14] Quite apart from that, there are, in my judgment, powerful arguments in favour of the view that the forensic process will be assisted by her participation as a party rather than as a mere witness. To adopt some words used by Lord Wilson of Culworth in *Re LC (Children) (Reunite International Child Abduction Centre Intervening)*, at para [54], Jessica's evidence "is evidence which, although the mother might have a valuable perspective on it, neither of the parents can give" and Jessica "has a standpoint incapable of being represented by either of the adult parties".'

Child joined in proceedings

6.87 Jessica was joined. Her advocate had cited FPR 2010, r 16.2(1) as the statutory basis for this. Not only was her evidence likely to be relevant; but it, and her standpoint, was such that it was unlikely to be represented by the adult parties. This comes back full circle to the point made by Briggs LJ of the seven-year old David in *Re D (A Child) (International Recognition)*;[103] and of the importance in law of the question of whether a child, even a seven-year-old, should be heard and should take some part in proceedings which were to have such 'very large implications' for him:

> '[108] ... I do regard the failure even to consider whether to give D an opportunity to be heard as fully deserving being described as a violation of a fundamental principle[104] of the procedure of our courts. Although some might regard the age of 7 as lying near the borderline above which the giving of such an opportunity might be regarded as routine, the very large implications for him of the decision sought by his father, namely a complete change in his main carer and a move to a country in which he had not lived since very soon after his birth, cried out for consideration of the question whether he should be heard, all the more so since the mother, who might have been supposed to be likely to put the case for preserving the status quo, appeared to be taking no part in the appeal.'

Child's application alongside an existing care order

The guardian and Re W (Child's Representation)

6.88 The guardian's duty is to 'safeguard the interests of the child in the manner prescribed by [FPR 2010]'.[105] The Court of Appeal explained this in *Re*

103 [2016] EWCA Civ 12, [2016] 1 WLR 2469, [2016] 2 FLR 347.
104 An explanation of the term 'fundamental principle' in this context is at 4.28.
105 *CA 1989, s 41(2)*.

W (A Child) (Care Proceedings: Child's Representation) Practice Note.[106] The scheme for care proceedings depends on the assumption that the court will appoint a lawyer in the original care proceedings.[107] However in *Re W* FW (the 'child' who was 16 at the time of the appeal) was subject to a care order due to what was seen as the excessive extent of parental control over her.

6.89 In the original care proceedings, FW had disagreed with the guardian (R); and the solicitor (G) continued to take instructions from R (this is surprising in itself: FPR 2010, r 16.29(2) says G should have acted on instructions from the child). FW instructed her own solicitor (D). Later FW left her foster carers and was staying at her grandmother's house. She was attending school regularly, but was thought to be still under influence from her parents. The local authority applied for a recovery order.[108]

6.90 FW wished to oppose the recovery order sought by the local authority. In addition, she made her own application for discharge of the care order. R was re-appointed as guardian. R appointed G. (The question of whether R had any business appointing a lawyer at this stage does not seem to have been considered in the Court of Appeal: see further below.[109]) G now acted under a fresh legal aid certificate. FW, it was thought, could not instruct her own lawyer. The court directed that G should instruct a psychiatrist to report on FW's competence and on her capacity[110] independently to 'instruct a solicitor and conduct the proceedings separately from the children's guardian' (FW preferred to revise for exams than to go to see the psychiatrist). D acted for FW again, without legal aid and free of charge. In FW's absence the judge made the recovery order and, at a later hearing, refused FW's application to discharge the care order. The judge did not allow her to be separately represented. FW appealed against this decision.

6.91 On the issue of representation, Black LJ said that the parties had 'ultimately agreed' that it was FPR 2010, r 16.29(3) which governed the issue of FW's representation. For these purposes – though it is aimed at the solicitor who takes instructions form the child who disagrees with the guardian (as FW had done when the order was originally made) – rr 16.29(3) and 16.29(7) apply.[111]

6.92 Black LJ continued:

> '[22] The parties agreed that FPR 2010, r 16.29(2) establishes the test for whether the child should be allowed to instruct his or her own solicitor in

106 [2016] EWCA Civ 1051, [2017] 1 WLR 1027.
107 *CA 1989, s 40(1).*
108 *CA 1989, s 50.*
109 See 6.116.
110 Of this exercise Tomlinson LJ commented: '[41]... The word 'capacity' is a legal term of art the precise meaning of which may elude many of full age and capacity. Similarly, it is wise to explain in clear terms that being required to consult a psychiatrist does not involve casting aspersions upon the child's mental health. Beyond ensuring that FW was supplied with a copy of the order, which was not helpfully worded in this regard the court here delegated to [G] the task of explaining by letter to FW the purpose of her meeting with Dr Butler....'.
111 Set out at 6.60.

> circumstances such as those which arose here. It is, in fact, directed to the position of the child's solicitor, being drafted in terms of what that solicitor considers to be the position but, as I shall set out, it also sets the standard that the court must apply when involved under r 16.29(7).
>
> [21] By virtue of FPR 2010, r 16.29(2), if the solicitor appointed on the child's behalf, by the guardian in accordance with PD 16A or the court under s 41(3) of the CA 1989, 'considers', taking into account the matters set out in r 16.29(3), that the child wishes to give instructions which conflict with the guardian's instructions and 'is able, having regard to the child's understanding, to give such instructions' on his or her own behalf, the solicitor must conduct the proceedings in accordance with the child's instructions not the guardian's....'

6.93 Black LJ concluded that the basis for deciding on representation in the context of a fresh application in the same care proceedings was by reference to r 16.9(2); and therefore in this case it depended on an assessment of 'whether FW was "able, having regard to [her] understanding", to give her own instructions.'[112] 'Understanding' in this context will be considered in the next part of this chapter.

Assessment of understanding: welfare and rights

6.94 The conflict between welfare as against the rights of a child – FW in this case – was highlighted in *Re W*. In his very short judgment Tomlinson LJ pointed out that the judge had 'confused welfare with understanding'.[113] He doubted that the court needed assistance in assessing the level of a child's 'understanding'. The question of FW's welfare did not come into question at the stage of FW and her instructions to a lawyer.

6.95 Early on in her judgment Black LJ had drawn attention to the fact that there is nothing to be found in the law as to the meaning of 'understanding', or as to when a child may be 'considered able to give instructions'; though she referred to *Mabon*[114] and cases cited there as being of assistance. In the central passage of her judgment Black LJ considered 'understanding'. 'Understanding' forms a key, not only to whether the court (or eg a doctor or other professional[115]) accepts what a child says in proceedings; but in the present context, it may be determinative of whether a child has representation. It is therefore appropriate to break down what Black LJ said in her paragraph [36] on the subject.

6.96 Black LJ looked next at the importance of separate representation, and in particular, of how it affected the legal aid position.[116] That the child's 'point of view' be represented. It may be noted, this is not seen from the point of view of

---

112 §[21].
113 §[40].
114 *Mabon v Mabon* [2005] EWCA Civ 634, [2005] Fam 366, [2005] 2 FLR 1011; and see 6.81.
115 See Ch 8.
116 See further Part 6 of this chapter on legal aid.

the rights of a child in FW's position or of those of a mature child to a fair trial of her case:[117]

> '[36] ... It is worth noting particularly that, given the public funding problems, the judge will have to be sure to take whatever steps are possible to ensure that the child's point of view in relation to separate representation is sufficiently before the court. The judge will expect to be guided by the guardian and by those solicitors who have formed a view as to whether they could accept instructions from the child....'

6.97 Black LJ had assumed from the outset of the passage in her judgement on understanding, that it was for the court to determine the issue of a child's understanding:

> '[36] ... Then it will be for the judge to form his or her own view on the material available at that stage in the proceedings, sometimes (but certainly not always) including expert opinion on the question of understanding (see *Re H (A Minor) (Care Proceedings: Child's Wishes)* [1993] 1 FLR 440, at 450[118]).'

6.98 So what influences a view of a child's understanding?

> '[36] ... Understanding can be affected by all sorts of things, including the age of the child, his or her intelligence, his or her emotional and/or psychological and/or psychiatric and/or physical state, language ability, influence etc. The child will obviously need to comprehend enough of what the case is about (without being expected to display too sophisticated an understanding) and must have the capacity to give his or her own coherent instructions, without being more than usually inconsistent.'

---

117 On a child's fair trial under European Convention 1950 jurisprudence and under EU law see Ch 7.

118 In *Re H (A Minor) (Care Proceedings: Child's Wishes)* [1993] 1 FLR 440, Thorpe J dismissed an appeal against a decision of Bexley Family Proceedings (Magistrates') Court six months after the coming into operation of CA 1989; and commented on the representation of a 16-year-old (at 448 and 450): 'I turn now to what seems to me the real point to this appeal. Was S properly represented? Was his case properly advocated in view of the widening gulf between the guardian ad litem's views and his wishes? The determination of that question seems to me to lie within rr 11 and 12 of the Family Proceedings Courts (Children Act 1989) Rules 1991. Rules 12(1)(a) [in similar terms to FPR 2010 r 16.29(1)] provides: "A solicitor appointed... shall represent the child... in accordance with instructions received from the guardian ad litem (unless the solicitor considers, having taken into account the views of the guardian ad litem and any direction of the court... that the child wishes to give instructions which conflict with those of the guardian and that he is able, having regard to his understanding, to give such instructions on his own behalf, in which case he shall conduct the proceedings in accordance with the instructions received from the child)..."'

> 'It seems to me [continued Thorpe LJ] that in these cases involving intelligent, articulate but disturbed children it is necessary for the court to apply [r 11] realistically to ensure that not only is the professional voice of the guardian heard through an advocate's presentation, but that also the wishes and feelings of the child, however limited the horizon, should be similarly presented. If there is any real question as to whether the child's emotional disturbance is so intense as to destroy the capacity to give coherent and consistent instructions, then I think that question should be the subject of specific expert opinion from the expert or experts who are already involved in the case.'

5 CHILD AND CIVIL PROCEEDINGS

Children's litigation friend in civil proceedings

6.99 Civil Procedure Rules 1998, r 21.2 requires that a child take proceedings in civil court by a litigation friend. The rule provides as follows:

> '21.2 Requirement for litigation friend in proceedings by or against children…
>
> (2) A child[119] must have a litigation friend to conduct proceedings on his behalf unless the court makes an order under paragraph (3).
>
> (3) The court may make an order permitting a child to conduct proceedings without a litigation friend.
>
> (4) An application for an order under paragraph (3) –
>
> (a) may be made by the child;
>
> (b) if the child already has a litigation friend, must be made on notice to the litigation friend; and
>
> (c) if the child has no litigation friend, may be made without notice.'

6.100 Formally a child must have a litigation friend to pursue an appeal in the Court of Appeal, where only CPR 1998 apply; but the court may 'regularise' that by ordering representation without a litigation friend.[120]

6.101 CPR 1998, r 21.4[121] defines a litigation friend as follows:

> '(3) …. a person may act as a litigation friend [without a court order] if he –
>
> (a) can fairly and competently conduct proceedings on behalf of the child or protected party;
>
> (b) has no interest adverse to that of the child or protected party; and
>
> (c) where the child or protected party is a claimant, undertakes to pay any costs which the child or patient may be ordered to pay in relation to the proceedings, subject to any right he may have to be repaid from the assets of the child or protected party.'

Care proceedings guardian cannot be litigation friend

6.102 A child's guardian in the care proceedings cannot be the same child's litigation friend under CPR 1998, r 21.2. This was considered by Cobb J *SW & TW (Human Rights Claim: Procedure)*[122].

119 A child for the purposes of CPR 1998 is a 'person under: CPR 1998, r 21.1(2)(b).

120 CPR 1998, r 21.2(3) and (4); and see, eg, *Re W (A Child) (Care Proceedings: Child's Representation) Practice Note* [2016] EWCA Civ 1051, [2017] 1 WLR 1027 at §[3] (this case is considered further at 6.88).

121 From which FPR 2010, rr 16.9(2) and 16.24(5) are derived.

122 [2017] EWHC 450 (Fam) at §§33–37. The judge's italics have been retained.

> '[33] Part 21 of the CPR 1998 sets out the "special provisions" which apply in relation to civil proceedings involving children and protected parties; it specifically provides that a child "must" have a litigation friend (CPR 1998 21.2(2)), unless the court (in defined circumstances, not relevant here) orders otherwise (CPR 1998 r 21.2(3)). The rules are clear that it is essential that the formalities are observed from the very earliest stage, as (see CPR 1998 21.3) no step can or should be taken in the proceedings until the child has a litigation friend appointed in accordance with r 21.6. A person may act as a litigation friend without court order provided that he/she can fulfil certain requirements, including the offering of an undertaking to pay any costs which the child may be ordered to pay in relation to the proceedings (rule 21.4(3)(c)). The Local Authority made a formal offer not to seek costs against the children here, but this was not of itself sufficient to overcome other insuperable obstacles to the appointment of Ms. O as litigation friend.'

6.103 Further, for a guardian to act in this way is advised against by *Guidance – the role of Cafcass in Human Rights Claims* (April 2016).[123] Further in *C v Bury Metropolitan BC*,[124] as Cobb J pointed out (adding his own emphasis) at [2] by the then President of the Family Division (Dame Elizabeth Butler-Sloss P):

> 'There is a jurisdictional difficulty for the guardian in making the human rights application for K, in that such an application does not appear to come within the duties of a guardian' (judge's underlining).

6.104 The court has a parallel power, if it has made an order under r 21.2(3), to re-appoint a litigation friend:

> '(5) Where –
>
> (a) the court has made an order under paragraph (3); and
>
> (b) it subsequently appears to the court that it is desirable for a litigation friend to conduct the proceedings on behalf of the child,
>
> the court may appoint a person to be the child's litigation friend.'

123 Per Cobb J: '[35] ... emphasises that the statutory functions of Cafcass (i.e. those covered by *section 12* of the *CJCSA 2000*) are confined to enabling Cafcass to act on behalf of a child in any "family proceedings" in which "the welfare of children ... is or may be in question". Quite apart from the fact that a *HRA 1998* application is not ‹family proceedings› (see above), Cafcass takes the view that a claim brought under the *HRA 1998* is not one in which the court is being asked to consider issues of welfare; a *HRA 1998* claim is concerned with declarations (and/or awards of damages) on the basis that a public authority has acted unlawfully in the exercise of their powers. The Guidance document goes on: «Cafcass cannot act as Litigation Friend in proceedings in which the welfare of the child is not in question, although it is within the scope of the guardian›s role to advise on pursuing a claim and if this is not resolved without making an application it must be the Official Solicitor (if there is no alternative) who should act for the child».'

124 [2002] EWHC 1438 (Fam) [2002] 2 FLR 868 per Dame Elizabeth Butler-Sloss P at §2.

6 LEGAL AID

Legal aid for children proceedings

Availability of legal aid

6.105 Legal aid for children proceedings is available in three main categories of case:

- Special *Children Act 1989* cases (non-merits non-means tested).
- Public law children cases (ie public law cases which are not special *Children Act 1989* cases), and
- General (mostly private law) children proceedings.

6.106 Provision of 'civil legal services' under the *Legal Aid Sentencing and Punishment of Offenders Act 2012* (*LASPOA 2012*) *s 9* (provision of legal aid for civil proceedings) normally depends on three factors:

- That legal aid is available for the proceedings in question as defined by *LASPOA 2012, Sch 1*. The effect of *LASPOA 2102* is to proscribe the forms of legal aid which might be available to parties to proceedings; and children (outside special *Children Act 1989* cases) are in no different position to other litigants.
- That the means of a legal aid applicant are below a certain level; and
- That the merits of the case (as defined by Civil Legal Aid (Merits Criteria) Regulations 2013) justify grant of legal aid.

6.107 For legal aid scheme purposes a 'child' is a person under 18; so that if a child applicant is under 18[125] – whatever may be anyone's or the court's view of the child's 'understanding' – a representative must complete application forms. Thus Civil Legal Aid (Procedure) Regulations 2012, reg 30(2) states:

> '(2) An application on behalf of a child must be made by—
>
> (a) a person who is, or proposes to be, the child's litigation friend, professional children's guardian or parental order reporter; or
>
> (b) the proposed provider if the application is made in relation to proceedings which the child may conduct without—
>
> (i) a children's guardian or litigation friend in accordance with rule 16.6 of the Family Procedure Rules 2010; or
>
> (ii) a litigation friend in accordance with rule 21.2 of the Civil Procedure Rules 1998.'

125 See, eg, reference to age in *LASPOA 2012, Sch 1, Pt 1, para 15(5)*; or at Civil Legal Aid (Procedure) Regulations 2012 re 2.

Special Children Act 1989 cases

6.108 Special *Children Act 1989* cases under Civil Legal Aid (Merits Criteria) Regulations 2013, reg 2 (interpretation regulation) are defined as:

> '"special Children Act 1989 case" means any matter described in paragraph 1(1)(a), (b) or (c) of Part 1 of Schedule 1 to the Act[126] (care, supervision and protection of children), to the extent that it relates to any of the following provisions of Children Act 1989—
>
> (a) section 25 (use of accommodation for restricting liberty), to the extent that the individual to whom civil legal services may be provided is the child who is or would be the subject of the order;
>
> (b) section 31 (care and supervision orders), to the extent that the individual to whom civil legal services may be provided is the child who is or would be the subject of the order, that child's parent or other person with parental responsibility for that child;
>
> (c) section 43 (child assessment orders), to the extent that the individual to whom civil legal services may be provided is the child who is or would be the subject of the order, that child's parent or other person with parental responsibility for that child;
>
> (d) section 44 (orders for emergency protection of children), to the extent that the individual to whom civil legal services may be provided is the child who is or would be the subject of the order, that child's parent or other person with parental responsibility for that child; or
>
> (e) section 45 (duration of emergency protection orders and other supplemental provisions)(12), to the extent that the individual to whom civil legal services may be provided is the child who is or would be the subject of the order, that child's parent or other person with parental responsibility for that child,
>
> but does not include appeals from final orders made under any of those provisions of the Children Act 1989...'

6.109 For the avoidance of doubt, the definition concludes with the provision, that the term 'special Children Act 1989 cases' does not apply to appeals from decisions in such cases.

---

126 Care, supervision and protection of children:
1(1) Civil legal services provided in relation to—
(a) orders under section 25 of the Children Act 1989 ("the 1989 Act") (secure accommodation);
(b) orders under Part 4 of the 1989 Act (care and supervision);
(c) orders under Part 5 of the 1989 Act (protection of children);

Merits and means tests: public law children proceedings

6.110 In the case of special *Children Act 1989* cases (defined below) and child abduction for the applicant in the UK there is no merits[127] and no means test.[128] The application of this to parties in special *Children Act 1989* cases is explained below. In the case of child abduction applications, the respondent parent will be subject to the usual means and merits test.[129] A child who is joined, or who applies to join in the High Court application, will be assessed within the terms of 'other forms of legal aid' (below).

6.111 As the list of special *Children Act 1989* cases shows, applicants for legal aid for special case legal aid are not only restricted by the types of case which qualify as 'special' (listed above), but are restricted to certain categories of case within that and to certain characteristic within each category. Thus:

- That in the case of the majority of the categories of case the concession on merits and means testing is limited to specific parties (who in practice will comprise the majority of those involved). These are (1) 'the child who is or would be the subject of the order, and [(2)] to that child's parent or other person with parental responsibility for that child'. Other carers, grand-parents or others who may be joined in the proceedings must apply as applicants for ordinary merits and means-tested legal aid.
- That it does not operate in the case of appeals against orders in special *Children Act 1989* cases: these are within the definition of public law children case.
- In the case of an application for secure accommodation (*CA 1989, s 25*) only an application for the child who is the subject of the application can be a special *Children Act 1989* case.

Public law children cases: legal aid

6.112 In the case of public law children cases there is a merits test which is less stringent than the normal test.[130] These cases are defined as:

127 Civil Legal Aid (Merits Criteria) Regulations 2013, reg 65.

128 Civil Legal Aid (Financial Resources and Payment for Services) Regulations 2013, reg 5 '(1) The following forms of civil legal services may be provided without a determination in respect of an individual's financial resources— ...(c)legal representation in a special Children Act 1989 case;... (h) legal representation in relation to any matter described in paragraph 17(1)(a) and (b) (EU and international agreements concerning children) of Part 1 of Schedule 1 to the Act, to the extent that the matter relates to an applicant under the 1980 European Convention on Child Custody or 1980 Hague Convention.

129 For an example of how this may work against a respondent parent see *Kinderis v Kineriene* [2013] EWHC 4139 (Fam), Holman J.

130 The extent to which the limitations of legal aid caused by a parent's slight excess over means entitlement in public law children cases (as defined by the legal aid scheme) was considered by Sir James Munby P in *Q v Q; Re B (A Child); Re C (A Child) (Practice Note)* [2014] EWFC 31, sub nom *Q v A; Re B; Re C (Private Law: Public Funding)* [2015] 1 FLR 324.

'"public law children case" means any matter which is described in either of the following paragraphs of Part 1 of Schedule 1 to the Act (civil legal services)—

(a) paragraph 1 (care, supervision and protection of children), to the extent that the matter is not a "special Children Act 1989 case"; or

(b) paragraph 9 (inherent jurisdiction of High Court in relation to children and vulnerable adults), to the extent that the matter relates to a child;...'

6.113 Examples of cases which fall outside the definition of special *Children Act 1989* cases but may be within the definition 'public law children cases' will include:

- Appeals against all special *Children Act 1989* cases orders, as appellant and respondent.
- Applications to discharge an order (*CA 1989, s 39*), by a child and other parties.
- Grandparent whose grandchild, or other relative of the child who, is involved in special *Children Act 1989* case proceedings.

Other forms of legal aid for children in family proceedings

6.114 For the second main category of legal aid case (described as 'General' above: ie not public law children cases) for which application might be made by a child, the application for legal aid is made on behalf of the child. That is, application must be by a children's guardian[131] (other than a CAFCASS guardian;[132] or application may be accepted from a child's solicitor, if the child acts alone. It is the child's means which determine eligibility, not those of the representative

6.115 In the case of children proceedings, whether civil proceedings, under *CA 1989* or otherwise in the family courts, civil legal services (legal aid) may be available (subject to merit and means) where children are parties to such proceedings. *LSPOA 2012* deals with this as follows:

'*Children who are parties to family proceedings*

15(1)Civil legal services provided to a child in relation to family proceedings—

(a) where the child is, or proposes to be, the applicant or respondent;

(b) where the child is made a party to the proceedings by a court under rule 16.2 of the Family Procedure Rules;

(c) where the child is a party to the proceedings and is conducting, or proposes to conduct, the proceedings without a children's guardian or litigation friend in accordance with rule 16.6 of the Family Procedure Rules.'

131 Civil Legal Aid (Procedure) Regulations 2012, s 30(2) set out at 6.107 above.
132 *SW & TW (Human Rights Claim: Procedure)* (above).

Legal aid and public law proceedings: an example

Recovery order not 'specified proceedings'

6.116 Finally an attempt will be made to show how *CA 1989, s 41*, FPR 2010, Pt 16 and legal aid provisions interact for the grant – or not – of a civil legal services certificate for a mature child. Loosely applied, the example will be based on such facts as are known of *Re W (A Child) (Care Proceedings: Child's Representation) Practice Note*.[133] However, as Black LJ records, the procedural history of the case 'is not as clear as it might be',[134] so facts will be imposed for the sake of the example which may not be correct. The child concerned will be called Fiona. She was 15 at the time of the events in question and was subject to a care order. She had returned to live with her parents. The local authority was unhappy with this arrangement and applied for a recovery order under *CA 1989, s 50*.

6.117 As mentioned above,[135] the application is not specified proceedings under *CA 1989, s 41(6)*, and – unless formally joined by the court – Fiona is not a party to the application.[136] There is therefore no basis in law that the court can appoint a children's guardian – whatever the provisions of *CA 1989, s 41* – since only a party to court proceedings can have a guardian. In *Re W* it appears FW was treated as a party (but this may be wrong: the report is unclear); and a children's guardian seems to have been appointed where there was no power in the court – even if the judge regarded it as 'necessary' – so to appoint.

Discharge of care order

6.118 Upon hearing of the application for a recovery order Fiona seeks legal advice and applies for a discharge of the care order. Her solicitor assesses her to be of sufficient understanding to be involved in her own right in the discharge application.[137] *CA 1989, s 39(1)(b)* gives the child a right to apply for discharge of a care order; and this does not expressly depend on age and understanding but will doubtless require the child to proceed by a litigation friend;[138] though this will be subject, surely, to what is said next about a children's guardian (the law is not clear). An application for discharge is 'specified proceedings'.[139] *CA 1989, s 41(1)* therefore applies: the court must consider whether it is 'necessary' to appoint a children's guardian.

6.119 In Fiona's case the court knows – or the local authority will have been able to tell the court – the following:

133 [2016] EWCA Civ 1051, [2017] 1 WLR 1027; the facts of the case are set out in outline at 6.88.
134 §[11].
135 See 6.12.
136 FPR 2010, r 12.3; and row 41 of the table to r 12.3.
137 On analogy with FPR 2010, r 16.29; and see *Re CT (A Minor) (Wardship: Representation)* [1993] 2 FLR 278, sub nom *Re T (A Minor) (Child: Representation)* [1994] Fam 49, [1993] 3 WLR 602, CA (above).
138 FPR 2010, Pt 16, Ch 5.
139 *CA 1989, s 41(6)(c)*.

- That Fiona has a solicitor who is on the court record on the care order discharge application.
- That Fiona had that solicitor when the care order was made and that there was a clear conflict between her and the children's guardian.

6.120 The court must consider judicially and give reasons for its decision as to whether, and if so why, it considers that a children's guardian should be appointed 'to safeguard [Fiona's] interests'.

6.121 There is no need for the court to appoint a solicitor[140] since the court knows Fiona already has one.

Legal aid for proceedings

6.122 Fiona, in this example, was not joined in the recovery order proceedings, so she was not a party. (It is not known whether FW was joined in the real case.) Fiona cannot therefore have legal aid in any form in relation to the recovery order application.

6.123 Fiona's discharge application is not a special *Children Act 1989* case;[141] so it is a 'public law children case'.[142] Fiona's application is therefore subject to a merits test. Her solicitor can apply for legal aid in her name, based on Fiona's own means (which in this case are nil). In *Re W* it is not known whether FW's lawyer applied for legal aid; but clearly had the lawyer appointed by the children's guardian applied it would not have been a legitimate application (unless FW had been formally joined in the recovery order proceedings) since FW was already represented by a solicitor.[143]

---

140 *CA 1989, s 41(3).*
141 See categories of special *Children Act 1989* cases at 6.108.
142 See 6.112.
143 *CA 1989, s 41(3)(a).*

7

CHILDREN'S RIGHTS: INTERNATIONAL LEGISLATION AND EU WITHDRAWAL

1 INTRODUCTION

Law and fundamental rights

7.1 This chapter will assume that children's rights and remedies operate on and apply under the following systems of law and definitions of rights:

- English common law and the children law statutory regime (mostly in *Children's Act 1989* (*CA 1989*)).
- Convention for the Protection of Human Rights and Fundamental Freedoms 1950 ('European Convention 1950') so far as it is incorporated into English law by the *Human Rights Act 1998* (*HRA 1998*).
- United Nations Convention on the Rights of the Child 1989 ('UN Convention').
- Convention on the Civil Aspects of International Child Abduction 1980 ('Hague Convention') as applied by *Child Abduction and Custody Act 1985*.
- Charter of Fundamental Rights of the European Union (2000/C 364/01) ('the EU Charter').
- Council Regulation (EC) No 2201/2003 of 27 November 2003 Concerning Jurisdiction and the Recognition and Enforcement of Judgments in Matrimonial Matters and in Matters of Parental Responsibility ('Brussels IIA').

7.2 Of these the last two will directly affect the rights of children living in the EU when the UK withdrawal goes ahead. At present the extent to which these effects will be felt is speculative. What this chapter seeks to do is to look at the rights which are now protected by European law and to suggest, briefly, what may happen to the extent that these rights cannot be reproduced in English law upon EU withdrawal (see consideration of *R (Miller & anor) v Secretary of State for Exiting the European Union*[1] ('*Miller*') later in this chapter).

1 [2017] UKSC 5, [2017] 2 WLR 583; and see further at 7.7.

7.3 A brief introduction to the European Union (Withdrawal) Bill is included in **Chapter 1**. In 'Providing a cross-border civil judicial cooperation framework (a future partnership paper) HM Government August 2017[2] refers to eg Council Regulation (EC) No 2201/2003 of 27 November (Brussels IIA); see **7.26**. This paper does not explain how the Government imagines it can secure, and enforce, co-operation from EU courts over, for example, children matters.

Children's European and international rights

7.4 Art 24 of the EU Charter gives rights to children which include that they be heard when decisions are to be made about them and that their views 'shall be taken into consideration on matters which concern them in accordance with their age and maturity'. Art 24(3) states that every child has the right to maintain a relationship 'with both… parents, unless that is contrary to his or her interests.' Accordingly, this chapter also looks at rights which are replicated by other conventions or charters. Children's rights will be looked at, particularly, in the contexts of Brussels IIA and the EU Charter, and these will be contrasted with the statutory and common law principles on which English law is based.

7.5 The question of survival of rights balanced by their loss will be considered here in the context of: first, the right of a child to have his/her 'views taken into consideration' (Art 24(1); and, secondly, 'the right [of a child] to maintain… a personal relationship and direct contact with both his or her parents'; and of the effect on children and their parents that the rights guaranteed by the Charter and of Brussels IIA no longer applying directly to the UK.

7.6 This chapter looks at children's rights as follows:

- **Part 2** considers the creation of rights in European and international legislation. It looks at the way the subject of rights was considered by the Supreme Court in *Miller* and explains the extent to which Parliamentary legislation is required to change fundamental rights, including those which affect children.
- **Part 3** looks at the EU and international legislation which affect children's rights, including the EU Charter, Brussels IIA and the United Nations Convention on the Rights of the Child 1989; and on their operation.
- **Part 4** deals with children's rights in operation under EU and international law in children cases in English courts.
- The chapter ends (**Part 5**) with brief reflections on application of international law and consequences of EU withdrawal.

2 www.gov.uk/government/uploads/system/uploads/attachment_data/file/639271/Providing_a_cross-border_civil_judicial_cooperation_framework.pdf.

2 INTERNATIONAL AND EUROPEAN LEGISLATION

European legislation: creation of rights

Miller, *rights and EU withdrawal*

7.7 *Miller* was decided at a hearing attended by all eleven of the Supreme Court justices, and was decided by a majority consisting of eight[3] ('the majority'). The main issue in the case concerned the ability of government ministers to exercise a prerogative power to withdraw from international treaties without parliamentary approval.[4] Further, to what extent may ministers change domestic law, other than by statute. The passage which defined this second strand of the case and which is of direct concern in this chapter was:

> '[5] … The second feature is that ministers are not normally entitled to exercise any power they might otherwise have if it results in a change in UK domestic law, unless statute, ie an Act of Parliament, so provides. The argument against the Secretary of State is that this principle prevents ministers withdrawing from the EU Treaties, until effectively authorised to do so by a statute.'

7.8 It is with the sources of law and consequent rights created by *European Communities Act 1972* (*ECA 1972*) and the UK's accession to what is now the European Union ('EU') with which this chapter is concerned. So far as rights are concerned, the question for the Supreme Court was: to what extent can a government by triggering steps to leave the EU (by giving notice under Treaty of European Union Art 50[5]) at the same time, and as a consequence of that, directly affect the rights of individuals. The majority in the Supreme Court held that the Government could not do this without parliamentary authority. This part looks at how the Supreme Court regarded rights in EU law generally; and the remainder of the chapter looks at how children's rights may ultimately be affected by EU withdrawal.

European Communities Act 1972: a 'source of law'

7.9 The effect of *ECA 1972* was, said the majority, that it set up a 'dynamic process' by which law was created:

> '[60] … It authorises a dynamic process by which, without further primary legislation (and, in some cases, even without any domestic legislation), EU

3 Lord Neuberger, Lady Hale, Lords Mance, Lord Kerr, Lord Clarke, Lord Wilson, Lord Sumption and Lord Hodge leaving Lord Reed, Lord Carnwath and Lord Hughes (who each gave separate judgments) in the minority.

4 §[5].

5 Treaty of European Union (TEU) Art 50 provides: "1 Any member state may decide to withdraw from the Union in accordance with its own constitutional requirements. 2 A member state which decides to withdraw shall notify the European Council of its intention....".

law not only becomes a source of UK law, but actually takes precedence over all domestic sources of UK law, including statutes. This may sound rather dry or technical to many people, but in constitutional terms the effect of the 1972 Act was unprecedented….'

7.10 The effect of *ECA 1972* and the European Legislation which followed was to create a new source of law enforceable in the UK: '… where EU law applies in the United Kingdom, it is the EU institutions which are the relevant source of that law'.[6] This can be seen, as will be explained,[7] in Brussels IIA and its operation and in the separate (though not directly applicable here) enforcement provisions of the Maintenance Regulation 2009.[8] The critical points of the effect of joining the EU and the rights which it created was as follows:

> '[62] The 1972 Act did two things which are relevant to these appeals. First, it provided that rights, duties and rules derived from EU law should apply in the United Kingdom as part of its domestic law. Secondly, it provided for a new constitutional process for making law in the United Kingdom. These things are closely related, but they are legally and conceptually distinct. The content of the rights, duties and rules introduced into our domestic law as a result of the 1972 Act is exclusively a question of EU law. However, the constitutional processes by which the law of the United Kingdom is made is exclusively a question of domestic law.'

7.11 Thus, so long as *ECA 1972* 'remains in force, its effect is to constitute EU law an independent and overriding source of domestic law'.[9] In effect *ECA 1972* delegates enforceable law-making powers to EU institutions. UK citizens are then bound by those laws.

Divisional court and rights

7.12 In *Miller* in the Divisional Court[10] the judge's explained three categories or rights which would be affected by EU withdrawal.[11] The Supreme Court explained this categorisation as follows:

> '[69] The Divisional Court concluded that, because ministers cannot claim prerogative powers to take an action which would result in a change in domestic law, it was not open to ministers to withdraw from the EU Treaties, and therefore to serve Notice, without authorisation in a statute. In that connection, the Divisional Court identified three categories of right:
>
> (1) Rights capable of replication in UK law;

6 *Miller* at §[61].
7 See 7.26.
8 Council Regulation (EC) No 4/2009 ('Maintenance Regulation').
9 §[65].
10 *R (Miller & Anor) v The Secretary of State for Exiting the European Union* [2016] EWHC 2768 (Admin), [2017] 2 WLR 583.
11 At §[57] *et seq.*

(2) Rights derived by UK citizens from EU law in other member states;

(3) Rights of participation in EU institutions that could not be replicated in UK law.'

7.13 Of these the Divisional Court identified 'category (ii)' rights as follows:

> '[60] The second category of rights is those enjoyed by British citizens and companies in relation to their activities in other Member States, as provided for by EU law, for example pursuant to rights of free movement of persons and of capital and rights of freedom of establishment ("category (ii) rights"). If a British citizen resides in another Member State pursuant to EU rights of free movement, EU law requires the authorities and courts of that Member State to respect and give effect to those rights. It also prohibits the authorities in the United Kingdom from placing impediments in the way of the exercise of such rights.'

7.14 The Supreme Court refined this category of right by referring it specifically in the following terms:

> '[71] The second category may appear to be irrelevant for present purposes as the rights within it arise from the incorporation of EU law into the law of other member states, and not from UK legislation. However, some rights falling within one category may be closely linked with rights falling within another category. For example, the rights under Council Regulation (EC) No 2201/2003, *concerning jurisdiction and the recognition and enforcement of judgments in matrimonial matters and the matters of parental responsibility* (known as "Brussels II Revised" [ie 'Brussels IIA']), would be undermined if a domestic judgment governing the residence of a child could not be enforced outside the UK.' (italics in judgment)

7.15 As can be seen, Brussels IIA is specifically identified amongst the EU instruments, loss of which will directly impact those affected by it. Amongst those affected will be children and their rights under EU legislation, as will be explained later.[12]

Sources of law and European Union

7.16 In terms of UK law and rights, what are its sources of law as defined and provided for by EU legislation; and what will be the effect of EU withdrawal on those sources of law? The majority in the Supreme Court defined the ceasing of EU law as a source of law as follows:

> '[80] One of the most fundamental functions of the constitution of any state is to identify the sources of its law.... The 1972 Act effectively constitutes EU law as an entirely new, independent and overriding source of domestic

12 See 7.26.

law, and the Court of Justice as a source of binding judicial decisions about its meaning.... Upon the United Kingdom's withdrawal from the European Union, EU law will cease to be a source of domestic law for the future (even if the Great Repeal Bill provides that some legal rules derived from it should remain in force or continue to apply to accrued rights and liabilities), decisions of the Court of Justice will (again depending on the precise terms of the Great Repeal Bill) be of no more than persuasive authority, and there will be no further references to that court from UK courts. Even those legal rules derived from EU law and transposed into UK law by domestic legislation will have a different status. They will no longer be paramount, but will be open to domestic repeal or amendment in ways that may be inconsistent with EU law.'

7.17 Just as the EU as a source of law will go, so too will references to the EU Court of Justice as arbiter and reviewer of decisions in the areas governed by EU law. The result of this was that in terms of rights, in particular, the Divisional Court had been right to hold that changes to be effected to domestic rights would form a separate justification for the conclusion that prerogative powers would not be enough to operate Art 50.[13]

Fundamental rights and law reform

Reform only by Parliament by express words

7.18 Fundamental rights can only be changed by Parliament by express words, and not by general words. The majority recalled Lord Hoffman in *R v Secretary of State for the Home Department, exp Simms*:[14]

'[87] ... As Lord Hoffmann explained in *R v Secretary of State for the Home Department, Ex p Simms* [2000] 2 AC 115, 131, "the principle of legality means that Parliament must squarely confront what it is doing and accept the political cost", and so "fundamental rights cannot be overridden by general ... words" in a statute, "because there is too great a risk that the full implications of their unqualified meaning may have passed unnoticed in the democratic process". Had the Bill which became the 1972 Act spelled out that ministers would be free to withdraw the United Kingdom from the EU Treaties, the implications of what Parliament was being asked to endorse would have been clear, and the courts would have so decided...'

13 §[83].

14 [1999] UKHL 33, [2000] 2 AC 115, [1999] 3 WLR 328. *Exp Simms* was commented upon by the Divisional Court thus: '[83] ... Another example [of statutory interpretation], is the principle of legality, i.e. the presumption that Parliament does not intend to legislate in a way which would defeat fundamental human rights: see *R v Secretary of State for the Home Department, ex p. Pierson* [1998] AC 539 at 573G, 575B-G (Lord Browne-Wilkinson) and *R v Secretary of State for the Home Department, ex p. Simms* [2000] 2 AC 115, 131D-G (Lord Hoffmann).'

7.19 The *ECA 1972* had not '"squarely confronted" the notion' that it was giving ministers 'the far-reaching and anomalous right to use a treaty-making power to remove an important source of domestic law and important domestic rights'.[15]

7.20 EU treaties 'are a source of domestic law, and they are a source of domestic legal rights many of which are inextricably linked with domestic law from other sources'.[16] Two questions remain for children and their EU law rights, therefore: to what extent will any of these EU laws, and the rights which they import, be positively reproduced in domestic law; and to what extent may any rights be lost as reciprocal arrangements between UK and European courts are lost as a result of EU withdrawal? Attempts will be made in **Part 3** to answer these questions once children's rights under existing law and the present jurisdiction arrangements have been considered.

7.21 The present government answered the Supreme Court majority judgment by introducing a very short European Union (Notification of Withdrawal) Act[17] which received Royal Assent on 16 March 2017. Art 50 – notification of withdrawal – was triggered on 29 March 2017 so that the process of UK withdrawal from the EU formally then began. Meanwhile a government white paper has outlined plans for EU withdrawal,[18] since overtaken to an extent by an intervening General Election in early June 2017. Following that election, a short Queen's Speech in June 2017, introduced by the now minority Conservative government, which included:

> 'A bill will be introduced to repeal the European Communities Act and provide certainty for individuals and businesses. This will be complemented by legislation to ensure that the United Kingdom makes a success of Brexit, establishing new national policies on immigration, international sanctions, nuclear safeguards, agriculture, and fisheries.'

Rights which may be lost on EU withdrawal

7.22 Nothing was said of rights which may be lost on EU withdrawal. Eight bills to achieve this are understood to be required to secure withdrawal. The detail of those bills must be awaited.[19] The intended 'Repeal Bill'[20] is proposed as follows:[21]

---

15 §[87].

16 §[86].

17 See www.legislation.gov.uk/ukpga/2017/9/contents.

18 'The United Kingdom's exit from and new partnership with the European Union' (Cm 9417), February 2017 www.gov.uk/government/uploads/system/uploads/attachment_data/file/589191/The_United_Kingdoms_exit_from_and_partnership_with_the_EU_Web.pdf.

19 See briefing paper issued by the Prime Minister's Office on 21 June 2017: 'The Queen's Speech and associated background briefing, on the occasion of the opening of Parliament' – www.gov.uk/government/uploads/system/uploads/attachment_data/file/620838/Queens_speech_2017_background_notes.pdf.

20 Described as the 'Great Repeal Bill' by the Government lawyers in the Supreme Court in *Miller.*

21 Page 11 of briefing paper.

> '*Repeal Bill*
>
> This Bill will allow for a smooth and orderly transition as the UK leaves the EU, ensuring that, wherever practical, the same rules and laws apply after exit and therefore maximising certainty for individuals and businesses. The Bill will:
>
> - repeal the European Communities Act 1972 and convert EU law into UK law as we leave the EU;
> - create temporary powers for Parliament to make secondary legislation, enabling corrections to be made to the laws that do not operate appropriately once we have left the EU. It will also allow changes to be made to domestic law to reflect the content of any withdrawal agreement under Article 50;...
>
> The Bill does not put any constraints on the withdrawal agreement we will make with the EU and further legislation will be introduced to support such an agreement if and when required.'

7.23 This proposal in terms of an initial bill has now produced the European Union (Withdrawal) Bill as explained in **Chapter 1**. However, this bill does not provide the detail which, for example, children and their lawyers, need to know how the former EU law will survive, or not survive, following EU withdrawal.

3 RIGHTS CONVENTIONS AND LEGISLATION

EU Charter

7.24 The Charter of Fundamental Rights of the European Union (2000/C 364/01) (the EU Charter) is based on the principles that 'the peoples of Europe' plan to create 'ever closer union among them' whilst preserving their 'diversity of cultures and traditions'. It guarantees a variety of rights which are treated as fundamental as between members. It became binding under the Lisbon Treaty of 2007. The Charter will no longer apply in its specific terms to the UK (though some of the rights it protects exist in common law, in UK statute law or are guaranteed by the European Convention 1950).

7.25 On rights of a child to express views, the EU Charter says:

> '*Article 24*
>
> **The rights of the child**
>
> 1 Children... may express their views freely. Such views shall be taken into consideration on matters which concern them in accordance with their age and maturity.'

Brussels IIA

Introduction

7.26 A number of the rights of individuals will be lost upon EU withdrawal.[22] Some can be reproduced in UK law; but others depend on co-operation from courts and other agencies within Europe, which co-operation cannot be guaranteed on behalf of UK nationals. Save to the extent that rights of UK nationals, including UK children, can be replicated in domestic legislation, various rights under European legislation will go: things like employment rights, cross-border arrangements for health and other rights which EU nationals take for granted may go, or be modified for UK nationals in EU and for EU citizens in the UK. Brussels IIA is amongst the examples of such legislation. It cannot be replicated. Its operation as far as UK court proceedings and enforcement are concerned depend upon the co-operation guaranteed by EU law of co-operation between courts and other agencies.

7.27 A question therefore remains, as to what extent children's rights – to take an important example – will be protected in any way under UK law as they are now under EU law; or will those rights, where different than under UK law, be lost with the UK's departure from the EU?

7.28 Brussels IIA came into force on 1 March 2005 in all 28 Member States of the EU (other than Denmark). It replaced Brussels II (Council Regulation (EC) No 1347/1000) concerning jurisdiction and the recognition and enforcement of judgments and matrimonial matters and in matters of parental responsibility for children of both spouses. Brussels IIA is an EU Regulation and is therefore directly applicable in Member States. It does not need implementation through UK legislation, and it prevails over domestic law.

7.29 The structure of Brussels IIA is that it consists of a series of 'recitals' or preambles which set out the bases on which it is formulated, for example Recitals (5) and (6), dealing with children and relationship/marriage breakdown provides:

'(5) In order to ensure equality for all children, this Regulation covers all decisions on parental responsibility, including measures for the protection of the child, independently of any link with a matrimonial proceeding.

(6) Since the application of the rules on parental responsibility often arises in the context of matrimonial proceedings, it is more appropriate to have a single instrument for matters of divorce and parental responsibility.'

Structure of Brussels IIA

7.30 The recitals are followed by the Articles which are the legislative or operative parts of the Regulation. How this works in practice will be seen later.[23]

22 See, eg, 7.47.
23 7.42.

The Articles are broken down into a series of 'chapters'. After definitions (Arts 1 and 2), Chapter II (Arts 3–20) deals with intended jurisdiction of the courts of Member States under the Regulation. Section 2 of Chapter I (Arts 8–15) relates to jurisdiction in the context of children and parental responsibility. Section 3 of Chapter II (Arts 16–20) contains provisions which are common to both divorce (dealt with in Section1) and parental responsibility; and in particular such matters as determination of which court shall have jurisdiction in an individual case.

7.31 Chapter III (Arts 21–52) goes on to deal with recognition and enforcement of judgements. Chapter V (Arts 59–63) deals with the relationship of Brussels IIA with other instruments (eg the Hague Conventions).

7.32 If a right is protected by EU law, but is not reproduced in UK law, then – as EU legislation now stands – it is enforceable in the UK. Brussels IIA is an example of this. However, where rights guaranteed in EU courts are in question upon EU withdrawal, the answer will depend on whether EU withdrawal negotiation secures agreement of all remaining EU members as to whether (say) reciprocal enforcement should continue.

Children's rights under Brussels IIA

7.33 In *Re F (Children)*[24] Sir James Munby P (sitting with Arden LJ in the Court of Appeal) provided a coda to a judgement on a 14-year-old child's participation in child abduction proceedings.[25] In that he described Art 11(2) (alongside UN Charter Art 12(2)) as providing the starting point of any review of a child's opportunity to participate (this conclusion to his judgment will be considered later in this chapter[26]): whether it be to give evidence or to express a view.

7.34 Brussels IIA Art 11(2) states:

> '2 When applying Articles 12 and 13 of the 1980 Hague Convention, it shall be ensured that the child is given the opportunity to be heard during the proceedings unless this appears inappropriate having regard to his or her age or degree of maturity.'

7.35 Article 11(2) applies specifically to Hague Convention applications; but it is clear from the context in which he considers it – both as to his reference to the UN Charter, and to later English decisions – that Sir James regards it as part of a continuum of law reform and jurisprudence which applies to children's participation in proceedings generally.

---

24 [2016] EWCA Civ 546.
25 See 7.43.
26 See 7.50.

Brussels IIA and EU withdrawal

7.36 As a general conclusion to this, Professor Nigel Lowe concludes with his view[27] that the UK – and therefore its children – will be better able to solve international family law problems by remaining, if possible, within the EU instruments he discusses, than outside:[28]

> 'Without denying that there are some alternative international instruments which can provide some remedies in the absence of EU Regulation, particularly the Hague Protection Convention (but also the other Hague Conventions already mentioned), it is strongly argued that the UK will better be able to solve international family law disputes by opting to be bound by the above mentioned EU instruments and particularly Brussels IIA (recast). It will not be good enough to adopt the strategy of enacting these instruments domestically since their efficacy depends on reciprocity and orders that are not enforceable are not worth the paper they are written on. The prospect of losing the ability not just to enforce orders throughout the EU but do so efficiently would surely be a huge deficit to every user in the European context of the International Family Justice System.'

United Nations Convention on the Rights of the Child 1989

7.37 As Collins J said of the UN Convention and of the duties of the UK under it in *R (on the application of DA & ors) v Secretary of State for Work and Pensions*[29] (of the benefit cap in relation to children under two):

> '[29] The defendant [Secretary of State] relies, as we have seen, on the need to incentivise parents to work so that children do not suffer from living in workless families. It is difficult to see how that is realistic in relation to children under two. It is surely in their interests that they should have adequate food, shelter, warmth and care since deprivation of such will produce much greater harm. Evidence from Professor Maggie Atkinson, who was Children's Commissioner for England between 2010 and 2015, deals with the [United Nations Convention on the Rights of the Child 1989], which has been ratified by all nations save the USA. The UK ratified in 1991 and so is committed to promote and protect children's rights....'

7.38 Of a child's right to express views, where the child is capable of forming them, and of that child's entitlement to have an opportunity to be herd, the UN Convention says:

27 'Some reflections on the options for dealing with international family law following Brexit', Professor Nigel V Lowe in [2017] *Family Law* at 399.

28 At 405.

29 [2017] EWHC 1446 (Admin).

'**Article 12**

1. States Parties shall assure to the child who is capable of forming his or her own views the right to express those views freely in all matters affecting the child, the views of the child being given due weight in accordance with the age and maturity of the child.
2. For this purpose, the child shall in particular be provided the opportunity to be heard in any judicial and administrative proceedings affecting the child, either directly, or through a representative or an appropriate body, in a manner consistent with the procedural rules of national law.'

Other instruments

7.39 *Convention for the Protection of Human Rights and Fundamental Freedoms 1950* (the Convention) – the position of the child and the European Convention 1950 is dealt with in **Chapter 5**. Save for references to the Convention in this chapter, no more need be said here.

7.40 *Children Act 1989* – the rights of the child protected by *CA 1989* are dealt with throughout this book, especially in **Chapters 4** and **5**. Again, no more need be said here.

7.41 *Hague Convention* – in relation to the views of a child, and when these should be taken into account in court proceedings, there are frequent mentions of case law especially in **Chapter 4**. In *Re Rinau (Case C-195/08)*[30] the European Court made comments on their view of the Hague Convention. *Re Rinau* was a referral to the European Court of Justice for rulings on a number of preliminary points in relation to jurisdiction and children proceedings. In the course of their decision the Court made 'preliminary observations' prior to their rulings, as to the purpose and intent of the Hague Convention and the EU Regulations, especially (at [48]) as to their view as to the 'paramount importance' of children's interests:

'*Preliminary observations*

> [47] The Brussels Convention of 27 September 1968 on Jurisdiction and the Enforcement of Judgments in Civil and Commercial Matters (OJ 1978 L 304, p 36), which has subsequently been amended on several occasions, sought to facilitate the recognition and enforcement of judgments in civil and commercial matters as between the Contracting States. To that end, it introduced rules on jurisdiction and procedures for the recognition and enforcement of judgments in those matters. Those rules were based on the principle of the trust of the courts of one Contracting State in the decisions taken by the courts of another Contracting State and vice versa. According to Art 1 thereof, that Convention is not to apply as regards the status or legal capacity of natural persons and rights in property arising out of a matrimonial relationship.

30 [2009] Fam 51, [2009] 2 WLR 972, [2008] 2 FLR 1495.

[48] The 1980 Hague Convention was adopted on the basis that the interests of children are of paramount importance in matters relating to their custody and that it is necessary to protect children internationally from the harmful effects of their wrongful removal or retention and to establish procedures to ensure their prompt return to the State of their habitual residence, as well as to secure protection for rights of access.

[49] The guiding principles of the Conventions referred to in the two previous paragraphs were taken over, in matrimonial matters and matters of parental responsibility, by the Regulation [ie Brussels IIA]. The Regulation is applicable in civil matters relating to divorce, legal separation or marriage annulment and to the attribution, exercise, delegation, restriction or termination of parental responsibility.'

4 CHILDREN'S RIGHTS IN OPERATION

Children's rights and EU withdrawal

7.42 The way in which children's right to have their views heard by the courts is considered in **Chapter 4**. Here it is necessary to consider those rights in the context of EU legislation and to see how the rights may be effected by EU withdrawal.

7.43 In *Re F (Children)*[31] Sir James Munby P (sitting with Arden LJ in the Court of Appeal) provided a coda – obiter – to his judgement on appeal concerning a deputy High Court judge's decision not to allow a child aged 14 to be separately represented. The appeal proceedings related to L (14), F (7) and G (4). Their parents (M and F) are Hungarian. Their marriage broke down. Proceedings followed the Hungarian court. M brought the children to the UK unlawfully (for Hague Convention purposes). F started Hague proceedings. M defended on two grounds: (1) under Art 13, that L and F objected to being returned to Hungary; and (2) under Art 13(b), that there was a grave risk that returning the children to Hungary would expose them to physical or psychological harm or otherwise place them in an intolerable situation.

7.44 By the time of a pre-trial review L had been interviewed by an experienced CAFCASS officer (P). M said L should be separately represented in the proceedings; but the judge refused her application; and there was no appeal against that decision. The case came on for hearing before a deputy judge two weeks later, by which time P had also interviewed F. The judge had read both of P's reports and of hearing P's oral evidence. The judge gave judgment that day. He rejected the Art 13(b) defence; found that L and F both objected to being returned to Hungary, but exercised his discretion to order their return. His order provided that the children were to be returned to Hungary two weeks later.

31 [2016] EWCA Civ 546.

7.45 By that time the mother had applied for permission to appeal (which was given by Black LJ); and a stay of the judge's order was directed by her. Subsequently, L applied to the Court of Appeal for permission to appeal against both the refusal of separate representation order and the order of the deputy judge. At the end of February 2016 Black LJ refused L permission to appeal against Newton J's order but gave both L and her mother permission to appeal against the judge's order.

7.46 On undertakings given by F the both appeals were dismissed.[32] The mother was to obtain a judgement in the Hungarian court as soon as possible; and in those circumstances F would not enforce his interim custody order there.

Right to participate in proceedings

7.47 In the conclusion to his judgement Sir James commented on the submissions made to the court on behalf of the child as to her rights to participate in proceedings which concern the child. As already mentioned[33] he took Brussels IIA, Art 11(2), with UN Charter Art 12(2),[34] as 'the starting point' for a child's participation and for the court to ensure that a child 'is given the opportunity to be "heard"'.[35] He referred to the emotional harm which might occur to a child if the child was denied the 'knowledge of and participation in the continuing proceedings'.[36]

7.48 This case has been reviewed in the context of the law on 'Children's Views' in **Chapter 4**.[37] Here it is necessary to extract from Sir James's comments the elements of what he says, by way of review of a child's participation in proceedings which concern her and the extent to which that engages EU law principles. These revolve mostly around the question of a right to be heard; not just the expectation (eg in *CA 1989, s 1(3)(a)*) that a child's 'wishes and feelings' will be taken into account).

Child to be heard more frequently

7.49 Sir James referred, in particular, to two House of Lords/Supreme Court cases where respectively a child's views in Hague Convention proceedings and evidence in care proceedings were concerned:[38]

> '[37] ...In *Re D (A Child) (Abduction: Rights of Custody)* [2006] UKHL 51, [2007] 1 AC 619, §[57]-[61], the House of Lords had indicated that merely enabling the child to meet the judge might not be sufficient. Having observed (§[59])

32 §[34].
33 §[36].
34 See text at 7.34.
35 §[36].
36 §[36]; and by reference to Thorpe LJ in *Mabon v Mabon* [2005] EWCA Civ 634, [2005] Fam 366, [2005] 2 FLR 1011.
37 See 4.10.
38 For *Re D* in relation to views see 4.36 and *Re W* in relation to evidence see 3.54.

that "children should be heard far more frequently in Hague Convention cases than has been the practice hitherto. The only question is how this should be done", Baroness Hale of Richmond continued (§[60]):'There are three possible ways of doing this. They range from full scale legal representation of the child, through the report of an independent CAFCASS officer or other professional, to a face-to-face interview with the judge.

[38] The Supreme Court returned to the topic, this time in the context of care proceedings, in *Re W (Children) (Family Proceedings: Evidence)* [2010] UKSC 12, [2010] 1 WLR 701, holding that there is no longer a presumption, or even a starting point, against children giving evidence in family proceedings.'

7.50 In the light of these cases, and of other reviewed by him, Sir James concluded that there had been a 'sea change' in attitudes to children in proceedings.[39] How much of this 'sea change' – if indeed it exists – is referable to the approach of judges in the family courts to rights under EU law? It must also be seen in the light of the 'acid observation' of McFarlane LJ in *E (A Child)*[40] to which Sir James drew attention:

'[40] Finally, I refer to the very recent decision of this court in *Re E A Child)* [2016] EWCA Civ 473, §§46-48, 56-63, and, in particular, McFarlane LJ's acid observation (paras 48, 56) that Baroness Hale's judgment in *In re W* "would seem to have gone unheeded in the five or more years since it was given" and that "the previous culture and practice of the family courts remains largely unchanged with the previous presumption against children giving evidence remaining intact."'

7.51 In particular, Sir James referred to *Re D (A Child) (International Recognition)*[41] – perhaps his only reference in this case to any '"right" of participation' a child affected by proceedings might be entitled to. That case, he felt, illustrated:

'[39] ... the obligation of the court to ensure that the child is given the opportunity to be heard and "the right of the child to participate in the process that is about him or her" were said to be fundamental principles of universal application, "reflected in our legislation, our rules and practice directions and our jurisprudence" and where it was said that "the theme of the case law is an emphasis on the 'right' of participation of those 'affected' by proceedings."'

7.52 Assessment of children's rights and of L's rights to participate in the case in the light of the Court of Appeal decision in *Re F* is limited. The appeal turned on a test of the deputy judge's powers in relation to the case, rather than an objective test of how he decided it. Mostly the appeal turned on whether the judge had 'improperly fettered a discretion' which was available to him, and that he was

39 Discussed further at 4.12.

40 [2016] EWCA Civ 473.

41 [2016] EWCA Civ 12, [2016] 1 WLR 2469, [2016] 2 FLR 347.

wrong in law in the way he approached the case.[42] The Court of Appeal held that he had indeed taken into account the matters he must decide in the context of the case and the procedure by which it should be decided. The appeal – for which permission was given on the papers[43] – should be disallowed. The deputy judge's decision must be read and reviewed on appeal as a whole, the Court of Appeal said.[44] It should not be interfered with on appeal.[45]

7.53 The case does not therefore provide authority for any proposition of law; save that it does provide an authoritative commentary from Sir James Munby P on the essentials of legal principle in relation to participation of children in proceedings which concern them (at §§[36]–[44] as outlined above[46]).

Unified rules to govern jurisdiction across Member States; 'opportunity to be heard'

7.54 What of the rights of a child to be heard by the court? In *Re D (A Child) (International Recognition)*[47] the Court of Appeal considered whether a Romanian court order should be enforced where a child was not given 'an opportunity to be heard' on parental responsibility. The child had not been given this opportunity in Romania, as required by Brussels IIA, Art 23(b), so his father could not enforce the order in this country. The decision depended on reciprocal arrangements between the English and Romanian courts under Brussels IIA. This cannot be expected to survive Brexit; even though, if families break up and go to different EU countries (with one of them remaining or being resident in the UK), family litigation will increase.

7.55 Ryder LJ explained the inter-relationship of EU and English law.[48] The starting point, he said, was Brussels IIA; but Art 24 of the Charter also applied. Brussels IIA establishes 'a scheme by which jurisdiction is determined in accordance with unified rules that are directly applicable to the assumption and exercise of jurisdiction across all Member States'. He explained the context of the case within EU legislation (which, he said, was not controversial as between the parties):

---

42 §§[13], [22], [23] and [32].

43 §[1].

44 Sir James Munby P: [22] Like any judgment, the judgment of the Deputy Judge has to be read as a whole, and having regard to its context and structure. The task facing a judge is not to pass an examination, or to prepare a detailed legal or factual analysis of all the evidence and submissions he has heard. Essentially, the judicial task is twofold: to enable the parties to understand why they have won or lost; and to provide sufficient detail and analysis to enable an appellate court to decide whether or not the judgment is sustainable. The judge need not slavishly restate either the facts, the arguments or the law. To adopt the striking metaphor of Mostyn J in *SP v EB and KP* [2014] EWHC 3964 (Fam), [2016] 1 FLR 228, para 29, there is no need for the judge to 'incant mechanically' passages from the authorities, the evidence or the submissions, as if he were 'a pilot going through the pre-flight checklist.'

45 §[32].

46 See 7.49.

47 [2016] EWCA Civ 12, [2016] 2 FLR 347.

48 He adopts, or quotes from, much of what is said in passages in *Re Rinau (Case C-195/08)* [2009] Fam 51, [2009] 2 WLR 972, [2008] 2 FLR 1495 (see 7.41).

> '[13] … The governing instrument in EU Member States concerning jurisdiction in matters about parental responsibility is Council Regulation (EC) No 2201/2003 of 27 November 2003 Concerning Jurisdiction and the Recognition and Enforcement of Judgments in Matrimonial Matters and in Matters of Parental Responsibility, repealing Regulation (EC) No 1347/2000 (Brussels IIA) (2003) OJ L 338/1 (BIIA or the Regulation). The Regulation establishes a scheme by which jurisdiction is determined in accordance with unified rules that are directly applicable to the assumption and exercise of jurisdiction across all Member States.... The Articles concerning parental responsibility that are the Articles relevant to this appeal, are set out at Arts 8–15.'

7.56 Ryder LJ explained the context and rationale for the scheme as set out in the preamble, or recitals, to Brussels IIA, first by reference to the mutual trust on which recognition and enforcement was predicated:

> '[14] The recitals in the preamble to the Regulation explain the rationale for the Articles, ie the rationale for the jurisdictional rules and the supporting scheme for recognition, registration and enforcement of the decisions made in one Member State by each other Member State. Recital 21 deals with recognition and enforcement:
>
> "The recognition and enforcement of judgments given in a Member State should be based on the principle of mutual trust and the grounds for non-recognition should be kept to the minimum required."'

7.57 As he pointed out,[49] recitals (12) and (13) 'deal with the underlying philosophy which is decision making based on the best interests of the child'. These recitals are as follows:

> '(12) The grounds of jurisdiction in matters of parental responsibility established in the present Regulation are shaped in the light of the best interests of the child, in particular on the criterion of proximity. This means that jurisdiction should lie in the first place with the Member State of the child's habitual residence, except for certain cases of a change in the child's residence or pursuant to an agreement between the holders of parental responsibility.
>
> (13) In the interest of the child, this Regulation allows, by way of exception and under certain conditions, that the court having jurisdiction may transfer a case to a court of another Member State if this court is better placed to hear the case....'

7.58 In particular, said the judge, recital (33) asserts that Brussels IIA recognises the rights and principles set out in the EU Charter, and in particular Art 24 (in

49 §[15].

relation to the rights of the child: the judge sets out Art 24 in full[50]). Recital (33) and its specific reference to the 'fundamental rights of the child' is as follows:

> '(33) [Brussels IIA] recognises the fundamental rights and observes the principles of the [EU Charter]. In particular, it seeks to ensure respect for the fundamental rights of the child as set out in Article 24 of the Charter of Fundamental Rights of the European Union....'

7.59 Each State is expected to interpret the jurisdictional rules in the same way to achieve the object of 'mutual trust'.[51] That is reflected in the concept of autonomous interpretation of Brussels IIA, as distinct from interpretation in accordance with domestic legal concepts. A consequence is that the approach of 'mutual trust' between courts helps to 'avoid an erroneous focus on the domestic process of the Member State of origin' when the focus should be on 'compliance with inter-continentally applicable procedural rules'.[52]

7.60 'Mutual trust' and reciprocally enforceable rules can no longer be guaranteed under EU withdrawal. An English Parliament – for all its sovereignty – cannot make law, as the EU Commission can, which draws together the European courts. It cannot replicate Brussels IIA so that jurisdictions work together to help couples in different European court jurisdictions.

Operation of fundamental principle

7.61 Having considered general questions of principle in relation to Brussels IIA and the children conventions, the court was required to apply these to the question of whether in that case the child had been given an opportunity to be heard before a decision as to his return under Brussels IIA, Art 23(b)[53] (in particular). This question and the issue of what is a 'fundamental principle' are considered in **Chapter 4**.[54] Here the interrelation of the EU and international law in relation to a child's views will be considered.

7.62 Ryder LJ explained that *CA 1989, s 1(3)(a)* (requiring the court to have regard to the wishes and feelings of a child before making a decision in relation to the child's welfare) was a fundamental principle of procedure. So how did this principle link with the principles in the UN Charter and those in Brussels IIA? The concept of 'opportunity to be heard' (in the *United Nations Convention on the*

---

50 The text of Art 24 is at 7.25.

51 §[16].

52 §[17]; and see reference to 'mutual trust' in *Re Rinau (Case C-195/08)* [2009] Fam 51, [2009] 2 WLR 972, [2008] 2 FLR 1495, European Court of Justice considered at 7.41.

53 Art 23(b) in the context of *Re D* is discussed at 4.28. The Article is as follows: 'A judgment relating to parental responsibility shall not be recognised:...(b) if it was given, except in case of urgency, without the child having been given an opportunity to be heard, in violation of *fundamental principles of procedure* of the Member State in which recognition is sought;...' (italics added).

54 See 4.28.

Rights of the Child 1989, Art 12[55]) and of a child's 'wishes and feelings' (in *CA 1989, s 1(3)(a)*) were part of the same 'recognition of [a child's] autonomy'.[56]

7.63 This, said Ryder LJ, confirms that the law 'includes the right of a child to participate' in proceedings which concern the child. That is a fundamental principle' of English law (see italicised passage in quotation below):

> '[44] That is rightly an acceptance that the rule of law in England and Wales includes the right of the child to participate in the process that is about him or her. *That is the fundamental principle that is reflected in our legislation, our rules and practice directions and our jurisprudence.* At its most basic level it involves asking at an early stage in family proceedings whether and how that child is going to be given the opportunity to be heard.' (emphasis added)

7.64 This is subject, as always, to the qualification, he said – both under *CA 1989, s 1(3)(a)* and *Art 12(1)* – that any decision about a child must be based on 'the weight to be put upon a child's wishes and feelings, not their participation'.[57]

Progression in English law: the right of the child to participate in proceedings

7.65 In reply to the suggestion from the father that a 'more liberal approach' (ie more restrictive of taking child's views) should apply to Hague Convention cases, Ryder LJ said the argument was 'unsustainable'.[58] Cases such as *Re D (Abduction: Rights of Custody)*[59] in the House of Lords and *Re F (Abduction: Child's Wishes)*[60] – all cited by Ryder LJ[61] – were, he said, part of a progression in English law which recognised the right to participation of the child 'affected' by the proceedings. And he traced that back to comments of Thorpe LJ in *Mabon v Mabon*[62] (considered in **Chapter 6**[63]) and the linking by that judge, in 2005, of the UN Convention Art 12 rights of (in that case) and 'articulate teenager':

> '[28]... Unless we in this jurisdiction are to fall out of step with similar societies as they safeguard Article 12 rights, we must, in the case of articulate teenagers, accept that the right to freedom of expression and participation outweighs the paternalistic judgment of welfare.'

7.66 Ryder LJ concluded this passage of his judgment by drawing on the significance of a child's European Convention 1950, Art 8 rights:[64]

55 The text of Art 12 is at 7.38.
56 §[43].
57 §[44].
58 §[46].
59 [2006] UKHL 51, [2007] 1 FLR 961.
60 [2007] EWCA Civ 468, [2007] 2 FLR 697.
61 In §[46].
62 [2005] EWCA Civ 634, [2005] Fam 366, [2005] 2 FLR 1011 especially at §[28].
63 Especially at 6.81.
64 Explained further at 5.96.

> '[48] The involvement in proceedings of children whose interests are affected was specifically highlighted by Baroness Hale in *Re D* (above) and in *ZH (Tanzania) v Secretary of State for the Home Department* [2011] UKSC 4, [2011] 2 AC 166, [2011] 1 FLR 2170. These dicta were brought together by Sir James Munby P in *Cambra v Jones* [2014] EWHC 913 (Fam), [2015] 1 FLR 263. [He said] '[18] ... If and to the extent that [the child's] Article 8 rights are engaged, then that will carry with it the important procedural right to be "involved in the decision-making process, seen as a whole, to a degree sufficient to provide [her] with the requisite protection of [her] interests" see *W v United Kingdom* (1988) 10 EHRR 29, para 64....'

Child's right to be heard

7.67 And what of the child's right to be heard in Europe? The *United Nations Convention on the Rights of the Child 1989, Art 12* (by which UK will still be bound, so far its provisions are enforceable) is in similar terms to Art 23 of the Charter as to a child's right to be heard in 'judicial proceedings', and where that child is capable of forming his or her own views.

7.68 In UK law, the child's wishes and feelings are considered by the court in the light of the child's 'age and understanding' (a factor to be considered in **Part 3**). It may be a distinction without any real difference; but the Charter and UN Convention express these principles as a right. In the UK it is permissive. The present *Guidelines on Judges Meeting Children who are subject to Family Proceedings April 2010* [2010] 2 FLR 1872 set out their purpose as being to encourage judges to enable children to feel more involved in proceedings which affect them and to ensure judges have understood their wishes and feelings.

7.69 In *Re D (Abduction: Rights of Custody)* [2006] UKHL 51, [2007] 1 FLR 961 Lady Hale spoke (at §[57]) of the importance of a mature child's views and of how these could be considered by the courts. In her speech to Association of Lawyers for Children in November 2015 (available on the Supreme Court website) she explained the variable way in which judges approach this task. In none of these UK sources is there mention of a child's rights. Ryder LJ is more emphatic in *Re D* [2016], when he speaks of 'the right of a child to participate in a process about him or her' and of *CA 1989, s 1(3)(a)* as 'a fundamental principle of procedure' of UK law.[65]

7.70 The Charter will go as far as UK cases are concerned with EU withdrawal. It remains to be seen whether UK judges develop its concept of child's rights; or take the more passive approach implied by the UK sources referred to above. Certainly, had the judge in *Re W (a Child)* [66]looked at that case in terms of W's Charter rights – which in 2016 she should have done – it is difficult to see how the decision not to join the child in her return order proceedings could have been made.

65 §§[42]–[49].

66 *Re W (A Child) (Care Proceedings: Child's Representation) Practice Note* [2016] EWCA Civ 1051, [2017] 1 WLR 1027.

Children's lost EU rights

7.71 Rights, for example to comity of enforcement of orders and recognition of court proceedings in relation to children of EU nationals coming to, or one of them taking proceedings in England, are unlikely to have the same reciprocal arrangements which cross-EU border proceedings enjoy now under Brussels IIA. If a nine-year old (C) lives in England, but her parent (F) goes to France, then if F were to start proceedings there and Brussels IIA no longer applied to his child in England, he could probably expect the French courts to hear his application. If the English court made a contact order it could be overridden by a French order if C went to stay with F in France. Now only one European court can have jurisdiction.

7.72 If the child speaks to the French judge, he or she may gain a different view of the case from the Family Court judge in England, who may feel inhibited from speaking directly with the child. The child will not decide the outcome; but her views may be more faithfully represented in France (under Art 24 principles). As Lady Hale said in *Re D (A Child)*:[67]

> '[57] … As any parent who has ever asked a child what he wants for tea knows, there is a large difference between taking account of a child's views and doing what he wants…. There is now a growing understanding of the importance of listening to the children…. It is the child, more than anyone else, who will have to live with what the court decides. Those who do listen to children understand that they often have a point of view which is quite distinct from that of the person looking after them. They are quite capable of being moral actors in their own right.'

Enforcement and EU law

7.73 *Re M (Children)*[68] concerned enforcement of an Estonian order, and may provide an example of the challenge which faces child law reformers if rights are to be preserved for children and their parents on EU withdrawal. In that case, the Court of Appeal was confronted by a question of enforcement under Brussels IIA of an Estonian court order. Black LJ defined the issue before the court as that Moylan J had refused to order enforcement, because:

> '[1] … The order provided for the father to have contact "in the presence of a third party being a competent child welfare authority of the UK" but there was no child welfare authority or child care professional willing to supervise the contact and Moylan J concluded that there was no order he could make to compel this.'

7.74 The father's appeal was therefore dismissed; but not till the court had fully considered what steps might be taken to make contact work; and Black LJ's

67 [2006] UKHL 51 sub nom *Re D (Abduction: Rights of Custody)* [2007] 1 FLR 961.
68 [2017] EWCA Civ 891.

extensive review of authorities under Brussels IIA. It was for the Estonian court to lay the foundations for a supervised contact order:

> '[72] ... The Estonian court had decided that the way to get contact established was by supervised contact of the type it imposed. If that was not feasible, it was for the Estonian court to reconsider and decide whether it would be appropriate to involve an independent social worker, or an organisation such as the Anna Freud Centre to assist...'

7.75 The main operative EU law provision is Art 47 of Brussels IIA, which is as follows:

> '*Article 47*
>
> **Enforcement procedure**
>
> 1. The enforcement procedure is governed by the law of the Member State of enforcement.
> 2. Any judgment delivered by a court of another Member State and declared to be enforceable in accordance with Section 2 or certified in accordance with Article 41(1) or Article 42(1) shall be enforced in the Member State of enforcement in the same conditions as if it had been delivered in that Member State.
>
> In particular, a judgment which has been certified according to Article 41(1) or Article 42(1) cannot be enforced if it is irreconcilable with a subsequent enforceable judgment.'

7.76 This plainly envisages co-operation between Member State's courts – which in *Re M* was not sufficient, for technical reasons, to secure supervised contact. However, survival of this level of co-operation between EU countries' courts cannot be guaranteed following EU withdrawal.

5 SURVIVAL OF CHILDREN'S RIGHTS AND EU LAW

Survival of rights

7.77 This final part is a short selection of instances where children's rights in international legislation are instrumental in court decisions. In *Re D (Abduction: Rights of Custody)*[69] Lady Hale put the question of the child's views in the context of Brussels IIA, Art 11.2 and of the UK's obligations under the UN Convention Art 12:[70]

69 [2006] UKHL 51, [2007] 1 FLR 961.
70 See 7.36.

> '[58] Brussels II Revised recognises this by reversing the burden in relation to hearing the child. Article 11.2 provides: "When applying articles 12 and 13 of the 1980 Hague Convention, it shall be ensured that the child is given the opportunity to be heard during the proceedings unless this appears inappropriate having regard to his or her age or degree of maturity." Although strictly this only applies to cases within the European Union (over half of the applications coming before the High Court), the principle is, in my view, of universal application and consistent with our international obligations under Art 12 of the United Nations Convention on the Rights of the Child 1989. It applies, not only when a "defence" under art 13 has been raised, but also in any case in which the court is being asked to apply Art 12 and direct the summary return of the child – in effect in every Hague Convention case.'

7.78 Thus she said, concluding §[58], Art 11.2 'erects a presumption that the child will be heard [by some means or another] unless this appears inappropriate'. However, she stressed: 'Hearing the child is, as already stated, not to be confused with giving effect to his views.' In Hague Convention cases children should be heard more often:

> '[59] It follows that children should be heard far more frequently in Hague Convention cases than has been the practice hitherto. The only question is how this should be done. It is plainly not good enough to say that the abducting parent, with whom the child is living, can present the child's views to the court. If those views coincide with the views of the abducting parent, the court will either assume that they are not authentically the child's own or give them very little independent weight. There has to be some means of conveying them to the court independently of the abducting parent.'

Child's evidence discounted by the judge

7.79 In *Re S (a Child)*[71] the Court of Appeal considered the appeal of a mother (M) which, in part, concerned the evidence of an eight-year-old child. Indeed, only ground of appeal allowed related to that evidence. That ground related to whether or not her eight-year-old son (A) may have been physically abused by his father (F). M had moved to Ireland, but returned to pursue a relocation claim in England. Assuming that M is able to relocate, the case raises the question of what may happen if Brussels IIA no longer applies mutuality between English and EU decisions and court orders.

7.80 M had not opposed F's contact in principle but wanted it to be safe for the child. (Though A (the child) was represented before the judge, he seems not to have appealed, nor to have made representations in the Court of Appeal.) By the time of the first instance hearing M had left the UK to live with her husband in Ireland; but, after A was made a ward, she returned to UK to apply to the UK court to relocate.

71 [2017] EWCA Civ 44.

7.81 The parents had a short relationship which had ended in August 2010. The appeal related to findings made by the judge before whom a series of contact applications had been made. He had a schedule of 14 allegations made by M. He found three proved and rejected the rest. The first two were general, namely that F had behaved in a controlling way towards M throughout their relationship and that he was violent towards her, this being exacerbated by drink. The third proved allegation related to a specific event when the father assaulted the mother, grabbing her around the neck and throwing her to the floor. The last item on the schedule was a recital of police cautions and convictions of the father, which the father accepted was accurate and the judge treated as a matter of record.

Evidence from the child: mother's case rejected by the judge

7.82 Of the remaining ten sets of allegations made by M, all but the ground which related to the child's evidence was rejected by the by the Court of Appeal; though this had not been accepted by the judge. (He seems not to have heard what the child said about it, a matter to be considered later.[72]) The evidence, accepted as justifying the appeal, arose from what A had said to a family support worker (S), combined with the fact of a 'conditional caution' – for which there must be an admission by a suspect – that F had injured the child.

7.83 Black LJ (who gave the main judgment) explained the factual back-ground when S had talked with A and had heard the evidence, as follows.

> [27] ... The judge had available to him [S's] written report of what A said to her. In it, S explained that she had been working with the family since February 2013, helping to "manage their high levels of anxieties". It seems that the visit during which the material conversation occurred was her third visit and took place around mid-July 2013. There is no suggestion in her report that the visit was in any way a response to A's account of his father's actions during contact. Ms Solway described how, during the visit, she spent some time with A in the kitchen and then in his bedroom. She said that he was enjoying a story book when he asked "unexpectedly" whether she was going to help him to get a particular person to stop hurting him, demonstrating to her how the person had grabbed his arm. He identified the person concerned by his forename only, the forename being the same as the father's.

7.84 The judge had said that 'the allegation was a serious one'; but had then rejected it. He had not given it proper consideration said Black LJ:

> '[30] ... It seems to me that his handling of the issue fell short in a number of ways. It was incumbent upon him, I think, to deal more fully with what was quite a graphic description by Ms Solway of A's apparently spontaneous

72 At 7.86.

demonstration of events to her. The judge stated baldly that he was unable to rely upon what A had said and gave very little explanation as to why he took that view, except perhaps that there was no mark on A. As for the caution, he said in responding to the request for clarification that he "took no account of [the father's] previous physical chastisement of children" (my emphasis). He might ultimately have concluded that the father's actions in relation to the other children did not assist him particularly in his decision about what happened to A, but he did need, in my view, to consider the evidence about those actions specifically and to explain expressly how he dealt with it in making his decision. Furthermore, the judge should also, in my view, have given consideration to whether the findings that he had made about the father's violence towards the mother contributed anything to the issue in relation to A.'

7.85 Black LJ therefore set aside the finding that the assault on A did not take place. She remitted the allegation for hearing by another circuit judge. No direct reference was made by the Court of Appeal to Art 24 of the EU Charter; nor was any reference made as to how the court intended A's evidence to be received by the next judge, if other than the hearsay evidence mentioned to the judge.

Evidence and child's rights

7.86 So what were A's rights in these proceedings; what light could he have shed on what happened; and what (if anything) will happen to those rights with EU withdrawal? A child's evidence may be as to relevant facts, or as to expression of a view on outcome. Had A been permitted to 'express a view' in these proceedings (as Art 24(2) guarantees: it is not clear from the report whether the first instance judge offered this).

7.87 If it is appropriate he could still speak to the judge at any further hearing. However, his evidence about the case will have to be received in such a way as gave F a fair opportunity to challenge it (perhaps short of cross-examination or asking direct questions of A). For example, what had happened during the period when he was 'hurt' by F? He is competent to give evidence; but as to how this should be done is a matter for the judge.

7.88 If M is able to move with A to Ireland, she will remain in the EU; but if the UK leaves the reciprocal arrangements between courts which exist under Brussels IIA it cannot be relied on to remain. A is left, on this simple example, of the possibility of F obtaining a contact order in England, and M having a different order from an Irish court. F's means of enforcement may be inhibited since enforcement may depend on the authorities in a jurisdiction which has made a different order.

7.89 UK legislation cannot prevent this, since the UK Parliament has no power to bind the courts or enforcement agencies in Ireland.

Rights to be heard and EU withdrawal

7.90 As to rights to be heard: the Charter will go with EU withdrawal. It remains to be seen whether UK judges develop its concept of child's rights (as distinct from their views being taken into account); or whether they will take the more passive approach implied by the UK sources referred to above. Beyond that, it whether any of the rights now attached in English proceedings, will be depend on the EU withdrawal legislation; or will English and European courts develop differing rights of issue and enforcement of proceedings following EU withdrawal?

8

CONFIDENTIALITY

1 INTRODUCTION

Children's confidentiality

8.1 A range of guidance exists for professionals who receive confidences from mature children. This may be in connection with children they deal with in the course of their work. It may be specifically in relation to court proceedings. For example, guidance comes from *Working Together*[1] ('sharing' information concerning work with children); *GMC Guidance on Confidentiality* for treating children;[2] and the law outlined in *Gillick v West Norfolk and Wisbech AHA* ('*Gillick*')[3], especially for doctors. It includes legal advice privilege, which protects confidences of mature children in their discussions with lawyers. Each of these creates different legal principles.

8.2 Alongside this variety of guidance and law is the fact differences of professional culture may lead to differences of the legal principles[4] as between (say) the absolute privacy accorded to lawyer's advice privilege as against the 'sharing' principle – which can be the antithesis of confidentiality – required of professionals who work with and for children and as required by the statutory guidance in *Working Together*.

8.3 The terminology and rationale behind *Gillick* remains central to assessment of the 'understanding' – a word taken directly from the opinions in *Gillick* – of a mature child. That understanding then dictates the extent to which a doctor must treat as entirely confidential information provided by a child (subject to any

1 *Working together to safeguard children*; A guide to inter-agency working to safeguard and promote the welfare of children March 2015 (HM Government) (amendments February 2017) (www.gov.uk/government/uploads/system/uploads/attachment_data/file/592101/Working_Together_to_Safeguard_Children_20170213.pdf) *CA 2004, s 11*.

2 See www.gmc-uk.org/guidance/ethical_guidance/children_guidance_contents.asp.

3 [1985] UKHL 7, [1986] 1 AC 112, [1986] 1 FLR 224; and see Ch 2, Pt 4.

4 The contrast between the various professional rules is considered in outline in 'Child confidentiality: a clash of professional rules' by David Burrows, *Family Law* [2017] June at 638.

overriding public interest duty[5] of the doctor to pass on information[6]). How far do the confidentiality principles on which *Gillick* is based apply to all professionals who work with children? If *Gillick* is inconsistent with *Working Together*, how much is this so; and which – *Gillick* or *Working Together* – should guide the professional?

8.4 This chapter proceeds as follows:

- **Part 2** looks particularly at a definition of the confidentiality of the mature child (child of age and understanding); and of how this is affected by European Convention 1950 principles.
- **Part 3** considers the right to legal professional privilege of a mature child.
- **Part 4** considers confidentiality in the context of medical treatment and of the Guidance provided to doctors and other health professionals.
- **Part 5** explains circumstances in which a professional, especially a doctor, may override or breach confidentiality.
- **Part 6** looks at the question of 'sharing information' as provided for in *Working Together*; and questions the appropriateness of some 'information sharing' advice in the context of a mature child.
- **Part 7** considers the factors a professional should consider when confronted with a possibility of having to breach a child's – of child patient/client's – confidentiality.

Gillick: confidentiality and 'sharing'

8.5 The main outline of *Gillick* is dealt with in **Chapter 2, Part 4**. Its importance – and continuing importance – in dealing with confidentiality, especially for children of age and understanding and in relation to medical treatment, is dealt with throughout this chapter.

8.6 On *Gillick* principles, the same rules apply for the doctor as to any other professional given confidential information by a mature child; and this is despite what may be said to the contrary in *Working Together*. If there is a clash of professional cultures between 'sharing' under *Working Together* and confidentiality in *Gillick*, then the common law as it now stands puts *Gillick* before departmental guidance where a child's privacy and their Art 8 rights are concerned.

5 *GMC Guidance on Confidentiality*: '47 A disclosure is in the public interest if the benefits which are likely to arise from the release of information outweigh both the child or young person's interest in keeping the information confidential and society's interest in maintaining trust between doctors and patients.' This and the lawyer's comparable public duty is explained at 8.99.

6 *GMC Guidance* www.gmc-uk.org/guidance/ethical_guidance/children_guidance_47_50_public_interest.asp, paras 47-50; *W v Egdell* [1989] EWCA Civ 13, [1990] Ch 359, [1990] 2 WLR 471; and see Pt 3.

2 CONFIDENTIALITY OF THE MATURE CHILD

Confidentiality: a definition

8.7 Confidentiality was defined by Lord Goff in *Att Gen v Guardian Newspapers Ltd (No 2)*[7] (the *Spycatcher* case) – a formulation which, despite Lord Goff's modesty for it, has since been generally treated as authoritative – as follows:

> 'I start with the broad general principle (which I do not intend in any way to be definitive) that a duty of confidence arises when confidential information comes to the knowledge of a person (the confidant) in circumstances where he has notice, or is held to have agreed, that the information is confidential, with the effect that it would be just in all the circumstances that he should be precluded from disclosing the information to others.... The existence of this broad general principle reflects the fact that there is such a public interest in the maintenance of confidences, that the law will provide remedies for their protection.'

8.8 The principle of confidentiality, especially in relation to children proceedings, is the source of the privacy in which most family proceedings under FPR 2010 are heard.[8] It is fundamental to a doctor's relationship with a patient, subject to the public interest exception considered later.[9] In the case of a mature child, confidentiality defines the ability of the under 16-year old to consent to medical treatment (as decided in *Gillick*).

8.9 The importance of confidentiality in relation to treatment of a patient is stressed by GMC Guidance to doctors. This defines 'Principles of confidentiality' in relation to children as:

> '42 Respecting patient confidentiality is an essential part of good care; this applies when the patient is a child or young person as well as when the patient is an adult. Without the trust that confidentiality brings, children and young people might not seek medical care and advice, or they might not tell you all the facts needed to provide good care.'

Breach of confidence and the public interest

8.10 In the *Spycatcher* case[10] Lord Goff explained that there were three important 'limiting principles' on the description of confidentiality which he had proposed:

7 [1990] 1 AC 109 at 281, [1988] UKHL 6.
8 *Administration of Justice Act 1960, s 12(1)*; FPR 2010 r 27.10; and see, eg, *Allan v Clibbery* [2002] EWCA Civ 45, [2002] Fam 261 sub nom *Clibbery v Allan* [2002] 1 FLR 565.
9 See 8.47.
10 See 8.45.

'The third limiting principle is of far greater importance. It is that, although the basis of the law's protection of confidence is that there is a public interest that confidences should be preserved and protected by the law, nevertheless that public interest may be outweighed by some other countervailing public interest which favours disclosure. This limitation may apply, as the learned judge pointed out, to all types of confidential information. It is this limiting principle which may require a court to carry out a balancing operation, weighing the public interest in maintaining confidence against a countervailing public interest favouring disclosure. Embraced within this limiting principle is, of course, the so called defence of iniquity. In origin, this principle was narrowly stated, on the basis that a man cannot be made "the confidant of a crime or a fraud": see *Gartside v. Outram* (1857) 26 LJCh 113, 114, per Sir William Page Wood VC. But it is now clear that the principle extends to matters of which disclosure is required in the public interest...'

8.11 Privilege is absolute (save where advice is sought in pursuit of a crime); whilst the right to privacy derived from confidentiality may be overridden in the public interest. In European Convention 1950 terms it is an Art 8 right which may be overridden in the public interest (where, for example, the right to legal professional privilege is derived from Art 6 and the right to a fair trial).

8.12 The importance of not breaching confidentiality, but of recognising its place in the context of human rights principles was explained by the Court of Appeal in *HRH Prince of Wales v Associated Newspapers Ltd*[11] by Lord Phillips (giving the judgment of the court, with Sir Anthony Clarke MR and May LJ):

'[32] Before the Human Rights Act 1998 came into force, the English law of confidence had recognised that there were circumstances where the public interest in disclosure overrode the duty of confidence, and that these circumstances could differ depending upon whether the duty was owed to a private individual or to a public authority....'

8.13 There was a public interest in confidences being protected, including those of children who want their information kept confidential.[12] But exceptional circumstances[13] might override a duty of confidence in the public interest:

'[67] There is an important public interest in the observance of duties of confidence. Those who engage employees, or who enter into other relationships that carry with them a duty of confidence, ought to be able to be confident that they can disclose, without risk of wider publication, information that it is legitimate for them to wish to keep confidential. Before the Human Rights Act 1998 came into force the circumstances in

11 [2006] EWCA Civ 1776, [2008] Ch 57: Prince Charles had released in confidence to a member of his staff particular confidential journals. Prince Charles's confidentiality, in that case, overrode the freedom of expression (Art 10) of the media to whom the journals were released by the member of staff.

12 See, eg, HI in *Local Authority X v HI and Others* [2016] EWHC 1123 (Fam), [2017] 1 FLR 1362, Roberts J considered at 10.48.

13 Such as those considered in Pt 5.

which the public interest in publication overrode a duty of confidence were very limited. The issue was whether exceptional circumstances justified disregarding the confidentiality that would otherwise prevail. Today the test is different. It is whether a fetter of the right of freedom of expression is, in the particular circumstances, "necessary in a democratic society". It is a test of proportionality.'

8.14 In *Re A (Sexual Abuse: Disclosure)* [2012] UKSC 60, [2013] 1 FLR 948 Lady Hale looked at the question of whether a putative witness (X) in a private law children case should have her confidentiality breach by social workers in whom she had confided. She explained the issues before the Supreme Court as follows:

'[1] We are asked in this case to reconcile the irreconcilable. On the one hand, there is the interest of a vulnerable young woman (X) who made an allegation in confidence to the authorities that while she was a child she had been seriously sexually abused by the father of a little girl (A) who is now aged 10. On the other hand we have the interests of that little girl, her mother (M) and her father (F), in having that allegation properly investigated and tested. These interests are not only private to the people involved. There are also public interests, on the one hand, in maintaining the confidentiality of this kind of communication, and, on the other, in the fair and open conduct of legal disputes. On both sides there is a public interest in protecting both children and vulnerable young adults from the risk of harm.'

8.15 The Supreme Court, all of whose justices agreed with Lady Hale's judgment, resolved the issue by saying that X's confidentiality should be overridden. She could be required to give evidence – albeit, as appropriate, with special measures in place[14] – as she had been required by the father by witness summons to do.

Gillick and Roddy: consent of a child under 16

8.16 *Gillick* defines the circumstances in which a child under 16 may consent to treatment. The case also regulates the relationship between mature children and professionals dealing with them. Munby J explained this in *Re Roddy (A Child) (Identification: Restriction on Publication)*[15] ('*Roddy*'). In the latter case Angela Roddy was 16. Her child had been taken into care and she had been made the subject of

14 '[36]... There are many ways in which her evidence could be received without recourse to the normal method of courtroom confrontation. Family proceedings have long been more flexible than other proceedings in this respect [which] could include the facility to have specific questions put to the witness at the request of the parties.... Oral questioning could be arranged in ways which did not involve face-to-face confrontation. It is not a requirement that the father be able to see her face. It is, to say the least, unlikely that the court would ever allow direct questioning by the father, should he still (other than in this court) be acting in person. The court's only concern in family proceedings is to get at the truth. The object of the procedure is to enable witnesses to give their evidence in the way which best enables the court to assess its reliability. It is certainly not to compound any abuse which may have been suffered'.

15 *Re Roddy (A Child)(Identification: Restriction on Publication)* [2003] EWHC 2927, [2004] 2 FLR 949 Munby J.

a care order when she was 13. She wanted to tell her story to the press, but it was assumed she needed court permission.[16]

8.17 Munby J said[17] of Angela Roddy and of older children generally, that the general principles for decisions as to her choice as to privacy and release of her confidentiality depended on the varying extent to which parental control could legitimately be exercised over them. Finding a definition of those principles started with Lord Fraser in *Gillick*, who had said:[18]

> '... Moreover, the degree of parental control actually exercised over a particular child does in practice vary considerably according to his understanding and intelligence and it would, in my opinion, be unrealistic for the courts not to recognise these facts. Social customs change, and the law ought to, and does in fact, have regard to such changes when they are of major importance.'

8.18 Munby J cited Lord Scarman:[19]

> 'The law relating to parent and child is concerned with the problems of the growth and maturity of the human personality. If the law should impose upon the process of "growing up" fixed limits where nature knows only a continuous process, the price would be artificiality and a lack of realism in an area where the law must be sensitive to human development and social change ... The underlying principle of the law ... is that parental right yields to the child's right to make his own decisions when he reaches a sufficient understanding and intelligence to be capable of making up his own mind on the matter requiring decision.'

Reality: judge's sensitivity to a child's developmental change

8.19 In the context of a mature child who wanted to tell her story to the press Munby J emphasised the importance of judges and public bodies generally facing 'reality' (as also discussed in **Chapter 5**):

> '[56] The courts must face reality. We must, as Lord Scarman said, be sensitive to human development and social change. Angela may not yet be quite 17 years old but she is a young woman with a mind of her own and, as her solicitor B has said, a mature and articulate young person. We no longer treat our 17-year-old daughters as our Victorian ancestors did, and if we try to do so it is at our – and their – peril. Angela, in my judgment, is of an age, and has sufficient understanding and maturity, to decide for herself whether that which is private, personal and intimate should remain private or whether it should be shared with the whole world.'

16 The *Roddy* case is considered fully in Ch 5.
17 Quoted by Munby J at §[50].
18 [1986] 1 FLR 224 at 236.
19 [1986] 1 FLR 224 at 250, quoted by Munby J at §[51].

8.20 Angela, he said was seeking 'to tell her story to the world – a right, and it is nothing less, securely founded in Arts 8 and 10'.[20] So what were Angela's rights and on what jurisprudence were they based? If she was competent then she was entitled to make her own decisions on her own confidentiality. Save to the extent that it affected anyone else's rights – in that case there was the father of Angela's child, the father and the child's adoptive family[21] – then the court had no power to interfere with Angela's private rights.

3 THE CHILD AND LEGAL PROFESSIONAL PRIVILEGE

Legal professional privilege and the mature child

8.21 A lawyer (solicitor or barrister) can guarantee confidentiality, in the form of legal professional privilege, for his or her child client,[22] in a way which is not possible for other professionals. This right to privilege[23] was emphasised by McFarlane LJ in *Re E (A Child)* (below): a child is 'entitled to the same protection afforded to all other individuals who undertake communications with their lawyers'.

8.22 The extent of the right to privilege and its relationship to confidentiality was explained by Lord Nicholls in *R v Derby Magistrates' Court exp B*.[24] He identified two public interests in the administration of justice on which it depended: the need for individuals confidentially to obtain legal advice and assistance balanced against the requirements 'that all relevant material should be available to courts when deciding cases'.[25]

8.23 Lord Nicholls explained the working of legal professional privilege as follows:

> 'Legal professional privilege is concerned with the interaction between two aspects of the public interest in the administration of justice. The public interest in the efficient working of the legal system requires that people should be able to obtain professional legal advice on their rights and liabilities and obligations.... Similarly, people should be able to seek legal advice and assistance in connection with the proper conduct of court proceedings. To this end communications between clients and lawyers must be uninhibited. But, in practice, candour cannot be expected if disclosure of the contents of communications between client and lawyer may be compelled, to a client's prejudice and contrary to his wishes. That is one aspect of the public interest. It takes the form of according to the client a right, or privilege as it

20 §[47].

21 As explained at 5.70.

22 And see Lady Hale to Association of Lawyers for Children (ALC), 20 November 2015, *Are we nearly there yet?* ([2016] Fam Law 320; http://alc.org.uk/uploads/Keynote_speech_2015.pdf): 'The only person who can give the child a guarantee of confidentiality is her own lawyer'.

23 See italicised passage in the comments of Lord Nicholls in the *Derby Justices* case below.

24 [1995] UKHL 18, [1996] 1 AC 487, [1996] 1 FLR 513 at 529-530 (*Derby Justices* case).

25 This subject is considered further in Chs 9 and 10.

is unhelpfully called, to withhold disclosure of the contents of client-lawyer communications. In the ordinary course the client has an interest in asserting this right, insofar as disclosure would or might prejudice him.'

8.24 Legal professional privilege is a single privilege with two branches: advice privilege and litigation privilege. The privilege with which this Chapter is concerned is advice privilege.[26] This privilege, or confidentiality, enables a client to speak frankly to his or her lawyer about legal matters. The client is then entitled to assume that, subject to narrow exceptions, that the content of their discussions cannot without the client's consent be passed on to a third party.[27] It represents an absolute right for the client which is justified on grounds that the administration of justice demands that an individual is must be able to speak openly where legal advice is sought.[28] The advice can be in any 'relevant legal context'.[29] That is to say, so the advice need not relate only to litigation, but can be legal advice on any subject.

Child's advice privilege in care proceedings

8.25 *Re E (A Child)(Evidence)*[30] confirms, if there were any doubts on the subject, that a child is as entitled to these rights as is any other individual. In that case the Court of Appeal was critical of the way the judge dealt with confidential evidence in care proceedings; and a solicitor was criticised for failing properly to respect the advice privilege of A the solicitor's 14-year-old client. In *Re E* the oldest child's solicitor (S) was criticised for failing properly to respect the child's confidentiality – legal advice privilege – of the oldest child in the case (A, born in 2001).[31]

8.26 On privilege in the Court of Appeal McFarlane LJ started from the premise that:

'[90] … A, as a party to the proceedings, who is represented by his own solicitor, must be entitled to the same protection afforded to all other individuals who undertake communications with their lawyers. No suggestion was made in the hearing of this appeal that any different standard or approach should be taken to A either because he is a child or because he may lack the capacity to instruct his solicitor directly.'

---

26 For a fuller account of legal advice privilege in family proceedings, see *Evidence in family proceedings* by David Burrows (2016, Family Law/LexisNexis) Ch 14.

27 *Anderson v Bank of British Columbia* (1876) 2 ChD 644.

28 *R v Derby Magistrates' Court exp B* [1995] UKHL 18, [1996] 1 AC 487, [1996] 1 FLR 513; *Three Rivers District Council and ors v Governor and Company of the Bank of England (No 6)* [2004] UKHL 48, [2004] 3 WLR 1274.

29 *Balabel v Air India* [1988] Ch 317, CA.

30 [2016] EWCA Civ 473, [2017] 1 FLR 1675, [2016] 4 WLR 105.

31 But see *Wolverhampton City Council v JA & Ors* [2017] EWFC 62 (18 August 2017), where Keehan J ordered a child's former solicitor to file evidence as to an interview without regard to the legal professional privilege consequences or to whether the solicitor was entitled to waive any confidentiality to which her client might be entitled.

8.27 McFarlane LJ went on to cite[32] Lord Taylor in *R v Derby Magistrates' Court exp B*[33] on the extent to which legal professional privilege applies. In the *Derby justices'* case Lord Taylor said:

> 'The principle which runs through all these cases, and the many other cases which were cited, is that a man must be able to consult his lawyer in confidence, since otherwise he might hold back half the truth. The client must be sure that what he tells his lawyer in confidence will never be revealed without his consent. Legal professional privilege is thus much more than an ordinary rule of evidence, limited in its application to the facts of a particular case. It is a fundamental condition on which the administration of justice as a whole rests.'

8.28 The circumstances in which the advice privilege arose, occurred during a visit by the solicitor, S, and A's guardian. The main object of that meeting was to enable S to go through with A the evidence against him. The advice privilege with which McFarlane LJ was concerned arose as follows:

> '[91] The express purpose of [the visit] was to go through the evidence against him for the purposes of the forthcoming hearing. It is not apparent from the guardian's statement or any other material that we have seen that the question of legal professional privilege was considered or discussed with A. The following day the fact that the visit had occurred was made known to the court and the judge directed the guardian to file a statement giving an account of it. There is no indication that that direction was contested or that the solicitor and guardian expressly purported to waive A's legal professional privilege on his behalf.... The result was that the full details of A's meeting with his solicitor to discuss these allegations, such as it was, became fully known to the court.'

8.29 McFarlane LJ made a number of criticisms of the interview. He considered that the subject of privilege was not even discussed by S with his client. He explains this, first as a failure of S:

> '[91] ... It is obviously most important that, in the case of a vulnerable young person, those who are instructed to act on his behalf where he or she is facing serious factual allegations are utterly clear as to their professional responsibilities and astute to ensure that their young client's rights are properly acknowledged and protected.'

8.30 McFarlane LJ then turned his attention to the way in which the judge had dealt with privilege. He was critical of her for not taking account of the extent to which legal advice privilege had been breached and how this affected A's

32 At §[90].
33 [1995] UKHL 18, [1996] 1 FLR 513.

Article 6[34] rights. And, the order she made for filing evidence by the guardian as to the meeting with A (see italicised passage below):

> '[97] ... Whilst the judge may have been correct that the mere formulation of aspects of the existing evidence into a more detailed threshold document was not a breach of A's rights under Article 6, her judgment does not engage with the processes adopted by the social worker, guardian and solicitor in the context of those rights. That this is so is not altogether the fault of the judge, as no party seems to have been aware of that aspect of the case during the hearing. *Nevertheless the judge did make an order requiring a party's representative to file a statement setting out what transpired at a meeting expressly established to elicit that party's instructions to his lawyers on serious allegations of abuse.* That is a significant and highly unusual order to make and, irrespective of the position of the parties, the judge ought to have questioned the basis of the proposed order and been aware of the need to protect A's Art 6 rights and his entitlement to legal professional privilege (italics supplied).'

8.31 Amongst the court's seven numbered reasons for allowing the appeal[35] was: '(v) A's right under ECHR, Article 6 to a fair trial and his right to the protection of legal professional privilege were breached to a substantial degree'. By this route McFarlane LJ brought this aspect of the case back to privilege and – what is at the root of the reason for privilege – the public interest in the administration of justice, to which he had referred in relation to Lord Taylor's speech in *R v Derby Magistrates' Court exp B.*[36]

4 DOCTORS: CONFIDENTIALITY AND A MATURE CHILD AS PATIENT

GMC Guidance to doctors

8.32 Where does this leave a medical professional who is working with a mature child? *Gillick* refers specifically to doctors; but what it says has been applied to practice, including the practice of lawyers, in a variety of fields where dealing with mature children. The GMC has issued Guidance ('GMC Guidance'). It deals with doctors and their treatment of children as a subject which spans children of all ages: *0-18 years guidance.*[37] The subjects which arise here are dealt with in the Guidance as follows:

34 European Convention 1950, Art 6. Gloster LJ concurred with McFarlane LJ, and emphasised what he had said on the Art 6 point: '[100] I agree that this appeal should be allowed for the reasons given by McFarlane LJ. I would, in particular, endorse his concerns about... the disregard of A's Art 6 European Convention rights by those who were meant to be safeguarding his interests.'

35 Para [98].

36 [1995] UKHL 18, [1996] 1 FLR 513; and see passage cited at 8.22.

37 The link to the contents page is www.gmc-uk.org/guidance/ethical_guidance/children_guidance_contents.asp.

- Principles of confidentiality (§§42 and 43);
- Sharing information with the consent of a child or young person (§44);
- Sharing information without consent (§§45–46);
- 'Public interest' and passing on of information (§§47–50);
- Sources of law on confidentiality, data protection and privacy.[38]

8.33 The first paragraph of the GMC Guidance on 'The ethical and legal duties of confidentiality'[39] asserts the important role of confidentiality in the role of the doctor: 'Trust is an essential part of the doctor-patient relationship and confidentiality is central to this'. In relation to children – that is, all children between '0 and 18' – the GMC Guidance goes on to explain circumstances in which information sharing – that is the passing on of information, and thus the breaching of a patient's confidentiality, including the passing on information to colleagues and nursing staff, for research, or where a child might be at risk.

8.34 In particular the GMC Guidance stresses the importance of a practitioner being required to pass on information where this is required by law or the public interest demands it.[40] This Part will consider the Guidance generally, followed in the next Part by a review of the public interest and other legal exceptions to confidentiality. (As will be explained in **Part 5** a doctor's duty to override of confidentiality can apply equally for lawyers in their duty – where the question arises – to override legal professional privilege.)

8.35 The GMC Guidance summarises the process of a doctor's assessment of the child's capacity as follows:

> **'Young people who have capacity**[41]
>
> 29 You should encourage young people to involve their parents in making important decisions, but you should usually abide by any decision they have the capacity to make themselves (see paragraphs 30 to 33[42] and paragraphs 46 to 52)....'

---

38 www.gmc-uk.org/guidance/ethical_guidance/30627.asp.

39 www.gmc-uk.org/guidance/ethical_guidance/30591.asp.

40 See, eg, *W v Egdell* [1989] EWCA Civ 13, [1990] Ch 359, where the Court of Appeal said a doctor was justified in passing on information to the Home Office about a prisoner-patient whom he regarded to be a threat to the community if he was released from prison.

41 www.gmc-uk.org/guidance/ethical_guidance/children_guidance_29_capacity_to_consent.asp.

42 30 Respect for young people's views is important in making decisions about their care. If they refuse treatment, particularly treatment that could save their life or prevent serious deterioration in their health, this presents a challenge that you need to consider carefully.
31 Parents cannot override the competent consent of a young person to treatment that you consider is in their best interests. But you can rely on parental consent when a child lacks the capacity to consent.

Confidentiality: sharing medical information with and without consent

8.36 Patient trust applies as much if the patient is a child as it does if the patient is an adult; and the same duties arise for the child as for the adult. The GMC Guidance defines 'Principles of confidentiality'[43] in relation to children as:

> '42 Respecting patient confidentiality is an essential part of good care; this applies when the patient is a child or young person as well as when the patient is an adult. Without the trust that confidentiality brings, children and young people might not seek medical care and advice, or they might not tell you all the facts needed to provide good care.'

8.37 The Guidance then goes on to explain when information as to a child or young person can be shared: with and without consent of the patient. First the Guidance, under the heading 'Sharing information with the consent of a child or young person' states the following:[44]

> '44 Sharing information with the right people can help to protect children and young people from harm and ensure that they get the help they need. It can also reduce the number of times they are asked the same questions by different professionals. By asking for their consent to share relevant information, you are showing them respect and involving them in decisions about their care.
>
> 45 If children and young people are able to take part in decision-making, you should explain why you need to share information, and ask for their consent. They will usually be happy for you to talk to their parents and others involved in their care or treatment.'

8.38 'Sharing information without consent' in the GMC Guidance deals with the question of 'disclosure'[45] – passing on of information – as a matter of public interest or of law:[46]

---

43 www.gmc-uk.org/guidance/ethical_guidance/children_guidance_42_43_principles_of_confidentiality.asp.

44 www.gmc-uk.org/guidance/ethical_guidance/children_guidance_44_45_consent_of_young_person.asp.

45 Of the term 'disclosure' in this context it is worth noting, in passing, the following:
(1) The disparaging comment of MacDonald J in *AS v TH (False Allegations of Abuse)* [2016] EWHC 532 Fam, MacDonald J: '[33] … I pause to note that despite the fact that the use of the term "disclosure" to describe a statement or allegation of abuse made by a child has been deprecated since the Cleveland Report due to it precluding the notion that the abuse might not have occurred (see para 12.34(1)), *every* professional who gave evidence in this case (except the Children's Guardian) used the term "disclosure" to describe what the children had said to them'; and
(2) That to a lawyer (see eg in Chs 9 and 10) the terms disclosure has a specific mean applied to informing other parties to the case that documents and information are held by one party, as in 'privilege from disclosure' (see Part 3).

46 www.gmc-uk.org/guidance/ethical_guidance/children_guidance_46_sharing_info_without_consent.asp.

'46 If a child or young person does not agree to disclosure there are still circumstances in which you should disclose information:

(a) when there is an overriding public interest in the disclosure

(b) when you judge that the disclosure is in the best interests of a child or young person who does not have the maturity or understanding to make a decision about disclosure

(c) when disclosure is required by law.'

8.39 The questions of law and of public interest will be dealt with in **Part 5**. Paragraph 46(b) leaves the doctor in a very similar position to that of the lawyer confronted with the decision of whether a child is of understanding to proceed with a court application.[47] The doctor, like the lawyer, is required to make the judgment as to the child's level of 'maturity or understanding'.

8.40 Amongst the factors in assessment of a child's 'best interests' the Guidance includes the following:[48]

'12 An assessment of best interests will include what is clinically indicated in a particular case. You should also consider:

(a) the views of the child or young person, so far as they can express them, including any previously expressed preferences

(d) the views of parents

(c) the views of others close to the child or young person

(d) the cultural, religious or other beliefs and values of the child or parent'[49]

---

47 FPR 2010, r 16.6(3)(b).

48 www.gmc-uk.org/guidance/ethical_guidance/children_guidance_12_13_assessing_best_interest.asp.

49 The footnote to para 12(d) in the GMC Guidance refers to *Re A (A minor) (Wardship: Medical Treatment)* [1993] 1 FLR 386, perhaps intending a reference to *Re E (A Minor) (Wardship: Medical Treatment)* [1993] 1 FLR 386, Ward J of which Munby LJ commented in *Re G (Education: Religious Upbringing)* [2012] EWCA Civ 1233, [2013] 1 FLR 677 as follows: '[81] The point arises in its most obvious and extreme form where the issue before the court is whether to require a teenager to submit against their wishes to lifesaving medical treatment. There, as Nolan LJ once observed (*Re W (A Minor) (Medical Treatment: Court's Jurisdiction)* [1993] Fam 64, [1992] 3 WLR 758 at 94 and 781respectively), the duty of the court is to ensure so far as it can that children survive to attain the age of 18 at which an individual is free to do with his life what he wishes. A poignant example is provided by the aftermath of *Re E (A Minor) (Wardship: Medical Treatment)* where Ward J (as he then was) had required a 15¾-year-old Jehovah's witness to have a blood transfusion despite his, and his parents', vehemently expressed religious objections. A few years later, not long after he had attained his majority, E's leukaemia returned. He refused a blood transfusion, going bravely to his death steadfast in his religious faith.'

5 PUBLIC INTEREST AND OVERIDING CONFIDENTIALITY

Public interest and the medical profession: passing on information without consent

8.41 The GMC Guidance deals with the passing on, or 'sharing' of information – what it calls 'disclosure'[50] but which means breaching confidentiality (or privilege in the case of a lawyer) – without a child's consent. It divides the subject into two main aspects:

- Passing on information without consent in the public interest, that is to say with justification; and
- Consideration of the benefits and possible harm to the child of passing on information.

8.42 Passing on of information is explained in the following way by the GMC Guidance:[51]

> '47 You can disclose, without consent, information that identifies the child or young person, in the public interest. A disclosure is in the public interest if the benefits which are likely to arise from the release of information outweigh both the child or young person's interest in keeping the information confidential and society's interest in maintaining trust between doctors and patients. You must make this judgement case by case, by weighing up the various interests involved.'
>
> '48 When considering whether disclosure would be justified you should:
>
> (a) tell the child or young person what you propose to disclose and why, unless that would undermine the purpose or place the child or young person at increased risk of harm
>
> (b) ask for consent to the disclosure, if you judge the young person to be competent to make the decision, unless it is not practical to do so.
>
> 49 If a child or young person refuses consent, or if it is not practical to ask for consent, you should consider the benefits and possible harms that may arise from disclosure. You should consider any views given by the child or young person on why you should not disclose the information. But you should disclose information if this is necessary to protect the child or young person, or someone else, from risk of death or serious harm….
>
> 50 If you judge that disclosure is justified, you should disclose the information promptly to an appropriate person or authority and record your discussions

50 See comments of MacDonald J in *AS v TH* (above) on use of the term 'disclose' in this context.

51 www.gmc-uk.org/guidance/ethical_guidance/children_guidance_47_50_public_interest.asp.

and reasons. If you judge that disclosure is not justified, you should record your reasons for not disclosing.'

8.43 Paragraph 47 sets the framework for this guidance, basing its advice on the public interest being served by passing on information without consent. This framework applies also to the legal profession. It should also apply – it is submitted – to any professional who has confidential information from a child which child is entitled to expect that his or her confidences will be kept. Whether the water-tightness of a child's confidence will always apply to other professionals covered by *Working Together* will be reviewed at the end of the next Part of this Chapter.[52]

Confidentiality and professional relationships

8.44 Where a professional relationship is concerned, confidentiality will arise as between the client/patient and the professional (privilege in the case of lawyers). Are there circumstances in which confidentiality or privilege can be overridden in the particular case?

8.45 A client's right to privilege – but not necessarily to confidentiality – is absolute.[53] There is in general terms a public interest in anyone who receives a confidence, in whatever relationship, being required to keep that confidence.[54] Consequently, there is a substantial duty on a professional person to maintain a confidence. The duty is particularly relevant to medical professionals; but the duty to protect confidences is as important for others involved as professionals with children.

8.46 The question of whether confidentiality can be overridden by an individual in a professional capacity and was considered by the Court of Appeal in *W v Egdell*;[55] and the points made by the court then concur with the factors rained by the GMC Guidance at §§47–50.[56]

Confidentiality and W v Egdell

8.47 In the *W v Egdell* case, W had shot and killed five people and seriously wounded two others. He pleaded guilty to manslaughter on the ground of diminished responsibility. He was in a special hospital where he remained at the time of the appeal. In 1984 a tribunal recommended steps to lead to W's eventual release. The Home Secretary did not accept the advice for transfer. W instructed solicitors to apply to a tribunal for a review of his case. Dr Egdell (E), a consultant psychiatrist, was instructed prepare a report. E considered that features of W's personality (eg a long-standing interest in explosives) had previously been

---

52 See 8.87.

53 *R v Derby Magistrates' Court exp B* [1995] UKHL 18, [1996] 1 AC 487, [1996] 1 FLR 513; and see 8.22

54 *Attorney-General v Guardian Newspapers Ltd (No 2)* [1988] UKHL 6, [1990] 1 AC 109, [1987] WLR 776; and see 8.7 for further consideration.

55 [1989] EWCA Civ 13, [1990] Ch 359 (Sir Stephen Baker P, Bingham LJ and Sir John May).

56 www.gmc-uk.org/guidance/ethical_guidance/children_guidance_47_50_public_interest.asp.

insufficiently appreciated. He did not favour W's transfer at that stage and so reported to W's solicitors. W withdrew his application to the tribunal; but did not want anyone to see the report. E wanted his report sent to W's hospital. The solicitors refused in view of their instructions.

8.48 When E sent a copy of his report to the Home Office, W issued a claim based on E's breach of his confidence. On an interim basis E was restrained from communicating the contents of his report save to W or with W's authority. The first instance judge discharged the interim injunction. W appealed against the order for discharge. Bingham LJ, who gave the main and most authoritative judgement, said any decision whether to restrain a breach of confidence depended on what the court ruled turned on how the court approached the question of the public interest in confidences being kept, in the individual case:[57]

> 'Where, as here, the relationship between doctor and patient is contractual, the question is whether the doctor's disclosure is or is not a breach of contract. The answer to that question must turn not on what the doctor thinks but on what the court rules. But it does not follow that the doctor's conclusion is irrelevant. In making its ruling the court will give such weight to the considered judgment of a professional man as seems in all the circumstances to be appropriate.
>
> The parties were agreed, as I think rightly, that the crucial question in the present case was how, on the special facts of the case, the balance should be struck between the public interest in maintaining professional confidences and the public interest in protecting the public against possible violence. Mr. Robertson submitted that on the facts here the public interest in maintaining confidences was shown to be clearly preponderant.'

Public interest in overriding privilege

8.49 In the final analysis, said Bingham LJ, where a professional person – in this case a consultant psychiatrist – considers that an individual with whom he has a confidential relationship poses a public risk, then public interest demands that he be entitled to breach confidentiality. He is then under a duty to take reasonable steps to pass on the confidential information 'to the responsible authorities' (see italicised passage below):

> 'There is one consideration which in my judgment, as in that of the judge, weighs the balance of public interest decisively in favour of disclosure. It may be shortly put. Where a man has committed multiple killings under the disability of serious mental illness, decisions which may lead directly or indirectly to his release from hospital should not be made unless a responsible authority is properly able to make an informed judgment that

57 See opinion of Lord Goff in *Attorney-General v Guardian Newspapers Ltd (No 2)* [1988] UKHL 6, [1990] 1 AC 109, [1987] WLR 776 considered at 8.7.

the risk of repetition is so small as to be acceptable. A consultant psychiatrist who becomes aware, even in the course of a confidential relationship, of information which leads him, in the exercise of what the court considers a sound professional judgment, to fear that such decisions may be made on the basis of inadequate information and with a real risk of consequent danger to the public is entitled *to take such steps as are reasonable in all the circumstances to communicate the grounds of his concern to the responsible authorities.* I have no doubt that the judge's decision in favour of Dr. Egdell was right on the facts of this case.' (italics added)

8.50 In assessing the balance to be weighed where a decision on public interest is concerned, Bingham LJ drew attention to European Convention 1950 rights (not then formally part of English law): that Art 8 applied; but that these might be overridden in the interests of 'public safety or the interest of crime'.

'No reference was made in argument before us (nor, so far as I know, before the judge J to the European Convention of Human Rights, but I believe this decision to be in accordance with it. I would accept that Article 8(1) of the Convention may protect an individual against the disclosure of information protected by the duty of professional secrecy. But Article 8(2) envisages that circumstances may arise in which a public authority may legitimately interfere with exercise of that right in accordance with the law and where necessary in a democratic society in the interests of public safety or the prevention of crime. Here there was no interference by a public authority. Dr Egdell did, as I conclude, act in accordance with the law. And his conduct was in my judgment necessary in the interests of public safety and the prevention of crime.'

Confidentiality and children

8.51 If the interests of children are in issue, their interests predominate where a privacy balance falls to be decided:[58]

'[73] The court reiterates that in judicial decisions where the rights under Art 8 of parents and those of a child are at stake, the child's rights must be the paramount consideration. If any balancing of interests is necessary, the interests of the child must prevail (see *Elsholz v Germany* (2002) 34 EHRR 58, [2000] 2 FLR 486 at para [52] and *TP and KM v United Kingdom* (2002) 34 EHRR 2, [2001] 2 FLR 549 at para [72]). This applies also in cases such as the present.'

58 See *Yousef v The Netherlands* (Application No 33711/96), [2003] 1 FLR 210; and see *ZH (Tanzania) v Secretary of State for the Home Department* [2011] UKSC 4, [2011] 1 FLR 2170; *H(H) v Deputy Prosecutor of the Italian Republic, Genoa (Official Solicitor intervening)* [2012] UKSC 25, [2013] 1 AC 338 concerning children's 'interests' and European Convention 1950 decisions.

8.52 It remains to be seen whether a similar loss of privilege – if it arose in the first place[59]– may arise where children are concerned. For example, it might be said that the welfare of a child created a public interest which was in a wholly different category to any other in this Chapter. The public interest in the welfare and protection of a child might be said to override litigation privilege (as has been the case where care proceedings are concerned). In an appropriately extreme case, as McFarlane J mentions in *Re T (Wardship: Impact of Police Intelligence)*[60] that it may be appropriate for a lawyer to decide override the confidentiality of a client where the welfare of a child is engaged.

8.53 In cases of urgency a lawyer or other professional may have to make his/her own decision quickly and proceed accordingly (eg prompt contact with the police or a children's department). In other cases, as with *W v Edgell* there may be time to give notice of the intention to breach confidentiality and then for the professional to await a court order restraining breach of confidence if the client/patient applies.

6 SHARING OF INFORMATION: *WORKING TOGETHER*

Introduction to working together

Guidance for professionals working with children

8.54 Since the Cleveland Report (*Report of the inquiry into child abuse in Cleveland 1987* Cm 412, HMSO) successive versions of guidance have been issued; and this series has, to date, concluded with *Working together to safeguard children*[61] (Department of Education, March 2015) ('*Working Together*'). The difference of approach to the confidences of a mature child as between the GMC guidance and *Working Together* must now be considered.

8.55 Failure to pass on information, and for professionals to act together, was at the root of the problems exposed by Cleveland in 1987. Thirty years later similar problems persist, as Cobb J showed in *GD and BD (Children) and ors v Wakefield MDC and West Yorks Police.*[62] His 'executive summary', included as Appendix C to the case report, records that the claim was one for damages under Human Rights Act 1998 arising from circumstances which 'exposed serious and systemic flaws in the decision-making and information-sharing of a joint investigation involving

59 See, eg, *Ramsbotham v Senior* (1869) FLR Rep 591 where a solicitor was ordered to reveal an address in the interests of the child concerned in the proceedings, considered further at 9.24.

60 [2009] EWHC 2440 (Fam), [2010] 1 FLR 1048.

61 *Working together to safeguard children, A guide to inter-agency working to safeguard and promote the welfare of children* (March 2015, Department of Education) www.gov.uk/government/uploads/system/uploads/attachment_data/file/419595/Working_Together_to_Safeguard_Children.pdf ('*Working Together*').

62 [2016] EWHC 3312 (Fam), [2017] Fam Law 283; and see opening remarks in the judgment of MacDonald J in *AS v TH (False Allegations of Abuse)* [2016] EWHC 532 Fam on failures to take account of the Cleveland Report.

West Yorkshire Police and Wakefield Metropolitan District Council'. Two children, aged seven and two were removed from their home under police protection, following arrest of their parents on suspicion of involvement in the downloading and distribution of indecent images of children. They were made the subject of interim care orders. Their father later pleaded guilty to six specimen counts relating to these offences, and was later sentenced to a term of imprisonment.

8.56 Cobb J's summary continues by explaining in outline – which he considers in more detail in a lengthy judgment – the failures within the police and with the local authority over the departments' working together. The judge's summary includes:

> '3 At the time of the parents' arrest, the officer in charge of the investigation from the West Yorkshire Police (DS Hudson) expressed himself to be 90% certain that the children's mother (MD) was a woman (Woman X) recorded on video (the short video) performing oral sex with a young female child who it was believed to be GD; this video footage was found on the parents' computer. The police officer further believed (with 99% certainty) that GD had been photographed in a sexually provocative pose displaying her genitals, on a still image also found on the parents' computer (Girl Y).
>
> 4 For a period of many days after their reception into care, the children had no contact with their parents; when contact was reinstated it was closely supervised. The children remained in foster care, separated from their parents, for 9½ months returning to live with their mother in December 2015.
>
> 5 The history now apparent reveals that on 31 March 2015, DS Hudson had been advised by forensic experts that the mother was not Woman X and had been "eliminated" on the basis of expert assessment. This was later confirmed in a written report from the forensic expert on 12 June 2015. The Police did not divulge this information to the Local Authority until 24 June, and not to the mother until 9 July 2015.
>
> 6 On 10 June 2015, a second (longer) video recording was discovered by the West Yorkshire Police in the context of a different investigation, of which the first (short) video was clearly an excerpt. This was a crucial discovery. This longer video showed: (a) that the film was recorded in the United State of America, (b) that the mother was definitively not Woman X, and that (c) that GD was definitively not the girl being abused. This information was not shared with the Local Authority, nor with the Respondent parents, until the final hearing. At a meeting on 21 August 2015 DS Hudson advised representatives of the Local Authority (its solicitor, Ms Anne McMullan, and the instructed counsel Mr Ian Shiels) in passing that the short video probably originated in the USA. He did not refer to the existence of the longer video. It was only on the second day of the final hearing of the public law applications some months later, on 18 November 2015, that the Local Authority advised the mother, father and Children's Guardian of the American origin of the video, and on the same day, the Police informed all parties (the Local Authority and

the respondent parents) for the first time of the existence of the longer video.'

Systemic failures

8.57 Cobb J identified the systemic failures at work in this case as including:

'[124] ... I am not sure that the failures in this case can or should be explained simply by a loss of objectivity. Rather they can and should be explained by a combination of the following factors...:

i) There was no strategic leadership in this joint investigation; each arm of the inquiry lacked direction, and there was no one individual taking responsibility for the co-ordination of the inquiries. Insofar as this role was fulfilled by the Officer in the Case, I consider that he allowed his own beliefs about the likely involvement of MD in abuse to cloud his judgment. The Local Authority was beholden to the police in relation to the information sought, and thereby at times found itself partially disabled from conducting any effective case management;

ii) There were poorly defined lines of communication within each of the authorities (social services/police and their respective legal departments) and between the authorities; within each authority different individuals took responsibility for similar functions, none of whom had a comprehensive grasp of the totality of the case;

iii) There was a lack of care and accuracy in record keeping, and in the management of information;

iv) Many key individuals (including the lawyers) had a partial knowledge of the case, which led to incoherent decision-making.

v) Insofar as this was ever a joint investigation (which is debatable) it lacked structure and cohesion. The police took an overly defensive stance in relation to information, and the Local Authority an over-ambitious position encouraged by an experienced police officer (DS Hudson) who lacked discipline in the information sharing.

vi) A lack of discipline and rigour in the evaluation of the evidence; and

vii) A casual regard, and in some respects total disregard, of ordinary principles of good professional practice.'

8.58 As a result children remained separated from their mother for much longer than need be; and in consequence that they and their mother were entitled to the *Human Rights Act 1998* damages claimed.[63] *GD and BD* may be an extreme example of things going wrong; but the operation of *Working Together* must be judged by its unreported successes, and its failures (as in that case).

63 See Cobb J at §[128].

Working together: statutory guidance

Working Together: *'sharing' information in relation to children*

8.59 *Working Together* is 'a guide to inter-agency working to safeguard and promote the welfare of children'. Amongst its 'key principles' is 'a child-centred and coordinated approach to safeguarding' of children. *Children Act 2004, s 11* places duties to safeguard children and to promote their welfare on specified public bodies including local authorities, health authorities and the police (*CA 2004, s 11(1)*). Each of these bodies are required to 'make arrangements for ensuring that their functions are discharged having regard to the need to safeguard and promote the welfare of children' and to make arrangements to promote co-operation between the agencies concerned with children.

8.60 *CA 2004, s 11(4)* requires anybody to which s 11(1) applies to discharge their duty under the section in such a way as to 'have regard to any guidance' issued by the Department of Education:

> '(4) Each person and body to whom this section applies must in discharging their duty under this section have regard to any guidance given to them for the purpose by the Secretary of State.'

8.61 *Working Together* is the guidance issued under s 11(4). It applies to a child defined by *CA 2004, s 65(1)* as in *CA 1989* as 'a person under the age of eighteen'. It deals with guidance over safeguarding, help and assessment for all ages of children. The guidance strongly advocates the need to listen to a child's views. It urges the sharing of information concerning children. There is no clear reference to dealing with the confidences of the mature child, as *Gillick* requires. For any professional who deals with mature children – treating them, teaching them, advising them, mediation – this provision as to 'sharing' information raises the question of confidentiality of mature children.

8.62 *Working Together* does not consider the subject of 'confidentiality' in any specific or clear way; though guidance is provided to its opposite, 'sharing' of information, in *Information sharing: Advice for practitioners providing safeguarding services* etc.[64] *Working Together* explains the 'early sharing of information' as being 'the key to providing effective early help where there are emerging problems'. If child protection – as distinct from their confidences – is the only criterion, this must surely be right? But 'Fears about sharing information cannot be allowed to stand in the way of the need to promote the welfare and protect the safety of children' says para 24 of *Working Together*. This betrays an approach to confidentiality which is not necessarily consistent with the common law.

64 *Information sharing Advice for practitioners providing safeguarding services to children, young people, parents and carers* (HM Government, March 2015) www.gov.uk/government/uploads/system/uploads/attachment_data/file/419628/Information_sharing_advice_safeguarding_practitioners.pdf).

Role and function of statutory guidance

8.63 Guidance, such as *Working together* – even though provided for by statute – cannot alter the common law.[65] Only express statutory provision, or a court higher than that which expressed the common law principle,[66] can do that. The ambit of confidentiality and the extent to which it is regarded as in the public interest is summarised by Lord Goff in *Att Gen v Guardian Newspapers Ltd (No 2)*.[67] The common law which asserts that confidentiality principles can apply to children of age and understanding is set out in *Gillick*.[68] Insofar as the confidentiality of any mature child is protected by the principles set out in that case, it cannot be overridden by anything which suggests that confidentiality can be overridden it is outside the scope (*ultra vires*) what the guidance in *Working Together* can empower.

8.64 Of the common law position, Lord Scarman explained his view as follows:[69]

> 'Although statute has intervened in respect of a child's capacity to consent to medical treatment from the age of 16 onwards, neither statute nor the case law has ruled on the extent and duration of parental right in respect of children under the age of 16. More specifically, there is no rule yet applied to contraceptive treatment, which has special problems of its own and is a late-comer in medical practice. It is open, therefore, to the House to formulate a rule.'

8.65 He and Lord Fraser then went on to explain their views of the law, generally, as to the rights of mature children – of 'intelligence and understanding – and of their right to confidentiality in particular. This is considered fully in **Chapter 2**; but the extent to which the judgment in *Gillick* turned on confidentiality and consent to medical treatment can be seen from the passage in the previous passage. So, said Lord Scarman, of the extent to which the law – in relation to a mature child's confidentiality – must adjust itself according to the facts of each individual case:[70]

> 'If the law should impose upon the process of 'growing up' fixed limits where nature knows only a continuous process, the price would be artificiality and a lack of realism in an area where the law must be sensitive to human development and social change.... Unless and until Parliament should think fit to intervene, the courts should establish a principle flexible enough to enable justice to be achieved by its application to the particular circumstances proved by the evidence placed before them.'

---

65 See 1.25.

66 As explained at 1.22.

67 [1990] 1 AC 109, [1988] UKHL 6, [1987] WLR 776, (*Spycatcher case*); see 8.7.

68 [1985] UKHL 7, [1986] 1 AC 112, [1986] 1 FLR 224; as affirmed in *R (Axon) v The Secretary of State for Health and anor* [2006] EWHC 37 (Admin), [2006] 2 FLR 206, Silber J.

69 [1986] 1 FLR 224 at 250.

70 [1986] 1 FLR 224 at 250.

Information sharing and a mature child's confidentiality

8.66 Privacy and rights of a mature child engage European Convention 1950 Art 8 (respect for family life). This creates a tension between the law (based on *Gillick*) and the Departmental guidance in *Working Together*. What rights to confidentiality does the child have in this situation?

8.67 A mature child's right to privacy was considered by Keehan J in *PD v SD & Anor.*[71] (PD was a gender change 16-year-old who sought an order in wardship that no information should be given by his carer local authority should not pass on information about his to his adoptive parents.) Keehan J held that the Art 8 rights of the child and his parents were engaged, and that the rights of PD prevailed over his parents:

> '[23] … I take particular account of the decision of the European Court of Human Rights in *Yousef v Netherlands* [2003] 1 FLR 210, that where there is a tension between the Article 8 rights of the child, on the one hand, and the parents, on the other, the rights of the child prevail…'.

8.68 He should therefore focus, said Keehan J, on the competing Article 8 rights of P and of his parents; and he did so, in the first instance, by referring (at §[26]) to the view of Lord Scarman in *Gillick* as to the limits of parental responsibility:

> 'The rights of a parent exist primarily to enable the parent to discharge his duty of maintenance, protection and education until he reaches such an age as to be able to look after himself and make his own decisions.'

8.69 As did the common law in *Gillick*, so in *PD v SD* (and there, with Art 8 in mind), the rights of the mature child were held to have priority over parental responsibility. It is likely that if the same balance were struck as between private rights and the *Working Together* guidance preference for sharing confidential information in respect of a mature child the same respect for a child's confidentiality at common law would prevail. And this is the more so in the light of Lord Goff's comment in *Spycatcher* (above): that there is always 'a public interest in the maintenance of confidences'.

71 [2015] EWHC 4103 (Fam), Keehan J

Sharing as against confidentiality

Guidance over safeguarding in the context of a child's confidentiality

8.70 *Working Together* deals with guidance over safeguarding.[72] It is intended to assist professionals with assessment for children of all ages. This chapter must review the guidance from the point of view of a mature child. Thus the way *Working Together* considers a mature child's views will dictate how its statutory guidance treats confidentiality.

8.71 Of the views of children and under the heading 'A child-centred approach' *Working Together* states:[73]

> '20 Effective safeguarding systems are child centred. Failings in safeguarding systems are too often the result of losing sight of the needs and views of the children within them, or placing the interests of adults ahead of the needs of children.
>
> 22 Children want to be respected, their views to be heard, to have stable relationships with professionals built on trust and to have consistent support provided for their individual needs. This should guide the behaviour of professionals. Anyone working with children should see and speak to the child; listen to what they say; take their views seriously; and work with them collaboratively when deciding how to support their needs….'

8.72 *Working Together* strongly advocates the need to listen to a child's views; but so too does it urge the sharing of information concerning children, without any overt reference to *Gillick* and the needs for the confidential information from mature children to be respected. This may create a tension between the law and the guidance in *Working Together* which must be considered here.

Children act 2004: working together and the duty to safeguard

Promoting welfare of children

8.73 *Children Act 2004, s 11* places the duties to safeguard children and to promote their welfare on specified public bodies including local authorities, health authorities and the police.[74] Each of these bodies are required to 'make

72 Cobb J stressed the importance of 'safeguarding' children in *AZ, BZ and CZ v Kirklees Council (Human Rights Claim: Costs)* [2017] EWFC 11 in relation to HRA 1998 claim in the following general terms: '[1] Local authorities responsible for safeguarding children carry a heavy obligation to ensure that they perform their statutory duties at all times in a manner which is compatible with the rights of the individuals and their families who they are assigned to help, specifically the rights which individuals enjoy under the *European Convention on Human Rights (ECHR) – Article 6* and *Article 8*. Any violation of these *Convention* rights is of course unlawful (*section 6 Human Rights Act 1998 'HRA 1998'*); when such an alleged violation occurs, those affected are entitled to bring claims under *section 7* and *8* of the *HRA 1998* for relief, including declarations and/or damages (judge's italics)'.

73 *Working Together* Introduction para 20 and 22 p 9.

74 *CA 2004, s 11(1).*

arrangements for ensuring that their functions are discharged having regard to the need to safeguard and promote the welfare of children'.[75] *CA 2004, s 10* requires each local authority to 'make arrangements to promote co-operation between' the agencies concerned with children: within the local authority, 'the authority's relevant partners'[76] and any other body they consider appropriate.[77]

8.74 These arrangements are to be made to improve 'the well-being of children in the authority's area', including in relation to 'physical and mental health and emotional well-being [and] protection from harm and neglect'. *CA 1989, s 47*, for example, places on a local authority the duty to investigate in response to a report under these sections has a duty to investigate and to establish whether the child in question is in need of local authority 'action to safeguard or promote [the child's] welfare'.[78]

'Well-being of children'

8.75 In exercise of their functions under *CA 2004, s 10* or in discharge of their duties under s 11, each body to whom these sections apply must 'have regard to any guidance given to them for the purpose by the Secretary of State'.[79] *Working Together* has been produced as statutory guidance under *CA 2004, ss 10* and *11*.[80] The 2004 Act is concerned with the 'well-being of children' which is described by s 10 as follows:

---

75 *CA 2004, s 11(2)(a)*.

76 *CA 2004, s 10(4)* defines 'relevant partner' as:
- (a) where the authority is a county council for an area for which there is also a district council, the district council;
- (b) the local policing body and the chief officer of police for a police area any part of which falls within the area of the local authority;
- (c) a local probation board for an area any part of which falls within the area of the authority;
- (ca) the Secretary of State in relation to his functions under sections 2 and 3 of the Offender Management Act 2007, so far as they are exercisable in relation to England;
- (cb) any provider of probation services that is required by arrangements under section 3(2) of the Offender Management Act 2007 to act as a relevant partner of the authority;
- (d) a youth offending team for an area any part of which falls within the area of the authority;
- (e) a Strategic Health Authority and Primary Care Trust for an area any part of which falls within the area of the authority;
- (f) a person providing services in pursuance of section 68 of the Education and Skills Act 2008 in any part of the area of the authority;
- (fa) the governing body of a maintained school that is maintained by the authority… ;
- (fb) the proprietor of a school approved by the Secretary of State under section 342 of the Education Act 1996 and situated in the authority's area;
- (fc) the proprietor of a city technology college, city college for the technology of the arts or Academy situated in the authority's area;
- (fd) the governing body of an institution within the further education sector the main site of which is situated in the authority's area;…

77 *CA 2004, s 10(1)*.

78 *CA 1989, s 47(1)*.

79 *CA 2004, ss 10(8A)* and *11(4)*.

80 The full list of statutory provisions under which *Working Together* has been produced as guidance is at para 3 on p 7.

'(2) The arrangements are to be made with a view to improving the well-being of children in the authority's area so far as relating to—

(a) physical and mental health and emotional well-being;

(b) protection from harm and neglect;

(c) education, training and recreation;

(d) the contribution made by them to society;

(e) social and economic well-being.

(3) In making arrangements under this section a local authority in England must have regard to the importance of parents and other persons caring for children in improving the well-being of children.'

8.76 It is not proposed to analyse each of these components of s 10. Perhaps 'protection from harm' can be seen as a central aspect of 'well-being' of a child; so a brief review of how this term has been analysed by the courts under *CA 1989, s 31(2)* will follow.

'Harm' and the welfare of a child

8.77 'Harm' is the term used, broadly, for that which is against the welfare of a child. *CA 1989, s 31(9)* defines 'harm' as 'ill-treatment or the impairment of health or development including, for example, impairment suffered from seeing or hearing the ill-treatment of another'. 'Significant harm' defines the first limb of the statutory basis for making a care or supervision order. *CA 1989, s 31(2)* provides as follows:

'(2) A court may only make a care order or supervision order if it is satisfied –

(a) that the child concerned is suffering, or is likely to suffer, significant harm; and

(b) that the harm [etc is attributable to parental care or lack of control].'

8.78 'Any harm which [the child] has suffered or is at risk of suffering'[81] is one of the factors to be considered by a court where decisions about the future of a child are to be considered.

Harm under Children Act 2004

8.79 The test under the *CA 2004, s 10(3)* is 'protection from harm'. Nothing is to be gained from seeking some legal distinction between 'significant harm' and 'harm' simpliciter. The point to stress is that each case will depend on its facts, the more so when the child in question is of an age to understand the significance of his or her confidences.

81 *CA 1989, s 1(3)(e)*.

8.80 The test is objective. What is 'harm' must be judged according to principles not guided by the particular child in question. This was explained by Hughes LJ in *Re D (Care Order: Evidence)*:[82]

> '[25] .... The test under s 31(2) is and has to be an objective one. If it were otherwise, and the 'care which it is reasonable to expect a parent to give' were to be judged by the standards of the parent with the characteristics of the particular parent in question, the protection afforded to children would be very limited indeed, if not entirely illusory. It would in effect then be limited to protection against the parent who was fully able to provide proper care but either chose not to do so or neglected through fault to do so. That is not the meaning of s 31(2). It is abundantly clear that a parent may unhappily fail to provide reasonable care even though he is doing his incompetent best.'

6 INFORMATION SHARING

'Early help assessment'

8.81 A main concern of *Working Together* is to ensure effective early help for children where this is needed and to be clear that local agencies have processes in place for children who may need early help for appropriate services.[83] *Working Together* requires local agencies work together cooperatively 'to put processes in place for the effective assessment of the needs of individual children who may benefit from early help'; and to co-ordinate early help assessment accordingly. It may ultimately become the responsibility for the local authority children's department to provide services to a child in need who has been assessed in this way.[84]

8.82 However, 'sharing' (as defined below) of a mature child's information passed to a local authority professional, by definition may mean breaching confidence if the sharing is done without consent. How does the local authority's 'early help assessment' impact on question of the confidentiality of the mature child? *Working Together* explains how it considers the assessment should be carried out in general terms:

> '10 For an early help assessment to be effective:
>
> - the assessment should be undertaken with the agreement of the child and their parents or carers. It should involve the child and family as well as all the professionals who are working with them;
> - a teacher, GP, health visitor, early years' worker or other professional should be able to discuss concerns they may have about a child and family with a social worker in the local authority. Local authority

82 [2010] EWCA Civ 1000, [2011] 1 FLR 447.
83 *Working Together* Ch 1 paras 7-11, p 13.
84 *CA 1989, s 17(1).*

children's social care should set out the process for how this will happen; and

- if parents and/or the child do not consent to an early help assessment, then the lead professional should make a judgement as to whether, without help, the needs of the child will escalate. If so, a referral into local authority children's social care may be necessary.

11 If at any time it is considered that the child may be a child in need as defined in the Children Act 1989, or that the child has suffered significant harm or is likely to do so, a referral should be made immediately to local authority children's social care. This referral can be made by any professional.'

8.83 This must be read subject to the clear proviso: that if the professional considers the child to be of age and understanding, then that professional must go on to consider with the child whether the child agrees to any aspect of the child's confidentiality should be overridden. If a child does not consent to information being passed on, but the professional considers that confidentiality must be breached, then he or she will be required to go on to balance the competing rights of the child to a private life as against the public interest.[85]

Information 'sharing'

8.84 *Working Together* requires all professionals who work with children[86] and who have a role in early identification of problems which may be suffered by them, to 'share information with other professionals'. This is stated in *Working Together* as follows:[87]

'3 Local agencies should have in place effective ways to identify emerging problems and potential unmet needs for individual children and families. This requires all professionals, including those in universal services and those providing services to adults with children, to understand their role in identifying emerging problems and to share information with other professionals to support early identification and assessment.'

8.85 This provision as to 'sharing' information immediately raises the question of confidentiality of mature children. It is submitted here that the government advice – *Information sharing advice*[88] – does not differentiate the consequences in terms the law on confidentiality as between the rights of a mature child and those of a dependent child (ie a child not yet of age and understanding). Particular care must be exercised where a mature child thinks his or her confidentiality can be

85 As explained at 8.41; and see *W v Egdell* [1989] EWCA Civ 13, [1990] Ch 359, [1990] 2 WLR 471 at 8.47.

86 See, eg, the list in *CA 2004, s 10(4)* at 8.73.

87 *Working Together* Ch 1 para 3 p 12.

88 For full title and discussion see 8.88.

guaranteed by a professional; but where the duties of the professional are treated – eg by advice in *Working Together* – as being overridden.[89]

8.86 As ever, in a consideration of whether to override the confidentiality of a mature child, the professional will need to consider the public interests under *W v Edgell* and also reasons for interference with the child's rights, as explained here.[90] The lawyer who gives legal advice will need to be clear as to whether advice privilege adds another dimension or layer of privacy to any decision as to whether to override confidentiality.

8.87 The emphasis in *Working Together* is that professionals should work for prompt passing on of information amongst those covered by its guidance.[91] In the vast majority of cases of dependent children,[92] this will be justified from the point of view their welfare. They will be treated as not being in a position to have confidences. However, once a child is of age and understanding on the issue concerned that child will be entitled to claim privacy for confidential information; and he or she is entitled to have those confidences respected.

Confidentiality and Working Together

8.88 *Working Together* does not appear to consider the concept of 'confidentiality' in any clear way. It explains its opposite – 'information sharing' – in its Chapter 1[93] paras 22–25 and by reference to further guidance, namely *Information sharing: Advice for practitioners providing safeguarding services to children, young people, parents and carers* March 2015[94] (*'Information sharing advice'*). *Working Together* explains the 'early sharing of information' as being 'the key to providing effective early help where there are emerging problems' and later to put 'in place effective child protection services'.[95]

8.89 If child welfare, regardless of the views of the child, were the issue, that would be understandable. The concern here must be to question this approach where the child is mature, and ask what confidentiality rights that child might have.

8.90 *Working Together* para 24 continues:

> 'Fears about sharing information cannot be allowed to stand in the way of the need to promote the welfare and protect the safety of children. To ensure effective safeguarding arrangements:
>
> - all organisations should have arrangements in place which set out clearly the processes and the principles for sharing information between each other, with other professionals and with the LSCB; and

89 See, eg, *Re A (A Child)* [2012] UKSC 60.
90 See 8.41.
91 For a summary of professionals concerned see 8.73.
92 'Dependent children': as explained at 8.85.
93 Page 16.
94 Published by HM Government.
95 Para 23.

- no professional should assume that someone else will pass on information which they think may be critical to keeping a child safe. If a professional has concerns about a child's welfare and believes they are suffering or likely to suffer harm, then they should share the information with local authority children's social care.'

8.91 The statement in *Working Together* para 24 concerning 'fears about sharing information' standing 'in the way of the need to…protect' children (the passage italicised above) must now be seen in the context of how this relates to the mature child and the balance which must be struck by the professional who is in contact with the child. For readers of *Working Together* the main source of further information is *Information sharing advice*; so how far does this comply with the law so far as confidentiality and the mature child is concerned?

Information sharing advice

8.92 *Working Together* contains statutory guidance. *Information sharing advice* is non-statutory (though it derives from statutory guidance). It is designed to support practitioners in their decision-making 'when sharing information to reduce the risk of harm to children and young people'. It is described as being advice:

> 'This advice is for all frontline practitioners and senior managers working with children, young people, parents and carers who have to make decisions about sharing personal information on a case by case basis. It might also be helpful for practitioners working with adults who are responsible for children who may be in need.'

8.93 Page 4 of the advice sets out what are described as 'seven golden rules to sharing information' appropriately. These rules include the following:

> '4 Share with informed consent where appropriate and, where possible, respect the wishes of those who do not consent to share confidential information. *You may still share information without consent if, in your judgement, there is good reason to do so, such as where safety may be at risk.* You will need to base your judgement on the facts of the case. When you are sharing or requesting personal information from someone, be certain of the basis upon which you are doing so. Where you have consent, be mindful that an individual might not expect information to be shared.'

8.94 The italicised passage above is the critical feature of this advice. For the mature child or for any adult who may confide in a professional who works in line with this advice, this is likely to be the criterion by which they decide to share information. The advice goes on:[96]

96 Page 5; this advice is repeated at page 7.

'Fears about sharing information cannot be allowed to stand in the way of the need to safeguard and promote the welfare of children at risk of abuse or neglect.'

8.95 In law the advice given by *Working Together* in relation to mature children must be seen in the light of the following:

'(1) The consent of a mature child being given to information – that is their confidences – being 'shared' (see Part 4); but also

(2) That any confidence, in the public interest can be overridden, as explained in **Part 4**.'

7 CONFIDENTIALITY OF A CHILD

Overriding the confidentiality of a mature child

8.96 Steps which therefor must be taken by the individual professional, and minuted as they are taken (or immediately afterwards)[97] Will be considered in this final part of this chapter. What follows is a variation on Lord Kerr's 'sequencing' in the *H(H)* case where a decision is to be made to infringe a child's rights.[98]

8.97 Lord Kerr held that, once the subject child or children have been identified, a sequencing test should be applied to assess or define a child's rights (including rights to privacy and confidentiality[99]). As appropriate Lord Kerr's test has been adapted into the following sequence:

'(1) The child or children whose confidentiality is in issue or who are otherwise thought to be at risk of harm must be identified individually. Each will be assessed separately.

(2) If they are mature (ie of age and understanding), but under (say) 16, why does the assessing professional (eg doctor, lawyer, social worker) think they are mature. This will also depend on definition of the issue(s) relevant to their case(s) (see (3) below).

(3) What is the issue, or issues, on which it may lead to a breach the child's confidentiality (ie to interfere with his/her Art 8(1) rights).

(4) What rights of the child are engaged (ie Art 8(1) rights to confidentiality) derived from the issue(s) defined at (3)?[100]

---

97 See, eg, GMC Guidance considered at 8.42.

98 *H(H) v Deputy Prosecutor of the Italian Republic, Genoa (Official Solicitor intervening)* [2012] UKSC 25, [2013] 1 AC 338: [144] ... This calls for a sequencing of, first, consideration of the importance to be attached to the children's rights (by obtaining a clear-sighted understanding of their nature), then an assessment of the degree of interference and finally addressing the question whether extradition justifies the interference.

99 The application of this sequencing in the human rights context is explained at 5.47.

100 Examples of the way these rights can be defined are provided by Lady Hale in *Re A (Sexual Abuse: Disclosure)* [2012] UKSC 60, [2013] 1 FLR 948 at §[1] and by Munby J in *Re Roddy (A Child)(Identification: Restriction on Publication)* [2003] EWHC 2927, [2004] 2 FLR 949 (see 5.67).

(5) Is any interference with the confidentiality (ie Art 8 rights) of the child(ren) by the person carrying out the assessment?

(6) What is the importance of the child's rights, relative to rights of others (including any public interest) engaged by the particular confidentiality issue(s)? This may include the rights of another adult, mature or dependent child.

(7) What is the degree of any proposed interference with the child's Art 8(1) rights (and see per Lord Steyn pointed out in *Re S*, para [25], it is 'necessary to measure the nature of the impact … on the child' of what is in prospect[101])?'

8.98 If these steps are followed and minuted as they are taken the record of why confidentiality is to be breached (if that is the decision of the professional concerned), and the justification for a breach of confidentiality, can be explained in the case of each individual child.

8.99 It is clear from the approaches of the law and of clinical practice on the one hand and the approach of *Information sharing advice* to a child's confidentiality is appreciably different, in that the guiding principles or priorities of each are different. The first emphasis that each case, each child, must be judged according to general principles applied to the individual; whereas it may be thought that *Sharing* starts from the – entirely laudable, perhaps – general principle that the end is child protection only.

Differences of professional cultures

8.100 What is the position in relation to confidentiality if a child of understanding – the Mabon[102] boys (for example) – wants to discuss his or her personal circumstances and any concerns that child may have in relation to (say) court proceedings between their parents. The child wants to discuss this on terms of absolute confidentiality; and on terms that what the child says will not be passed on to third parties, save with their permission? That is an absolute pre-condition of their discussion with any professional: lawyer, doctor, social worker or other.

8.101 Their confidence will be protected absolutely if they speak with a lawyer where he or she considers that the child can give instructions in proceedings.[103] It is likely, if the child is regarded by a doctor as of 'sufficient understanding' – that is, *Gillick*-competent – that the child can speak confidentially to that doctor. Their confidences will be protected if there is no public interest in them being overridden.[104]

101 Considered at 5.46; and see in particular the review of the importance of child's interest in *PJS v News Group Newspapers Ltd* [2016] UKSC 26, [2016] AC 1081, [2016] 2 FLR 251, [2016] 2 WLR 1253 as discussed at 5.32.

102 *Mabon v Mabon* [2005] EWCA Civ 634, [2005] Fam 366, [2005] 2 FLR 1011: see 6.81 for further consideration of this case.

103 FPR 2010, r 16.6(3).

104 GMC Guidance at §§47-50; see 8.42.

8.102 On *Gillick* principles, the same rules apply for the doctor as to any other professional given confidential information by a mature child; and this is despite what may be said to the contrary in *Working Together.* If there is a clash of professional cultures between 'sharing' under *Working Together* and confidentiality in *Gillick,* then the common law as it now stands puts *Gillick* before departmental guidance where a child's privacy and their Art 8 rights are concerned.

Confidentiality and evidence in child sexual abuse cases

8.103 The differences in professional cultures[105] are highlighted by *Wolverhampton City Council v JA & Ors*[106] where Keehan J dealt with a care case which involved allegations of sexual abuse of two young girls, aged 13 (X) and 12 (Y) at the time of his judgment. This was the first part of a split trial ('findings of fact' and 'welfare') where there had been a variety of allegations against the children's father (F) and two males (YQ and ZK), and of the mother (M) and her mother (G) dating back nearly ten years. Keehan J summarised his conclusion on the facts he had found: that the girls had been subjected to 'sustained and prolonged sexual abuse' by F and YQ and ZK; they were subject to physical abuse by F; and M and G had failed to protect them ([288]).

8.104 The case raised a number of questions in relation to evidence,[107] especially in relation to allegations of child sexual abuse and how they should be dealt with by family courts. At paras [10] to [17] Keehan J set out the applicable law in relation to such proceedings. The burden of proof, to the civil standard, is upon the applicant local authority.[108] Lies may be told for a number of reasons and that the lie, which is uncorroborated, does not – on its own – prove a fact against the person who is held to be lying.[109] Findings must be based on evidence; and failing that, on inferences which can properly be drawn from evidence (see eg *Re A (Fact-Finding: Disputed Findings)*[110]).

---

105 See, eg, 'Child confidentiality: a clash of professional rules' by David Burrows, *Family Law* [2017] June at 638.

106 [2017] EWFC 62.

107 The subject of evidence in family proceedings generally is dealt with in *Evidence in family proceedings* by David Burrows (2016, Family Law/LexisNexis) especially at Ch 14 (Confidentiality) and 15 (Legal professional privilege)).

108 *Re B (Children)* [2008] UKHL 35 [2009] 1 AC 11, sub nom *Re B (Care Proceedings: Standard of Proof)* [2008] 2 FLR 141.

109 *R v Lucas (Ruth)* [1981] QB 720, CA Crim per Lord Lane: 'To be capable of amounting to corroboration the lie told out of court must first of all be deliberate. Secondly it must relate to a material issue. Thirdly the motive for the lie must be a realisation of guilt and a fear of the truth. The jury should in appropriate cases be reminded that people sometimes lie, for example, in an attempt to bolster up a just cause, or out of shame or out of a wish to conceal disgraceful behaviour from their family. Fourthly the statement must be clearly shown to be a lie by evidence other than that of the accomplice who is to be corroborated, that is to say by admission or by evidence from an independent witness.'

110 [2011] EWCA Civ 12, [2011] 1 FLR 1817.

ABE interviews and child sexual abuse cases

8.105 In relation to ABE interviews[111] (*Achieving Best Evidence in Criminal Proceedings Guidance on interviewing victims and witnesses..., March 2011* Ministry of Justice: applicable also to family proceedings) Keehan J reflected upon the approach he should adopt when he was to consider the allegations made by the two girls (see [17]). Where there are practice deviations from ABE guidance the court must be especially careful to analyse the reliability of the evidence;[112] though in *Wolverhampton* Keehan J concluded of the ABE interviews (at [287](d)]:

> 'Having read the girls' ABE interviews and, in particular, viewed the relevant parts of their DVDs I was left with a clearly determined conclusion that what they were saying, despite all of the lack of detail and clarity was true: it was an expression, on however many occasion and whatever circumstances, of what they had experienced or seen their sibling experience;...'

8.106 Keehan J referred to MacDonald J's 'extremely helpful summary of the principles' to be applied in child sexual abuse allegation cases in *AS v TH (False Allegations of Abuse)*.[113] Keehan J exhaustively reviewed the evidence he had heard. He concluded as stated above as to the sex abuse; and that M, F and G had failed to protect the girls. All family adults (save for F who had been adjudged to lack litigation capacity ([9])) had lied in different ways: M (see [126]); G ([136]); ZK ([155]) and YQ ([171]). ZK and YQ had been successfully prosecuted for their part in what had happened to X and Y.

Legal professional privilege, self-incrimination privilege and the child care lawyer

8.107 Keehan J was critical of the way that the children's first solicitor (SN), and to a lesser extent the children's original guardian, had interviewed them both. The criticism is clear. It may be the subject of separate disciplinary proceedings (though no self-incrimination privilege warning was given to SN by the judge, if that may be the case).

8.108 There remain questions as to why confidential information – perhaps covered by legal professional privilege – was released by SN to other parties and to the court; though the position of the original children's guardian as to confidentiality should be clear (see *Working Together*[114]).

111 See further Ch 3, Part 6.

112 *Re E (A Child)(Evidence)* [2016] EWCA Civ 473, [2017] 1 FLR 1675, [2016] 4 WLR 105.

113 [2016] EWHC 532 Fam (a dispute over contact with children which involved serious emotional abuse by their mother).

114 See Part 6.

9

DISCLOSURE IN CHILDREN PROCEEDINGS

1 INTRODUCTION

Disclosure in children proceedings

9.1 All relevant material should be available to a judge when the court decides a case. 'Courts should not have to reach decisions in ignorance of the contents of documents or other material which, if disclosed, might well effect the outcome' said Lord Nicholls in *R v Derby Magistrates' Court exp B*.[1] This is subject to a number of exceptions or exemptions – such as those dictated by the rules of privilege (especially legal advice privilege, considered in **Part 2** of this chapter) and public interest immunity (covered separately in **Chapter 13**).

9.2 Confidentiality is an important aspect of children law, and of the rules in relation to legal professional privilege. These subjects have been considered, especially in relation to mature children, in **Chapter 8**.

9.3 This chapter looks at the principles which apply to disclosure in children proceedings: the definitions of terms in Family Procedure Rules 2010 (FPR 2010) Pt 21; the extent to which the rules are extended by Civil Procedure Rules 1998 (CPR 1998) and at the extent to which confidential information may be released to other authorities. It proceeds as follows:

- **Part 2** explains how 'disclosure' and other terminology is defined in FPR 2010, Pt 21; and the extent to which for family proceedings the subject is regulated also by CPR 1998, Pt 31. Exemptions from disclosure – privilege, confidentiality and public interest immunity are outlined.
- **Part 3** covers the subject of obtaining disclosure from third parties: by statute and in the inherent jurisdiction of the court, and especially in relation to the recovery of children.
- **Part 4** deals with release of information about children proceedings to the police and others (*PD12G*); and with restrictions on release of such information.

1 [1995] UKHL 18, [1996] 1 AC 487, [1996] 1 FLR 513; considered further at 9.14.

This is followed by a consideration of the law in relation to release of documents to those not covered by *PG12G*. The meaning of 'use' (publication) by a party of documents disclosed in proceedings is explained.

- **Part 5** concludes the chapter with the special rules in relation to self-incrimination privilege in children proceedings and the exceptions to it explained by *Re EC (Disclosure of Material)*[2] and the case law which has followed it.

9.4 This chapter is not concerned directly with the following aspects of passing on of information from proceedings, which are covered elsewhere:

- 'Sharing' of information about a mature child with others concerning possible harm to a child; and considerations of privilege and confidentiality in relation to that. This subject is dealt with alongside confidentiality in **Chapter 8**.[3]
- Restricting or withholding documents and information and closed material procedures in children proceedings are dealt with respectively in **Chapters 10** and **11**.
- Release of 'hearing documents' to the press and others who may attend a children hearing is dealt with in **Chapter 13**.[4]

2 DISCLOSURE AND CHILDREN PROCEEDINGS

Duty of disclosure

Disclosure and Family Procedure Rules 2010

9.5 The rules about disclosure are dealt with only briefly in FPR 2010: three rules as against over twenty in CPR 1998, Pt 31 (which regulates disclosure in civil proceedings). These rules must be extensively supplemented by the common law. This can be said to be summarised in CPR 1998, Pt 31 (which cannot directly be applied to family proceedings[5]); and that CPR 1998 for practical purposes therefore applies equally to family proceedings as to civil proceedings. For example, the extent to which a party has a continuing duty of disclosure up to the hearing of an appeal, applies in family proceedings as it does in civil proceedings under CPR 1998, r 31.11; and the law in relation to 'use' of documents – the 'implied undertaking' as to documents disclosed in a case – which were produced for family proceedings is defined by the jurisprudence which arises from CPR 1998, r 31.19.

9.6 The formal provision for 'disclosure' in FPR 2010 is in Pt 21, entitled miscellaneous 'Miscellaneous rules about disclosure and inspection of documents'. It starts with a definition of its terms (mostly derived from CPR 1998 Pt 31):

2 [1997] Fam 76, [1997] 2 WLR 322, [1996] 2 FLR 725.
3 See especially 8.59 and 8.70.
4 See especially 13.10.
5 CPR 1998, r 2.1(2),

- *Disclosure* – In law, 'disclosure' means only that a party states that he or she knows that a document 'exists or has existed'.[6] Any duty to produce for inspection[7] or hand over copies, strictly speaking, does not arise until later. Documents include electronic documents in appropriate cases.[8] The step in relation to documents which most people think of as 'disclosure' – the handing over of a document – is formally known as 'production'.
- *Production* – Production means the act of producing documents that have been inspected at court, for example, mostly in a court bundle.

Disclosure and a fair trial

9.7 The general rule of disclosure and production is that a fair trial demands that the court makes its decision on the basis of all available relevant evidence, which includes documentary evidence (to which disclosure is addressed). In *R v Derby Magistrates' Court exp B*[9] Lord Nicholls explained the public interest in legal professional privilege as related to two public interests in the administration of justice.[10] These include that:

> '... All relevant material should be available to courts when deciding cases. Courts should not have to reach decisions in ignorance of the contents of documents or other material which, if disclosed, might well affect the outcome.'

9.8 Certain material may be exempt from disclosure. It may be exempt because it is confidential (including privilege) or because of immunity due to other public interests (public interest immunity).

9.9 Once proceedings have begun, a duty of disclosure continues throughout. CPR 1998, r 31.11 stresses the common law rule that 'disclosure continues until the proceedings are concluded'.[11] Thus if relevant documents or information comes into the hands of, or to the attention of, one party they have a duty to the court and to the other party to tell them. (As already explained, the common law applies equally to family, as to any other, court proceedings.) In respect of relevant evidence, a child as party to proceedings will be exactly the same as any other party – so far as a child may have access to relevant documents and information; just as a child will be entitled to the same protection for evidence which is covered by privilege or confidentiality.[12]

---

6 FPR 2010, r 21.1(1); and see CPR 1998, r 31.2.

7 FPR 2010, r 21.1(2).

8 And see CPR 1998, practice direction *PD36B* on electronic documents.

9 [1995] UKHL 18, [1996] 1 AC 487, [1996] 1 FLR 513 at 530

10 His first is: 'The public interest in the efficient working of the legal system requires that people should be able to obtain professional legal advice on their rights and liabilities and obligations...'.

11 As explained by Stuart Smith LJ in *Vernon v Bosley (No 2)* [1999] QB 18, [1998] 1 FLR 304. In *Vernon* the relevant information was medical evidence in children proceedings (subsequent to the first instance damages proceedings) which, if disclosed on the appeal in his damages proceedings, was likely to have had an appreciable effect – contrary to his interests – on the amount of damages

12 See, eg, *E (A Child)* [2016] EWCA Civ 473; *PD v SD & Anor* [2015] EWHC 4103 (Fam), Keehan J; and see Ch 8.

Exemptions from disclosure

Immunity from disclosure: confidentiality and privilege

9.10 Confidentiality arises where one person reposes confidence in another. The subject is explained fully in **Chapter 8**; but its important aspect where legal advice is concerned, of legal professional privilege will be developed further here. A definition of confidentiality was provided by Lord Goff in *Att Gen v Guardian Newspapers Ltd (No 2)*,[13] namely that:

> '... information comes to the knowledge of a person (the confidant) in circumstances where he has notice, or is held to have agreed, that the information is confidential, with the effect that it would be just in all the circumstances that he should be precluded from disclosing the information to others.'

9.11 There is a public interest in confidentiality being maintained, but it may be overridden, for example, by a competing right (eg to a fair trial[14]); by statutory requirement, such as the revealing of the whereabouts of a child;[15] or because of a competing and superseding public interest.[16] Confidentiality arises in the context of discussions between doctors and other professionals who deal with children, as explained in **Chapter 8**. It is a component of legal professional privilege, which is the particular form of confidentiality provided by members of the legal profession.[17] Confidentiality does not on its own give rise to privilege.

Privilege from disclosure

Privilege: advice, negotiations and court proceedings

9.12 'Privilege' means that a party to proceedings can withhold from the court otherwise relevant evidence. The forms of privilege to be commented on here are each quite different in origin and result. In summary they are:

- Legal professional privilege, consisting of two separate categories: legal advice privilege and litigation privilege.
- Without prejudice privilege (or immunity).
- Self-incrimination privilege.

---

13 [1990] 1 AC 109, [1988] UKHL 6, [1987] WLR 776; and see 8.7.

14 See, eg, *Re A (Sexual Abuse: Disclosure)* [2012] UKSC 60, [2013] 1 FLR 948.

15 *Family Law Act 1996, s 33(1)* and *(2)* and *CA 1989, s 48(1)*; and see consideration of *Ramsbotham v Senior* (1869) FLR Rep 591 at 9.24 and *Re T (Wardship: Impact of Police Intelligence)* [2009] EWHC 2440 (Fam), [2010] 1 FLR 1048, McFarlane J at 11.41.

16 See, eg, *W v Egdell* [1989] EWCA Civ 13, [1990] Ch 359, [1990] 2 WLR 471, considered fully at 8.47.

17 *R (Prudential plc and anor) v Special Commissioner of Income Tax* [2013] UKSC 1, [2013] 2 AC 185.

9.13 The separate subject of public interest immunity will be considered alongside privilege and confidentiality; though it is important to appreciate that it raises quite different issues of principle to confidentiality. The feature public interest immunity shares with privilege is that it exempts relevant documents from disclosure in proceedings; but it does so in circumstances which are based on public law principles and which exclude even the judge from sight of the immune documents.

Legal professional privilege

9.14 Legal professional privilege confers an absolute right, on the person entitled to it, not to have produced in court otherwise relevant confidential information or documents.[18] It comprises two distinct categories of material: respectively material covered by legal advice privilege and by litigation privilege.

9.15 Legal advice privilege attaches to, and exempts from disclosure, advice in any 'relevant legal context'[19] and whether or not court proceedings are in prospect. It enables any client to obtain advice in complete privacy[20] and to ensure that, for the proper administration of justice, they have genuine independent assistance.[21] So long as it is legal advice, it is covered by privilege. It is not necessary that it be advice in connection with litigation.

9.16 By contrast, litigation privilege applies only where proceedings are in prospect or are already under way and where the dominant purpose of the evidence to which it attaches is the proceedings.[22] However, it has been held that reports in children proceedings, where these are obtained with permission of the court for report to the court and though their dominant purpose is litigation, are not covered by litigation privilege.[23]

Without prejudice rule immunity

9.17 Without prejudice rule immunity rarely applies in children proceedings, since it is designed to assist parties to negotiate a settlement of their litigation, a

---

18 *R v Derby Magistrates' Court exp B* [1995] UKHL 18, [1996] 1 AC 487, [1996] 1 FLR 513; *Three Rivers District Council and ors v Governor and Company of the Bank of England (No 6)* [2004] UKHL 48, [2004] 3 WLR 1274.

19 *Balabel v Air India* [1988] Ch 317, CA.

20 *Anderson v Bank of British Columbia* (1876) 2 ChD 644.

21 *Ventouris v Mountain (The Italia Express (No 1))* [1991] 1 WLR 607, CA.

22 *Waugh v British Railways Board* [1980] AC 521.

23 *Re L (Police Investigation: Privilege)* [1997] AC 16, [1996] 1 FLR 731: per Lord Jauncey at [1996] 1 FLR at 738: 'In these circumstances I consider that care proceedings under Part IV of the Act are so far removed from normal actions that *litigation privilege has no place in relation to reports* obtained by a party thereto which could not have been prepared without the leave of the court to disclose documents already filed or to examine the child (emphasis added).'

concept which will mostly be inappropriate in children cases.[24] It is based on public policy: first, that parties should be encouraged to settle their litigation (or disputes that might lead to litigation); and, secondly, on an implied contractual term that they agree that any admissions by either of them against their own interest cannot be disclosed to the court. The rule is subject to a number of exceptions which were summarised by the Court of Appeal in *Unilever PLC v The Procter & Gamble Company*.[25]

9.18 There is no specific privilege for mediation or other non-court dispute resolution, although the proceedings may be confidential as between mediator and the parties;[26] so that they can only be breached for good reason or by order of the court.

Self-incrimination privilege: right to silence

9.19 Self-incrimination privilege is based on the common law principle that a party in legal proceedings cannot be required to make a case against him- or herself; or to answer questions which make such a case.[27] Where there is a requirement to provide evidence to the court then, subject to any higher public interest, self-incrimination privilege will apply.[28]

9.20 As explained more fully in **Part 5**, *Children Act 1989* (*CA 1989*) *s 98* provides a form of self-incrimination privilege for proceedings *CA 1989*, *Pts 4* and *5* (care, interim care and emergency protection proceedings). Its aim is to encourage frankness in witnesses and parties by preventing the use, or admissibility, of evidence given in children proceedings in subsequent criminal proceedings (other than criminal proceedings for perjury in the children proceedings).

Waiver of privilege

9.21 The right to privilege, or privilege for the particular information, document or advice, is that of the client. It can be waived – that is, dispensed with – expressly by the particular client; or in certain circumstances it can be waived by implication

---

24 That said, one of the earliest Court of Appeal cases on mediation was a children case, *Re D (Minors) (Conciliation: Privilege)* [1993] 1 FLR 932: Where mediation ('conciliation') was in progress, immunity from that evidence being placed before the court applied as much in children proceedings as in any other litigation: 'evidence may not be given in [CA 1989] proceedings ... of statements made by one or other of the parties in the course of meetings held or communications made for the purpose of conciliation save in the very unusual case where a statement is made clearly indicating that the maker has in the past caused or is likely in the future to cause serious harm to the well-being of a child' (per Sir Thomas Bingham MR).

25 [2000] 1 WLR 2436.

26 *Farm Assist Ltd v Secretary of State for the Environment, Food and Rural Affairs (No 2)* [2009] EWHC 1102 (TCC), Ramsey J.

27 As explained by Lord Mustill in *R v Director of Serious Fraud Office, exp Smith* [1993] AC 1 at 30–31, [1992] 3 WLR 66.

28 *Brown v Stott (Procurator Fiscal, Dunfermline) and another* [2000] UKPC D3, [2003] 1 AC 681.

from a client's actions.[29] In the case of the without prejudice rule, the benefit of the immunity is joint. It can therefore only be waived effectively by both parties; and a mediator is bound by such waiver.[30]

9.22 This question of waiver of privilege is quite separate from that of when a child's privilege or confidentiality may be overridden. This is dealt with separately in **Chapter 8**.

Privilege, 'iniquity' and the welfare of the child

9.23 Privilege may be held not to have existed at all, where the advice is sought to further a crime or other iniquitous intent (whether or not the lawyer who advises knows that he or she is consulted for 'iniquitous purposes').[31] This would include advice given – perhaps unwittingly – by a solicitor in relation to child abduction (eg as to residence) where the purpose of seeking the advice was help the proposed abduction. Such advice would not be covered by privilege.

9.24 In *Ramsbotham v Senior*[32] Sir R Malins V-C sitting in the Court of Chancery dealing with the address of a ward held, when it was argued that information as to the address of a ward's mother held by a solicitor was not covered by privilege, akin to the iniquity exception. He took the view, not that privilege is overridden, but that it did not arise in the first place.[33] Of the 'rule' in relation to legal professional privilege he said:

> 'The rule has no application to the case of concealing the residence of a ward, which may lead to the utter ruin or destruction of that ward.... [In this case the solicitor] does not know [the ward's address], but he is in possession of documents which may by possibility lead to its being ascertained. Those documents, for the reasons I have already stated, I am clearly of opinion he is bound to produce. The order must be made according to the summons.'

Public interest immunity

Public law and immunity from disclosure

9.25 Public interest immunity arises as a matter of public law[34] which arises as of right for public bodies, to protect documents which in the public interest

29 See, eg, *Re D (Care Proceedings: Legal Privilege)* [2011] EWCA Civ 684, [2011] 2 FLR 1183, CA, where a mother in care proceedings had, by referring to part of the documents and notes that arose from an interview with her lawyers, impliedly waived privilege in respect of the rest.

30 *Farm Assist Ltd v Secretary of State for the Environment, Food and Rural Affairs (No 2)* [2009] EWHC 1102 (TCC), Ramsey J.

31 *R v Cox and Railton* (1884) 14 QBD 153.

32 (1869) FLR Rep 591 at 593.

33 This decision is in line with *Re T (Wardship: Impact of Police Intelligence)* [2009] EWHC 2440 (Fam), [2010] 1 FLR 1048 (considered at 11.41) where McFarlane J was clear that the court had power to make an order for disclosure as to a child's whereabouts; but that without the order a solicitor did not necessarily have a duty to produce information.

34 *Conway v Rimmer* [1968] AC 910; but see *D v National Society for the Prevention of Cruelty to Children* [1978] AC 171, (1977) FLR Rep 181 for a rare example of public interest immunity applied to a private body.

should not be published in court. The immunity applies where the public body seeks an order from the court which makes them immune from disclosing certain specific relevant documents; or where the court, of its own motion, directs that documents of a public body should not be disclosed. Grounds for the immunity are that disclosure to the court and the parties to the case might harm the public interest. This is considered in **Chapter 12**.

Procedure for disclosure

9.26 Procedure for disclosure in children proceedings is minimal. The rules[35] prescribe that documents must be produced with court application papers. If specific disclosure is sought there is no procedure prescribed in FPR 2010, Pt 21; so that a procedure akin to that set out in CPR 1998, Pt 31, in the case of a dispute is likely to have to be followed;[36] or specific orders made under FPR 2010, Pt 12.[37]

9.27 Specific procedures for dealing with orders for disclosure against a person not a party to the proceedings (third parties) (FPR 2010, r 21.2) and to withhold inspection or disclosure (FPR 2010, r 21.3) are dealt with in **Part 3**.

3 OBTAINING INFORMATION FROM THIRD PARTIES

Disclosure under family procedure rules 2010

Disclosure from a 'person not a party'

9.28 FPR 2010, r 21.2 enables a party to proceedings to obtain a court order for disclosure of documents or information an order for an individual or body which is not a party to proceedings can be made for production of documents and for information as to the whereabouts of a child, in three main sets of circumstance:

(1) An application to court by the procedure in r 21.2 where statute permits an order against a third party (including information as to the whereabouts of a child);

(2) A witness summons which requires production of documents,[38] normally at trial (subject as explained below);

(3) An application for an order in the inherent jurisdiction of the court, and

(4) An application for information as to the whereabouts of a child under Family Law Act 1996 (FLA 1996) s 33 and CA 1989, ss 48 and 50.

9.29 The main operative part of FPR 2010, r 21.2 provides as follows:

35 FPR 2010, r 5.2.

36 *Tchenguiz-Imerman v Imerman* (Rev 1) [2013] EWHC 3627 (Fam), Moylan J.

37 See, eg, FPR 2010, r 12.12.

38 FPR 2010, r 24.2(1)(b).

'21.2 Orders for disclosure against a person not a party

(1) This rule applies where an application is made to the court under any Act for disclosure by a person who is not a party to the proceedings.

(2) The application –

(a) may be made without notice; and

(b) must be supported by evidence.

(3) The court may make an order under this rule only where disclosure is necessary in order to dispose fairly of the proceedings or to save costs.'

9.30 Of the four categories in para 9.28 (above) it will be necessary to consider the second, third and fourth. Examples of statute permitting third party disclosure are very rare,[39] save in the cases of *FLA 1996* and *CA 1989* (considered in the fourth category).

Witness summons to produce documents

9.31 FPR 2010, Pt 24 deals with issue of a witness summons by the court. This includes FPR 2010, r 24.2(1) which enables the court to require a witness – who, by definition is not a party to proceedings – to attend court and to '(b) produce documents to the court'. Production of documents to the court may be on the date fixed for a hearing or on such other date as the court may direct.[40]

9.32 So, for example, if medical records are required by the court, a summons could be addressed to a suitable person who holds the records. If the witness cannot release documents unconditionally, the court may decide that the documents are better produced on a specific date, maybe at an address where the records are held; and in any event in advance of a final hearing. They can then be inspected by the parties to the application in this way.

9.33 Only documents which could be required at the final hearing can be ordered to be produced.[41] Documents covered by privilege would be excluded from production, as would most documents covered by confidentiality.[42] Only documents which are relevant to the issues in the case will be permitted to be ordered.

Setting aside a witness summons

9.34 A third-party witness who is ordered to produce documents is able to apply to the court to 'set aside or vary a witness summons'.[43] The witness may

39 Eg, *Bankers Book Evidence Act 1879* applicable only in financial applications (ie not children) and then only very rarely used.
40 FPR 2010, r 24.2(4).
41 FPR 2010, r 24.2(5).
42 For explanation of confidentiality and privilege in this context see Ch 8, Part 2.
43 FPR 2010, r 24.3(4).

not have to produce the documents which the summons ordered. The court has a discretion to say, for example, that production would be oppressive, not relevant to an issue before the court or otherwise not necessary to its 'fair disposal'.[44]

9.35 In *Morgan v Morgan*[45], Watkins J defined the test for setting aside a witness summons (subpoena) issued to the wife's father (which he applied to set aside) as that the court must balance the need to have the information necessary to get the answer as near as possible right (amount of a lump sum); as against the 'rights of the citizen ... to keep to himself ... details of his wealth and what he intends to do with it' (wife's father had been subpoenaed to produce his will).

9.36 Put in terms of the European Convention 1950, following introduction by the *Human Rights Act 1998* (*HRA 1989*), this translates – and for modern purposes can be translated – as: that the rights of the husband to a fair trial of his claim for a lump sum, must be balanced against the Art 8 of the father to keep his personal information private. The need for disclosure to secure a fair trial, can be balanced with the right of a non-party witness to privacy. If the witness is a child, and especially if the child is a party, his interests are likely to override those of any other party (such as his parents).[46]

Disclosure under inherent jurisdiction

Inherent jurisdiction of the High Court

9.37 That there is an inherent jurisdiction to make orders against non-parties in children proceedings is not in question; but the limits of that jurisdiction are not clear nor is the basis of the jurisdiction judicially defined. For example, in slightly different circumstances to routine children proceedings, in *A Health Authority v X (Discovery: Medical Conduct)*[47] Munby J dealt with a health authority for third part y disclosure in relation to earlier care proceedings. The health authority wanted to consider compliance by a GP practice involved in the care proceedings. Munby J ordered disclosure on strict conditions. He commented, in passing, on the extent to which documents could be ordered to be disclosed in the Family Division.

9.38 Counsel for the health authority had argued the case for a type of public interest approach. A public body can apply, said counsel and as the judge explained it, for 'a mandatory order requiring the delivery up to it by anybody of documents required by it for the purpose of carrying out its public or regulatory functions'.[48] Munby J rejected the idea that there was any such wide jurisdiction. It was not

44 See *South Tyneside Borough Council v Wickes Building Supplies Ltd* [2004] EWHC 2428 (Comm) for what is 'necessary for the fair disposal' of a case.

45 [1977] Fam 122, (1976) FLR Rep 473.

46 *Yousef v The Netherlands (Application No 33711/96)* (2003) 36 EHRR 20, [2003] 1 FLR 210, ECtHR; *Local Authority X v HI and Others* [2016] EWHC 1123 (Fam), [2017] 1 FLR 1362, Roberts J; and see further at 10.48.

47 [2001] 2 FLR 673.

48 Para [59].

possible to obtain documents from an 'innocent third party' save in very restricted circumstances. Indeed, he concluded:

> '[60] ... Neither at common law nor in equity does any independent action (that is, an action unlinked with any sustainable claim for substantive relief) lie against an innocent third party for the purpose of obtaining papers or information. The only permissible course is to issue a [witness summons]....'

9.39 In *A London Borough Council v K & Ors,*[49] Baker J comments on police production of evidence in a case which had started as private law (contact proceedings) and had later involved the local authority. The police had investigated allegations by the mother, but had decided not to press charges against the father. Of the police's co-operation with the court the judge concluded:

> '[159] ... The deficiencies in the police disclosure in this case were alarming. It was only during the evidence of the fourth and last police witness, DI Jeffries, who was the senior officer who gave evidence, that it became apparent that a large amount of material had not been disclosed... If a family court orders disclosure, that order must be obeyed. All the disclosure orders contain a liberty to apply clause, and if the police have an objection on grounds of public interest immunity or otherwise, they must apply to the judge to amend the order...'

9.40 Plainly Baker J considers that he has a discretion to order production by the police (a non-party in this case). He does not approach the question on the basis of authority. Co-operation and 'sharing' between those concerned with safeguarding children is a quasi-statutory duty.[50] Whether this extends to a blanket power to order a third party to disclose remains unresolved. As can be seen from the views of Munby J in *A Health Authority v X (Discovery: Medical Conduct)* (above), the power to order non-parties to produce documents is unclear.

Information as to a child's whereabouts

Whereabouts of a child: recovery of children

9.41 The jurisdiction to order non-parties to produce documents may or may not be limited. Where recovery of children is concerned the Family Division and the Family Court[51] – have an inherent power to order information to be provided from third parties. The court has statutory powers also. Both aspects of the family courts' jurisdiction must now be explained.

49 [2009] EWHC 850.

50 See discussion of *Children Act 1989, ss 10* and *11* and *Working together* in Ch 8; and of police involvement in care proceedings in the *2013 Protocol* at 9.52.

51 *MFPA 1984, s 31E(1).*

9.42 The inherent jurisdiction to order third parties to provide information Munby LJ[52] in *Re HM (Vulnerable Adult: Abduction)*[53] said of the High Court's inherent jurisdiction concerning children and information from third parties:

> '[36] It has long been recognised that, quite apart from any statutory jurisdiction (for example under s 33 of the Family Law Act 1986 or s 50 of the Children Act 1989), the Family Division has an inherent jurisdiction to make orders directed to third parties who there is reason to believe may be able to provide information which may lead to the location of a missing child. Thus orders can be made against public authorities (for example, Her Majesty's Revenue and Customs, the Benefits Agency, the DVLA, local authorities or local education authorities, etc, etc) requiring them to search their records with a view to informing the court whether they have any record of the child or the child's parent or other carer. Similar orders can be directed to telephone and other IT service providers, to banks and other financial institutions, to airline and other travel service providers – the latter with a view to finding out whether the missing child has in fact left the jurisdiction and, if so, for what destination – and to relatives, friends and associates of the abducting parent....'

Statutory provisions

9.43 Examples of statutory provision for production of information in relation to children exist in *FLA 1986, s 33* and *CA 1989, s 48*. Applications under these statutory provisions are covered procedurally by FPR 2010, r 21.2;[54] but will be considered separately here under children proceedings disclosure provisions.

9.44 *FLA 1986* gives power to the Family Court to order information as to the whereabouts of a child who is the subject of proceedings under the Act be produced. Section 33(1) and (1) is as follows:

> **'33 Power to order disclosure of child's whereabouts**
>
> (1) Where in proceedings for or relating to a Part I order in respect of a child there is not available to the court adequate information as to where the child is, the court may order any person who it has reason to believe may have relevant information to disclose it to the court.
>
> (2) A person shall not be excused from complying with an order under subsection (1) above by reason that to do so may incriminate him or his spouse of an offence; but a statement or admission made in compliance with such an order shall not be admissible in evidence against either of them in proceedings for any offence other than perjury.'

52 Sitting as a judge of the Family Division.
53 [2010] EWHC 870 (Fam), [2010] 2 FLR 1057.
54 Text at 9.29.

9.45 An order under s 33(1) can be addressed to individuals who are not parties to the proceedings including the manager of a women's refuge, a person's doctor[55] or the police, as well as relatives or friends of a person who may be keeping the child. The person's access to information as to a child's whereabouts is the critical factor.

9.46 *CA 1989, ss 48* and *50* both provide the family courts with powers to order that information be provided as to the whereabouts of children who may be in need of emergency protection or who, it is thought, have been abducted and in respect of whom the court has ordered recovery. In each case the orders for providing information are ancillary to existing children proceedings; and require third parties who have information to provide it direct to the 'applicant', that is the local authority which is taking the care proceedings. To give effect to this, *CA 1989, s 48(1)* provides:

> '(1) Where it appears to a court making an emergency protection order[56] that adequate information as to the child's whereabouts –
>
> (a) is not available to the applicant for the order; but
>
> (b) is available to another person,
>
> it may include in the order a provision requiring that other person to disclose, if asked to do so by the applicant, any information that he may have as to the child's whereabouts.'

9.47 *CA 1989, s 50(1)* gives power to the court to make a 'recovery order' where a child has been taken away unlawfully, has run away or is missing. By *CA 1989, s 50(3)(c)* the making of a recovery order 'requires any person who has information as to the child's whereabouts to disclose that information, if asked to do so, to a constable or an officer of the court'. By definition, such a person will not be a party to the proceedings.

4 PASSING ON INFORMATION TO THIRD PARTIES

Children documents to police

Information and court proceedings

9.48 **Chapter 8** considered the role of confidentiality of a child's information, as between the child and a professional person: a lawyer, a doctor, a social worker, teacher or other local authority professional. It was not essential that there be court proceedings: confidences can be made to professional people by children in a variety of situations; and many will be before any question arises. In many

55 This may be subject to a doctor's claim of confidentiality; but this may be required to be balanced against the welfare of a child in the proceedings.

56 *CA 1989, s 44.*

circumstances, especially of medical confidences, it is unlikely that there would be court proceedings.

9.49 This part assumes that there are court proceedings. In consequence disclosure is regulated by the common law (supplemented by the rules, as applicable). The court is procedurally in control of the disclosure process. There will be circumstances in which information in relation to children can be passed on to specified third parties.[57] This process may, for example, be sanctioned by the rules[58] and confirmed by judicial approval.[59]

Communication of information: police and care proceedings

9.50 If care proceedings are in contemplation whilst there are simultaneous criminal proceedings, or one or other sets of proceedings are concluded, the arrangements for communication of information are governed against a background of the contempt of court restrictions of the *Administration of Justice Act 1960 (AJA 1960) s 12(1)(a)*.[60] The rules and guidance which deal specifically with release of information as between courts, police and the local authority consist of the following:

- Family Procedure Rules 2010, r 12.73.
- FPR 2010, *Practice Direction 12G – Communication of Information.*
- *Protocol and Good Practice Model: Disclosure of information in cases of alleged child abuse and linked criminal and care directions hearings* (October 2013:[61] 'the *2013 Protocol*').

9.51 Its object is to provide a framework to set up an exchange of information between, in particular, the local authority and the police; and to ensure full co-operation, between the authorities involved in child protection. It sets up procedures for information and notification of proceedings from police and CPS; and for the passing on of information from the family justice system to the police (summarised in its *Part 3: Aims and objectives*).

Disclosure of child abuse information to the police

9.52 The *2013 Protocol* is divided into three parts:

(a) Part A: *Police information for care proceedings* – disclosure by the police of information into the care proceedings; confirmation by the police of the issue of criminal proceedings; and provision for court orders for disclosure by the police;

---

57 See FPR 2010, r 12. And, especially, the table in *PG12G*.
58 FPR 2010, r 12.73 and *PG12G* (considered at 9.68).
59 See, eg, *Re X and Y (Disclosure of Judgment to Police)* [2014] EWHC 278 (Fam), [2015] 1 FLR 1218, Baker J (considered at 9.53).
60 For text of s 12(1) see 13.19.
61 See www.cps.gov.uk/publications/docs/third_party_protocol_2013.pdf.

(b) Part B: *Information for criminal proceedings from care proceedings* – disclosure from care proceedings into the criminal justice system; disclosure of information by the local authority to the police; and provision for formal application by the police to the Family Court for release of information and the court's judgment.

(c) Part C: *Linked directions hearings* – 'linked criminal and care directions hearings' are to be considered by the allocated case management judge in the Family Court; and the local authority lawyers, in such cases, must liaise with the CPS as to what its then current position is in care proceedings (para 16.6). Part 17 sets out what must be considered at any linked directions hearing.

The protocol: co-operation and the investigation of crime

9.53 The operation of *2013 Protocol* and of FPR 2010, r 12.73 can be seen in *Re X and Y (Disclosure of Judgment to Police)*.[62] Baker J was dealing with an application by the police who wanted to see a judgment in which he had recorded that the father of a child had admitted, after the making of a care order, that he had perpetrated the injuries on one of three children. The judge had found – in the first of a series of judgments – that the injuries in question were probably caused by one of the parents. He encouraged both parents to reflect; and hoped that eventually they would be more frank with the court about what had really happened. Two days later the father confessed that he had caused the injuries to the child. The parents separated.

9.54 Baker J delivered a further judgment in the case, in which he said:

> '[5]... The matter was therefore restored before me... The father duly filed a statement in which he described in detail the circumstances in which he had come to inflict the injuries. The mother filed a statement setting out her response to the father's confession. Two experts filed addendum reports in which they accepted that the injuries could have been sustained in the incidents described by the father.'

9.55 Following a resumed hearing, at which judgment was transcribed, but not released for publication nor communicated to the police, the judge concluded 'on a balance of probabilities, that the injuries had been inflicted by the father in the manner described in his statement'.[63] The mother was exonerated. The children remained in her care subject to a supervision order.

9.56 The father applied for an order prohibiting the local authority or any other party from communicating any information to the police or CPS. The police filed a statement asking for 'disclosure of any information that had come to light in these proceedings indicating the perpetrator of [the child's] injuries "in order that the

62 [2014] EWHC 278 (Fam), [2015] 1 FLR 1218.
63 §[6].

decision to prosecute that person can be taken"'.[64] The court was dealing with the father's restraint application since, as will be seen, over the entitlement of a party to proceedings to pass information to the police.

Release of child protection information to the police by CAFCASS

9.57 *S v SP and CAFCASS*[65] deals with the extent to which a Cafcass officer may provide child protection information to when asked for it. SP, the Cafcass officer in question was asked to provide information to the police about a mentally unstable parent in private law proceedings. Confronted by an application for committal by the father of Cafcass and their officer, Baker J emphasised the importance of a children's guardian (ie the 'Cafcass officer') being able to pass on information to the police 'in furtherance of child protection'. This was entirely within the meaning of the terms 'child protection' in FPR 2010, r 12.73.[66]

9.58 In *S v SP* a father ('S') had been permitted only indirect contact with his children. There were concerns as to his mental health. He was not permitted directly to communicate with the mother or children. He made a complaint concerning SP, their Cafcass officer, as to her conduct of the case. She had received a call about S from a police officer and in the course of it gave to the police officer certain information about the proceedings. Acting in person, S applied for findings of contempt against SP and against Cafcass, for 'deliberately disclosing inappropriate information'.

9.59 The judge gave short shrift to S's argument that this passing on of information was 'publication' as anticipated by *AJA 1960, s 12(1)*[67] and that is could therefore contempt within the terms of s 12(1). He dwelled however on the meaning of FPR 2010, r 12.73(1)(a)(viii): that for any alleged contempt in relation to children proceedings, 'information… may be communicated [by] (viii) a professional acting in furtherance of the protection of children…'.[68]

9.60 In *S v SP*, as he had done in *Re X and Y*, Baker J stressed the importance of professionals working together to share information. If in doubt before passing on information, a professional should make application in the children proceedings.[69] In this case, the guardian was not acting unlawfully in passing on the information, said the judge; and neither SP nor CAFCASS were in contempt of court in any way. On the contrary, in passing on information to the police the guardian was acting entirely in accordance with what was intended by FPR 2010, r 12.73(1)(b).

64 §[7].
65 [2016] EWHC 3673 (Fam) Baker J.
66 See *S v SP* at §[37]. For the text of r 12.73(1) see 9.61.
67 For the text of s 12(1) see 13.19.
68 *S v SP* at §[24].
69 §[38]; FPR 2010, r 12.73(1)(b).

Restrictions on release

Communication of information in children proceedings: application to restrict release

9.61 In *Re X and Y* Baker J explains the working of r 12.73 and the practice direction. FPR 2010, r 12.73(1) provides as followed:

> '**12.73 Communication of information: general**
>
> (1) For the purposes of the law relating to contempt of court, information relating to proceedings held in private (whether or not contained in a document filed with the court) may be communicated –
>
> (a) where the communication is to [various individuals and bodies such as the legal representative of a party, Legal Aid Agency, a court appointed expert etc, formally entitled to receive information];
>
> (b) where the court gives permission; or
>
> (c) subject to any direction of the court, in accordance with rule 12.75 and Practice Direction 12G.'

9.62 *PD12G* provides three tables which set out what communications in children proceedings can be passed on to particular bodies or individuals. Paragraph 2.1 is the first of these and sets out a table which deals with 'any information relating to the proceedings'. The rule and *PD* table enable information to be passed on by specified individuals – for example, a party, a legal representative or others lawfully in possession of the information – to other individuals or bodies and for specified purposes, other than the proceedings (eg information to a person conducting 'an approved research project').

9.63 Any communication in accordance with the provisions of *PD12G* is, by para 1.2, 'Subject to any direction of the court....', which means that communication under the practice direction is subject to any other 'direction of the court' or court order. It is such other order which the father applied for in *Re X and Y*.

9.64 The local authority – one of the specified individuals, as a party to the proceedings, in para 2.1 – did not need permission under r 12.73(1)(b) to release information to the police. The judgment was required by the police 'for the purpose of a criminal investigation' and thus – subject to any contrary order – was eligible for communication within the terms of para 2.1. The resultant position under the rules, as summarised by Baker J, was therefore as follows:

> '[16] Thus the scheme of the current rules is that communication of information relating to care proceedings falls into three categories:
>
> (1) communications under r 12.73(1)(a), which may be made as a matter of right;

(2) communications under r 12.73(1)(c) and PD 12G paras 1 and 2, which may be made, but are subject to any direction by the court, including, in appropriate circumstances, a direction that they should not be made; and

(3) other communications, which under 12.73(1)(b) may only be made with the court's permission.

Plainly, whereas the onus in respect of proposed communications under r 12.73(1)(b) lies on the party seeking permission to communicate, the onus in respect of communications that would otherwise be permitted under r 12.73(1)(c) and Practice Direction 12G paras 1 and 2 lies on the party contending that such communication should not be permitted.'

Re EC *and disclosure of material from care proceedings*

9.65 Baker J treated *Re EC (Disclosure of Material)*[70] as still the leading authority on release of information to the police; though the relative importance of the factors identified in *Re EC* might shift with the passage of time. That case was decided under a much earlier version of the rules for children proceedings. It was likely that the current rules and case law would make the courts more, rather than less, disposed towards release to the police.

9.66 The factors in *Re EC* listed by Swinton Thomas LJ,[71] and as relevant in the present context, are:

'(1) The welfare and interests of the child or children concerned in the care proceedings. If the child is likely to be adversely affected by the order in any serious way, this will be a very important factor.

(2) The welfare and interests of other children generally.

(3) The maintenance of confidentiality in children cases.

(4) The importance of encouraging frankness in children's cases....

(5) The public interest in the administration of justice. Barriers should not be erected between one branch of the judicature and another because this may be inimical to the overall interests of justice.

(6) The public interest in the prosecution of serious crime and the punishment of offenders, including the public interest in convicting those who have been guilty of violent or sexual offences against children. There is a strong public interest in making available material to the police which is relevant to a criminal trial. In many cases, this is likely to be a very important factor.

70 *Re C (A Minor) (Care Proceedings: Disclosure)* [1997] Fam 76, [1997] 2 WLR 322, sub nom *Re EC (Disclosure of Material)* [1996] 2 FLR 725, CA.

71 At 85 and 733 respectively.

(7) The gravity of the alleged offence and the relevance of the evidence to it. If the evidence has little or no bearing on the investigation or the trial, this will militate against a disclosure order.

(8) The desirability of co-operation between various agencies concerned with the welfare of children, including the social services departments, the police service, medical practitioners, health visitors, school, etc. This is particularly important in cases concerning children.

(9) ...

(10) Any other material disclosure which has already taken place.'

9.67 Any order for communication in *Re X and Y* would be limited to 'criminal investigation', said Baker J. Any further communication by the police (for example, for disclosure in a criminal trial) would only be with permission from the court, as the judge made clear.[72]

Release of documents to third parties outside PD12g

Release of information to the security services

9.68 In *X, Y and Z (Disclosure to the Security Service)*[73] McDonald J dealt with an application by the Metropolitan Police (MPS) to release a judgment and mother's statement in un-concluded care proceedings to the security services (ie MI5). The child was aged three and it was suspect that her mother wanted to take her to Islamic State. MPS had received the documents on their own earlier application. MI5 were not a party to that application. MPS wanted to release the documents, and to do so unconditionally, in case MI5 could assist them in their own enquiries (eg to provide them with information about any criminal, including radicalisation, information about the mother).

9.69 The case turned on whether there should be, and if so what, conditions upon release by the police to MI5. MPS said release should be unconditional. On behalf of the child it was said release should be conditional. McDonald J agreed. He explained the background law (providing an excellent summary in the process) at paras [16] to [35]. He said that release of documents in the proceedings was not a 'binary issue': to disclose or not to disclose. He explained this:

> '[26] ...The court may order disclosure but impose appropriate conditions on the disclosure of documents where such conditions are necessary to ensure fair balance between the rights engaged (*Re X (Children)* [2007] EWHC 1719, [2008] 1 FLR 589 [Munby J] at [38] and *Re X and Y (Disclosure of Judgment to Police)* [[2014] EWHC 278 (Fam), [2015] 1 FLR 1218, Baker J] at [21] and [38]).'

---

72 Paras [21] and [25].

73 [2016] EWHC 2400 (Fam), McDonald J.

Conditional release of documents in family proceeding

9.70 McDonald J ordered release but subject to conditions which essentially maintained control of confidentiality in the documents with the court. And an essential aspect of the judge's decision-making turned on the right of the parties and child, or children, to confidentiality. Further, the security services are not in the lists in *PD12G*. They must therefore make application – or, in this case, the police on their behalf. In making any order for release, the court will be concerned to preserve, as far as possible, the parties' rights and any confidentiality in documents.

Collateral use of disclosed documents

Use outside proceedings of disclosed documents

9.71 The extent to which a party to proceedings of any sort may 'use' (ie pass on to a third party (eg the press) or otherwise publish) disclosed documents in any civil proceedings (including family proceedings) has for many years been covered by an 'implied undertaking' that disclosed documents cannot be released.

9.72 The implied undertaking is intended to be absorbed and reproduced by CPR 1998, r 31.22(1). which provides as follows:

> **'31.22 Subsequent use of disclosed documents...**
>
> (1) A party to whom a document has been disclosed may use the document only for the purpose of the proceedings in which it is disclosed, except where –
>
> (a) the document has been read to or by the court, or referred to, at a hearing which has been held in public;
>
> (b) the court gives permission; or
>
> (c) the party who disclosed the document and the person to whom the document belongs agree.'

9.73 Thus, there are only certain circumstances in which a party may 'use' a document within the terms of r 31.22(1), unless the court orders.[74] In the case of children proceedings, even if parties were to agree, there would still be the question of obtaining permission from the court (subject to the extent to which release is permitted by FPR 2010, r 12.73 and *PD12G*[75]).

---

74 Explained further by Sir James Munby P in eg, *Re J (A Child)* [2013] EWHC 2694 (Fam) sub nom *Re J (Reporting Restriction: Internet: Video)* [2014] 1 FLR 523.

75 See 9.68 for further explanation of *PD12G*.

Passing on of information by the courts to appropriate outside agency

9.74 There is modest case law on the question of the courts, on their own initiative, passing on of information by the courts to relevant authorities. This mostly occurs in the context of financial relief proceedings. The subject was fully explored by Charles J in *A v A; B v B*.[76] Though strictly speaking what Charles J said was obiter, its content has been approved in subsequent proceedings – namely that the court does have power to refer on abuses by a party to appropriate authorities (in *A v A; B v B* it was HM Revenue and Customs).

9.75 In *Re Jones (Alleged Contempt of Court)*[77] Sir James Munby P[78] approved the approach of Charles J in *A v A; B v B* and confirmed his support for the view that it was open to the court itself to report abuses to appropriate government authorities. So, said Sir James, this allowed the court to refer matters to an outside agency, such as the police, Crown Prosecution Service or HM Revenue and Customs (as set out in the italicised passage below):

> '[12] It is well known that, on occasions, judges refer the papers in a case which has been before them to some outside agency with a view to that agency considering whether or not to take any steps arising out of the matters referred by the judge. Sometimes the papers are referred to the police, the CPS or the DPP with a view to the possible commencement of criminal proceedings. Sometimes the referral is to some professional or other regulator. Sometimes the referral is to HMRC. Sometimes, as here, the referral is to the Law Officers. No doubt there are other instances. Although the basis upon which such referrals are made has not very often been explored in any depth – the judgment of Charles J in *A v A; B v B* [2000] 1 FLR 701 is an exception – *there can be no question about the right of the judges to act in this way*. Nor, in my judgment, can there be any objection to a judge, as here, referring the papers to the Law Officers with a view to them considering whether or not to bring proceedings for contempt; and, I should make clear, whether the contempt is criminal or, as in the present case, civil....'. (italics added)

9.76 In *Re Jones* the court had referred papers in a children case to the Solicitor General to consider proceedings for contempt in respect of a mother who appeared to be in contempt of a child abduction order. The mother's advocate questioned whether it was appropriate for the judge to have referred papers to the law officers. Though Sir James gives no authority for his assertion that reference to the appropriate 'outside agency' was open to the judge, he was quite clear that an important aspect of the case was the extent to which the law officers are required to receive referrals and to represent the public interest – in that in *Re Jones* to the extent of considering committal proceedings against a mother in child abduction proceedings:

---

76 [2000] 1 FLR 701.

77 [2013] EWHC 2579 (Fam) sub nom *The Solicitor General v J M J (Contempt)* [2014] 1 FLR 852, Sir James Munby P; court's invitation to the Attorney-General to apply for committal of a mother in child abduction proceedings.

78 Who represented the husbands in *A v A; B v B*.

> '[15] It is... clear that, apart only from certain statutory rights conferred on local authorities, the Law Officers have the exclusive right to represent the public interest. As Lord Diplock said in *Attorney-General v Times Newspapers Ltd*,[79] at 311, speaking of the Attorney-General: "He is the appropriate public officer to represent the public interest in the administration of justice". In *Gouriet v Union of Post Office Workers*,[80] at 481, Lord Wilberforce... said: "That it is the exclusive right of the Attorney-General to represent the public interest – even where individuals might be interested in a larger view of the matter – is not technical, not procedural, not fictional. It is constitutional."'

9.77 Information had been correctly passed on to the law officers by the court. On the particular facts of the case the mother was not committed for contempt.

5 SELF-INCRIMINATION PRIVILEGE AND CHILDREN PROCEEDINGS

Incriminating evidence and children proceedings

9.78 *CA 1989, s 98* provides an immunity which is particular to proceedings under *CA 1989, Pts 4* and *5* (care, interim care and emergency protection proceedings). It is intended to encourage frankness in witnesses and parties to public law children proceedings. This frankness is encouraged by preventing the use, or admissibility, of evidence given in children proceedings in subsequent criminal proceedings (other than criminal proceedings for perjury in the children proceedings). However, it does not prevent the evidence which emerges in the proceedings, or in connection with them, being used in criminal investigations arising, nor does it prevent a prosecution based on the evidence of the children proceedings. It merely ensures that the evidence in the children proceedings is not admissible in the later proceedings.

9.79 *CA 1989, s 98* provides as follows:

> **'98 Self-incrimination**
>
> (1) In any proceedings in which a court is hearing an application for an order under Part IV or V, no person shall be excused from –
>
> (a) giving evidence on any matter; or
>
> (b) answering any question put to him in the course of his giving evidence,
>
> on the ground that doing so might incriminate him or his spouse or civil partner of an offence.

---

79 *Attorney-General v Times Newspapers Ltd* [1974] AC 273, [1973] 3 WLR 298, [1973] 3 All ER 54.
80 *Gouriet v Union of Post Office Workers* [1978] AC 435, [1977] 3 WLR 300, [1977] 3 All ER 70.

(2) A statement or admission made in such proceedings shall not be admissible in evidence against the person making it or his spouse or civil partner in proceedings for an offence other than perjury.'

9.80 The immunity given by s 98(2) is in respect of 'a statement or admission' made, and of its subsequent use in 'proceedings for an offence'. This does not prevent a judge from permitting disclosure of the evidence to third parties (as will be explained below). It only prevents the evidence itself being admissible as evidence against him or her. It does not prevent the same case being made against the parent or witness, which they will have to defend again in another court (or in some other forum[81]). It will then be a matter for the judge at any subsequent criminal trial as to whether the content of that interview was admissible under *CA 1989, s 98(2)* in the later trial.

Disclosure of confidential material

9.81 *Re EC (Disclosure of Material)*[82] provides the test for deciding how the court should deal with evidence covered by s 98(2). The case applies whether application is made in the course of proceedings or as a subsequent application for release is made to the court for release of the children proceedings evidence to the police or for any of the other types of reason outlined above.

9.82 The court must balance the desirability of privacy which is protected by self-incrimination privilege, on the one hand, as against the public interest in making information available for a criminal trial:[83]

> '[That is] between the importance of maintaining confidentiality in family cases and the public interest in making available material information for the purposes of a criminal trial, taking into account the purpose for which the information was required, its weight and significance,... and the gravity of the offence.'

9.83 *Re EC* concerned care proceedings for a child aged three. The child's baby sister had been injured and had died. There were five members of the child's family who came under suspicion for killing the younger child. Each gave evidence at the hearing; and each was told of the effects of s 98(2). In the Court of Appeal judgment, Swinton Thomas LJ explained his understanding of the meaning of *CA 1989, s 98(2)*, and of what it meant in the context of the confidentiality of the care proceedings:[84]

---

81 See, eg, the doctor in *A County Council v W and Others (Disclosure)* [1997] 1 FLR 574.

82 *Re C (A Minor) (Care Proceedings: Disclosure)* [1997] Fam 76, [1997] 2 WLR 322, sub nom Re EC (Disclosure of Material) [1996] 2 FLR 725, CA.

83 At 732 per Swinton Thomas LJ; and see comments of Wall J in *Re AB (Care Proceedings: Disclosure of Medical Evidence to Police)* at 9.84.

84 At 732.

> 'The proceedings themselves are confidential but subject to the power of the judge, in appropriate circumstances, to order disclosure. Nothing in s98 detracts from that power. Section 98(2) gives protection only against statements being admissible in evidence in criminal proceedings except for an offence of perjury. *Accordingly, the judge could not give any guarantee for all time as to confidentiality, even had he wished to do so because the law makes no provision which would enable him to do so.* It may well be that in fairness to persons giving evidence in these circumstances judges may wish to point this out to a witness to whom the warning is given and, almost certainly, a legal adviser should do so.' (emphasis added)

Balance: parental frankness against public interest in prosecution

9.84 In *Re AB (Care Proceedings: Disclosure of Medical Evidence to Police)*,[85] Wall J was asked by the police for evidence from care proceedings. He described the difficulties for the court as follows:

> 'This case raises in an acute and unusual form the well-recognised tension in care proceedings between, on the one hand, the desirability of encouraging frankness on the part of parents suspected of killing or injuring their children and, on the other, the public interest in the prosecution of serious crime and the punishment of offenders, including the public interest in convicting those who have been guilty of violent or sexual offences against children.'

9.85 In *Re AB* a mother had been advised by the lawyers instructed by her in criminal proceedings to restrict the terms on which she was willing to be seen by a doctor in connection with the proceedings. The doctor, Professor David, objected that the mother had been put in this position, to protect herself in criminal proceedings; but that this was at the cost of the frankness necessary for the interests of her own child. Wall J felt he was bound by the Court of Appeal decision in *Re EC* and could not override the police request for any evidence arising from the interview with the doctor.

9.86 He set out the position in which he found himself in *Re AB*. At the end of a long and careful judgment, he explained how *Re EC* applies in a case like this; but pointed out that the protection provided by s 98(2) must not be underestimated by parties and their lawyers:

> '[134] … It may be that the extent and effect of the protection given by s 98(2) are currently being underestimated by family lawyers. Section 98 gives substantial protection to any parent who wishes to be frank, and who makes a self-incriminating statement either to an expert witness or in the witness-box.'

85 [2002] EWHC 2198 (Fam) [2003] 1 FLR 579.

10

RESTRICTING OR WITHHOLDING DISCLOSURE

1 INTRODUCTION

Disclosure and closed procedures

10.1 In **Chapter 9** the subject of disclosure generally was reviewed; and in **Chapter 11** closed material procedures are dealt with. This chapter deals with the intermediate question of how documents or other relevant information or evidence may be withheld (partly or completely) from disclosure to one or more of the other parties; and with the procedural means by which this can be done.

10.2 This chapter considers the extent to which the court may restrict disclosure of a document or of other relevant information in children proceedings. For example, this may be by restricting the extent to which one or more parties has access to documents, because of privilege or confidentiality; or because evidence is treated by the court as irrelevant. Apart from the exclusion of evidence which is regarded as not relevant, the withholding of otherwise relevant evidence can arise in the way outlined below.

10.3 This chapter proceeds as follows:

- **Part 2** introduces the subject of why disclosure should not be exempted, and then the procedure by which application can be made for material to be withheld in family proceedings under FPR 2010, r 21.3 (derived from CPR 1998, r 31.19).
- **Part 3** describes the legal principles on which the withholding of evidence (privilege, confidentiality and public interest immunity (but see also **Chapter 12**)) is based. Non-disclosure is the exception not the rule; and European Convention 1950 jurisprudence.
- **Part 4** deals with the powers of the court to prevent release of confidential information outside court proceedings.
- **Part 5** deals with the law and practice – governed by law or discretion? – of judicial control of evidence (FPR 2010, r 22.1).

Disclosure, control of evidence and the rules

10.4 As mentioned in the previous chapter, FPR 2010, rr 21.1 and 21.2 is all that there is (other than r 21.3) on the subject of 'disclosure'. The provisions set out there are very light. Law and procedure must be deduced from CPR 1998, Pt 31. By contrast the remaining rules of evidence follow CPR 1998 closely and are relatively full. They include:

- FPR 2010, r 21.3 (considered in **Part 2** of this chapter).
- FPR 2010, Pt 22 which includes the power to control evidence (r 22.1: see **Part 6** below), and various rules about how witnesses evidence can be adduced before the court and in statements.
- FPR 2010, Pt 23 (described as 'Miscellaneous rules about evidence') which includes rules in relation to hearsay (not likely to be relevant in children proceedings).[1]
- FPR 2010, Pt 24 which contains rules about witness summonses, depositions and evidence from the EU.

2 PROCEDURE FOR WITHHOLDING DISCLOSURE

Disclosure and a fair trial

Disclosure: part of the right to a fair trial

10.5 Disclosure of all material – documents and information – on which the court is to decide a case is part of a party's right to a fair trial;[2] and the principle is protected also by European Convention 1950, Art 6(1). Disclosure in these terms ensures that all parties and the court are able to consider the same material before the court makes a decision.

10.6 Disclosure is an important aspect of the open justice principle. In *Bank Mellat v Her Majesty's Treasury (No. 1)*,[3] under the heading 'Open justice and natural justice' (in a case predominantly about closed material procedures) the common law principle of documents being available to all parties to a case, was explained by Lord Neuberger:

> '[2] The idea of a court hearing evidence or argument in private is contrary to the principle of open justice, which is fundamental to the dispensation of justice in a modern, democratic society. However, it has long been accepted that, in rare cases, a court has inherent power to receive evidence and

---

1 As explained at 1.18.

2 See, eg, the comments of Lord Nicholl in *R v Derby Magistrates' Court exp B* [1995] UKHL 18, [1996] 1 AC 487, [1996] 1 FLR 513 considered at 9.1 and 9.7.

3 [2013] UKSC 38, [2014] AC 700 per Lord Neuberger, with whom Lady Hale, Lord Clarke, Lord Sumption and Lord Carnwath agreed (Lord Hope, Lord Kerr and Lord Reed dissenting).

> argument in a hearing from which the public and the press are excluded, and that it can even give a judgment which is only available to the parties. Such a course may only be taken (i) if it is strictly necessary to have a private hearing in order to achieve justice between the parties, and, (ii) if the degree of privacy is kept to an absolute minimum: see, for instance Independent News and Media Ltd v A [2010] 1 WLR 2262, and H v News Group Newspapers Ltd (Practice Note) [2011] 1 WLR 1645.'

10.7 Lord Neuberger concluded this passage by emphasising that such cases 'include litigation where children are involved [and] where threatened breaches of privacy are being alleged'.

Exemptions form disclosure

10.8 In **Chapter 9** the bases for a claim that relevant evidence should be excepted from disclosure – privilege, confidentiality and public interest immunity – were explained. This chapter considers the procedure by which a claim to withhold information is dealt with (in this part); and the law upon which such decisions are based in children proceedings (**Part 3**).

10.9 Any restriction on disclosure to a party may conflict with Art 6(1); and can only be justified by the balancing of any greater, but higher and conflicting right or interest, or public interest. This might include the children's interests (in exceptional circumstances) or, for example, national security or police information. The public interest was explained by Lord Bingham in *Secretary of State for the Home Department v MB* by reference to classic and well tested case law:[4]

> '[29] In Kanda v Government of Malaya [1962] AC 322, 337, the Privy Council (per Lord Denning) described the right to be heard as one of the essential characteristics of natural justice. But he pointed out: "If the right to be heard is to be a real right which is worth anything, it must carry with it a right in the accused man to know the case which is made against him. He must know what evidence has been given and what statements have been made affecting him: and then he must be given a fair opportunity to correct or contradict them … It follows, of course, that the judge or whoever has to adjudicate must not hear evidence or receive representations from one side behind the back of the other." Lord Morris of Borth-y-Gest repeated this ruling in Ridge v Baldwin [1964] AC 40, 113–114: "It is well established that the essential requirements of natural justice at least include that before someone is condemned he is to have an opportunity of defending himself, and in order that he may do so that he is to be made aware of the charges or allegations or suggestions which he has to meet: Kanda v Government of Malaya. My Lords, here is something which is basic to our system: the importance of upholding it far transcends the significance of any particular case."'

4 [2007] UKHL 46 [2008] 1 AC 440, [2007] 3 WLR 681.

10.10 Lord Bingham brought the position up-to-date by reference to post-*HRA 1998* authority:

> '[29] Much more recently, and in a Convention context, Lord Hope of Craighead described the right to a fair trial as "fundamental and absolute" (Brown v Stott [2003] 1 AC 681, 719) and in DS v HM Advocate [2007] UKPC D1 (22 May 2007), para 6, Lord Hope referred to and reaffirmed earlier observations to the effect that "the overriding right guaranteed by article 6(1) was a fundamental right which did not admit of any balancing exercise, and that the public interest could never be invoked to deny that right to anybody in any circumstances."'

10.11 However, as will be explained in **Part 3**,[5] though the right to a fair trial is absolute, its component aspects – such as the right to disclosure of relevant documents – may not be. It may be possible, and necessary, as Munby J explained in *Re B (Disclosure to Other Parties)*,[6] to distinguish the component aspects of the right to a fair trial from the whole, and to find that disclosure of otherwise relevant material can be withheld because of a higher interest than the disclosure right.

10.12 So what steps does a party take if he, she or a local authority believe that they have relevant material; but material which they consider should not be disclosed because it is covered by a principle of law which enables it to be excluded (privilege); or, the material being confidential, they should not be required to disclose it. Separately there is the question of whether a public body should be required to disclose information which may immune from disclosure in the public interest (public interest immunity: see **Chapter 12**).

Procedure for withholding disclosure

Onus of proof in privilege applications

10.13 The burden of establishing that material can be withheld from disclosure rests on the party who claims to withhold. In the conclusion to his judgment in *West London Pipeline and Storage Ltd v Total UK Ltd*[7] ('*WLP*') Beatson J summarised his understanding of the law on the burden of establishing that material should be withheld (in *WLP* it was a question of litigation privilege) as follows:

> '[86] The burden of proof is on the party claiming privilege to establish it.... A claim for privilege is an unusual claim in the sense that the party claiming privilege and that party's legal advisers are, subject to the power of the court to inspect the documents, the judges in their or their own client's cause. Because of this, the court must be particularly careful to consider how the claim for privilege is made out and affidavits should be as specific as possible without making disclosure of the very matters that the claim for privilege

5 See especially 10.25.
6 [2001] 2 FLR 1017.
7 [2008] EWHC (Comm) 1729 Beatson J.

is designed to protect: *Bank Austria Akt v Price Waterhouse* (unreported 16 April 1997 Neuberger J) *Sumitomo Corp v Credit Lyonnais Rouse Ltd* [2001] 151 NLJ 272 [Andrew Smith J].'

10.14 CPR 1998, r 31.19 and FPR, 2010 r 21.3 together (respectively in civil and in family proceedings) deal with claims for immunity from disclosure. In the case of both sets of rules, they include in one rule public interest immunity[8] claims alongside claims by a party seeking to override inspection of documents. The conflation can be unhelpful, particularly since it blurs two quite different forms of immunity: privilege is a matter of private law and rights; whilst public interest immunity raises mostly public law questions.

10.15 FPR 2010, r 21.3 is directly derived from CPR 1998, r 31.19 and is as follows:

'Claim to withhold inspection or disclosure of a document

21.3 (1) A person may apply, without notice, for an order permitting him to withhold disclosure of a document on the ground that disclosure would damage the public interest.

(2) Unless the court orders otherwise, an order of the court under paragraph (1) –

(a) must not be served on any other person; and

(b) must not be opened to inspection by any other person.

(3) A person who wishes to claim that he has a right or a duty to withhold inspection of a document, or part of a document, must state in writing –

(a) that he has such a right or duty; and

(b) the grounds on which he claims that right or duty.

(4) The statement referred to in paragraph (3) must be made to the person wishing to inspect the document.

(5) A party may apply to the court to decide whether a claim made under paragraph (3) should be upheld.

(6) For the purpose of deciding an application under paragraph (1) (application to withhold disclosure) or paragraph (3) (claim to withhold inspection) the court may –

(a) require the person seeking to withhold disclosure or inspection of a document to produce that document to the court; and

(b) invite any person, whether or not a party, to make representations.

(7) An application under paragraph (1) or paragraph (5) must be supported by evidence.

8 See Ch 12.

(8) This Part does not affect any rule of law which permits or requires a document to be withheld from disclosure or inspection on the ground that its disclosure or inspection would damage the public interest'

The application for immunity

10.16 In the *WLP* case Beatson J surveyed recent case law on the subject of claims for privilege and considered the procedure for claiming that material should be withheld; and in that case, the court's options where privilege is claimed. The claim was for litigation privilege arising from the litigation following the explosion and fire at Buncefield Oil Terminal in December 2005. The procedure proposed by Beatson J, it is submitted, would cover any claim by a party – such as HI in the *HI* case[9] – for material to be withheld under FPR 2010, r 21.3(3). That said, it must be recalled that in proceedings under FPR 2010, including all children proceedings, the silence in Pt 21 is such that there is no standard disclosure; and that the only requirement for asserting a right to privilege is in r 21.3(4).

10.17 In making an application, a party to proceedings who claims privilege must be sensitive to the fact that the court is being asked to make an order on their assertions as to the content of the documents; unless – as in *HI* – a separate judge is deputed to try the withholding question as a preliminary issue. Other parties will not generally see the documents (unless the claim is not upheld); and it is possible, likely even, that they will be suspicious of the assertions of the party claiming the confidentiality. It follows that any challenge to the claim will be made without the underlying evidence being seen by other parties, and often by the judge. (A separate procedure for closed material is explained in **Chapter 11**.)

10.18 Rule 21.3(7) requires that the application 'be supported by evidence'. This rule and the duties it dictates is explained fully by Beatson J. It is clear that Beatson J expects affidavit evidence (ie not merely a statement). The affidavit should comply with the following:

> '[53] ...Affidavits claiming privilege whether sworn by the legal advisers to the party claiming privilege as is often the case, or, as in this case, by a Director of the party, should be specific enough to show something of the deponent's analysis of the documents or, in the case of a claim to litigation privilege, the purpose for which they were created. It is desirable that they should refer to such contemporary material as it is possible to do so without making disclosure of the very matters that the claim for privilege is designed to protect....
>
> [54] Notwithstanding these threshold requirements, and the care the court must show, once it is established that a communication was made when litigation was contemplated or pending and for the dominant purpose of obtaining legal advice, the privilege cannot be overridden by another public interest.'

9 See 10.48.

10.19 If the court is uncertain whether on the basis of the affidavit evidence that the claim to withhold has been made out, it may consider it necessary to go behind the affidavit. In these circumstances, says Beatson J,[10] its options are as follows:

(a) It may be held that there is no right to withhold, so that the passing on of the information, or filing of the evidence, is ordered.

(b) A further affidavit may be ordered by the court to deal with matters which the earlier affidavit does not cover or on which it is unsatisfactory.

(c) The court may look at the documents.[11] Inspection by the court should be a solution of last resort; and should only be undertaken if there is credible evidence that those claiming privilege have either misunderstood their duty, or are not to be trusted with the decision making, or there is no reasonably practical alternative.[12]

Confidential information: an example

10.20 The above procedure in r 21.3 applies equally to material covered by privilege (as was the case in the *WLP* case) and to material covered by confidentiality. So, for example, what is to happen if 'Amelia', a thirteen-year-old – who in this instance is *Gillick*-competent – has discussed confidential (to her) matters with a school teacher? Under the rule in *Gillick v West Norfolk and Wisbech AHA*[13] – but perhaps not under the principle in *Working together*[14] – it cannot be released to third parties on ordinary confidentiality principles.[15] However, if it is relevant evidence (eg a statement by Amelia as to improper behaviour (short of sexual intercourse) by her step-father) the fact of the confidential information (ie that it exists) must be disclosed by the local authority.[16] So far as it is confidential its content and detail can be withheld unless the court orders otherwise.

10.21 The steps for the local authority to take in the care proceedings are to tell all parties that the material exits: for example, that it is in notes made by the teacher and is evidence which the teacher could give were she called as a witness. Details of the evidence need not be given; but the information that the evidence exists must be 'stated in writing'.[17] The grounds on which the local authority claim to be entitled to withhold full disclosure and the calling of the evidence – the confidentiality of Amelia – must be set out at this stage.

10 §[86](4).
11 CPR 1998, r 31.19(6)(a); FPR 2010, r 21.3(6)(a).
12 *National Westminster Bank plc v Rabobank Nederland* (above); *Atos Consulting Ltd v Avis plc (No. 2)* [2007] EWHC TCC 233, Ramsay J.
13 [1985] UKHL 7, [1986] 1 AC 112, [1986] 1 FLR 224.
14 See discussion at 8.80.
15 See, eg, *Local Authority X v HI and Others* [2016] EWHC 1123 (Fam), [2017] 1 FLR 1362, Roberts J considered at 10.48.
16 FPR 2010, r 21.1(1).
17 FPR 2010, r 21.3(3).

10.22 It is then open to a party – the father and step-mother, for example, as in *Re HI* – to apply to the court to decide whether the claim by the local authority to withhold the evidence 'should be upheld'.[18] An affidavit should be filed explaining in outline why the information is confidential, and why Amelia's confidentiality should not be overridden; but not stating any detail as to what the confidential information is. This affidavit will be considered by the judge.

10.23 What may not happen,[19] the case law authorities assert, is that confidential evidence is seen only by the parties' lawyers, to the exclusion of the parties themselves.[20] This is explained in **Chapter 11**. Otherwise what is happening is a form of closed material procedure; and the documents which are not produced can only be seen, as far as the respondents are concerned, by special advocates.[21] The more conventional, common law and rules-based approach, which does not call for a separate judge and a preliminary issue hearing,[22] is as outlined above. As can be seen this approach is based on r 21.3 and is drawn from Beatson J's common law approach as set out by him in the *WLP* case.

3 WITHHOLDING DISCLOSURE: LEGAL PRINCIPLES

Non-disclosure the exception not the rule

The test in Re D *– the historical starting point*

10.24 *Re D* concerned adoption proceedings where a judge at first instance, upheld by the Court of Appeal, had ordered that a mother should be excluded from disclosure of certain evidence as to what her children had said in a court report. The House of Lords allowed the mother's appeal; and in so doing Lord Mustill – who gave the only reasoned speech – concluded with a series of 'propositions' which were accepted by his fellow Lords:[23]

> '1 It is a fundamental principle of fairness that a party is entitled to the disclosure of all materials which may be taken into account by the court when reaching a decision adverse to that party. This principle applies with particular force to proceedings designed to lead to an order for adoption, since the consequences of such an order are so lasting and far-reaching.
>
> 2 When deciding whether to direct that notwithstanding r 53(2) of the Adoption Rules 1984 a party referred to in a confidential report supplied

18 FPR 2010, r 21.3(5).

19 Despite what was ordered in *Local Authority X v HI and Others* [2016] EWHC 1123 (Fam), [2017] 1 FLR 1362, Roberts J, see 10.48.

20 *Somerville and others v Scottish Ministers (HM Advocate General for Scotland intervening)* [2007] UKHL 44, [2007] 1 WLR 2734; *Browning v The Information Commissioner & Anor* [2014] EWCA Civ 1050, [2014] 1 WLR 3848.

21 As explained in Ch 11.

22 As happened in *Local Authority v HI*.

23 [1995] 2 FLR 701. Roberts J numbers these propositions as Lord Mustill does not. The numbering has been adopted here.

by an adoption agency, a local authority, a reporting officer or a guardian ad litem shall not be entitled to inspect the part of the report which refers to him or her, the court should first consider whether disclosure of the material would involve a real possibility of significant harm to the child.

3 If it would, the court should next consider whether the overall interests of the child would benefit from non-disclosure, weighing on the one hand the interest of the child in having the material properly tested, and on the other both the magnitude of the risk that harm will occur and the gravity of the harm if it does occur.

4 If the court is satisfied that the interests of the child point towards non-disclosure, the next and final step is for the court to weigh that consideration, and its strength in the circumstances of the case, against the interest of the parent or other party in having an opportunity to see and respond to the material. In the latter regard the court should take into account the importance of the material to the issues in the case.

5 Non-disclosure should be the exception and not the rule. The court should be rigorous in its examination of the risk and gravity of the feared harm to the child, and should order non-disclosure only when the case for doing so is compelling.'

Disclosure: a right within the right to a fair trial

10.25 The House of Lords considered *Re D* (amongst a variety of other case law) in *Secretary of State for the Home Department v MB*[24] and in the context of closed material procedures under prevention of terrorism legislation. They held that, although the right to a fair trial required that a person be informed of the case against him and that he or she be permitted to respond to it, such right was not absolute and might (in that case) be limited in the interests of national security. Only such measures for restricting a party's rights as were strictly necessary were permissible. Any difficulties the party suffered in making his or her case were to be sufficiently counterbalanced by the procedures employed by the court. Its task on appeal, was decide whether, looking at the process as a whole, a procedure had been used which involved appreciable injustice to the person excluded from disclosure.

10.26 Lord Bingham considered the European jurisprudence on limiting disclosure, and in particular:

> '[31] In *McMichael v United Kingdom* (1995) 20 EHRR 205 §[80], a family case concerning a child, the court said: "Nevertheless, notwithstanding the special characteristics of the adjudication to be made, as a matter of general principle the right to a fair—adversarial—trial 'means the opportunity to have knowledge of and comment on the observations filed or evidence adduced by the other party'." *Lobo Machado v Portugal* (1996) 23 EHRR 79 was a civil

24 [2007] UKHL 46 [2008] 1 AC 440, [2007] 3 WLR 681.

case concerning the applicant's right, in an adversarial hearing, to see and reply to material before the court. "That right", the court ruled, at §[31]: "means in principle the opportunity for the parties to a criminal or civil trial to have knowledge of and comment on all evidence adduced or observations filed, even by an independent member of the national legal service, with a view to influencing the court's decision."…'

10.27 From this Lord Bingham concluded, again by reference to European jurisprudence, that disclosure – as 'constituent right embodied in Art 6(1)' – is not, in itself, an absolute right. It may give way to competing interests, 'such as national security or the need to protect witnesses at risk of reprisals or keep secret police methods…; [but] only where strictly necessary':

'[32] … The Strasbourg court has repeatedly stated that the constituent rights embodied in article 6(1) are not in themselves absolute. As it was put in *Jasper v United Kingdom* (2000) 30 EHRR 441 §[52], and *Fitt v United Kingdom*(2000) 30 EHRR 480 §[45]: "However, as the applicant recognised, the entitlement to disclosure of relevant evidence is not an absolute right. In any criminal proceedings there may be competing interests, such as national security or the need to protect witnesses at risk of reprisals or keep secret police methods of investigation of crime, which must be weighed against the rights of the accused. In some cases it may be necessary to withhold certain evidence from the defence so as to preserve the fundamental rights of another individual or to safeguard an important public interest. However, only such measures restricting the rights of the defence which are strictly necessary are permissible under article 6(1). Moreover, in order to ensure that the accused receives a fair trial, any difficulties caused to the defence by a limitation on its rights must be sufficiently counterbalanced by the procedures followed by the judicial authorities."'

10.28 By parity of reasoning – as Lady Hale's comments in *MB* (touched on below) and *Re B* (below) show – it will be said here that the interests of children or their and other parties' Art 8 rights may, where 'strictly necessary', demand similar limitation of a parties' Art 6(1) rights; and in particular a limitation on a party's rights to disclosure.

Just result in a just manner

10.29 In *Secretary of State for the Home Department v MB*[25] Lady Hale started from the premise that 'The object of all legal proceedings is to do justice according to law'; but, she went on, justice 'means not only arriving at a just result but arriving at it in a just manner'.[26] She recalled[27] the words of Lord Devlin in *Re K (Infants)*,[28] that:

25 [2007] UKHL 46 [2008] 1 AC 440, [2007] 3 WLR 681.
26 §[57].
27 §[58].
28 [1965] AC 201 at 238.

> '... a principle of judicial inquiry, whether fundamental or not, is only a means to an end. If it can be shown in any particular class of case that the observance of a principle of this sort does not serve the ends of justice, it must be dismissed; otherwise it would become the master instead of the servant of justice.'

10.30 The basic requirement is for the party concerned to know the case against him or her, said Lady Hale in *MB*; and to have a fair opportunity to meet it:

> '[58] ... If, as in [*Re K (Infants)* (above)], the whole object of the proceedings is to protect and promote the best interests of a child, there may be exceptional circumstances in which disclosure of some of the evidence would be so detrimental to the child's welfare as to defeat the object of the exercise: the modern principles are explained in *In re D (Minors)(Adoption Reports: Confidentiality)* [1996] AC 593, [1995] 2 FLR 687.'[29]

Parallel: children and national interests

10.31 In relation to the court's assessment of closed material and partial disclosure principles, Lady Hale explained the parallel between restrictions on disclosure in the national interest (police or defence secrets, for example) and in children law:

> '[59] I mention these examples, not because they are factually similar to the present case, but to show that the problem is not a new one and that there are courts which have long been doing their best to try cases justly even though the ordinary principles of judicial inquiry identified by Upjohn LJ cannot be observed in every particular. If procedure is the servant rather than the master, then dealing with some cases "justly" may sometimes require a rather different approach....
>
> [60] The examples of cases concerning children and mental patients fall fairly and squarely within the problem which now confronts us in the control order cases. They too are hearings in which civil rights and obligations are determined for the purpose of article 6(1)....'

10.32 Lady Hale says: modern principles for limits on disclosure are set out in *Re D (Minors) (Adoption Reports: Confidentiality)*.[30] It remains the starting point for a court's decision as to whether or not to restrict disclosure. It must also be seen also in the light of the European Convention 1950 principles, as explained by Munby J in *Re B* (see below).

---

29 For further consideration of *Re D* see 10.24.

30 [1996] AC 593, sub nom *Re D (Adoption Reports: Confidentiality)* [1995] 2 FLR 687.

Non-disclosure: European convention jurisprudence

European Convention 1950 principles and restraints on disclosure

10.33 In *Re B (Disclosure to Other Parties)*[31] the principles for restraining disclosure in family proceedings was reviewed fully by Munby J. Subsequently to the decision in *Re B* the Court of Appeal have approved Munby J's approach and its reference to Convention principles (as will be seen later[32]), for example in *A Local Authority v A*[33] where, in a joint judgment, Etherton and Sullivan LJJ said:

> '[38]... The incorporation of the Convention into our law by the Human Rights Act 1998 has inevitably raised awareness that the relevant principles apply to the rights of all those, in addition to the child, who would be adversely affected by disclosure or non-disclosure: *Re B (Disclosure to Other Parties)* [2001] 2 FLR 1017.'

10.34 In *Re B* the mother's four children were in care under interim orders. The mother had been married to the father of the eldest two, and had not married the father of the third child. She was now married to the father of the fourth child. The unmarried father ('R') of the third child was joined in the care proceedings. He wanted to see all the filed documents. He was seeking contact with his child, now aged 6 (his parental responsibility and contact applications had already been dismissed). The mother alleged that serious violence had been inflicted by R on both her and the children, including his own child. She wished to limit the ambit of disclosure to him (not to other). She said it would violate her and the children's privacy.

10.35 Munby J summarised the mother's case; and made clear his own view of her predicament. He quoted from her statements as to why she wanted disclosure limited, and then went on:

> '[13] The mother concluded [her statement] by saying: "...the situation regarding [the applicant father having access to her papers is that] he has not been involved with my family for many years, and when he was involved it was as a violent and frightening man. He has no need for any information relating to myself, [K, S or B] and only a very limited need for information regarding [H]. I therefore request that this court acknowledge and protect my family's right to privacy."
>
> [14] That, if I may say so, is a powerful and moving plea which I find wholly understandable in human terms. Lawyers and others who spend their professional lives dabbling in the stuff of other people's misery may not always appreciate as much as they should the embarrassment and worse – sometimes, understandably, the shame, humiliation and anger – that someone in the mother's position must feel as strangers pick over and dissect

31 [2001] 2 FLR 1017.

32 See 10.45.

33 [2009] EWCA Civ 1057, [2010] 2 FLR 1757, considered further at 10.45.

the most intimate aspects of private and family life. Recognition of that reality of course underlies the restrictions which the Family Division traditionally imposes on the public dissemination of information relating to proceedings in chambers, more particularly when those proceedings concern children….'

10.36 That was the judge's view 'in human terms'. He then went on to examine the law. He summarised the balance which must be struck on the mother's withholding argument in Convention terms as:

> '[21] Formulated in the polarised terms to which the forensic pressures of even supposedly non-adversarial proceedings in the Family Division so often lead, the case is therefore one of a conflict or contest between R's asserted right to a fair trial and the mother's, and her children's asserted rights to privacy. Put in Convention terms the contest is said to be one between R's rights under Art 6 and the mother's and children's rights under Art 8.'

10.37 He referred to *Re D* as part of the pre-*HRA 1998* law, and recited in full Lord Mustill's five propositions.[34] He emphasised the importance of the children's Art 6 rights in the context of Lord Mustill's third proposition – 'the overall interests of the child would benefit from non-disclosure'; and of the extent to which the children's interests in disclosure might help the court to reach the truth:

> '[31] … I should mention another, and as it seems to me important, point which emerges from Lord Mustill's reference in his para 3 to 'the interest of the child in having the material properly tested'. Expressing the point in terms of the parties to the present dispute, it is not only R's right to a fair trial which points in the direction of disclosure of the documents to him. So also, it might be said, the children's (and indeed everyone else's) right to a fair trial points in the same direction, for only if there is disclosure to all concerned can the children, and indeed all the parties to the proceedings, be confident that the material has been properly tested.
>
> [32] Put in Convention terms, although the precise nature of the rights in play may differ, it is not merely R's Art 6 rights which are implicated. The Art 6 rights of the mother and W, and more importantly for present purposes, because the mother and W can waive those rights, the Art 6 rights of the children are also implicated. Indeed, the children's Art 6 right, as part of their right under Art 6 to a fair trial, to have the materials properly tested, might be said … to point in the same direction as R's right, as part of his Art 6 right to a fair trial, to have access to the materials so that he can properly test them.'

10.38 So, said the judge,[35] the contest is not merely between the father's Art 6 rights and the mother's and children's Art 8 rights. Also in the balance are the children's Art 6 rights. In one sense, therefore, 'disclosure of the documents to R is not merely for his benefit'. It must also be recalled that, in appropriate cases (of

34 See 10.24.
35 At §[32].

which this was not one) disclosure, 'may also, as Lord Mustill recognised, be for the benefit of the children'.

European Convention 1950 and restricted disclosure

10.39 Munby J set out the then European Convention 1950 jurisprudence fully; but concentrated his conclusions on the Art 6 balance where interests of those other than a party – such as the children, in this case – come into play.[36] In *Montgomery v Her Majesty's Advocate; Coulter v Her Majesty's Advocate and Another*[37] Lord Hope said that 'primacy must be given to the right to a fair trial'. Art 6 does not 'permit, a balance to be struck between the rights which it sets out and other considerations such as the public interest.' In *Brown v Stott (Procurator Fiscal, Dunfermline) and Another*[38] Lord Bingham commented on the procedure required for fairness:

> 'What a fair trial requires cannot, however, be the subject of a single, unvarying rule or collection of rules. It is proper to take account of the facts and circumstances of particular cases, as the European Court has consistently done.'

10.40 From this Munby J deduced the following in respect of fairness and disclosure of documents:

> '[56] ... Although R has an absolute right under Art 6 to a fair trial, and although his absolute right to a fair trial cannot be compromised or watered down by reference to Art 8, he does *not* necessarily have an absolute and unqualified right to see all the documents in the case.

Balancing of Convention rights: fairness and disclosure

10.41 Munby J concluded his assessment of the European Convention 1950 balance in *Re B* by relying on two principles, which can be taken to represent the modern law:[39]

(1) That a party's right to see documents is not absolute;

(2) That in Convention terms the children are no longer the 'only interests capable of denying a litigant access to the documents'.

10.42 Of the right to see documents, said the judge, R did not have an absolute right to see all documents in the case:

> '[64] ... This seems to me to follow quite clearly from the Court's decisions in *Doorson v The Netherlands* (1996) 22 EHRR 330 and *Campbell and Fell v United Kingdom* (1984) 7 EHRR 165 (as from the Commission's earlier

36 §§[54]–[63].
37 [2001] 2 WLR 779 at 806H.
38 [2001] 2 WLR 817 at 824D.
39 As explained at 10.44.

decision in *Hendriks v The Netherlands* (1983) 5 EHRR 223) and from what the Privy Council said in *Brown v Stott (Procurator Fiscal, Dunfermline) and Another* [2001] 2 WLR 817. On this aspect of the matter I see nothing in subsequent Convention jurisprudence to cast any doubt on what the House of Lords said in *Re D (Minors) (Adoption Reports: Confidentiality)* [1996] AC 593, sub nom *Re D (Adoption Reports: Confidentiality)* [1995] 2 FLR 687.'

10.43 To that extent, said Munby J, what was said by the House of Lords in *Re D* remained of full effect in a consideration of whether a party should be excluded from seeing evidence. However, its role in giving priority to children's interests and rights was no longer the same – if ever they truly were predominant after *Re D* – in assessing a party's rights; so long as that party has Art 8 rights which are engaged. For the court to act otherwise, and to ignore a Convention right engaged by the application would be contrary to *HRA 1998, s 6(3)(a)*.

> '[66] Secondly, however, I am satisfied that there is no longer, if there ever was, any warrant for saying that the only interests capable of denying a litigant access to the documents in a proper case are the interests of the *child(ren)* involved in the litigation.... The Act accordingly, in my judgment, requires me to have regard in this context to the Art 8 rights of the mother and W as well as of the children. Section 2(1) of the Act requires me to "take into account" any judgment of the European Court of Human Rights which is "relevant to the proceedings" with which I am concerned.... There can be cases, in my judgment, where a litigant's right to see the documents may have to give way not merely in the interests of the child(ren) involved but also, or alternatively, to the Art 8 rights of one or more of the adults involved, whether as victim, party or witness.'

10.44 So, said Munby J, if – and only if – *Re D* said that only a child's interests determined the disclosure issue, it was inconsistent with European Convention 1950 and *HRA 1998*. It cannot, said Munby J,[40] 'stand as authority for the proposition that only the child(ren)'s interests can be taken into account'.

European convention and rights of children

Convention rights and effects on children

10.45 Limitations on disclosure, and with European Convention 1950 principles in mind, can be seen in *A Local Authority v A*.[41] In that case, a local authority had concerns about the mother's care for A. The parents came from Pakistan. When the mother returned from a holiday abroad with her sister, her aunt and the child, she told the social worker that she had had sex with three different men, one occasion while A was in the room. The authority regarded the information as relevant to the mother's parenting capacity. The women were adamant that the male members of the family should not be told anything about the conversation: the truth would

---

40 At §[66].

41 [2009] EWCA Civ 1057, [2010] 2 FLR 1757.

bring 'dishonour' on the family. They feared for their wellbeing, even their lives. The mother's confidentiality – and therefore her Art 8 rights – was engaged.

10.46 In the care proceedings, the mother and father made a joint application to care for the child as a family unit. The local authority applied for permission not to disclose the relevant information to the father. Some was served inadvertently on the father's solicitors, but they, rather than releasing it to the father (their client), sought guidance from the court. The father consented (on a temporary basis) not to see the document. The judge agreed with the father's lawyers that in law the information should be passed on to the father; and the judge so ordered.

10.47 The Court of Appeal allowed the local authority's appeal and set aside the direction for passing on of information to the father. As already mentioned, Etherton and Sullivan LJJ gave a joint judgement.[42] They explained the law on limiting disclosure and the historical importance of *Re D*:

> '[38] The basic principles which the court applies to determine whether or not to prohibit disclosure of relevant information in this type of case are clear and now well established. While the historical starting point is the speech of Lord Mustill in *Re D (Minors) (Adoption Reports: Confidentiality)* [(above)], the incorporation of the Convention into our law by the Human Rights Act 1998 has inevitably raised awareness that the relevant principles apply to the rights of all those, in addition to the child, who would be adversely affected by disclosure or non-disclosure: *Re B (Disclosure to Other Parties)* [2001] 2 FLR 1017. The fundamental objective of the court in every case is to strike a fair balance between the various rights and interests in the context of achieving a fair trial.'

Restricting or withholding disclosure

10.48 In *Local Authority X v HI and Others*[43] Roberts J was trying a preliminary issue as to whether evidence – which might or might not be relevant to an issue of a mature child's care proceedings – should be disclosed to all parties, including to the child's parents, by the local authority. HI (known as 'I' in the judgment) a 15-year-old – nearly 16 – was in foster care. There were care proceedings in respect of him. HI had said things, in confidence, to professionals which he wanted them to be prevented from disclosing to his father and step-mother, with whom he had previously been living. As parties to the care proceedings they pressed for disclosure, as they were entitled to do.

10.49 Roberts J considered an application by his guardian on behalf of HI for the withholding of the evidence.[44] (The thrust of the case is blunted, since Russell J thought the evidence to be of only tangential relevance; and its disclosure could have been refused on that ground alone.) The local authority asked whether they

42 The lead judgment was from Wilson LJ.

43 [2016] EWHC 1123 (Fam), [2017] 1 FLR 1362, Russell J.

44 It might be though that the application would proceed under FPR 2010, r 21.3; but this provision was not mentioned by Roberts J.

should pass on the information in any event (an application which was open to them under FPR 2010, r 21.3). HI wanted to ensure that what he had said to remain confidential.

Withholding disclosure as a preliminary issue

10.50 The preliminary issue was set up in the following way (Holman J was to be the judge who tried the care application):

> '[10] When the matter came before Holman J on 18 April 2016, none of the three respondents had been given notice of the guardian's application. In those circumstances, and following the guidance given in *Re M (Disclosure)* [1998] 2 FLR 1028 and *Official Solicitor to the Supreme Court v K and Another* [1965] AC 201, (1963) FLR Rep 520,[45] the matter was adjourned to today on the basis that the respondents would be served with notice of the application. In accordance with the practice recommended in those authorities, his Lordship directed that the papers were to be released to counsel instructed to attend today but on the basis that those legal representatives should not disclose the papers or the information contained in them to their respective clients. Pending adjudication of the issue, the local authority were (*sic*) ordered not to disclose the information to any of the respondents.'

10.51 The 'guidance given by *Re M*[46] etc', with respect to Roberts J, has been overtaken by:

(1) Formal provision in FPR 2010, r 21.3 for the withholding of evidence by a party (as discussed here, and by the procedure outlined by Beatson J in the *WLP* case[47]); and

(2) In respect of the release of closed documents to advocates only, by such cases as *Browning* and the jurisprudence in relation to closed procedures[48] (which she was in effect operating).

10.52 *Re M* turned on whether the judge should have heard from the party to whom material was not to be disclosed (in this case the parents). That the judge should have heard from that party before making the order is clear from, for example, Pill LJ (who sat with Thorpe LJ):[49]

> 'It is essential that any party to whom it is proposed information is not to be revealed should have the opportunity of making representations to the court. In *Re C (Disclosure)* [1996] 1 FLR 797 Johnson J stated at 801F that:

45 *Re K (Infants)* [1965] AC 201, also *Official Solicitor to Supreme Court v K* [1963] 3 WLR 408, (1963) FLR Rep 520.
46 *Re M (Disclosure)* [1998] 2 FLR 1028.
47 *West London Pipeline and Storage Ltd v Total UK Ltd* [2008] EWHC (Comm) 1729 Beatson J.
48 Dealt with in Ch 11.
49 At 1033.

> "… the procedure in each case will be determined by the court in the light of the particular circumstances and demands of the particular case."'

10.53 As consideration of, for example, *MB* and *Re B* shows, the law has probably moved on since *Re K*, save to the extent that its emphasis on disclosure demonstrates. For example, the following passage shows that the emphasis in *Re K* was on the exceptional procedure in wardship, which modern children procedure overrides; and as the following passage from Lord Devlin demonstrates:[50]

> 'But it is, I think, with respect, erroneous to suppose that because the inquiry is judicial, all the ordinary principles of a judicial inquiry must be observed. In the jurisdiction parens patriae there are unquestionably some principles of judicial inquiry which are not observed. Contrary to ordinary principles, all wardship proceedings, either final or interlocutory, are held in camera and the practice permits the judge to see by himself not only the ward but also each parent separately.'

Information and the advocates only

10.54 It can be seen that the judge and all parties' lawyers, but not the lay adult parties, had read H's information; but on terms that the lawyers could not discuss the content of the information with their clients. Holman and Roberts JJ were operating what amounted to, in all but name, a closed material procedure. However, it was not termed that, and procedures designed for such procedures were not adopted. The comparison between this procedure and the procedure under the rules will be considered later.[51]

10.55 The judge took account of the fact that H was *Gillick*-competent. His views 'deserve the court's respect' (§[60]); but he was but one party in relation to the disclosure issue. The rights of his parents, affected by her decision, must also be taken into account.

10.56 The judge dealt with reasons for her decision not to give full disclosure to all parties in the case under four categories:

- The relevance of the evidence.
- The extent to which H might suffer 'significant harm' if the information was disclosed to the parties themselves in the proceedings.
- Benefits to the interests of H – the *re D* test.
- Weighing of the interests of the various parties in European Convention 1950 terms.

50 *Re K (Infants)* [1965] AC 201 at 239.
51 See 10.70.

10.57 *Relevance* – The judge had 'significant concerns' as to whether or not the evidence was relevant to an issue before the court, anyway;[52] but she did not decide the application on that issue. She therefore went on to consider the withholding application on the basis that the evidence had at least tangential relevance.

10.58 *Significant harm to HI* – The judge summarised the difference on harm to HI between his guardian and the local authority as that both accepted there would be some harm: the question was how 'significant'.[53] She held that, in her view, there was 'a real possibility of significant harm to HI if the information is disclosed'; and this might inhibit any rehabilitation with his father and step mother which the professionals might be able to achieve.[54]

10.59 *The* Re D *test* – To consider the '*Re D*[55] test' the judge said she must look at the extent to which the interests of HI might benefit from *non-disclosure*. This was a subjective test. It depended entirely on the court's assessment of the effects of the particular disclosure on the child concerned. Of HI and the risk of 'harm' to him, the judge concluded as follows (ie the fifth proposition in *Re D*):

> '[55] … There is ample evidence in the papers to substantiate the positive benefits which have already flowed from his ability to confide in others. I regard both the magnitude of the risk of harm occurring and the gravity of that harm if it does occur as being substantial and significant. The balance at this point clearly falls in favour of non-disclosure. Indeed, I can find no positive benefits to I whatsoever in disclosure at this stage.'

Non-disclosure and Article 6 rights

10.60 *European Convention 1950 rights* – The Art 8 rights of the parents could not take precedence over HI's Art 8 rights which were paramount. The judge explained this: 'As *Yousef* makes clear, the child's rights are the paramount consideration in any balancing of competing Art 8 rights.'[56] As to the parents' Art 6 rights: Roberts J had the jurisprudence discussed by Lord Bingham and Lady Hale in *MB* [57] and by Munby J in *Re B* in mind when she said:

52 §[44].

53 §[49].

54 §[53].

55 *Re D (Minors) (Adoption Reports: Confidentiality)* [1996] AC 593, sub nom *Re D (Adoption Reports: Confidentiality)* [1995] 2 FLR 687.

56 §[57]; *Yousef v The Netherlands* (Application No 33711/96) (2003) 36 EHRR 20, [2003] 1 FLR 210, ECHR.

57 *Secretary of State for the Home Department v MB* [2007] UKHL 46 [2008] 1 AC 440, [2007] 3 WLR 681, considered at 10.25.

> '[58] … The [parents'] rights to a fair trial are, of course, absolute but, as Hale LJ acknowledged in *Re X*,[58] in deciding how to conduct a fair trial, it is perfectly reasonable to take account of the facts and circumstances of the particular case with which the court is dealing. The concept of a fair trial is inviolable but the *content* (including the evidence) which is placed before the court is flexible and depends upon context and the issues with which the court is dealing. Whilst I accept that any departure from the usual requirements in relation to the disclosure of evidence in an adversarial trial must be for a legitimate aim and proportionate to that aim, the Court of Appeal has held that protecting the welfare of vulnerable young persons is a specific and undoubtedly a legitimate aim.'

10.61 Thus, the procedure for the fair trial will normally depend on the facts of the particular case; and the procedure adopted must be proportionate to its aims. The right to a fair trial was absolute, but denying the father and step-mother access to the information here – even so far as it was relevant – would not deprive them of a fair trial. The harm which would be caused to HI would, said Roberts J, be 'wholly disproportionate to any legitimate forensic purposes served.'[59]

4 WITHHOLDING RELEASE OF INFORMATION

Injunctions to prevent passing on of information: inherent jurisdiction

10.62 In the cases considered above there were court proceedings; and the question of disclosure arose in those proceedings. What is the position if there are no proceedings but a person – say, a mature child – wants information kept confidential, where it has been passed on by him or her in confidence to a public authority. Can the court prevent a local authority – which is normally required to 'share' such information – from doing so? Can the court make an order which overrides any duty that confidential information be passed on, or shared, by the body with that information (say the local authority); and even though the law may require that the local authority does so?[60]

58 *Re X (Adoption: Confidential Procedure)* [2002] EWCA Civ 828, [2002] 2 FLR 476: a case where prospective adopters, who were known to the natural parents, nevertheless wanted their adoption to be anonymous. Of the fair trial aspect, Hale LJ said: **[13]** Unlike the right to respect for family and private life in Art 8, the right to a fair trial in Art 6 is absolute and unqualified. But the content of a fair trial in any particular case is more flexible and depends upon the context: as Lord Bingham of Cornhill said in *Brown v Stott (Procurator Fiscal, Dunfermline) and Another* [2001] 2 WLR 817, at 824:'What a fair trial requires cannot, however, be the subject of a single unvarying rule or collection of rules. It is proper to take account of the facts and circumstances of particular cases, as the European Court has consistently done.' Departures from the usual requirements of an adversarial trial must, of course, be for a legitimate aim and proportionate to that aim. Protecting the welfare of these very vulnerable children is undoubtedly a legitimate aim.

59 §[59].

60 See, eg, *CA 1989, s 22(4)* at n 54 below.

10.63 In *PD v SD & Anor*[61] there was no issue as between the parties that Keehan J, in the Family Division, had the power to make an order of the type referred to in the previous paragraph. The question for the judge was: in his discretion, should he do so? That is to say, should he accede to the wishes of the 16-year-old child PD. As Keehan J explained, he was dealing with a 'child' whose adoptive parents were the respondents to the application. PD was with foster carers. He had told his parents a year earlier that he wanted to be a boy and to change his identity. He changed his name from H. His parents had struggled to come to terms with P's decision. In the course of direct and indirect contact they called him H, to his very great annoyance and distress. He had therefore come to the clear conclusion that he no longer wanted his parents to be involved in his life. He did not want them to receive any information about his day-to-day life, nor about his assessment and possible treatment. Finally his parents agreed; save that they wanted quarterly updates as to P's progress, which he did not agree to their having. The local authority simply wished for the judge to define clarity on the extent to which it should fulfil its statutory obligations to consult with and give information about P to his parents.

10.64 Keehan J considered the ability of a 16-year-old to give valid consent. The *Family Law Reform Act 1969, s 8(3)*, the House of Lords recalled in *Gillick v West Norfolk and Wisbech AHA*[62] permits such consent by statute law. But for the fact that P was accommodated by the local authority and was not looked after by them, there would be no obligation on the local authority to provide information anyway. It was only because P was looked after by the authority that it must give information to parents and consult with them.[63]

10.65 To resolve the issues posed by this case Keehan J held that he must consider the competing European Convention 1950, Art 8 rights of parents and P. He had already held that the parents' and P's Art 8 rights were engaged.[64] But what, first were the parents' rights? To answer this he went back to *Gillick*: that the rights existed only till a child can look after himself and make his own decisions.[65]

Gillick *in the light of European Convention 1950*

10.66 Finally, Keehan J addressed what might be called the post *HRA 1998* review of *Gillick* in *Axon*[66] where he refers to Silber J's comments on the importance of

61 [2015] EWHC 4103 (Fam).

62 [1985] UKHL 7, [1986] 1 AC 112, [1986] 1 FLR 224.

63 *CA 1989, s 22*: (4) Before making any decision with respect to a child whom they are looking after or proposing to look after the local authority shall, so far as it is reasonably practicable, ascertain the wishes of – (a) the child;(b) his parents;...regarding the matter to be decided.

64 [23] The Article 8 Convention rights of P and of his parents are engaged. I take particular account of the decision of the European Court of Human Rights in *Yousef v Netherlands* [2003] 1 FLR 210, that where there is a tension between the Article 8 rights of the child, on the one hand, and the parents, on the other, the rights of the child prevail.

65 At §[26], *Gillick* [1986] 1 AC 112 at 185E.

66 *R (Axon) v The Secretary of State for Health and anor* [2006] EWHC 37 (Admin), [2006] 2 FLR 206, Silber J.

children's rights[67] and of the part they play in the importance of the confidentiality of children:

> '[64] It is appropriate to bear in mind that the European Court of Human Rights attaches great value to the rights of children. Furthermore, the ratification by the United Kingdom of the United Nations Convention on the Rights of the Child in November 1989 was significantly showing a desire to give children greater rights. The ECHR and the UNC show why the duty of confidence owed by a medical professional to a competent young person is a high one and which therefore should not be overridden except for a very powerful reason. In my view, although family factors are significant and cogent, they should not override the duty of confidentiality owed to the child. It must not be forgotten that this duty was described in *Z v Finland*[68] as a vital principle in the legal system of all Contracting Parties to the Convention.'

10.67 As can be seen, Silber J refers to the 'vital principle' in *Z v Finland*. In that case and in rejecting a patient's claim that her confidentiality had been overridden by Finnish criminal laws (a requirement that her records be made available to a criminal court by her doctors), the European Court of Human Rights explained the crucial importance of confidentiality in assessment of Art 8 rights:

> '[96] In this connection, the Court will take into account that the protection of personal data, not least medical data, is of fundamental importance to a person's enjoyment of his or her right to respect for private and family life as guaranteed by Article 8 of the Convention (art. 8). Respecting the confidentiality of health data is a vital principle in the legal systems of all the Contracting Parties to the Convention. It is crucial not only to respect the sense of privacy of a patient but also to preserve his or her confidence in the medical profession and in the health services in general.…The domestic law must therefore afford appropriate safeguards to prevent any such communication or disclosure of personal health data as may be inconsistent with the guarantees in Art 8.'

5 POWER OF THE COURT TO CONTROL EVIDENCE

Proof by evidence

10.68 The general rule is that a fact which needs to be proved by a witness's evidence must be proved by oral evidence 'at the final hearing', or 'at any other hearing, by their evidence in writing'.[69] This is subject to rules which exclude further proof of facts or challenges to existing judicial decisions. This evidence can be treated as if it had been already formally proved before the court.

67 And see 2.43.
68 *Z v Finland* 22009/93 – Chamber Judgment [1997] ECHR 10, (1998) 25 EHRR 371.
69 FPR 2010, r 22.2(1).

10.69 Evidence which is treated as already proved and which need not be proved again includes the following categories:

- *Judicial notice* – That is, that a fact is treated as proved, even where formal proof has not been called and even though that fact is in issue before the court. Judicial notice may be the general knowledge that can be imputed to the judge.
- *Estoppel: issue and cause of action estoppel (res judicata)* – Issue estoppel and cause of action estoppel prevent a party from denying what has already been tried and established against that party, either as part of the case (issue estoppel) or as to the final disposal of a case (cause of action estoppel). It operates where factors have been proved in a court of competent jurisdiction following a trial between the parties involved in the present litigation, where the earlier court was one of competent jurisdiction, and the trial – that decided the earlier proceedings – was on the merits, as between the parties.[70]
- *Admissions* – A party is generally bound by his or her admission. An admission made by a party does not need to be proved again.[71]

Power to control evidence

Control of evidence

10.70 FPR 2010, r 22.1, under the heading 'Power of court to control evidence' includes the following:

> '(1) The court may control the evidence by giving directions as to –
>
> (a) the issues on which it requires evidence;
>
> (b) the nature of the evidence which it requires to decide those issues; and
>
> (c) the way in which the evidence is to be placed before the court.
>
> (2) The court may use its power under this rule to exclude evidence that would otherwise be admissible…'

10.71 Rule 22.1 is derived from CPR 1998, r 32.1; and must be read subject to the common law and European Convention 1950 requirements of the right to a fair trial (Art 6(1)). In any case Art 6(1) rights will be engaged. In many cases Art 8 rights (respect for family life) will also be engaged. As Macur LJ said in *Re J (Children)*,[72] where a care order had been made by the judge in haste at a case management hearing:

70 Issue estoppel rarely apply in children proceedings: *Re B (Minors) (Care Proceedings: Issue Estoppel)* [1997] Fam 117, *sub nom Re B (Children Act Proceedings: Issue Estoppel)* [1997] 1 FLR 285, Hale J.

71 *Cf* notices to admit facts: FPR 2010, r 22.15.

72 [2017] EWCA Civ 398; and see 10.79.

'[22] … It is obvious that European Convention 1950, Art 6 and 8 rights necessarily will be engaged at every stage of the process; and that justice must not be sacrificed on 'the altar of speed'.[73]

Limits on judicial control: case management or a question of law

10.72 Any control of evidence by a judge must be exercised judicially and in accordance with the law; and not always as a matter only of discretion. Questions of a fair trial (or of 'fairness' as Sir James Munby P put it in *Re S-W* (below)) will often be in issue; and this generally raises a question of procedure – that is, due process – and thus of law for the court. Whether these are issues of law, or of judicial case management (ie giving a greater degree of discretion to the judge), is an issue which is live in recent Court of Appeal judgments. For the present, it is sufficient to illustrate the law or discretion question in case management issue from four recent cases.

10.73 In *Re S-W (Children)*[74] Lewison LJ and Sir James Munby P treated the question of control of evidence as one of 'robust case management'. However, as Sir James pointed out, the duty of the court remains to act fairly: 'robustness', said Sir James, 'cannot trump fairness':

'[52] Vigorous and robust case management has a vital role to play in all family cases, but as r 1.1 of the FPR 2010 makes clear, the duty of the court is to 'deal with cases justly, having regard to any welfare issues involved'. So, as my Lord has emphasised, robustness cannot trump fairness.

[53] In the context of case management, fairness has two aspects: first, the case management hearing itself must be conducted fairly; secondly, as I observed in the passage in *Re TG* [75] to which my Lord has referred, the task of the case management judge is to arrange a trial that is fair. Here, there was a failure in both respects.'

10.74 In *Re TG* [76] Sir James had stressed the question of fairness and specifically associated it with European Convention 1950 Art 6 and the overriding objective in FPR 2010, Pt 1:

'[37] … The task of the case management judge is to arrange a trial that is fair; fair, that is, judged both by domestic standards and by the standards mandated by Arts 6 and 8. The objective is that spelt out in r 1.1 of the Family Procedure Rules 2010, namely a trial conducted "justly", "expeditiously and fairly" and in a way which is "proportionate to the nature, importance and

73 Quoting Pauffley J in *Re NL (A Child) (Appeal: Interim Care Order: Facts and Reasons)* [2014] EWHC 270 (Fam) S.

74 [2015] EWCA Civ 27 sub nom *Re S-W (Care Proceedings: Case Management Hearing)* [2015] 2 FLR 136.

75 *Re TG (A Child)* [2013] EWCA Civ 5 sub nom *Re TG (Care Proceedings: Case Management: Expert Evidence)* [2013] 1 FLR 1250.

76 *Re TG (Care proceedings: Case Management; Expert Evidence)* [2013] EWCA Civ 5, [2013] 1 FLR 1250.

complexity of the issues", but never losing sight of the need to have regard to the welfare issues involved.'

10.75 Questions of fairness go to the root of the judicial task in any proceedings. They raise questions of law and of European Convention 1950. Control of evidence is not therefore a question only of judicial case management. It goes, as *Re TG* says, to the issue of dealing with a case justly and of fairness under Art 6(1). Where such case management decisions are to be made they must be approached as matter of law.

Case management or control of evidence

10.76 The question for a judge is: when does case management become control of evidence and involve questions of fairness, questions of law and not of discretion? In *Re B (A Child)*[77] the judge had limited the evidence to the two days for which the case had been listed, and which had to finish no later than 4.30 pm on the second day. He ordered that the five-year-old child should return to live with F. The judge did not permit the mother ('M') to call certain evidence which might have supported her case or thrown doubt on F's case.

10.77 It was not fair that the judge had refused to hear this evidence, even at an interim hearing. Black LJ explained the role of the judge in the decision to limit the evidence:

> '[35] It is always difficult for a judge faced, as this judge was, with an urgent decision to take and insufficient time in which to take it. It is a dilemma which family judges regularly have to confront. How they resolve it will depend upon the precise circumstances of the individual case. As this court has often observed, a judge making case management decisions has a very wide discretion and anyone seeking to appeal against such a decision has an uphill task.
>
> [36] However, in this case, I am very clearly of the view that the judge's case management decisions not only deprived [M] of the opportunity to answer the case against her but also deprived the court of evidence that was necessary to enable it to make reliable findings of fact. It is therefore necessary, in my judgment, for the judge's finding of fact and his consequential orders to be overturned and for the matter to be reheard in front of a different judge....'

10.78 Black LJ's attention may not have been draw to FPR 2010, r 22.1; but it is submitted that exclusion of evidence in this way by the judge is a matter of law and not a matter of judicial discretion. This is so, especially in the light of subsequent

77 [2012] EWCA Civ 1742 (unreported). Appeal in *CA 1989, s 8* proceedings by a father (F) in relation to a child (S) aged five. The local authority was involved because of their concern that the mother (M) was involved with Mr C who had been involved in proceedings for serious violence against his wife and three children. M said their relationship was at an end. F produced a statement from an enquiry agent which showed that C had been seen leaving the mother's house early in the morning.

judicial consideration of the point in such cases as *Re S-W (Children)*,[78] already considered. What was fair to the mother, and, probably, to the little girl, needed to be considered in terms of fairness. This required the judge to make the decision as a matter of law, not as an exercise of his discretion.[79] It would have been within the judge's case management powers to tailor and timetable the hearing within the confines of the two-day fixture[80] (not, perhaps, ungenerous for a section 8 application?). Fairness demanded the hearing of both sides fairly and, for example, ensuring that both parties were on an equal footing.[81]

10.79 A similar judicial attempt to short-circuit the evidence and impose a care order at an interim hearing can be seen in *Re J (Children)*.[82] As a matter of law, the local authority must prove its case under *CA 1989, s 31(2)* if a care order was to be made. Of the judges attempt to impose an early order Macur LJ said:

> '[35] It is entirely understandable that this judicial approach raised the collective hackles of all parties. The parties' united stance in this appeal demonstrates an objective unease at the lack of fairness in the process. The burden of proof rested on the local authority throughout, not only in relation to establishing the threshold for the making of statutory orders but also that the intervention in the family's life proposed in the care plans was necessary and proportionate. The local authority sought the outcome delivered but did not support the mechanism adopted to achieve it.'

Admissibility and control

Evidence relevant to the issues: admissibility

10.80 One of the features of an assessment in law of control of evidence will be its relevance to the issues before the court. This is touched upon in r 22.1(1)(a), which gives the court power to define the issues on which 'it requires evidence'. This leads on to the question of admissibility based on relevance: that only evidence which is sufficiently relevant to an issue before the court is admissible. Evidence which is irrelevant, or insufficiently relevant, should not be admitted.

10.81 The importance of defining the issues for trial as part of case management is clear from FPR 2010 r 1.4. Without that definition, parties cannot decide what evidence they need to prove their case, neither can they be sure – to prove an issue that is essential to the outcome of the case – that they have the evidence that the court will need and in a form that proves the point that the party wishes to make. If evidence is not admissible the court can exercise its powers of control to exclude it.

---

78 [2015] EWCA Civ 27 sub nom *Re S-W (Care Proceedings: Case Management Hearing)* [2015] 2 FLR 136.

79 See, eg, Lewison LJ in *Re TG (A Child)* [2013] EWCA Civ 5 sub nom *Re TG (Care Proceedings: Case Management: Expert Evidence)* [2013] 1 FLR 1250 at [47].

80 FPR 2010, r 1.4(2)(a): 'setting timetables or otherwise controlling the progress of the case'.

81 FPR 2010, r 1.2(c).

82 [2017] EWCA Civ 398.

10.82 As Lady Hale commented in *W (Children) (Abuse: Oral Evidence)*,[83] the aim of court proceedings must be to secure a fair trial and to determine the rights of all those involved in the proceedings. The court must admit all evidence which bears upon the questions relevant to that:

> '[23] The object of the proceedings is to achieve a fair trial in the determination of the rights of all the people involved. Children are harmed if they are taken away from their families for no good reason. Children are harmed if they are left in abusive families. This means that the court must admit all the evidence which bears upon the relevant questions: whether the threshold criteria justifying State intervention have been proved; if they have, what action if any will be in the best interests of the child? The court cannot ignore relevant evidence just because other evidence might have been better. It will have to do the best it can on what it has.'

83 [2010] UKSC 12, [2010] 1 FLR 1485.

11

CLOSED MATERIAL PROCEDURES

1 INTRODUCTION

Exclusion from disclosure to a party to proceedings

11.1 In the very rare circumstances where it may be used a closed material procedure permits the High Court to restrict disclosure of certain documents – to be defined in this chapter as 'sensitive material' – to one or more parties to the proceedings; and to specially appointed advocates for the parties not permitted to see the closed material. Generally speaking, only a statute can authorise a closed material procedure. It cannot be done in the inherent jurisdiction of the court. Children proceedings are probably an exception to this general rule.[1]

11.2 A closed material procedure was defined by Lord Neuberger *Bank Mellat v Her Majesty's Treasury (No 1)*[2] as:

> '[1] … A closed material procedure involves the production of material which is so confidential and sensitive that it requires the court not only to sit in private, but to sit in a closed hearing (ie a hearing at which the court considers the material and hears submissions about it without one of the parties to the appeal seeing the material or being present), and to contemplate giving a partly closed judgment (ie a judgment part of which will not be seen by one of the parties).'

11.3 The starting point in any case must always be to protect a party's right to an open trial and with all material which will be considered by the court available on the same terms to all parties. However, closed material procedures have been used to protect national security[3] and in proceedings before the Information Commissioner where sensitive information is required to be protected.[4] In tightly controlled circumstances such procedures may be justified in children proceedings.[5]

---

1 See 11.10.
2 [2013] UKSC 38, [2014] AC 700.
3 See, eg, *Bank Mellat v Her Majesty's Treasury (No. 2)* [2013] UKSC 39, [2014] 1 AC 700.
4 *Browning v The Information Commissioner & Anor* [2014] EWCA Civ 1050, [2014] 1 WLR 3848.
5 As explained in *Al Rawi & Ors v The Security Service & Ors* [2011] UKSC 34 [2012] AC 531, [2011] 3 WLR 388 and considered at 11.10.

11.4 This chapter proceeds as follows:

- **Part 2** explains the severe restrictions on closed material procedures and that (save perhaps in children proceedings) such procedures should be strictly limited as provided for by statute.
- **Part 3** deals briefly with the circumstances in which a closed material procedure may be used in civil proceedings; and illustrates this with procedures under *Justice and Security Act 2013* (*JSA 2013*) and Civil Procedure Rules 1998 (CPR 1998) Pt 82 and appointment of special advocates.
- **Part 4** explains the common law's reluctance to permit a case to proceed on terms that a party's advocate only sees documents.
- **Part 5** concludes the chapter by touching on the subject of special advocates and the setting up of a closed material procedure in children proceedings

Closed material procedures and public interest immunity

11.5 The distinction between public interest immunity (see **Chapter 12**) and closed material procedures should be made clear at the outset. With closed material procedures, only the judge and certain parties (and perhaps special advocates for the parties who are not permitted to see the sensitive material) will see the sensitive material; though the excluded parties will not (by definition). By contrast, in the case of public interest immunity only the party who has the documents has access to the information they contain. This access is denied to the judge and to other parties to the proceedings: the court therefore decides the case with sight only of a part of the relevant evidence.

2 RULE AGAINST CLOSED MATERIAL PROCEDURES

Scope for closed material in children proceedings

Closed material procedures in civil proceedings

11.6 In *Al Rawi & Ors v The Security Service & Ors*[6] the Supreme Court held that the common law, on its own, could not – as a general rule – be used as authority for a closed material procedure. Such procedures can only be provided for by express statutory provision (the *Bank Mellat* case proceeded under the *Counter-Terrorism Act 2008*). The European Convention 1950 and the right to a fair trial does not on its own prevent closed material procedures, provided strict conditions as to the procedure are met.

11.7 In *Bank Mellat (No 1)* Lord Neuberger summarised the condition for use of a closed material procedures as follows:

6 [2011] UKSC 34 [2012] AC 531.

'[5] ...Those conditions, in very summary terms, would normally include the court being satisfied that (i) for weighty reasons, such as national security, the material has to be kept secret from the excluded party as well as the public, (ii) a hearing to determine the issues between the parties could not fairly go ahead without the material being shown to the judge, (iii) a summary, which is both sufficiently informative and as full as the circumstances permit, of all the closed material has been made available to the excluded party, and (iv) an independent advocate, who has seen all the material, is able to challenge the need for the procedure, and, if there is a closed hearing, is present throughout to test the accuracy and relevance of the material and to make submissions about it.'

11.8 In *Re A (Sexual Abuse: Disclosure)*[7] (a vulnerable young adult witness confronted by an argument that her confidentiality should be breached so she could give evidence against a father in children proceedings) Lady Hale dealt with a suggestion that closed material procedures could be used in a case where a vulnerable witness wanted to restrict a father's access to her evidence. Her reply was as follows:

'[34] ... It has been suggested that the court might adopt some form of closed material procedure, in which full disclosure was made to a special advocate appointed to protect the parents' interests, but not to the father himself. It faces two formidable difficulties. The first is that this Court has held that there is no power to adopt such a procedure in ordinary civil proceedings: *Al Rawi v Security Service (JUSTICE intervening)* [2011] UKSC 34, [2012] 1 AC 531.... It is arguable that a greater latitude may be allowed in children cases where the child's welfare is the court's paramount concern. But the arguments against making such an inroad into the normal principles of a fair trial remain very powerful...'.

11.9 Further, she went on to say, there are difficulties inherent in the fairness of the procedures; and, by definition, in relation to a person's ability to mount a defence which is based on all material available to the court and to some other parties. So, said Lady Hale:

'[34] ... The essential requirement of any fair procedure is that the person who stands to lose his rights has an opportunity effectively to challenge the essence of the case against him. There may be cases in which this can be done by offering him a "gist" of the allegations and appointing a special advocate to scrutinise the whole of the material deployed against him. In a case such as this, however, it is not possible effectively to challenge the allegations without knowing where, when and how the abuse is alleged to have taken place. From this information, it is inevitable that X's identity will be revealed. Even if it were theoretically possible to devise some form of closed material procedures, therefore, it would not meet the minimum requirements of a fair hearing in this case.

7 [2012] UKSC 60, [2013] 1 FLR 948.

Closed material procedures: children proceedings and Al Rawi

11.10 So where does that leave the possibility of the use of closed material procedures in children proceedings? *Al Rawi & Ors v The Security Service & Ors*[8] provides the starting point. The case arose as a preliminary issue on disclosure in a damages claim. The claimants said that the security services had been complicit in their detention and ill-treatment of them by foreign authorities, including at Guantanamo Bay. The pleaded causes of action included false imprisonment, trespass to the person, conspiracy to injure, torture and breach of the *Human Rights Act 1998* (*HRA 1998*).

11.11 The Security Service, the defendants, said that the disclosure question could not be dealt with on ordinary public interest immunity grounds. They said there was so much material: this might take three years just to decide in respect of which material PII should be claimed. The judge said a closed material procedure was permitted. The Court of Appeal disagreed; and the Supreme Court disallowed the Security Service's appeal from that decision (with Lord Clarke dissenting). In that case, and as a general rule in civil proceedings, it was held that closed material procedures could not be permitted save where statutory provision provided for it in a specific class of cases.

Objections to closed material procedures

11.12 Lord Dyson, who gave the main judgment for the majority in *Al Rawi*, summarised the open trial principles. First, he said, trials must be in public:

> '[10] There are certain features of a common law trial which are fundamental to our system of justice (both criminal and civil). First, subject to certain established and limited exceptions, trials should be conducted and judgments given in public. The importance of the open justice principle has been emphasised many times: see, for example, *R v Sussex Justices, Ex p McCarthy* [1924] 1 KB 256, at p 259, per Lord Hewart CJ, *Attorney General v Leveller Magazine Ltd* [1979] AC 440, at pp 449H–450B, per Lord Diplock, and recently *R (Mohamed) v Secretary of State for Foreign and Commonwealth Affairs (No 2) (Guardian News and Media Ltd intervening)* [2011] QB 218, paras 38–39, per Lord Judge CJ.'

11.13 Certain basic principles of natural justice must be observed by the courts:

> '[12]... A party has a right to know the case against him and the evidence on which it is based. [and] he is entitled to have the opportunity to respond to any such evidence and to any submissions made by the other side. The other side may not advance contentions or adduce evidence of which he is kept in ignorance....

8 [2011] UKSC 34 [2012] AC 531, [2011] 3 WLR 388.

> [13] ... The parties should be given an opportunity to call their own witnesses and to cross-examine the opposing witnesses. As was said by the High Court of Australia in *Lee v The Queen* (1998) 195 CLR 594, at para 32: "Confrontation and the opportunity for cross-examination is of central significance to the common law adversarial system of trial."'

11.14 As already mentioned, a closed material procedure must be distinguished from public interest immunity. With closed material procedures the judge, certain parties and perhaps special advocates for the parties kept out of the material will see the sensitive material; but the excluded parties themselves will not. By contrast, in the case of public interest immunity only the party who has the documents has access to the information they contain. This is denied to other parties and to the court. The court therefore decides the case with only a part of the relevant evidence.

Proceedings in private

11.15 It is not in question that proceedings in relation to children are one of the exceptions to the open justice principle.[9] Hearings will almost invariably be in private even though an anonymised version of the judgement may be published. Closed material procedures go much further than privacy. However, in *Al Rawi* Lord Dyson continued:

> '[27] It is one thing to say that the open justice principle may be abrogated if justice cannot otherwise be achieved. As Lord Bingham of Cornhill said in *R v Davis* [2008] UKHL 36, [2008] 1 AC 1128 at para 28, the rights of a litigating party are the same whether a trial is conducted in camera or in open court and whether or not the course of the proceedings may be reported in the media. It is quite a different matter to say that the court may sanction a departure from the natural justice principle (including the right to be present at and participate in the whole or part of a trial). *Scott v Scott* is no authority for such a proposition.'

11.16 Lord Dyson concluded his judgment by referring to the exceptions to the normal rule (defined by him above) as to disallowance of closed material procedures. He agreed with Lord Clarke's minority judgment to the extent explained below; and especially to the extent that it recognised that closed material procedures might in effect operate in wardship, and in other children cases (see italicised passage below):

> '[63] ... there are certain classes of case where a departure from the normal rule may be justified for special reasons in the interests of justice. Thus as Baroness Hale of Richmond said in *Secretary of State for the Home Department v MB* [2007] UKHL 46, [2008] 1 AC 440 at para 58:

9 As explained at 13.16.

> "If....the whole object of the proceedings is to protect and promote the best interests of a child, there may be exceptional circumstances in which disclosure of some of the evidence would be so detrimental to the child's welfare as to defeat the object of the exercise."
>
> Wardship proceedings are an obvious example of such a case: see *In re K (Infants)* [1965] AC 201, per Lord Devlin at p 241A. Cases involving children raise different considerations from those which arise in ordinary civil litigation. *That is because the interests of children are paramount. It follows that where the interests of the child are served, so too are the interests of justice.'* (emphasis added)

Children proceedings and wardship

11.17 In *Re K (Infants)*[10] the House of Lords considered whether, in wardship proceedings, they were entitled to deny to a mother access to a medical report which had been prepared specifically for the Official Solicitor. They held that a judge was entitled, as a matter of discretion, to deny access to information to a party, in the interests of a child. Lord Devlin started from 'the ordinary principles of a judicial inquiry' (as had Upjohn LJ in the Court of Appeal):

> 'They include [said Lord Devlin] the rules that all justice shall be done openly and that it shall be done only after a fair hearing; and also the rule that is in point here, namely, that judgment shall be given only upon evidence that is made known to all parties. Some of these principles are so fundamental that they must be observed by everyone who is acting judicially, whether he is sitting in a court of law or not; and these are called the principles of natural justice. The rule in point here is undoubtedly one of those.'

11.18 Lord Devlin explained the difference between the judge who sits – as in most cases –as 'arbiter between two parties'; and where a judge has a duty in respect of interests (as of a child) 'outside the conflict':[11]

> 'This is the essence of the matter. Where the judge sits as an arbiter between two parties, he need consider only what they put before him. If one or other omits something material and suffers from the omission, he must blame himself and not the judge. Where the judge sits purely as an arbiter and relies on the parties for his information, the parties have a correlative right that he should act only on information which they have had the opportunity of testing. Where the judge is not sitting purely, or even primarily, as an arbiter but is charged with the paramount duty of protecting the interests of one outside the conflict, a rule that is designed for just arbitrament cannot in all circumstances prevail.'

10 [1965] AC 201.
11 At 240–241.

11.19 Where the interests of a child require it, the position remains as it was in 1965: that the court can restrict disclosure to a party to protect the interest of a third party, the child. A form of closed material procedure can operate. But how far?

Closed material and justice and security act 2013

Justice and Security Act 2013: national security alongside interests of children

11.20 The *Justice and Security Act 2013* may provide a framework for closed material procedures which can be referred analogically in children proceedings. However, any question related to closed material must be considered always with the European Convention 1950, Art 6 fully in mind, including the extent to exclusion to open court principles can be overridden; for, as explained further in **Chapter 5**, Art 6 includes:

> '(1) … the press and public may be excluded from all or part of the trial in the interest of morals, public order or national security in a democratic society, where the interests of juveniles or the protection of the private life of the parties so require, or to the extent strictly necessary in the opinion of the court in special circumstances where publicity would prejudice the interests of justice.'

11.21 *JSA 2013* deals with national security. Public order and national security and 'the interests of juveniles [(ie the welfare of children)] or the protection of the private life of the parties' are bracketed in Art 6(1) as justifying exclusion of public and press. In a similar way in CPR 1998, r 39.2(3) 'national security'[12] is included with 'the interests of any child or protected party'[13] as amongst those proceedings where the court is able to consider ordering that a hearing should be in private. There seems to be no reason in underlying principle why similar criteria, at least in terms of evidence and procedure, should not be applied, in the very limited circumstances where it may be demanded, in children proceedings as in proceedings which concern national security under *JSA 2013* and CPR 1998, Pt 82.

3 CLOSED MATERIAL PROCEDURES IN CIVIL PROCEEDINGS

Prevention of access to disclosed documents

11.22 Closed material procedures arise mostly in cases where damage to national security is alleged; and to this end CPR 1998 has been amended to include Pt 82 (entitled 'Closed Material Procedure', in operation from June 2013) which is in support of *JSA 2013*. However, closed material procedures may arise in other

12 CPR 1998, r 39.2(3)(b).
13 CPR 1998, r 39.2(3)(d).

proceedings where state or other private interests are threatened where a party has access to highly sensitive information which is to be produced in court. It may arise in children proceedings where a child's welfare or the safety of a party to proceedings[14] is at risk if confidential material is produced.

11.23 To deal with restriction on production of documents which such a procedure may demand, CPR 1998, r 82.2 (in the context of *JSA 2013*) requires that the overriding objective in CPR 1998, r 1.1 'be read and given effect to in a way which is compatible'[15] with CPR 1998, r 82.2(2). Rule 82.2(2) provides as follows:

> '(2) The court must ensure that information is not disclosed in a way which would be damaging to the interests of national security.'

Closed material procedures in civil proceedings

11.24 An application for a closed material declaration, where this is made by the government (whether or not a party to the proceedings) or one of the parties, is such that a closed material application can be made:[16] that is to say, an application within the terms of CPR 1998, Pt 82. *JSA 2013, s 6(2)*:

> '(2) The court may make [a closed material] declaration—
>
> (a) on the application of—
>
> (i) the Secretary of State (whether or not the Secretary of State is a party to the proceedings), or
>
> (ii) any party to the proceedings, or
>
> (b) of its own motion.'

11.25 If both the conditions in s 6(3) and (4) are met in relation to material which should otherwise be disclosed in proceedings,[17] *JSA 2013, s 6(2)* permits the court to make a closed material declaration.[18] The conditions which are required to be met are set out in *JSA 2013, s 6(4)* and *(5)*.

11.26 Application for a closed material declaration can only be made in 'relevant civil proceedings' which means 'any proceedings (other than proceedings in a criminal cause or matter)' in the High Court, Court of Appeal or Supreme Court.[19] A consequence of a closed material declaration is that the court will give notice of the declaration to the Attorney-General who then has power to appoint a special

---

14 See, eg, *Re T (Wardship: Impact of Police Intelligence)* [2009] EWHC 2440 (Fam), [2010] 1 FLR 1048, McFarlane J (police believed there was a credible threat to the life of the mother of the wards); considered below at 11.41.

15 CPR 1998, r 82.2(1).

16 *JSA 2013, s 6(2)*.

17 *JSA 2013, s 6(6)*.

18 *JSA 2013, s 6(3)–(5)*.

19 *JSA 2013, s 6(11)*.

advocate.[20] But to what extent are the procedures under *JSA 2013* and CPR 1998, Pt 82 in any way helpful in the context of children proceedings?

Conditions for allowing a closed material procedure

11.27 Any order which completely restricts access of a party to documents seen by the court and by other parties will need to comply with conditions explained below. Each case will depend on its own facts, and will be assessed by an exacting proportionality and rationality test as explained by Lord Sumption in *Bank Mellat v Her Majesty's Treasury (No. 2)*:[21]

> '[20] The requirements of rationality and proportionality, as applied to decisions engaging the human rights of applicants, inevitably overlap. [That is] the question depends on an exacting analysis of the factual case advanced in defence of the measure, in order to determine (i) whether its objective is sufficiently important to justify the limitation of a fundamental right; (ii) whether it is rationally connected to the objective; (iii) whether a less intrusive measure could have been used; and (iv) whether, having regard to these matters and to the severity of the consequences, a fair balance has been struck between the rights of the individual and the interests of the community. These four requirements are logically separate, but in practice they inevitably overlap because the same facts are likely to be relevant to more than one of them.'

11.28 That is to say, in outline: does the closed material procedures means justify the non-disclosure end, having regard to the incursion on open justice principles which will result if a closed material declaration is made?

4 DISCLOSURE TO LEGAL REPRESENTATIVES ONLY

Disclosure only to a legal representative

11.29 In *Browning v The Information Commissioner & Anor*[22] the Court of Appeal heard an appeal from the Upper Tribunal (Administrative Appeals Chamber)[23] by a journalist, Jonathan Browning.[24] The appeal was against a refusal of the Information Commissioner to permit disclosure of information to Mr Browning because, said the Commissioner, it was not in the public interest that it should be disclosed. The question on appeal was whether the court (ie Upper Tribunal, in this particular case) could see material that neither the appellant nor his representative could see.

20 *JSA 2013, s 9(1)*; CPR 1998, r 82.9(1).
21 [2013] UKSC 39, [2014] 1 AC 700.
22 [2014] EWCA Civ 1050, [2014] 1 WLR 3848.
23 The unsuccessful appeal to the Court of Appeal was from an Upper Tribunal (UKUT 236 AC) consisting of Charles J, then President of the Chamber, Mitting J and Upper Tribunal Judge Andrew Bartlett QC.
24 Maurice Kay LJ described Mr Browning is a 'respected journalist'.

Neither the statute under which the tribunals are set up nor their rules[25] provide expressly for a closed material procedure. And, as Maurice Kay LJ acknowledged, the case was concerned with 'part of the substantive hearing' before the tribunal:

> '[32] ... the present case is not concerned with public interest immunity. Nor is it concerned with an interlocutory determination of what may or may not form part of a trial. The closed session with which we are concerned was part of the substantive hearing.'

11.30 In *Browning*, Mr Browning accepted that he should himself be excluded from sight of the material. The decision related to whether the material could be seen only by his legal representative, subject to the representative giving an undertaking not to disclose confidential material to his or her client.[26] Though the case did not directly concern closed material procedures it did relate to a particular means, sometimes used by courts, of limiting disclosure, or of preventing a party, personally, from seeing material.

11.31 Maurice Kay LJ gave judgment based on the question of whether Mr Browning's legal representative also should be excluded from seeing the undisclosed documents, which the court would see. He found[27] that the rules under the *Tribunals, Courts and Enforcement Act 2007* permitted the procedure used in this case to exclude the appellant and his legal representative from production of the documents. In any event, he continued, courts were generally averse to allowing lawyers to have access to documents which they could not disclose to their client. Thus, he made what amounted to a form of closed material declaration. It was not appropriate for a legal representative (as distinct from a special advocate: see **Part 5**) only to see documents from which his or her client was excluded.

Disclosure of documents to a party's legal representative only

11.32 The following relies on the assumption that a party has a legal representative (which is increasingly not the case). In *Browning v The Information Commissioner & Anor*[28] Maurice Kay LJ held:

> '[32] Our Courts have shown an aversion to permitting counsel to see or hear evidence which he is not at liberty to disclose to his client. In the context of criminal litigation, this is illustrated by *R v Davis* [1993] 1 WLR 613, 616 to 617, per Lord Taylor CJ; *R v Preston* [1994] 2 AC 130 at 152-153, per Lord Mustill; and *R v G* [2004] 1 WLR 2932, at paragraph 13, per Rose LJ.'

---

25 *Tribunals, Courts and Enforcement Act 2007* and Tribunal Procedure (First-tier Tribunal) (General Regulatory Chamber) Rules 2009.

26 As had been the case, said the Court of Appeal (at §[8]), *British Union for the Abolition of Vivisection v ICO and anor* EA 2010/0064.

27 At para [28].

28 [2014] EWCA Civ 1050, [2014] 1 WLR 3848.

11.33 However, said Maurice Kay LJ, this approach of courts being unwilling to let parties' advocates (only) see documents which their clients may not see, can arise also in civil litigation. The point was dealt with by Lord Rodger in *Somerville v Scottish Ministers*:[29,30]

> '[152] In terms of an agreement contained in a "protocol", under conditions of the strictest confidentiality, senior counsel for the petitioners was allowed to inspect the complete versions of the documents for which the respondents were claiming public interest immunity. Although devised with the best of intentions, this procedure was, in my view, wrong in principle. As a result, it not only gave rise to very real practical difficulties but led the court to adopt a mistaken approach to the inspection of the documents by the [judge].
>
> [153] If the respondents claim that, in the public interest, the redacted parts of the documents should not be revealed was valid, then, in normal course, it was valid against counsel ... who should therefore not have seen the full version. As it was, counsel ... was left in a very difficult situation where, as a result of reading the documents, he had information that he was not able to reveal to, or discuss with, his clients or instructing solicitors. He even felt inhibited from revealing it to the [judge].'

11.34 Lord Rodger concluded:[31] 'In agreement with all of your Lordships, I am satisfied that no such procedure should be followed in future'. Advocates should not see documents in circumstances where their clients are not permitted access to those documents (as appears to have been permitted in *Local Authority X v HI and Others* [32]).

5 SPECIAL ADVOCATES

Special advocates to the court

11.35 *JSA 2013, s 9* enables the Attorney-General to appoint a qualified lawyer 'to represent the interests of a party in any [closed material declaration application] from which the party (and any legal representative of the party) is excluded.'[33] The person 'appointed as a special advocate is not responsible to the party to the proceedings whose interests the person is appointed to represent'.[34]

29 *Somerville v Scottish Ministers (Scotland)* [2007] UKHL 44, [2007] 1 WLR 2734.
30 And see Lord Mance at [203].
31 At para [153].
32 [2016] EWHC 1123 (Fam), [2017] 1 FLR 1362, Roberts J; and see discussion at 10.48.
33 *JSA 2013, s 9(1)*.
34 *JSA 2013, s 9(4)*; and *cf* the duties of the advocate to the court appointed in civil proceedings: *Memorandum of 19 December 2001*, para 4: the 'advocate to the court represents no one'.

11.36 CPR 1998, Pt 82, Section II provides a procedure for appointment of a special advocate in civil proceedings.[35] FPR 2010, not surprisingly, provides no such procedure. A procedure analogous to that in CPR 1998, Pt 82 may work for children proceedings. Where application for a closed material declaration is made on behalf of a government department or a party to proceedings the Attorney-General will be notified.[36] The Attorney-General can then give consideration under *JSA 2013, s 9(1)* to arrangements for representation of the specially represented party.

11.37 The functions of the special advocate are to 'represent the interests of the specially represented party',[37] and are defined by CPR 1998, r 82.10 as follows:

> **'82.10 Functions of a special advocate**
>
> The functions of a special advocate are to represent the interests of a specially represented party by—
>
> (a) making submissions to the court at any hearing or part of a hearing from which the specially represented party and the specially represented party's legal representatives are excluded;
>
> (b) adducing evidence and cross-examining witnesses at any such hearing or part of a hearing;
>
> (c) making applications to the court or seeking directions from the court where necessary; and
>
> (d) making written submissions to the court.'

Sensitive material

11.38 CPR 1998, r 82.11 defines how a special advocate can communicate about the proceedings, and depends on the date on which a 'relevant person'[38] serves the material – 'the sensitive material'[39] – in respect of which a declaration is claimed. Before service of the material, the special advocate is permitted to

35 Appointment of a special advocate to the court in family proceedings is not dealt with in the *Attorney-General's Memorandum of 19 December 2001*, and, the President's guidance of 25 March 2015 explains appointment is by a separate procedure: *Special Advocates* – These are not the subject of [25 March 2015 guidance], or any, Memorandum. Usually a Special Advocate is required because a public body that is party to the litigation, often a local authority or the police, resist disclosure of sensitive documents. The Attorney General has asked that at the point of requesting him to instruct a Special Advocate the court should specifically consider and make provision (after, of course, hearing submissions from the parties) as to which party should pay the costs of the Special Advocate. The essential point is that this is not a service which the Attorney General will normally cover…

36 CPR 1998, r 82.9(1).

37 But *cf* the assertion in *JSA 2013, s 9(4)* that the 'special advocate is not responsible to the party to the proceedings whose interests the person is appointed to represent'.

38 *JSA 2013, s 6(8)* defines a 'relevant person' – eg the police in *Re T (Wardship: Impact of Police Intelligence)* [2009] EWHC 2440 (Fam), [2010] 1 FLR 1048 – as the person who held the material in respect of which a declaration under s 6 was to be sought.

39 'Sensitive material' under *JSA 2013, s 6(11)* is material the disclosure of which – under *JSA 2013* – would be damaging to the interests of national security.

communicate with the represented party. CPR 1998, r 82.11(1) and (2) provide as follows:

> **'82.11 Special advocate: communicating about proceedings**
>
> (1) The special advocate may communicate with the specially represented party or the specially represented party's legal representative at any time before a relevant person serves sensitive material on the special advocate.
>
> (2) After the relevant person serves sensitive material on the special advocate, the special advocate must not communicate with any person about any matter connected with the proceedings, except [as provided in r 82.11]…'.

11.39 The remainder of CPR 1998, r 82.11 deals with:

- With whom the special advocate may communicate, without direction of the court (r 82.11(3): eg the court, the relevant person or (where different) the government representative);
- That the special advocate may seek directions from the court to communicate with the specially represented party or his/her representative (r 82.11(4)); and in that case the court must notify the Secretary of State and the relevant person, and
- That the specially represented party may communicate with the advocate after service, but only 'in writing through the specially represented party's legal representative'; and the special advocate can only reply as directed by the court (r 82.11(6)).

'Scepticism and stringency'

11.40 The role of the special advocate in *JSA 2013* is defined in CPR 1998, r 82.10. The House of Lords has urged[40] scepticism on the part of special advocates and of the judge who is asked to make a closed material declaration:

> '[66] The [applicant] must give as full as possible an explanation of why she considers that the grounds [for a declaration] are made out. The fuller the explanation given, the fuller the instructions that the special advocates will be able to take from the client before they see the closed material. Both judge and special advocates will have to probe the claim that the closed material should remain closed with great care and considerable scepticism…. Both judge and special advocates will have stringently to test the material which remains closed. All must be alive to the possibility that material could be redacted or gisted in such a way as to enable the special advocates to seek the client's instructions upon it…. The nature of the case may be such that the client does not need to know all the details of the evidence in order to make an effective challenge.'

40 *Secretary of State for the Home Department v MB* [2007] UKHL 46, [2008] 1 AC 440 per Lady Hale.

6 SPECIAL ADVOCATE AND CHILDREN PROCEEDINGS

Special advocate and Re T

11.41 In *Re T (Wardship: Impact of Police Intelligence)*[41] McFarlane J explained his view of the role of the special advocate and on the basis of the case law then available (the judgment is dated 7 October 2009).[42] He drew, in particular, on *Secretary of State for the Home Department v MB*[43], especially on the speech of Lady Hale. He referred to the speech of Lord Hoffman (in which there are echoes, perhaps, of Lord Devlin in *Re K (Infants)*[44] and of the interests of others including children in limiting access to disclosed material): that there may be interests other than those of the parties only to consider in a closed material procedure decision:

> '[54] ... From the point of view of the individual seeking to challenge the order [the special advocate procedure] is of course imperfect. But the Strasbourg Court has recognised that the right to be informed of the case against one, though important, may have to be qualified in the interests of others and the public interest...'.

11.42 In *Re T (Wardship: Impact of Police Intelligence)*[45] a child, aged 5 at the time of the hearing, had been made a ward of court when he was taken to India by the father (F), but without the mother's (M) consent. F returned with the child to England two years later. Neither he nor his solicitors[46] disclosed the child's whereabouts to the court. The child was ultimately recovered by the police. F applied for contact from prison. His parents also applied for contact.

11.43 On the day a directions hearing was to take place, the police informed the family judge that there was credible intelligence that F had taken out a contract to have M murdered when she came to the hearing. The police had therefore decided to take M and the child into police protection; but this protection would be withdrawn if interim contact was ordered. The police initially requested that none of this information be disclosed to F, his family or any of the family's representatives. The court was required to investigate these allegations, whilst at the same time affording due protection to the police material. The police asserted that their material must, in the public interest, remain confidential and undisclosed to the parties; and, crucially, that it must remain undisclosed also to their representatives.

41 [2009] EWHC 2440 (Fam), [2010] 1 FLR 1048, McFarlane J.
42 Paras [19] to [28].
43 [2007] UKHL 46, [2008] 1 AC 440 (to what extent can the Special Immigration Appeals Commission restrict access to materials before them).
44 [1965] AC 201 at 240–241.
45 [2009] EWHC 2440 (Fam), [2010] 1 FLR 1048, McFarlane J.
46 There was no general duty, absent a court order, requiring solicitors to disclose information as to the whereabouts of a ward, in breach of the duty of confidentiality owed to a client: paras [102]–[105].

11.44 Special advocates were appointed – possibly for the first time in family proceedings, said the judge – to see the police material, and with that information then to represent the interests of F and his parents at the closed hearings. They filtered the evidence whose disclosure was resisted by the police. Following a proper evaluation by the court, the police eventually agreed to disclose the great bulk of its material at the non-closed fact-finding hearing; though certain information concerning the original intelligence as to the contract remained closed and known only to the judge and the special advocates throughout the process.

11.45 In wardship the family court had always had a duty to investigate all of the relevant circumstances that might touch upon the ward's future welfare, the wardship court could, unlike a criminal court, receive anonymous, hearsay evidence.[47] For the Family Division the question was the weight which could be given to such material. McFarlane J explained this as follows:

> '[89] [The court's] investigation must include receiving evidence, even if it is anonymous, hearsay evidence from an unknown individual, as part of the process. Thus, for the wardship court, it is not a case that a certain category of evidence cannot be acceptable or must be excluded, rather, it is a question of what weight is to be attached to that evidence when the court comes to evaluate it. During the exercise of determining the weight to be given to material ..., the principles underpinning the House of Lords decision in *R v Davis*[48] will be of substantial relevance and may well be determinative, but the issue will be weight rather than admissibility.'

Appointment of special advocate: procedure in Re T

11.46 In *Re T* the procedure favoured by the judge, in wardship (but procedurally there need be no difference between wardship and other children proceedings) was summarised by him.[49]

(1) The two special advocates retained were 'fully briefed' by the lawyers acting for F and for his parents (the two specially represented parties).

(2) The special advocates met their respective lay clients in conference. Thereafter the special advocates had little or no direct contact with the paternal family or their legal representatives.

47 And see 1.18 on weight to be given to hearsay evidence.

48 In *R v Davis* [2008] UKHL 36, [2008] 1 AC 1128, [2008] 3 WLR 125 the House of Lords held that in a criminal trial the use of anonymous evidence was not acceptable and did not satisfy the requirements of European Convention 1950, Art 6. In wardship the judge held (para [89]) there was a 'distinction between the criminal jurisdiction and the wardship jurisdiction. Unlike the criminal jurisdiction, where the sole issue before the court is determining the guilt or otherwise of the defendant on a particular charge, the wardship court has a duty to investigate all of the relevant circumstances that may touch upon the ward's future welfare. That investigation must include receiving evidence, even if it is anonymous, hearsay evidence from an unknown individual, as part of the process.' For the wardship court 'it is a question of what weight is to be attached to that evidence when the court comes to evaluate it.'

49 See especially paras [34]–[37].

(3) The parties' representatives remained able at all times to communicate with and pass information to the special advocates.[50]

(4) The special advocates could not communicate with the open parties save with their legal representatives in writing and with the permission of the court.

11.47 The next stage of the process, said the judge, was geared to the special advocates' challenge to the police assertion of public interest immunity:

> '[32] ... involved the police disclosing what was thought to be the entirety of their files to the special advocates. There followed a detailed discussion between the special advocates and the police as to which parts of the material could be disclosed to the 'open' parties, the role of the special advocates at this stage being to challenge the assertion of PII made by the MPS.'

11.48 It then became possible, as a result of the 'process of the special advocates and the [police] consideration of the detailed material' that the majority of undisclosed material could be disclosed to the 'open parties', and public interest immunity was accepted as being applicable to certain restricted categories of document (eg to protect arrangements for the mother and to avoid identification of informants).[51] The resulting material in full, redacted or 'gisted' (summarised) could then be disclosed to the open parties; and, said the judge:

> '[34] ... It is also right to record that this degree of disclosure had been achieved through discussion between the [police] legal team and the special advocates, and did not at any stage of that process require a ruling from the court on any disclosure issue.'

Statutory provision

11.49 As already mentioned, in *Al Rawi & Ors v The Security Service & Ors*[52] it was held by the Supreme Court that, in the absence of statutory authority, it was not open to the courts to set up closed material procedures, including in civil proceedings (save perhaps in children proceedings). In *Secretary of State for the Home Department v MB*[53] Lady Hale explained why, in her opinion, children proceedings might be different from other civil proceedings in terms of the court being able to order that not all material be disclosed to all parties:

> '[57] The object of all legal proceedings is to do justice according to law: but this is easily said and not so easily done. Doing justice means not only arriving at a just result but arriving at it in a just manner. The overriding objective of the Civil Procedure Rules is to enable the court to deal with cases justly: CPR r. 1.1(1). Of the fundamental importance of the right to a fair trial there can be no doubt. But there is equally no doubt that the essential

50 *Cf* CPR 1998, r 82.11.
51 Para [33].
52 [2011] UKSC 34 [2012] AC 531.
53 [2007] UKHL 46, [2008] 1 AC 440.

ingredients of a fair trial can vary according to the subject matter and nature of the proceedings.'

11.50 Thus, though the requirements of fairness in given cases vary according to the issues for hearing, the basic requirements remain: that a party knows the case against him or her, and that that party has an opportunity to meet that case. However, as Lord Devlin in the House of Lords stressed in *Re K (Infants)*:[54] a procedural rule must be the servant of justice, not its master:

> ' ... a principle of judicial inquiry, whether fundamental or not, is only a means to an end. If it can be shown in any particular class of case that the observance of a principle of this sort does not serve the ends of justice, it must be dismissed: otherwise it would become the master instead of the servant of justice.'

Best interests of children: special circumstances

11.51 If the requirement is to promote the best interests of a child, there might be exceptional circumstances where disclosure might harm the child. In *MB* Lady Hale continued:

> '[58] The basic requirement is to know the case against one and to have an opportunity of meeting it. But in *In re K (Infants)* [1963] Ch 381, 405, Upjohn LJ identified more detailed principles of a judicial inquiry: "the right to see all the information put before the judge, to comment on it, to challenge it and if needs be to combat it, and to try to establish by contrary evidence that it is wrong." However, as Lord Devlin pointed out in the same case in the House of Lords, at [1965] AC 201, 238 [per passage cited above]. If, as in that case, the whole object of the proceedings is to protect and promote the best interests of a child, there may be exceptional circumstances in which disclosure of some of the evidence would be so detrimental to the child's welfare as to defeat the object of the exercise: the modern principles are explained in *In re D (Minors)(Adoption Reports: Confidentiality)* [1996] AC 593, [1995] 2 FLR 687.'[55]

11.52 As Lady Hale says: modern principles for limits on disclosure are set out in *Re D (Minors) (Adoption Reports: Confidentiality)*,[56] by Lord Mustill in the House of Lords. *Re D* was an adoption case in which the question of whether a mother should see a section of a report in the proceedings relating to the children's wishes and feelings was in question. The judge held as a matter of his discretion that she should not. The House of Lords said the wider principles of openness, even within the privacy of adoption proceedings, should have been taken into account by the judge. They sent the case back for him to reconsider. Lord Mustill (who gave the only reasoned opinion) commented:

---

54 [1965] AC 201 at 238.

55 For further consideration of *Re D* see 10.24.

56 [1996] AC 593, sub nom *Re D (Adoption Reports: Confidentiality)* [1995] 2 FLR 687, HL.

> 'For my part I have no hesitation in saying that a strong presumption in favour of disclosing to a party any material relating to him or her is the point at which the judge should start. It is true, as frequently emphasised, that the requirements of natural justice are not invariable, and that circumstances must alter cases. Nevertheless the opportunity to know about and respond to adverse materials is at the heart of a fair hearing. Adoption is an unusual process, but it calls for fairness as much as any other, and indeed with special intensity, for the reasons already given.'

Closed material in children proceedings

11.53 In *Re A (Sexual Abuse: Disclosure)*[57] Lady Hale returned to the question of closed material, in the context of limitation of disclosure of material to a party, but instead to a special advocate 'to protect the parents' interests. The first objection to such a proposal was the *Al Rawi* point: that the Supreme Court had held that, save where permitted by statute, no such procedures were available in civil proceedings. There may be greater latitude for a closed material procedure in children cases she said; but arguments for such a procedure in any case must be 'very powerful':

> '[34] It is in this context that it has been suggested that the court might adopt some form of closed material procedure, in which full disclosure was made to a special advocate appointed to protect the parents' interests, but not to the father himself. It faces two formidable difficulties. The first is that this Court has held that there is no power to adopt such a procedure in ordinary civil proceedings: *Al Rawi v Security Service (JUSTICE intervening)* [2011] UKSC 34, [2012] 1 AC 531. That case can be distinguished on the ground that it was the fair trial rights of the state that were in issue, and the state does not enjoy Convention rights. It is arguable that a greater latitude may be allowed in children cases where the child's welfare is the court's paramount concern. But the arguments against making such an inroad into the normal principles of a fair trial remain very powerful.'

11.54 Secondly, she said, there were difficulties inherent in the procedures themselves:

> '[34] ... The essential requirement of any fair procedure is that the person who stands to lose his rights has an opportunity effectively to challenge the essence of the case against him. There may be cases in which this can be done by offering him a "gist" of the allegations and appointing a special advocate to scrutinise the whole of the material deployed against him. In a case such as this, however, it is not possible effectively to challenge the allegations without knowing where, when and how the abuse is alleged to have taken place. From this information it is inevitable that X's identity will be revealed. Even if it were theoretically possible to devise some form of closed material procedures, therefore, it would not meet the minimum requirements of a fair hearing in this case.'

57 [2012] UKSC 60, [2013] 1 FLR 948.

11.55 It remains the case that in the interests of a child, special procedures may be set up to prevent a party to children proceedings – it may be a parent, but it could be another family member who is a party to the case – having full access to material seen by the court and by other parties.[58] 'Very powerful' arguments will be needed to justify the extreme step of closed material procedures.[59] However, to deal with an application for a closed material declaration the Family Division, it is submitted, may wish to adjust McFarlane J's procedure in *Re T (Wardship: Impact of Police Intelligence)*[60] alongside the *Bank Mellat (No 1)* conditions[61] to the new procedures in CPR 1998, Pt 82 and *JSA 2013, Pt II.*

58 See, eg, *D (Minors)(Adoption Reports: Confidentiality)* [1996] AC 593, [1995] 2 FLR 687; *Secretary of State for the Home Department v MB* [2007] UKHL 46, [2008] 1 AC 440; *Re T (Wardship: Impact of Police Intelligence)* [2009] EWHC 2440 (Fam), [2010] 1 FLR 1048, McFarlane J.

59 *Re A (Sexual Abuse: Disclosure)* [2012] UKSC 60, [2013] 1 FLR 948 per Lady Hale at [34].

60 [2009] EWHC 2440 (Fam), [2010] 1 FLR 1048

61 *Bank Mellat v Her Majesty's Treasury (No 1)* [2013] UKSC 38, [2014] AC 700 at [5].

12

PUBLIC INTEREST IMMUNITY

1 INTRODUCTION

Claims to immunity in civil proceedings

12.1 As explained in **Chapter 10**, Family Procedure Rules 2010 (FPR 2010) r 21.3 regulates claims for withholding disclosure of documents in children proceedings. It does this as part of what is in effect the formal regulation of claims for public interest immunity for documents which may be held need not be disclosed in the public interest. Such claims will be almost exclusively from public bodies.[1]

12.2 The procedure for a claim to public interest immunity is the same as for documents covered by privilege and confidentiality (as considered in **Chapter 10, Part 2**); save that in the case of public interest immunity it is for the body seeking public interest immunity – or exceptionally for the judge to direct it – to apply to the court to withhold disclosure.[2]

12.3 This chapter proceeds as follows:

- **Part 2** explains public interest immunity and its meaning in recent case law.
- **Part 3** contrasts public interest immunity with private interests in disclosure; and considers third party orders for disclosure and public interest immunity in that context.
- **Part 4** Deals with procedure under FPR 2010, r 21.3 (related also to the similar procedure in withholding disclosure of private documents).

Public interest immunity and closed material procedures

12.4 The subject of closed material procedures (which, in certain cases may be considered in parallel with public interest immunity) is dealt with separately

1 A private law tort case claim was pursued by NSPCC in *D v National Society for the Prevention of Cruelty to Children* [1978] AC 171, (1977) FLR Rep 181; but this is a very rare example of a private claim, though in public law (investigation of alleged child abuse) circumstances.
2 See 12.36.

in **Chapter 11**. The important distinction between public interest immunity and closed material procedures is stressed there:[3] that where public interest immunity is ordered neither the court nor any party (save the party with the immune material) sees the material; whereas at least where closed material procedures are adopted all parties or their special advocates, albeit on a restricted basis, have access to the material.

2 PUBLIC INTEREST IMMUNITY

Public interests: confidentiality balanced against justice

12.5 In *Duncan v Cammell Laird*[4] Lord Simon pointed out that what had been known as 'Crown privilege' was not, in reality, anything to do with the law of privilege. It was a 'rule that the interests of the state must not be put in jeopardy by production of documents'. If necessary, it could be insisted upon by the judge 'even though no objection is taken at all' by the party entitled to seek the immunity.[5] Privilege, said Lord Simon, is for the protection of the individual litigant. It can be waived by him or her. In contrast, a rule that protects documents or information in the interests of the state was a matter for the administration of justice. It was quite unconnected with the private law interests of parties to court proceedings which define privilege.

12.6 The modern law on public interest immunity was explained by the House of Lords in *R v Chief Constable of the West Midlands, ex p Wiley*[6] (*'exp Wiley'*). In a short speech Lord Templeman emphasised the principle that the courts must balance the public interest in preserving confidentiality as against that of 'securing justice'. Disclosure must be the starting point. Specific documents covered by public interest may be immune from disclosure, but as a rule each document sought to be withheld will be tested for harm to the public interest:

> 'If public interest immunity is approached by every litigant on the basis that a relevant and material document must be disclosed unless the disclosure will cause substantial harm to the public interest, the distinction between a class claim and a contents claim loses much of its significance. As a general rule the harm to the public interest of the disclosure of the whole or part of a document dealing with defence or national security or diplomatic secrets will be self-evident and will preclude disclosure. On the other hand it is difficult to see how the disclosure of documents generated by the activities of the Police Complaints Authority can cause any harm.'

3 See 11.5.
4 [1942] AC 624.
5 At 641.
6 [1994] UKHL 8, [1995] AC 274.

Open justice – natural justice

12.7 In *Bank Mellat v Her Majesty's Treasury (No. 1)*,[7] under the heading 'Open justice and natural justice', the common law principle of documents being available in open court to all parties to a case, was explained by Lord Neuberger:

> '[2] The idea of a court hearing evidence or argument in private is contrary to the principle of open justice, which is fundamental to the dispensation of justice in a modern, democratic society…'.

12.8 But, said Lord Neuberger, there were 'rare cases' where the court has powers to override open justice – including, as he emphasised, in children cases:

> '[2] … However, it has long been accepted that, in rare cases, a court has inherent power to receive evidence and argument in a hearing from which the public and the press are excluded, and that it can even give a judgment which is only available to the parties. Such a course may only be taken (i) if it is strictly necessary to have a private hearing in order to achieve justice between the parties, and, (ii) if the degree of privacy is kept to an absolute minimum…. Examples of such cases include litigation where children are involved, where threatened breaches of privacy are being alleged, and where commercially valuable secret information is in issue.'

12.9 More fundamental still was the principle of natural justice: that all parties have the right to know the full case against them and to test the evidence of an opposing party:

> '[3] Even more fundamental to any justice system in a modern, democratic society is the principle of natural justice, whose most important aspect is that every party has a right to know the full case against him, and the right to test and challenge that case fully. A closed hearing is therefore even more offensive to fundamental principle than a private hearing. At least a private hearing cannot be said, of itself, to give rise to inequality or even unfairness as between the parties. But that cannot be said of an arrangement where the court can look at evidence or hear arguments on behalf of one party without the other party ("the excluded party") knowing, or being able to test, the contents of that evidence and those arguments ("the closed material"), or even being able to see all the reasons why the court reached its conclusions.'

Exp Wiley: rejection of class immunity for documents

12.10 In *Exp Wiley* the House of Lords rejected the concept of 'class' – or blanket – immunity for documents on any application by a public body. That is to say, they disapproved of any practice for giving blanket immunity, more or less regardless, to a category of documents held by a public body: such as 'all health records of…';

7 [2013] UKSC 38.

'all social work files of the ... family' etc. As far as possible documents must be considered individually if they are to be treated as immune.

12.11 'Class immunity' can be contrasted with contents immunity. The first applies immunity to a class or category of documents; whereas content immunity refers to immunity based on the content of particular documents. The House of Lords said – as subsequent case law has confirmed – that it will be rare, after *exp Wiley*, that public interest immunity will apply because a document falls into a category ('class') of documents (eg a social work file or medical records). The immunity, since *exp Wiley*, will generally only be ordered by reference to the specific content of individual documents.

12.12 This basis for disclosure was explained by Charles J in *Re R (Care: Disclosure: Nature of Proceedings)*:[8]

> 'Since *R v Chief Constable of West Midlands Police ex parte Wiley; R v Chief Constable of Nottinghamshire Police ex parte Sunderland* [1995] 1 AC 274, there has been a considerable review of the law, practice and approach relating to public interest immunity.... Part of that consideration was in respect of what was called a class claim to public interest immunity, as opposed to a contents claim. The result was that, in large measure, the class claim became a matter of history.'

12.13 Charles J summarised his review of the position since the *exp Wiley* case, and offered the following commentary and guidance:[9]

(a) Any case on public interest immunity that precedes *R v Chief Constable of West Midlands Police ex parte Wiley; R v Chief Constable of Nottinghamshire Police ex parte Sunderland* [1995] 1 AC 275 or post-dates it but does not include a careful consideration of that case and the developments in the law and practice relating to public interest immunity that followed should be regarded with caution and carefully reconsidered;

(b) General statements that one sees in textbooks and hears that social work records are covered by public interest immunity, which is a widely stated class claim, should now be consigned to history;

(c) Anyone advancing a claim to public interest immunity in respect of material held by a local authority should take advice and set out with particularity the harm that it is alleged will be caused to the public interest, for example the proper conduct of the duties of a local authority in respect of the protection of children, if material which passes the threshold test for disclosure is disclosed with or without appropriate redaction in the relevant proceedings,[10] and

8 [2002] 1 FLR 755 at 777; comments which were later approved obiter by Munby LJ in *Durham County Council v Dunn* [2012] EWCA Civ 1654, [2013] 1 WLR 2305 at §[44] (considered further below).

9 [2002] 1 FLR 755 at 777–8.

10 This procedural point will be considered further at 12.39.

(d) Before embarking on a claim to public interest immunity or another basis for opposing disclosure consideration should be given to the question whether the material passed the threshold test for disclosure and if so why.

12.14 Charles J concluded this passage by reference to the decision of Munby J in *Re B (Disclosure to Other Parties),*[11] Munby J:

> 'Generally, I make the point that, as Munby J emphasised in *Re B (Disclosure to Other Parties)* [2001] 2 FLR 1017, in respect of claims for non-disclosure based on Art 8 a compelling case for non-disclosure based on public interest immunity needs to be made out and any non-disclosure must go no further than is strictly necessary, having regard to the competing public interests.'

12.15 Charles J considered disclosure in children proceedings and to the then recent decision of Munby J in *Re B (Disclosure to Other Parties)*[12] where he considers the question of disclosure in the context of the European Convention 1950; and of the extent to which Art 8 rights might justify an order limiting disclosure:[13]

> 'In proceedings concerning children, significant harm to a child has been taken into account in the consideration of the competing interests involved when determining whether disclosure of relevant material known to the court but not to one of the parties can be refused....
>
> In a recent case, *Re B (Disclosure to Other Parties)* [2001] 2 FLR 1017, Munby J carried out a very helpful review of authorities and in particular those relating to the Convention. He concluded that the Art 8 rights of any person, if they are sufficiently engaged, could found an order that relevant material should not be disclosed. Thus, he concludes that there is room for a balancing of competing interests under Arts 6 and 8 and a conclusion based thereon that some relevant material should not be disclosed in proceedings.'

'Automatic immunity from production of' local authority records

12.16 In *Durham County Council v Dunn*[14] Munby LJ, obiter, explained that disclosure – as distinct from public interest immunity – is not 'simply a binary question: yes or no'. There might be cases where, so as to avoid the dumbing effect of public interest immunity, limited disclosure might be ordered (as he had

---

11 [2001] 2 FLR 1017. Charles J had earlier commented (at 776) on *Re B*, thus: 'In a recent case, *Re B (Disclosure to Other Parties)* [2001] 2 FLR 1017, Munby J carried out a very helpful review of authorities and in particular those relating to the Convention. He concluded that the Art 8 rights of any person, if they are sufficiently engaged, could found an order that relevant material should not be disclosed. Thus, he concludes that there is room for a balancing of competing interests under Arts 6 and 8 and a conclusion based thereon that some relevant material should not be disclosed in proceedings.'

12 [2001] 2 FLR 1017.

13 See also 10.33.

14 [2012] EWCA Civ 1654, [2013] 1 WLR 2305.

himself ordered in *Re B (A Child) (Disclosure)*[15]) but that this might be subject to 'effective and adequate safeguards' (as he explained in *Durham CC v Dunn*):

> '[50]... limiting the use that may be made of the documents and, in particular, safeguards designed to ensure that the release into the public domain of intensely personal information about third parties is strictly limited and permitted only if it has first been anonymised. Disclosure of third party personal data is permissible only if there are what the Strasbourg court in *Z v Finland* (1998) 25 EHRR 373, paragraph 103, referred to as "effective and adequate safeguards against abuse." An example of an order imposing such safeguards can be found in *A Health Authority v X (Discovery: Medical Conduct)* [2001] 2 FLR 673, 699 (appeal dismissed *A Health Authority v X* [2001] EWCA Civ 2014).'

3 PUBLIC AND PRIVATE INTERESTS

Suppression of evidence

12.17 Public interest immunity is a public law remedy. It is designed to protect public interests. It has been defined as 'Suppression of evidence in the public interest' (*Administrative Law* HWR Wade and CF Forsyth 10th Edition, Oxford, 2009). As a matter of fact, suppression of relevant documents and information on grounds of public interest is what the court is being asked to order. The application under FPR 2010, r 21.3(1) is that the applicant be permitted to 'withhold disclosure... on the ground that [it] would damage the public interest'.

12.18 In the case of each application under r 21.3(1) 'the court has a power and the duty to weigh the public interest of justice to litigants against [any] public interest asserted by the government',[16] where the authors were commenting on *Conway v Rimmer*[17] where the House of Lords commented that, if need be, the court must look at the documents themselves (without the claimant having seen them) to decide whether immunity should be ordered.[18]

Public interest immunity in the light of Human Rights Act 1998

12.19 The coming into operation of the *Human Rights Act 1998* (*HRA 1989*) and of the European Convention 1950 preceded *Re B (Disclosure to other parties)*.[19] In that case, Munby J set out three propositions in relation to restrictions on disclosure in children proceedings (as discussed fully in **Chapter 10**[20]).

15 [2004] EWHC 411 (Fam), [2004] 2 FLR 142.
16 *Administrative Law* (2014) Wade & Forsyth (11th Ed) at 721.
17 [1968] AC 910.
18 The House later looked at the documents (reports on a police probationer who was suing his former employers) and held that disclosure would not be against the public interest.
19 [2001] 2 FLR 1017.
20 Considered fully at 10.33.

(1) Entitlement to a fair trial under European Convention 1950, Art 6(1) is absolute. Disclosure of all relevant documents and information is an element of a fair trial. This does not mean that all parties, as a matter of right, are entitled to see all the documents in the case.

(2) It is not only the private interests of children involved in the litigation which may deny access to documents. The interests of anyone else who is involved, whether as victim, party or witness and who can demonstrate that their European Convention 1950, Art 8 rights are sufficiently engaged, may apply for documents to be withheld from a party to the proceedings.

(3) A limited qualification of the right to see the documents may be acceptable if directed towards a clear and proper objective. Non-disclosure must be limited to what the situation demands and is justified only when the case is compelling or strictly necessary. The court must be careful to balance the feared harm and any difficulty caused to the litigant counterbalanced by procedures designed to ensure a fair trial.

12.20 In *Chief Constable & Anor v YK & Ors*[21] Sir Nicholas Wall P considered public interest immunity in the context of two forced marriage protection order[22] applications. He poised the immunity problem at the outset of his judgment:

> '[10] The legal conundrum potentially thrown up by the instant case (and certainly likely to arise at some point in the future) is one which, potentially, goes to the root of family justice, namely how is it possible to achieve a fair hearing (i.e. comply with ECHR Article 6) if parts of the evidence which it is necessary for parties to know in order to enable them to meet allegations made against them cannot safely be revealed to them on the ground that disclosure of the information or its source is likely to identify the informant (and thus place him or her at risk)?'

Public interest immunity or non-party disclosure

12.21 In *Re C (A Child)*[23] ('*Tower Hamlets v M (No 1)*'), Pauffley J raises a number of issues over where the welfare of a child may be seen as in conflict with the needs of national security (as asserted by a government body known as SO15: the Counter Terrorism Command, a Special Operations branch within London's Metropolitan Police); and the extent to which the Secretary of State for the Home Department (SSHD) should disclose information, as a third party, to the parties in care proceedings. The case hints at a procedure for closed material procedure and refers to possibilities of an application for public interest immunity for the material in question. Since the first hearing the case has returned before Pauffley J as a public interest immunity application: *London Borough of Tower Hamlets v M & Ors*[24] ('*Tower Hamlets v M (No 2)*').

---

21 [2010] EWHC 2438 (Fam).

22 *Family Law Act 1996, Pt 4A.*

23 [2016] EWHC 3171 (Fam) (case heading: *London Borough of Tower Hamlets v M and F and ors*) ('*Tower Hamlets v M (No 1)*').

24 [2017] EWHC 692 (Fam) ('*Tower Hamlets v M (No 2)*').

12.22 In *Tower Hamlets v M (No 1)* care proceedings were started by the local authority as a result of information provided by SO15, including that on information from the passport office, they believed the father of a child held 'an Islamist extremist mind-set'. The local authority needed evidence to support their application: the onus of proving the care application was on them. They obtained a non-party disclosure order under FPR 2010, r 21.2 from Pauffley J, without notice to the Home Department (the reason for this was said 'dues to a need to progress the case'[25]). Pauffley J explained the court's request that SO15 provide information as follows:

> '[9] … The order sought 'all information … pertaining to the individuals listed below (the parents) including but not limited to all witness statements, interview records, exhibits, crime reports and Police National Computer records and including any information from other jurisdictions which it is at liberty to disclose.' (my [ie judge's] emphasis)

Public interest immunity and closed material procedures

12.23 The application before the court was by SSHD to discharge the non-party disclosure order. SSHD told the court that if the order was retained it might apply for public interest immunity for the material covered by it.[26] It will be recalled, that if public interest immunity is ordered by the court, no-one sees the material (save for the party with the material). If a closed material procedure is ordered (where the court has power to do this[27]) the excluded parties do not see the material, but at least the court, other parties and the special advocates do. The balance between a claim for public interest immunity or an application for CMP was explained by Pauffley J in relation to the Home Department decision-making as follows:

> '[16] [This] involves determining whether to claim PII or make an application under the Justice and Security Act 2013. This is a decision taken by the SSHD…. The decision maker will have to consider the importance of the information to the issues the court has to decide, and form a view as to whether the public interest in non-disclosure is outweighed by the public interest in disclosure, in order to do justice within the proceedings: "If a document is relevant and material then it must be disclosed … unless a breach of confidentiality will cause harm to the public interest which outweighs the harm to the interests of justice caused by non-disclosure" per Lord Templeman in *R v CC (West Midlands) ex parte Wiley* [1995] 1AC 274 at 281F.'

Procedure for third party disclosure as a prelude to public interest immunity

12.24 FPR 2010, r 21.2 (orders for disclosure against a person not a party) is rarely used in family proceedings. The rule enables the court – where statute

25 §[9].
26 §[17].
27 See Ch 11.

permits – to order disclosure against a non-party. The rule under review here is r 21.2(3)[28] is:

> '(3) The court may make an order under this rule only where disclosure is necessary in order to dispose fairly of the proceedings or to save costs.'

12.25 This stresses the discretionary nature of the jurisdiction. In *A Health Authority v X (Discovery: Medical Conduct)*,[29] Munby J explained the limited powers of even the Family Division to make orders against non-parties. Pauffley J emphasised the term 'necessary' which in most contexts might be thought to limit the ambit of the principle; but here, as seen by Pauffley J, depends on the view of the judge as to the need for information from non-parties.

12.26 The meaning of this rule – stressing, like Munby J above, that disclosure is the exception, rather than the rule – was explained in *Rowe & Ors v Fryers & Anor*[30] (where the appeal against non-party disclosure was dismissed):

> '[9] CPR 31.17 applies, as paragraph (1) makes clear, when disclosure is sought [from] a person who is not a party to the proceedings. Many and varied circumstances are envisaged. Examples that come readily to mind are records held by local authorities about children, police accident reports in road traffic cases and documents held by bodies such as the Health and Safety Executive, hospitals and so forth…
>
> [10] The word 'only' in paragraph (3) emphasises that disclosure from third parties is the exception rather than the rule. Disclosure will not be routinely ordered but only where the conditions there specified are met…'.

12.27 Rule 21.2 goes on to require that the court 'specify the documents or the classes of documents' to be disclosed.[31] It enables the court, in terms similar to CPR 1998, rr 31.17 and 31.19, to require a party to specify what documents are not in their control.[32] Disclosure could take place at a particular time and place.[33] A non-party cannot be compelled to disclose a document which is covered by privilege[34] or, perhaps, by confidentiality.

Home Department opposition to disclosure

12.28 The SSHD opposition to disclosure started from the President's *Radicalisation Guidance*[35] paras 10–12 and its emphasis – like *Children Act 2004*,

28 Derived from CPR 1998, r 31.17(3).
29 [2001] 2 FLR 673 especially §[60].
30 [2003] EWCA Civ 655, [2003] 1 WLR 1952.
31 FPR 2010, r 21.2(4)(a)).
32 FPR 2010, r 21.2(4) and (5).
33 FPR 2010, r 21.2(5)(b); and see r 24.2(2) for documents and a witness summons.
34 FPR 2010, r 21.2(6).
35 *Radicalisation cases in the family courts of 8 October 2015* issued by the President of the Family Division www.judiciary.gov.uk/wp-content/uploads/2015/10/pfd-guidance-radicalisation-cases.pdf.

s 11 and *Working Together* (2015) – on the need for co-operation between police and local authority.. It refers to the quote from Hayden J (cited by Pauffley J at §34) in *London Borough of Tower Hamlets v M and Others* [36] in which he said:

> '[18] … (iv) All involved must recognise that in this particular process it is the interest of the individual child that is paramount. This cannot be eclipsed by wider considerations of counter-terrorism policy or operations, but it must be recognised that the decision the court is being asked to take can only be arrived at against an informed understanding of that wider canvas. It is essential that the court be provided with that material in appropriate detail.'

12.29 On this first objection to disclosure, Pauffley J suggested that the SSHD had mounted a 'circular argument of the most bewildering kind'.[37] How could the local authority specify the information it wanted when the SSHD's failure to disclose made it impossible to know what information they held?[38] She rejected the SSHD submission.

12.30 In conclusion, Pauffley J said she had no wish to re-visit the passport office decision. However, the parents and child have a right to a fair trial, she said. The SSHD material might – it was impossible to tell, yet – assist the local authority in presenting their case. It might then assist the court in deciding that case and whether or not a child had suffered significant harm:

> '[41] … the information upon which the decision was based could be highly relevant to the fundamental question: whether there is a likelihood that this child would suffer significant harm if an order were not made. To that end, the local authority and the court have a legitimate interest in the material which founds the decision not to re-issue the father with a passport.
>
> [42] This child and these parents have a right to a fair trial. They have a right to respect for their private and family life. Unless there is a disclosure mechanism for receiving and considering relevant, highly sensitive material from the SSHD then it is difficult to envisage a future for this application.'

Public interest immunity application by the Home Department

12.31 *Tower Hamlets v M (No 2)* provides a return to the question of public interest immunity on the application – finally – of SSHD. After *Tower Hamlets v M (No 1)* the SSHD did not make an application for a closed material procedure under the *Justice and Security Act 2013* (*JSA 2013*) (as they had been ordered to do) but asked for a closed hearing before the judge so that they could to make submissions in relation to sensitive material. A small bundle was provided to the judge which she read.

36 [2015] EWHC 869 (Fam), [2015] 2 FLR 1431.
37 §§[25] and [29].
38 §[25].

12.32 In hindsight, the judge said she should not have done so. The father and local authority's counsel said that the SSHD was 'attempting to initiate a closed material procedure notwithstanding that no application for one had been made'.[39] This gave potential for unfairness; especially as the parties were unaware of what material was provided to the judge. Finally, in early March 2017, the SSHD did issue a public interest immunity application; and the consequential closed hearing was not opposed.

The ex parte Wiley balance

12.33 Pauffley J directed herself in accordance with *R v Chief Constable of the West Midlands, ex p Wiley*:[40]

> '[29] There are three required steps when the SSHD considers whether to make a claim for PII. First, whether the material is relevant and passes the threshold test for disclosure in the applicable proceedings.... Second, if the threshold test is passed, whether the material identified as relevant and subject to disclosure attracts PII. The test is whether there is a real risk that disclosure would cause "real damage" or "serious harm" to the public interest.... Third, if applying the "real damage" test, the material attracts PII, the question arises as to whether the public interest in non-disclosure is outweighed by the public interest in disclosure for the purpose of doing justice in the proceedings...'.

12.34 The court was satisfied the material was relevant. The court accepted the argument that disclosure would do 'serious harm' on the basis of closed materials. The court also accepted that there were significant reasons against disclosure on the basis that the material engaged considerations of national security and there was a real risk disclosure would damage it. Under the heading 'The Wiley balance – factors for and against disclosure' the judge summarised how the *Wiley* balance fell in her judgment:

> '[38] The last part of the Wiley exercise involves balancing the factors in favour of and against disclosure. The SSHD when considering the impact of non-disclosure takes into account three specific points – the nature of the material, the open and available material and other powers to protect the child.
>
> [39] The SSHD considers the factors in favour of disclosure to fall into two categories. First, the strong public interest in ensuring that children are protected from the risk of harm and that the material of potential relevance should be available to parties to family court proceedings. And second, that in general legal proceedings should be conducted openly; open justice principles are in play and are an important factor in protecting the rights of individuals and maintaining public confidence in the justice system.

---

39 §[6].

40 [1994] UKHL 8, [1995] AC 274; and see 12.10.

> [40] To my mind, the most significant, weighty and powerful of the factors militating against disclosure is that the material engages considerations of national security. The SSHD formed the view that disclosure would create a real and significant risk of damage to national security. I accord great respect to and share that assessment on the basis of the material made available to me in CLOSED session…
>
> [41] The conclusion of the SSHD that national security considerations are engaged… As Lord Templeman observed in *R v Chief Constable of the West Midlands Police, ex parte Wiley*[41] 'As a general rule the harm to the public interest of the disclosure of the whole or part of a document dealing with defence of national security or diplomatic secrets will be self-evident and preclude disclosure.'

12.35 The court accepted, from a realistic stand-point, that the SSHD arguments that the care proceedings could conclude and threshold criteria could be proved; and that this was perfectly possible even in the absence of disclosure. The local authority could still safeguard the child. The judge concluded, finally, that the material sought by the local authority would not advance their case to any significant degree.

4 PROCEDURE

Justice in a just manner

12.36 In *Secretary of State for the Home Department v MB and AF*,[42] in which the House of Lords were considering the solicitor advocate procedure in criminal trials, Lady Hale considered limitations on disclosure; and, in particular, she considered the importance of achieving a just result being seen also in the context also of a just procedure. The means – the procedure – by which justice is achieved can sometimes be as important as achieving the just result.

12.37 The essence of justice, said Lady Hale, was that the defendant or other party to proceedings, must know the case which is being presented to the court:

> '[57] The object of all legal proceedings is to do justice according to law: but this is easily said and not so easily done. Doing justice means not only arriving at a just result but arriving at it in a just manner:… the essential ingredients of a fair trial can vary according to the subject matter and nature of the proceedings.
>
> [58] The basic requirement is to know the case against one and to have an opportunity of meeting it. But in *In re K (Infants)* [1963] Ch 381, 405, Upjohn LJ identified more detailed principles of a judicial inquiry: "the right to see all

41 [1995] 1 AC 274 at 281.
42 [2007] UKHL 46, [2008] 1 AC 40.

the information put before the judge, to comment on it, to challenge it and if needs be to combat it, and to try to establish by contrary evidence that it is wrong." However, as Lord Devlin pointed out in the same case in the House of Lords, at [1965] AC 201, 238: " ... a principle of judicial inquiry, whether fundamental or not, is only a means to an end. If it can be shown in any particular class of case that the observance of a principle of this sort does not serve the ends of justice, it must be dismissed: otherwise it would become the master instead of the servant of justice."'

12.38 That said, where limitations on disclosure – or, as in this chapter, limitations based on public interest immunity – are directed 'is to protect and promote the best interests of a child' then exceptionally disclosure might be limited or withheld:

> '[58] ... If, as in that case, the whole object of the proceedings is to protect and promote the best interests of a child, there may be exceptional circumstances in which disclosure of some of the evidence would be so detrimental to the child's welfare as to defeat the object of the exercise: the modern principles are explained in *In re D (Minors) (Adoption Reports: Confidentiality)* [1996] AC 593....'[43]

Withholding disclosure: public interest immunity

12.39 The procedure for withholding inspection and disclosure under FPR 2010, r 21.3 has been considered fully in **Chapter 10**. That part of the procedure in r 21.3 which applies to public interest immunity specifically is as follows:

> '**Claim to withhold inspection or disclosure of a document**
>
> 31.19/21.3 (1) A person may apply, without notice, for an order permitting him to withhold disclosure of a document on the ground that disclosure would damage the public interest.
>
> (2) Unless the court orders otherwise, an order of the court under paragraph (1) –
>
> (a) must not be served on any other person; and
>
> (b) must not be opened to inspection by any other person.
>
> (6) For the purpose of deciding an application under paragraph (1) (application to withhold disclosure) ... the court may –
>
> (a) require the person seeking to withhold disclosure or inspection of a document to produce that document to the court; and
>
> (b) invite any person, whether or not a party, to make representations.
>
> (7) An application under paragraph (1)... must be supported by evidence.'

43 See also, *Re B (Disclosure to Other Parties)* [2001] 2 FLR 1017, Munby J. That case and *Re D (Minors) (Adoption Reports: Confidentiality)* are considered at 10.33 and 10.24, respectively.

12.40 As can be seen, it is the body which seeks the immunity – 'to withhold disclosure [on grounds that it] would damage the public interest' – which must seek the order. Subject to that the material concerned is subject to ordinary rules of open disclosure. It is not for the respondent in the proceedings – a parent or guardian on behalf of the child – to seek an order for specific disclosure.

12.41 Until there is an order on the subject of disclosure the material concerned must not be served on other parties nor be inspected by them, unless the court so orders.[44] If the court does so order, it should bear in mind the criticism of the House of Lords and Court of Appeal[45] where documents are ordered to be seen only by parties[46] lawyers.

Evidence in support of the application

12.42 The procedure for an application under CPR 1998, r 31.19, and thus by extension, FPR 2010, r 21.3, for consideration of whether documents were covered by legal professional privilege was considered fully by Beatson J in *West London Pipeline and Storage Ltd v Total UK Ltd* ('*WLP*').[47] Though in respect of privilege, and therefore of a different part of CPR 1998, r 31.19 (of FPR 2010, r 21.3) it is submitted that much of what Beatson J said applies equally to a public interest immunity claim (FPR 2010, r 21.3(1)) in children proceedings.

12.43 Further, it will be recalled that in *Re R* (above)[48] it was urged that a claim for public interest immunity be fully supported by an explanation of what harm, it is said, may accrue to the public interest if documents are disclosed; and if necessary with 'appropriate redaction':

> '(c) Anyone advancing a claim to public interest immunity in respect of material held by a local authority should take advice and set out with particularity the harm that it is alleged will be caused to the public interest, for example the proper conduct of the duties of a local authority in respect of the protection of children, if material which passes the threshold test for disclosure is disclosed with or without appropriate redaction in the relevant proceedings;'

12.44 In *WLP* Beatson J suggested:[49]

> '[53] ...Affidavits claiming privilege whether sworn by the legal advisers to the party claiming privilege as is often the case, or, as in this case, by a

44 FPR 2010, r 21.3(2).

45 *Somerville and others v Scottish Ministers (HM Advocate General for Scotland intervening)* [2007] UKHL 44, [2007] 1 WLR 2734; *Browning v The Information Commissioner & Anor* [2014] EWCA Civ 1050, [2014] 1 WLR 3848.

46 As was done recently, eg, in *Local Authority X v HI and Others* [2016] EWHC 1123 (Fam), [2017] 1 FLR 1362, Russell J; see 10.48.

47 [2008] EWHC (Comm) 1729.

48 See 12.12.

49 And see further at 10.13.

Director of the party, should be specific enough to show something of the deponent's analysis of the documents or, in the case of a claim to litigation privilege, the purpose for which they were created. It is desirable that they should refer to such contemporary material as it is possible to do so without making disclosure of the very matters that the claim for privilege is designed to protect…'.

12.45 The person who drafts the affidavit on the lines of these two judicial statements for documents in children proceedings will need to include:

- a statement of the harm anticipated by the local authority bearing in mind the competing Art 6 and Art 8 rights of the lay parties and the child or children;
- an analysis or summary of the documents concerned;
- a statement of whose confidentiality is affected by the documents;
- an assessment of harm to the child (if any anticipated) if the documents are or are not ordered to be immune from disclosure.

13

PRIVACY AND ANONYMITY IN CHILDREN PROCEEDINGS

1 INTRODUCTION

Child's right to confidentiality

13.1 A child has private law rights of confidentiality, no less than any other individual. The extent to which those rights may be asserted by the child will depend on the child's maturity (as explained in **Chapter 5**). This chapter considers the child rights to confidentiality, privacy and anonymity in the context of court proceedings.

13.2 This chapter proceeds as follows:

- **Part 2** contrasts the open justice principle for civil proceedings generally with the privacy provisions which apply in family and children proceedings.
- **Part 3** considers the various statutory and inherent jurisdiction remedies available which restrain publicity for children, especially in the light of the summary of these remedies provided by Sir James Munby P in *Re J (Reporting Restriction: Internet: Video)*.[1]
- **Part 4** looks at children's interests and their right to resect for family life in the context of the European Convention 1950 (a subject also considered in **Chapter 5, Part 8**); and of the possible shift in Supreme Court consideration of this subject in the past three years.
- **Part 5** explains the extent to which the media and others may attend court under Family Procedure Rules 2010 (FPR 2010) r 27.11 and the range of family law in relation to release of documents to those in court to help them to make sense of the proceedings.
- **Part 6** concludes the chapter with a summary of the law on press exclusion from children proceedings (FPR 2010 r 27.11(3)).

1 [2013] EWHC 2694 (Fam), [2014] 1 FLR 523.

Children's best interests and privacy

13.3 The privacy and anonymity of a child will be guaranteed in children proceedings; but their anonymity may be in question – or at least at risk – in other civil proceedings.[2] Concern for the welfare of children – whether concerned in proceedings or not – is a powerful factor in any decision by a court to anonymise a parent's names in proceedings, or whether to order privacy of the proceedings. The interests of children was considered by the Supreme Court in relation to an injunction sought by a parent in *PJS v News Group Newspapers Ltd.*[3] That case provides an opportunity for considering how far concern for children's interests have moved since *Re S (Identification: Restrictions on Publication)*[4] (as explained also in **Chapter 5**).

2 PRIVACY AND OPEN COURT PRINCIPLE

Open justice principle

Common law: open court principle

13.4 In this part the general open court principle rule will be contrasted with the privacy rule which applies to almost all children proceedings. Privacy and anonymity is almost invariably guaranteed for children hearings. Indeed FPR 2010, r 27.10 states baldly and without reference to common law principle, that all proceeding to which the family proceedings rules apply 'will be held in private':

> **'27.10 Hearings in private**
>
> (1) Proceedings to which these rules apply will be held in private, except –
>
> (a) where these rules or any other enactment provide otherwise;
>
> (b) subject to any enactment, where the court directs otherwise.'

13.5 Privacy will therefore apply for all children proceedings, subject to the exceptions which operate for a limited range of observers (including the media) who are permitted by FPR 2010, r 27.11 to have access to the family courts (as explained below).

2 See discussion in Court of Appeal (where a child's anonymity was guaranteed) in *X v Dartford and Gravesham NHS Trust (Personal Injury Bar Association and another intervening)* [2015] EWCA Civ 96, [2015] 1 WLR 3647.

3 [2016] UKSC 26, [2016] AC 1081, [2016] 2 FLR 251.

4 [2004] UKHL 47, [2005] 1 AC 593, [2005] 1 FLR 591.

The general rule on openness

13.6 The common law rule that all court proceedings should be in open court was explained in *Scott & Anor v Scott*'[5] which remains the case on which any modern discussion of the common law rests. The principle set out in *Scott*, bolstered by the European Convention 1950, Art 6(1) (right to a fair trial[6]) represent the modern law, and is frequently referred to in recent case law. For example, the open justice principle was explained by Toulson LJ in *R (Guardian News and Media Ltd) v City of Westminster Magistrates' Court (Article 19 intervening)*[7] where he emphasised the 'watchdog' role of the press:

> '[1] Open justice. The words express a principle at the heart of our system of justice and vital to the rule of law. The rule of law is a fine concept but fine words butter no parsnips. How is the rule of law itself to be policed? It is an age old question. Quis custodiet ipsos custodes – who will guard the guards themselves? In a democracy, where power depends on the consent of the people governed, the answer must lie in the transparency of the legal process. Open justice lets in the light and allows the public to scrutinise the workings of the law, for better or for worse. Jeremy Bentham said in a well-known passage quoted by Lord Shaw of Dunfermline in *Scott v Scott* [1913] 417 at 477: Publicity is the very soul of justice. It is the keenest spur to exertion and the surest of all guards against improbity. It keeps the judge himself while trying under trial.'

13.7 Of the history and importance of the rule, Toulson LJ continued:

> '[2] This is a constitutional principle which has been recognised by the common law since the fall of the Stuart dynasty, as Lord Shaw explained. It is not only the individual judge who is open to scrutiny but the process of justice…'.

13.8 The open justice principle or rule, is restated in Civil Procedure Rules 1998 (CPR 1998) 39.2(1), which then goes on to set out a number of exceptions where the court may direct that – in civil proceedings (ie not family proceedings) – a hearing, or part of it can be in private. CPR 1998, r 39.2 is as follows:

> '**39.2 General rule – hearing to be in public**
>
> (1) The general rule is that a hearing is to be in public.
>
> (2) The requirement for a hearing to be in public does not require the court to make special arrangements for accommodating members of the public.

---

5 [1913] UKHL 2, [1913] AC 417. As its title suggests *Scott* was a family case where questions of privacy in connection with nullity proceedings was not permissible; and Mrs Scott and her solicitor should not have been found in contempt of court for their alleged breach of a privacy order which had been imposed.

6 Set out in full at 5.15.

7 [2012] EWCA Civ 420, [2013] QB 618.

(3) A hearing, or any part of it, may be in private if –

(a) publicity would defeat the object of the hearing;

(b) it involves matters relating to national security;

(c) it involves confidential information (including information relating to personal financial matters) and publicity would damage that confidentiality;

(d) a private hearing is necessary to protect the interests of any child or protected party;

(e) it is a hearing of an application made without notice and it would be unjust to any respondent for there to be a public hearing;

(f) it involves uncontentious matters arising in the administration of trusts or in the administration of a deceased person's estate; or

(g) the court considers this to be necessary, in the interests of justice.

(4) The court may order that the identity of any party or witness must not be disclosed if it considers non-disclosure necessary in order to protect the interests of that party or witness.'

13.9 As can be seen, the list of types of hearing where the court may restrict openness includes that the evidence 'it involves confidential information (including information relating to personal financial matters) and publicity would damage that confidentiality' and that 'a private hearing is necessary to protect the interests of any child or protected party' (or person said to be lacking mental capacity (per the *Mental Capacity Act 2005* or 'lunatic' in the words of *Scott*). These are both exceptions which would, in family proceedings, comprise the majority of applications heard in the family courts.

Attendance at private hearings

Press attendance at court

13.10 A narrow range of individuals who are not parties to the proceedings – such as accredited press representatives and others whom the court permits[8] – may be permitted to attend court[9] (as explained in **Part 5**); but they must still recognise the anonymity and confidentiality rules which apply under the *Administration of Justice Act 1960* (*AJA 1960*) *s 12(1)*. To a limited degree Jeremy Bentham's watch-dog role for the press is intended to apply also to the press as Sir Mark Potter P explained in *Re Child X*:[10]

8 The range of those able to attend court is not wide. Apart from court officers, those acting for the parties or the press, the only additional category of individual permitted to attend court is '(g) any other person whom the court permits to be present' (perhaps a friend, relative of a party or an academic researcher).

9 FPR 2010, r 27.11(2), which is set out in full at 13.45.

10 [2009] EWHC 1728 (Fam), [2009] 2 FLR 1467.

'[38] … [to] exercise a role of "watchdog" on the part of the public at large and to observe family justice at work for the purpose of informed comment upon its workings and the behaviour of its judges…'.

13.11 Family judges lag behind their civil proceedings colleagues in allowing release of court documents to the press (or others who are permitted to attend the hearing). Release of certain documents to the press (eg skeleton arguments, position statements etc which will be read by the judge but which are not formally part of the pleadings or other court documents) to help them to understand court proceedings, was encouraged per Lord Scarman in *Harman v Secretary of State for the Home Department.*[11] Release of some documents has been attempted in children proceedings by Munby J to assist in press understanding of proceedings which they attend.[12]

13.12 By contrast documents from children proceedings may be released to a very limited range of non-parties such as the police, to CPS and the security services with appropriate conditions on any orders to protect confidentiality. Release of documents has been ordered in an exceptional case to enable a witness to pursue a damages claim arising from the way in which a judge dealt with children proceedings.[13]

Anonymity for children and parties to family proceedings

13.13 Suitably anonymised judgements at the appropriate level of court should be published (*Transparency in the family courts: publication of judgments: practice guidance issued on 16 January 2014;*[14] but there remains the issue as to the dangers of jig-saw identification of children if anonymisation is not carefully carried out.

13.14 And finally: 'what's in a name?' asked Lord Hope rhetorically in *In re Guardian News and Media Ltd.*[15] Recent examples of recent orders of anonymity include C in *R (on the application of C) v Secretary of State for Justice*[16] whose killing had placed him, a mental patient, compulsorily in mental hospital; and in *JX MX v Dartford & Gravesham NHS Trust & Ors*[17] to a child in an infant settlement. In *Birmingham City Council v Riaz, AB & Ors*[18] Keehan J granted a lifetime reporting restrictions order to a girl who had been the subject of child sexual abuse.

11 [1983] 1 AC 280, [1982] 2 WLR 338; and see *R (Guardian News and Media Ltd) v City of Westminster Magistrates' Court* (above).

12 *Norfolk County Council v Webster and Others* [2006] EWHC 2898 (Fam), [2007] 2 FLR 415.

13 FPR 2010, Pt 12, Ch 7; FPR 2010 *Practice Direction 12G; Re X and Y (Disclosure of Judgment to Police)* [2014] EWHC 278 (Fam), [2015] 1 FLR 1218, Baker J; *X, Y and Z (Disclosure to the Security Service)* [2016] EWHC 2400 (Fam), McDonald J. Release of documents to a social worker was ordered in *Re W (application by SW)* [2017] EWFC 61 after the findings of the Court of Appeal in *Re W (a Child)* [2016] EWCA Civ 1140, [2017] 1 FLR 1629.

14 See www.judiciary.gov.uk/wp-content/uploads/JCO/Documents/Guidance/transparency-in-the-family-courts-jan2014.pdf.

15 [2010] UKSC 1, [2010] 2 AC 697.

16 [2016] UKSC 2.

17 [2015] EWCA Civ 96, [2015] 1 WLR 3647.

18 [2015] EWHC 1857 (Fam), [2016] 1 FLR 797.

13.15 In *PJS v News Group Newspapers Ltd*[19] (interim injunction for well-known person's involvement in 'three-way sex') Lady Hale reflected on the importance of the interests of PJS's children in assessing whether his privacy should be protected.

> '[72] … Of course [children] cannot always rule the day. But they deserve closer attention than they have so far received in this case, for two main reasons. First, not only are the children's interests likely to be affected by a breach of the privacy interests of their parents, but the children have independent privacy interests of their own. They also have a right to respect for their family life with their parents. Secondly, by section 12(4)(b), any court considering whether to grant either an interim or a permanent injunction has to have "particular regard" to "any relevant privacy code". It is not disputed that the IPSO Code, which came into force in January, is a relevant Code for this purpose; [and which] provides that "editors must demonstrate an exceptional public interest to over-ride the normally paramount interests of [children under 16]".'

3 STATUTORY PROVISION FOR RESTRICTING PUBLICITY

Restrictions on publicity and children: naming children

13.16 In *Re J (A Child)*[20] Sir James Munby P summarised the legislative provisions which restrain publicity in respect of children. He started by pointing out the statutory – or, as he called them, the 'automatic constraints' – on publicity. The *Children's Act 1989* (*CA 1989*) *s 97* prohibits publication, but only till the conclusion of proceedings (*Clayton v Clayton*[21]); and the *AJA 1960, s 12* is limited to 'proceedings in private', including family proceedings, but narrows those proceedings to those in relation to children and only to 'proceedings before any court'.

13.17 The principal statutory and common law limitations on publicity in relation to publicity for children, and for children proceedings, are as follows:

- *AJA 1960, s 12.*
- *CA 1989, s 97.*
- *Children and Young Persons Act 1933, s 33.*
- Inherent jurisdiction of the High Court (*Senior Courts Act 1981, s 37*; and as extended by *County Courts Act 1984, s 37*).

13.18 The Crown Court has only very limited powers of restriction of publicity.[22]

19 [2016] UKSC 26, [2016] AC 1081, [2016] 2 FLR 251; considered further in Ch 5.
20 [2013] EWHC 2694 (Fam) sub nom *Re J (Reporting Restriction: Internet: Video)* [2014] 1 FLR 523.
21 [2006] EWCA Civ 878, [2006] 1 FLR 11.
22 See further at 13.33.

Administration of Justice Act 1960

13.19 *AJA 1960, s 12(1)* makes publicity of children cases an exception to the general rule as to publicity for court proceedings. Section 12 provides (as relevant here) that:

> '**Publication of information relating to proceedings in private**
>
> (1) The publication of information relating to proceedings before any court sitting in private shall not in itself be contempt of court except in the following cases, that is to say:
>
> (a) where the proceedings –
>
> (i) relate to exercise of the inherent jurisdiction of the High Court in respect of minors
>
> (ii) are brought under the Children Act 1989 or
>
> (iii) otherwise relate wholly or mainly to the maintenance or upbringing of a minor…
>
> (2) Without prejudice to the foregoing subsection, the publication of the text or summary of the whole or part of an order made by a court sitting in private shall not in itself be contempt of court except where the court (having power to do so) expressly prohibits publication….
>
> (4) Nothing in this section shall be construed as implying with any publication is punishable as contempt of court which would not be so punishable apart from the section and in particular where the publication is not so punishable by reason of being authorised by rules of court.'

13.20 In *Re B (A Child) (Disclosure)*[23] Munby J summarised his then understanding of the principles under s 12. Section 12(1)(a) prohibits publication of 'information relating to proceedings before any court sitting in private … where the proceedings (i) relate to the exercise of the inherent jurisdiction of the High Court with respect to minors; (ii) are brought under the Children Act 1989; or (iii) otherwise relate wholly or mainly to the … upbringing of a minor.' Publication of such information, where the person publishing knows that there are such proceedings, is a contempt; and to whomsoever the publication is made (eg to a journalist, MP, Minister of the Crown etc).

13.21 Section 12(1) does not, on its own, prohibit publication as in Munby J explains ((v) in his list):

> 'a) the fact, if it be the case, that a child is a ward of court and is the subject of wardship proceedings or that a child is the subject of residence or other proceedings under the Children Act 1989 or of proceedings relating wholly or mainly to his maintenance or upbringing;
>
> b) the name, address or photograph of such a child;

23 [2004] EWHC 411 (Fam), [2004] 2 FLR 142.

c) the name, address or photograph of the parties (or, if the child is a party, the other parties) to such proceedings;

d) the date, time or place of a past or future hearing of such proceedings;

e) the nature of the dispute in such proceedings;

f) anything which has been seen or heard by a person conducting himself lawfully in the public corridor or other public precincts outside the court in which the hearing in private is taking place;

g) the name, address or photograph of the witnesses who have given evidence in such proceedings;

h) the party on whose behalf such a witness has given evidence; and

i) the text or summary of the whole or part of any order made in such proceedings.'

13.22 On the other hand, s 12(1) prohibits the following (whether or not the documents concerned have been anonymised), says Munby J:

'a) accounts of what has gone on in front of the judge sitting in private;

b) documents such as affidavits, witness statements, reports, position statements, skeleton arguments or other documents filed in the proceedings, transcripts or notes of the evidence or submissions, and transcripts or notes of the judgment (this list is not necessarily exhaustive);

c) extracts or quotations from such documents;

d) summaries of such documents.'

Publication of information about children proceedings

13.23 Section 12 alone does not prevent publication of information about a ward;[24] or, by extension, about a child who is involved in *CA 1989* proceedings. If there is a contempt, it derives from publication of information about the proceedings. Thus, outside the court proceedings, a child involved in the proceedings has no more right than any other child to privacy. This was explained by Waite LJ in *R v Central Independent Television Plc* [25] as follows:

'No child, simply by virtue of being a child, is entitled to a right of privacy or confidentiality. That is as true of a ward of court (or child in respect of whom the inherent jurisdiction is otherwise invoked) as of any other child. Any element of confidentiality concerning a child in respect of whom the court's jurisdiction is invoked belongs not to the child but to the court. It is imposed to protect the proper functioning of the court's own jurisdiction, and will not be imposed to any further extent than is necessary to afford

24 *Re F (orse A) (a Minor) (Publication of Information)* [1977] Fam 58, [1976] 3 WLR 813, CA.
25 [1994] Fam 192 at 207-208 [1994] 2 FLR 151 at 166, CA.

that protection: *Scott v Scott* [1913] AC 417 and *Re F (Orse A) (A Minor) (Publication of Information)* [1977] Fam 58.'

13.24 Section 12 does not prevent the court from making such necessary privacy injunction orders in its inherent jurisdiction. Munby J stressed this point in *Re B*: the provisions of s 12 remained subject to 'any specific injunction or other order that a court of competent jurisdiction may have made in any particular case'. The section imposes statutory limitations, but does not prevent a court taking other steps to restrain or restrict publicity, should these be needed.

Children Act 1989, s 97

13.25 *CA 1989, s 97* (as amended) provides as follows:

'**Privacy for children involved in certain proceedings:**

(1) Rules made under Section 144 of the Magistrates' 1980 may make provision for a Magistrates' Court to sit in private in proceedings in which any powers under this Act the Adoption and Children Act 2002 may be exercised by the court with respect to any child.

(2) No person shall publish to the public at large or any section of the public any material which is intended, or likely, to identify –

(a) Any child as being involved in proceedings before the High Court, a County Court or a Magistrates' Court in which any power under this Act or the Adoption and Children Act 2002 may be exercised by the court with respect to that or any other child; or

(b) An address or school as being that of a child being involved in any such proceedings.

(3) In any proceedings for an offence under this section it shall be a defence for the accused person to prove that he did not know, and had no reason to suspect, the published material was intended, or likely, to identify the child.

(4) The court or the Lord Chancellor may, if satisfied that the welfare of the child requires it, by order dispense with the requirements of subsection (2) to such extent as may be specified in the order.

(5) For the purposes of this section –

"publish" includes –

(a) include in a programme service (within the meaning of the Broadcasting Act 1990); or

(b) caused to be published; and "material" includes any picture or representation.

(6) Any person who contravenes this section shall be guilty of an offence and liable on summary conviction to a fine not exceeding level 4 of the standard scale.'

13.26 On the basis of this provision, said Sir Mark Potter P in *Clayton v Clayton* (above) a construction of s 97, especially s 97(2), must be given by the court; and this must be compatible with the European Convention 1950. In particular the principles set out in Lord Steyn's opinion in *Re S (Identification: Restrictions on Publication)* ('*Re S* [2004]')[26] must be born in mind. Identification of a child who has been involved in court proceedings does not, on its own, necessarily involve harm to the child's welfare.[27] Sir Mark explained this as follows:

> '[51] It is plainly open to be argued in relation to s 97 that, headed as it is "Privacy for Children Involved in Certain Proceedings", the focus should be on Article 8 considerations and thus a Convention compatible construction should lead to an interpretation in accordance with previous judicial assumption that the wording, though inapt, should be read as extending to prevent publication of any material likely to identify the child as *having been* involved in the proceedings once complete.... I do not think that, as a generality, it is right to assume that identification of a child as having been involved in proceedings will involve harm to his or her welfare interests or failure to respect the child's family or private life.'

13.27 The period of any restriction under *CA 1989, s 97* cannot last beyond the 'duration of the proceedings' said Sir Mark in *Clayton v Clayton* ,[28] a view confirmed by Wall LJ in the same case:

> '[102] ... apart from the natural meaning of the words used in the section, I am, I think, particularly influenced by three factors. The first is the fact that the section creates a criminal offence (CA 1989, section 97(6)) and therefore needs to be construed strictly. The second is that the use of the phrase "as being involved in any proceedings" in CA 1989, section 97(2)(a) connotes the identification of a period when those proceedings are pending and not concluded. The third is that the thrust of the authorities ... is that there is no special privilege accorded to children who are the subject matter of proceeding save as is strictly necessary for their protection in the context of the proceedings themselves: see *R v Central Independent Television PLC* [1994] Fam 192 at 207 per Waite LJ.'

Children and Young Persons Act 1933

13.28 The *Children and Young Persons Act 1933, s 33* provides as follows:

> '(1) In relation to any proceedings in any court... the court may direct that:
>
> (a) No newspaper report of the proceedings shall reveal the name, address, or school, or include any particulars calculated to lead to

26 *Re S (Identification: Restrictions on Publication)* [2004] UKHL 47, [2005] 1 AC 593, [2005] 1 FLR 591 at §[17].

27 Though see discussion of this point especially in relation to *PJS* (above) at 5.49 and in the light of *Yousef v The Netherlands (Application No 33711/96)* (2003) 36 EHRR 20, [2003] 1 FLR 210, ECtHR.

28 [2006] EWCA Civ 878, [2007] 1 FLR 11 at §[26].

the identification, of any child or young person concerned in the proceedings, either as being the person by or against or in respect of whom proceedings are taken, or being a witness therein;

(b) No picture shall be published in any newspaper as being or including a picture of any child or young person so concerned in the proceedings as aforesaid; except in so far (if at all) as may be permitted by the direction of the court.'

13.29 The limits of this provision were recognised by Cobb J in *Z & Ors v News Group Newspapers Ltd (1)*.[29] Protection only applies to children and young persons involved in the proceedings and 'who are victims, defendants or witnesses [in those proceedings], but not otherwise' (para [30]). In that case, though the children's welfare benefits and their alleged disabilities were the subject of the criminal proceedings against their mother, none were covered by s 39. As Cobb J pointed out (at para [28]): '... the lives of the dependent children are the focus of the criminal trial, but the children do not attract the ordinary protections of [s 39]'.

Inherent jurisdiction

13.30 In the High Court and the Family Court,[30] and to the extent that *CA 1989, s 97* and *s 12* are inadequate, it remains open to the judge – if the judge considers it to be in the best interest of a child – to protect privacy within the terms of Art 8 by an injunction which can protect the child (as mentioned in connection with s 12, above). This could be, for example, for a period which extends well beyond the conclusion of the case, perhaps throughout childhood.[31] It is open to the child, later and if he or she wishes, to apply to vary or revoke the injunction, or otherwise to seek its review by the court.

13.31 Where the court is asked to exercise its inherent jurisdiction, it will have to balance the Art 8 rights of the child against those of the freedom of expression of the press or of others (eg a parent) under Art 10, as explained by Sir Mark Potter in *Clayton v Clayton* (above) as follows:

> '[54] ... However, in deciding to make a long-term injunction aimed at restricting the reporting and publication of proceedings involving children, the court is obliged in the face of challenge to conduct a balancing exercise between the Article 8 rights of the child and the Article 10 rights of the parent asserting such right, and/ or, where press or media interest is involved, the Article 10 right to report and discuss the circumstances surrounding, as well as the issues arising out of, a case of public interest...'.

29 [2013] EWHC 1150 (Fam); especially §§[27]–[31].

30 Matrimonial and Family Proceedings Act 1984 s 31E (Family Court has High Court and County Court powers; and see *County Court Act 1984, s 38*).

31 See, eg, reporting restrictions order of Keehan J in *Birmingham City Council v Riaz & Ors* [2014] EWHC 4247 (Fam), [2015] 2 FLR 763.

13.32 In weighing rights in the balance, the courts guide to the European Convention 1950 rights derives predominantly from *Re S (A Child) (Identification: Restrictions on Publication)*.[32] As Lord Steyn in the House of Lords explained in that case, authorities which are older and which may seek to explain the balance are of restricted limited application as precedents:

> '[23] The House unanimously takes the view that since the Human Rights Act 1998 came into force in October 2000, the earlier case law about the existence and scope of inherent jurisdiction need not be considered in this case or in similar cases. The foundation of the jurisdiction to restrain publicity in a case such as the present is now derived from convention rights under the European Convention. This is the simple and direct way to approach such cases. In this case the jurisdiction is not in doubt…'.

Crown Court proceedings and anonymity for children

13.33 In *R (Trinity Mirror) v Croydon Crown Court*[33] the Court of Appeal considered the extent to which the Crown Court has power to prevent publicity concerning a child. In that case, a Crown Court judge had made an order limiting reporting restrictions concerning a defendant's children under the *Contempt of Court Act 1981, s 11* where the defendant faced allegations that he had downloaded paedophile images. The judge's order was made for the protection of the defendant's own children. His jurisdiction to make the order was challenged by the press. The five judge Court of Appeal held that the judge in the Crown Court had no statutory jurisdiction to do this. They held further, that the Crown Court has no inherent jurisdiction to grant an injunction:

> '[30] …. Unless the proposed injunction is directly linked to the exercise of the Crown Court's jurisdiction and the exercise of its statutory functions, the appropriate jurisdiction is lacking.'

13.34 Thus, said the Court of Appeal, if such order were to be justified then the circumstances for an order to be made must be 'exceptional':

> '[33]… If the court were to uphold this ruling so as to protect the rights of the defendant's children under Article 8, it would be countenancing a substantial erosion of the principle of open justice, to the overwhelming disadvantage of public confidence in the criminal justice system, the free reporting of criminal trials and the proper identification of those convicted and sentenced in them. Such an order cannot begin to be contemplated unless the circumstances are indeed properly to be described as exceptional.'

---

32 [2004] UKHL 47, [2005] 1 AC 593, [2005] 1 FLR 591.

33 [2008] EWCA Crim 50, [2008] QB 770.

4 BEST INTERESTS OF A CHILD AND EUROPEAN CONVENTION 1950

Human rights balance in the case of children

13.35 If a comparison must be drawn between the protection of a child's right to family life (privacy), and the right of freedom of expression in relation to that child, human rights under the European Convention 1950 – Arts 8 and 10 – will require respectively to be balanced by the court. In the case of press freedom there is the additional protection provided by the *Human Rights Act 1998, s 12(4)*. This subject is considered here in relation to privacy of children proceedings and also in **Chapter 5** in relation to rights of mature children under the European Convention 1950.

13.36 In *Re S* [2004] Lord Steyn pointed out that of the Convention rights which might be in issue, Art 6 (right to a fair trial) applied to a limited extent only, in the general sense that 'The purpose of a public hearing is to guard against an administration of justice in secret and with no public scrutiny and to maintain public confidence'.[34] He went on:[35] 'It is, however, the interaction between Arts 8 and 10 which lies at the heart of this appeal.'

Publicity and children

13.37 Consideration of the rights of children in relation to press and publicity starts from *Re S* [2004]. The case concerned publicity for a criminal trial and the extent to which that might affect the welfare of a child whose mother was charged with the murder of his brother. Following the death of his brother, care proceedings were brought in relation to S (also called 'CS' in the reports), a boy aged five. His parents separated and he went to live with his father (under a care order). The death was caused by salt poisoning and the mother was charged with murder. S's guardian was concerned that the publicity about his mother and dead brother would have a detrimental effect on S's welfare. The guardian applied for an order under the court's inherent jurisdiction in the care proceedings.

13.38 On the application of three national newspapers, Hedley J made an order which prohibited any identification of S's name or the school he attended. He did not prevent reporting of the criminal trial or that it should contain the names or photographs of the mother or the dead child. On S's appeal to the Court of Appeal, by a majority, the court affirmed the judge's order: any interference with S's rights to respect for private and family life under Art 8 which might occur, was justified in the light of public interest and the rights of the press under Art 10. The House of Lords dismissed S's appeal and upheld the judge's and the Court of Appeal orders.

---

34 At §[15]. Lord Steyn cited *Axen v Germany* (1983) 5 EHRR 195at §[25] as authority for his proposition.
35 At §[16].

Interaction between European Convention 1950 rights: Arts 8 and 10

13.39 Lord Steyn gave the only reasoned speech. He dealt with the interaction between Arts 8 and 10. By *HRA 1998, s 12(4)*, he said, special provision had been made for freedom of expression, namely:

> '[16] ... That when considering whether to grant relief which, if granted, might affect the exercise of the Convention right to freedom of expression the court must have particular regard to the importance of the right.'

13.40 He drew attention to four propositions as to the 'interplay' of Arts 8 and 10 (drawn from his own assessment of the House's consideration of those articles in *Campbell v MGN Ltd*[36]):

> '[17] ... First, neither article has as such precedence over the other. Secondly, where the values under the two articles are in conflict, an intense focus on the comparative importance of the specific rights being claimed in the individual case is necessary. Thirdly, the justifications for interfering with or restricting each right must be taken into account. Finally, the proportionality test must be applied to each.'

13.41 Neither Art 8 nor Art 10 has precedence, one over the other, says Lord Steyn; though he does not specifically address the question of whether or not any priority should be given to the welfare of the child, where the interplay of Arts 8 and 10 are in issue over matters which directly involve the best interests of a child. The priority (if any) to be given to children's welfare has, however, received more recent consideration in the Supreme Court.[37] In cases where deportation or extradition of one or both a child's parents the question of the relative importance of a child's welfare and of his or her right to respect for a private life has been part of the court's consideration of the main issue before it.[38]

Children's family rights: 'a different order'

13.42 In *H(H) v Deputy Prosecutor of the Italian Republic, Genoa (Official Solicitor intervening)* [39] Lady Hale explains why the rights of children are different from those of adults:

> '[33] ... The family rights of children are of a different order from those of adults, for several reasons. In the first place, as *Neulinger* [[40] and *ZH (Tanzania)*

36 [2004] UKHL 22, [2004] 2 AC 457.
37 See, eg, *PJS v News Group Newspapers Ltd* [2016] UKSC 26, [2016] AC 1081, [2016] 2 FLR 251, [2016] 2 WLR 1253 considered at 5.50.
38 See, eg, *H(H) v Deputy Prosecutor of the Italian Republic, Genoa (Official Solicitor intervening)* [2012] UKSC 25, [2013] 1 AC 338.
39 [2012] UKSC 25, [2013] 1 AC 338.
40 *Neulinger* and *Shuruk v Switzerland Application No 41615/07* [2011] 1 FLR 122.

[41] have explained, Art 8 has to be interpreted in such a way that their best interests are a primary consideration, although not always the only primary consideration and not necessarily the paramount consideration. This gives them an importance which the family rights of other people (and in particular the extraditee) may not have. Secondly, children need a family life in a way that adults do not. They have to be fed, clothed, washed, supervised, taught and above all loved if they are to grow up to be the properly functioning members of society which we all need them to be. Their physical and educational needs may be met outside the family, although usually not as well as they are met within it, but their emotional needs can only be fully met within a functioning family. Depriving a child of her family life is altogether more serious than depriving an adult of his…'.

13.43 Lady Hale returned to the question of children's Art 8 rights balanced against those of the adults – of 'Depriving a child of her family life is altogether more serious than depriving an adult of his' – in the case in *PJS* as explained in **Chapter 5**.

5 CHILDREN PROCEEDINGS AND MEDIA REPRESENTATIVES

Press attendance

Press attendance at children hearings

13.44 A variety of special measures to help children to provide their best evidence are considered in **Chapter 3**. These are considered there in general in relation to proceedings in which children may be required to give evidence. The same measures may be of assistance in cases where the press is entitled to attend children proceedings; but in such proceedings the court retains the power to exclude any person permitted into court (such as the press) where this may be necessary.[42] Thus FPR 2010, r 27.10 states that all proceedings covered by the rules shall be in private save where otherwise provided.

13.45 The rule-makers have devised a scheme which enables certain further individuals – that is, beyond the parties and their representatives – to attend court, if they wish to do so. The scheme applies, in particular, to the media and to others who might be interested in the proceedings (eg friends and family; academics and other researchers etc). FPR 2010, r 27.11 represents a qualification to the privacy rule in FPR 2010, r 27.10 and provides exceptions to that rule. For present purposes rr 27.10 and 27.11(1) provide as follows:

41 *ZH (Tanzania) v Secretary of State for the Home Department* [2011] UKSC 4, [2011] 2 AC 166, [2011] 1 FLR 2170.
42 FPR 2010, r 27.11(3); and see further at 13.45.

'27.10 Hearings in private

(1) Proceedings to which these rules apply will be held in private, except –

(a) where these rules or any other enactment provide otherwise;

(b) subject to any enactment, where the court directs otherwise.

(2) For the purposes of these rules, a reference to proceedings held "in private" means proceedings at which the general public have no right to be present.

27.11 Attendance at private hearings

(1) This rule applies when proceedings are held in private, except in relation to –

(a) hearings conducted for the purpose of judicially assisted conciliation or negotiation;

(b) proceedings to which the following provisions apply –

(i) Part 13 (proceedings under section 54 of the Human Fertilisation and Embryology Act 2008);

(ii) Part 14 (procedure for applications in adoption, placement and related proceedings); and

(iii) any proceedings identified in a practice direction as being excepted from this rule.

(2) When this rule applies, no person shall be present during any hearing other than –

(a) an officer of the court;

(b) a party to the proceedings;

(c) a litigation friend for any party, or legal representative instructed to act on that party's behalf;

(d) an officer of the service or Welsh family proceedings officer;

(e) a witness;

(f) duly accredited representatives of news gathering and reporting organisations; and

(g) any other person whom the court permits to be present....

(6) This rule does not affect any power of the court to direct that witnesses shall be excluded until they are called for examination.

(7) In this rule "duly accredited" refers to accreditation in accordance with any administrative scheme for the time being approved for the purposes of this rule by the Lord Chancellor.'

'Duly accredited' press representative

13.46 A 'duly accredited'[43] press representative must obtain a card issued by the UK Press Card Authority to provide evidence of accreditation; though an unaccredited representative may be permitted to attend the hearing at the court's discretion.[44]

13.47 FPR 2010, r 27.11(3)–(5) deals with a set of provisions which enables the court on its own initiative, or the parties or witnesses or a child (if of age and understanding) to apply, to exclude the press where admitted under r 27.11(2)(f). PD27B – *Attendance or media representative at hearings in family proceedings (High Court and County Courts)* – supports r 27.11 and deals with hearings in private. It deals mostly with exclusion of the press. In particular r 27.11(3) and (4) enables the court to exclude members of the media, whether on the court's own initiative or on application by individuals listed in r 27.11(5):

> '(3) At any stage of the proceedings the court may direct that persons within paragraph (2)(f) shall not attend the proceedings or any part of them, where satisfied that –
>
> (a) this is necessary –
>
> (i) in the interests of any child concerned in, or connected with, the proceedings;
>
> (ii) for the safety or protection of a party, a witness in the proceedings, or a person connected with such a party or witness; or
>
> (iii) for the orderly conduct of the proceedings; or
>
> (b) justice will otherwise be impeded or prejudiced.
>
> (4) The court may exercise the power in paragraph (3) of its own initiative or pursuant to representations made by any of the persons listed in paragraph (5), and in either case having given to any person within paragraph (2)(f) who is in attendance an opportunity to make representations.
>
> (5) At any stage of the proceedings, the following persons may make representations to the court regarding restricting the attendance of persons within paragraph (2)(f) in accordance with paragraph (3) –
>
> (a) a party to the proceedings;
>
> (b) any witness in the proceedings;
>
> (c) where appointed, any children's guardian;
>
> (d) where appointed, an officer of the service or Welsh family proceedings officer, on behalf of the child the subject of the proceedings;
>
> (e) the child, if of sufficient age and understanding.'

43 FPR 2010, r 27.11(2)(f).
44 FPR 2010, r 27.11(2)(g).

To make sense of a hearing

Release of documents to non-parties to make sense of the proceedings

13.48 FPR 2010, rr 27.11 and 29.12 make no specific provision for hearing documents to be provided to the media of any of the other individuals who may be allowed into court. By 'hearing documents in this context, is meant documents which are produced by the parties and which are read by the court as part of the hearing of the case.[45] So how is an accredited journalist,[46] or (say) an academic or other researcher[47] to be able to understand what is happening in court if they are not able – as the judge and the parties have done – to read statements or skeleton arguments or other documents which are routinely produced by the parties. These 'hearing documents' are prepared to help the court to have a full picture of the case and are read by the judge prior to any hearing?

13.49 In *Norfolk County Council v Webster and Others*[48] an answer was provided – for that case – to some of these questions. Munby J had been asked to allow the press to read the local authority position statement which would explain their proposals for three children at the start of care proceedings. A court order was required for this release of information to the media, failing which they might be in contempt of court. The judge explained his view. 'It was essential' he said 'for me to [release the statement] if the media, and through the media the general public, were to understand what had gone on' in the proceedings.[49] Munby J was, in this way, adopting the press-making-sense-of-the-proceedings criterion in family proceedings which was foreseen by Lord Scarman[50] and referred to in *Guardian v Westminster.*

The common law and family proceedings

13.50 In relation to release of documents to the media, 'new ground' was broken in *R (Guardian News and Media Ltd) v City of Westminster Magistrates' Court (Article 19 intervening)*[51] ('*Guardian v Westminster*'):

45 And see further definition of this term at 13.63.
46 FPR 2010, r 27.11(2)(f).
47 FPR 2010, r 27.11(2)(g).
48 [2006] EWHC 2898 (Fam), [2007] 2 FLR 415 Munby J.
49 *Norfolk County Council v Webster and Others* [2006] EWHC 2898 (Fam), [2007] 2 FLR 415, Munby J at [43].
50 In *Harman v Secretary of State for the Home Department* [1983] 1 AC 280, [1982] 2 WLR 338.
51 [2012] EWCA Civ 420, [2013] QB 618 at para [90]: '...I recognise that this decision breaks new ground in the application of the principle of open justice, although not, as I believe, in relation to the nature of the principle itself.'

'[87] In this case the Guardian has put forward good reasons[52] for having access to the documents which it seeks. There has been no suggestion that this would give rise to any risk of harm to any other party, nor would it place any great burden on the court. Accordingly, its application should be allowed.'

13.51 If an observer were to apply alongside attendance at court, then on principles equivalent to *Guardian v Westminster* (save for references to the open justice principle) a court may be able, in children proceedings, to release suitable anonymised documents to a journalist, academic or other responsible person who is permitted to attend court in family proceedings. Paragraph 2.3 of the *Practice Direction* implies that permission of the court can be applied for. It does not provide the same clarity with which such an application will be dealt with, and disposed of, as does the reasoning in *Guardian v Westminster.*

'Evidence and argument must be publicly known'[53]

13.52 In *Harman v Secretary of State for the Home Department*[54] Lord Scarman[55] explained the importance, as he saw it, to open justice of understanding what went on in court:

'[There is] another important public interest involved in justice done openly, namely, that the evidence and argument should be publicly known, so that society may judge for itself the quality of justice administered in its name, and whether the law requires modification. When public policy in the administration of justice is considered, public knowledge of the evidence and arguments of the parties is certainly as important as expedition: and, if the price of expedition is to be the silent reading by the judge before or at trial of relevant documents, it is arguable that expedition will not always be consistent with justice being seen to be done.'

13.53 In *Smithkline Beecham Biologicals SA v Connaught Laboratories Inc*[56] Lord Bingham CJ developed Lord Scarman's concerns in relation to hearing documents. The case concerned a patent where documents had been disclosed by the defendants pursuant to court order. The question was whether each of these documents had been 'read to or by the Court, or referred to, in open Court' (in the language of the then applicable Rules of the Supreme Court 1965, Ord 24, r 14A, and as reproduced in CPR 1998, r 31.22(1)(a)). After the judge had pre-

52 Toulson LJ had summarised *The Guardian's* reasons thus: '[13] the Guardian submitted that it was wrong for it to be denied the documentation sought. In particular, (a) it had a serious journalistic purpose in seeking production of the documents, because the case raised issues of public interest; (b) allowing it to see the documents would not frustrate or render impracticable the administration of justice; and (c) allowing it to see the documents would not interfere with any rights of the parties to the case or of third parties.'

53 See Lord Scarman in citation form *Harman v Home Department.*

54 [1983] 1 AC 280 at 316.

55 Quoted by Toulson LJ in *Guardian v Westminster* at [33].

56 [1999] EWCA Civ 1781, [1999] 4 All ER 498.

read all that he had been given, the respondent abandoned their case and the patent in issue was revoked. The appeal turned on confidentiality in the disclosed documents (or their 'use' in terms of CPR 1998, r 31.22). The Court of Appeal held that they had been referred to in open court[57] and that therefore 'we do not order that they should not be disclosed'.

13.54 In answering the question as to the confidentiality of the documents, Lord Bingham CJ (giving the judgment of the court[58]) discussed the matters raised by Lord Scarman in *Harman* and which are of direct concern here:

> 'Since the date when Lord Scarman expressed doubt in *Home Office v Harman* as to whether expedition would always be consistent with open justice, the practices of counsel preparing skeleton arguments, chronologies and reading guides, and judges pre-reading documents (including witness statements) out of court, have become much more common. These methods of saving time in court are now not merely permitted, but are positively required, by practice directions. The result is that a case may be heard in such a way that even an intelligent and well-informed member of the public, present throughout every hearing in open court, would be unable to obtain a full understanding of the documentary evidence and the arguments on which the case was to be decided.'

13.55 In *Norfolk County Council v Webster and Others*[59] Munby J took up the same point as Lord Scarman and Lord Bingham CJ, when he justified his decision to permit the press to see a party's position statement:

> '[42] Today in the Family Division, as in the other divisions of the High Court and in the Court of Appeal, we have a system under which many matters that would in the days of purely oral advocacy have been spoken in court by counsel are now set out in written documents, prepared by counsel, which are pre-read by the judge before the hearing and which are therefore not read out in court during the hearing.... This system is intended to further the proper administration of justice. It does so in various ways including, in particular, by shortening hearings (and thereby increasing the throughput of cases through the court system)...'.

13.56 In *Norfolk v Webster* Munby J explained his decision on grounds of the importance to the press and therefore the public to understand the proceedings:

> '[41] For if the media, and indeed the public generally, are not permitted to see the position statement [of counsel for the County Council], the ability of

57 '... these were documents which had been referred to in open court. They were materials which the judge had read, on which SmithKline relied in seeking revocation of the patent and on which the judge must be taken to have relied, among other materials, when ruling that the patent should be revoked'.

58 Lord Bingham CJ and Otton and Robert Walker LJJ (passages cited here are also cited by Toulson LJ in *Guardian v Westminster* (at [34]) and by Bean J in NAB v Serco (at [26]).

59 [2006] EWHC 2898 (Fam), [2007] 2 FLR 415, Munby J.

the media, and through the media the ability of the public, to understand what took place during the hearing would be severely compromised. This outcome would defeat the very purpose of permitting the media to be present.'

Judge's pre-read documents

13.57 *Guardian v Westminster* was concerned with extradition proceedings in a magistrates' court. However, the decision is not confined to magistrates' court documents. It applies to all hearings documents where the issue is based on the common law open justice principle.[60] It applies to all proceedings where the court relies on documents which are pre-read by the judge: summaries, statements and affidavits, skeleton arguments, correspondence between parties. The default position will be that – as in *Guardian v Westminster* – any such documents should be available on application by a non-party, subject to a proportionality balance (see later). The criterion must be, as far as this aspect of release is concerned: if a journalist (say) or member of the public is allowed into court (ie for example, where the case is heard in open court), what does s/he need to read to make sense of the proceedings? (As will be seen, the principle at issue in *NAB v Serco* is slightly different and relates to a potentially wider spectrum of documents: in that case, required for a 'proper journalistic purpose'.[61])

13.58 As Munby J accepted in *Norfolk v Webster* to make sense of the proceedings, press and others permitted into court must see some documents. It remains to be seen (a) whether demand for documents will develop, for example from the press; and (b) whether, in children proceedings, a formula can be provided which preserves the privacy of children concerned in the proceedings.

6 EXCLUSION OF THE MEDIA

Exclusion of media representatives: Practice Direction PD27B

13.59 FPR 2010, r 27.11(7) states that in the rule '"duly accredited" refers to accreditation in accordance with any administrative scheme for the time being approved for the purposes of this rule by the Lord Chancellor.' Though it is not specifically approved by the Lord Chancellor, the practice direction *PD27B* which supports FPR 2010, Pt 27 sets out a scheme for *Attendance of media representatives at hearings in family proceedings*. Two aspects of this practice direction justify comment: first is the reference to a 'discretion to exclude' the media (para 3); and, secondly, is the reference to 'documents referred to in the course of evidence'. These and other 'hearing documents' will be explained below.

60 As discussed by Bean J in *NAB v Serco Ltd & Anor* [2014] EWHC 1225 (QB) at [36] and [38]).
61 *NAB v Serco Ltd & Anor* [2014] EWHC 1225 (QB) at [43].

13.60 Under the heading 'Aims of the Guidance' in *PD27B*, para 3.1 says:

> '3.1 This Practice Direction is intended to provide guidance regarding:
>
> - the handling of applications to exclude media representatives from the whole or part of a hearing; and
> - the exercise of the court's discretion to exclude media representatives whether upon the court's own motion or any such application.'

13.61 In *Re Child X (Residence and Contact: Rights of Media Attendance: FPR Rule 10.28(4))*[62,63] Sir Mark Potter P considered this practice direction and the rule on which it was based (now FPR 2010, r 27.11(3)). The case concerned an application from a 'celebrity' in private law children proceedings that the press be excluded from a part of the hearing dealing with psychiatric issues in relation to his family. He granted the application. In doing so he made some comments as to the nature of applications to exclude.[64] In particular he doubted that the reference in the practice direction to a 'discretion to exclude' is 'strictly speaking' correct (see (3) below).

13.62 Sir Mark's comments include:

(1) That an application in relation to the children of 'celebrities' is no different from applications in relation to any other child.[65] On the contrary, he said:

> 'the focus is upon the interests of the child and not the parents. It is almost axiomatic that the press interest in and surrounding the case will be more intense in the case of children of celebrities; and the need for protection of the child from intrusion or publicity, and the danger of leakage of information to the public will similarly be the more intense.'

(2) That the wording of what is now 27.11(3)(a)(i) requires the court to be satisfied that it is 'necessary' to exclude the press. This specifically picks up the balancing exercise required by the European Convention 1950:

> '[53] ... That is wording which picks up and reflects the provisions of the European Convention relevant to the balancing act which the court has to perform as set out in Arts 6(1), 8(2) and 10(2) of the European Convention. We are here concerned with a restriction on the freedom of expression of the media under Art 10(1), (namely the right

62 FPR 1991, r 10.28 was the predecessor to FPR 2010, r 27.11.

63 [2009] EWHC 1728 (Fam), [2009] 2 FLR 1467.

64 He did so, he said, because such exclusion '[59] ... is necessary in the interests of X as the child concerned in the proceedings: r 10.28(4)(a)(i). Also upon the basis that justice will otherwise be impeded: r 10.28(4)(b)' (now r 27.11(3)(a)(i) and (b)).

65 §[51]; 'In this respect, and in very different circumstances concerning the publication of the identity of a barrister who had been convicted of criminal offences, (*C v Crown Prosecution Service* [2008] EWHC 854 (Admin), (2008) *The Times* 20 February), Thomas LJ rejected the submission that, in conducting the *Re S* balancing exercise there involved the Court should have regard to the public profile of the appellant....'.

to receive and impart information and ideas without interference) for the purpose of the protection of the rights of the child to respect for her private and family life.'

(3) That so far as the practice direction was concerned:

'[56] … Its reference to the exercise of the court's *discretion* to exclude media representatives from all or part of the proceedings is, strictly speaking, not accurate.[66]… Thus references to the court's discretion in para [3.1] and in the heading to para [5] in the practice direction dated 20 April 2009 are a misnomer. Nonetheless, the balancing act involved in the weighing of the conflicting but interlocking rights and restraints embodied in Art 10 and Art 8 of the European Convention are highly fact-sensitive from case to case. Thus, in performing the necessary balancing act, and in particular the ultimate test of proportionality, it is the judge dealing with the case who is the person best placed to make the necessary decision.'

'Hearing documents'

13.63 The term 'hearing documents' is used in this chapter to describe documents which are not read out in open court but which are read by the judge and referred to during the course of a court hearing. Four separate categories of documents and information (including those defined by CPR 1998, rr 5.4C and 31.22) may be said to exist:

(1) *Court documents* – Court documents for which a non-party is entitled to apply as a matter of formality (CPR 1998 r 5.4C).

(2) *Hearing documents* – Court documents for which a non-party is entitled to apply: eg to make sense of the proceedings[67] or for a particular journalistic purpose.[68]

(3) *Disclosed documents* – Use, or other release, of documents whose production has been compelled by disclosure rules (CPR 1998, r 31.22(1)), and who release or other use the law restricts or may prevent, in cases of breach (r 31.22(2)).

(4) *Other documents and information* which a party is entitled to publish about proceedings where a court has sat in private.[69]

---

66 '[56] … In *Financial Times Ltd v Interbrew SA* [2002] EWCA Civ 274, [2002] 2 Lloyd's Rep 229 at para [58] Sedley LJ made clear that where the court has a duty to apply a test of necessity in relation to a series of questions as to legitimacy and proportionality, the duty of the court is to proceed through the balancing exercise, making a value judgment as to the conflicts which arise, rather than to regard the matter simply as an exercise of discretion as between two equally legitimate courses.'

67 *R (Guardian News and Media Ltd) v City of Westminster Magistrates' Court (Article 19 intervening)* [2012] EWCA Civ 420, [2013] QB 618.

68 See, eg, *NAB v Serco Ltd & Anor* [2014] EWHC 1225 (QB), Bean J.

69 Discussed, eg, in *Clibbery v Allan* [2002] EWCA Civ 45, [2002] 1 FLR 565.

13.64 Thus 'hearing documents' come somewhere between formal court documents (see eg FPR 2010, r 29.12[70]) and documents disclosed under FPR 2010, Pt 21. These hearing documents were the subject of the *Guardian*'s appeal in *R (Guardian News and Media Ltd) v City of Westminster Magistrates' Court (Article 19 intervening)*[71] (*Guardian v Westminster*) and are referred to in the cases referred to in the rest of this part of the chapter. In *Guardian v Westminster* Toulson J defined the issue and the documents in question as:

> '[6] In this case the question has arisen whether a District Judge, who made two extradition orders on the application of the US Government, had power to allow the Guardian Newspaper to inspect and take copies of affidavits or witness statements, written arguments and correspondence, which were supplied to the judge for the purposes of the extradition hearings. They were not read out in open court but they were referred to during the course of the hearings…'.

13.65 What hearing documents could be released to the press represented the issue before the Court of Appeal in *Guardian v Westminster*. However, the Court of Appeal's decision was not confined to magistrates' court documents.[72] It confirms that the common law, in respect of the applicable documents and information, applies to all court documents where the issue is based on the much wider common law open justice principle; and the case identifies an intermediate range between court documents (covered by FPR 2010, r 29.12(1)) and disclosed documents (disclosure not permitted: see **Chapter 9, Part 4**) to which the question of release – with court permission – may apply.

70 FPR 2010, r 29.12, as relevant, provides:

29.12 Access to and inspection of documents retained in court

(1) Except as provided by this rule or by any other rule or Practice Direction, no document or copy of a document filed or lodged in the court office shall be open to inspection by any person without the permission of the court, and no copy of any such document or copy shall be taken by, or issued to, any person without such permission.

(2) A copy of an order made in open court will be issued to any person who requests it.....

71 [2012] EWCA Civ 420, [2013] QB 618.

72 As discussed by Bean J in *NAB v Serco Ltd & Anor* [2014] EWHC 1225 (QB) at [36] and [38]).

INDEX

[*References are to paragraph number*]